WISDOM'S CHILDREN

SUNY series in
Western Esoteric Traditions

David Appelbaum, editor

WISDOM'S CHILDREN

A Christian Esoteric Tradition

ARTHUR VERSLUIS

STATE UNIVERSITY OF NEW YORK PRESS

Published by
State University of New York Press, Albany

For information, address State University of New York Press,
State University Plaza, Albany, NY 12246

Production and book design, Laurie Searl
Marketing, Nancy Farrell

Library of Congress Cataloging-in-Publication Data

Versluis, Arthur, 1959–
    Wisdom's children : a Christian esoteric tradition / Arthur
Versluis.
        p.   cm. — (SUNY series in Western esoteric traditions)
    Includes bibliographical references and index.
    ISBN 0-7914-4329-9 (hbk. : alk. paper). — ISBN 0-7914-4330-2 (pbk
: alk. paper)
    1. Mysticism. 2. Theosophy. I. Title. II. Series.
BV5083.V48 1999
248.2´2—dc21   99-24164
                                                                                CIP

10   9   8   7   6   5   4   3   2   1

To Antoine Faivre for his generosity and vast scholarship; to Wouter Hanegraaff and Robert Faas for sharing their knowledge and for their friendship; to Adam McLean for invaluable assistance in finding rare manuscripts and books; and to Joost R. Ritman and his daughter Esther, for their extraordinary library, the Bibliotheca Philosophica Hermetica, and for their help. Two chapters in this book were published elsewhere first, and so I gratefully acknowledge *Studies in Spirituality* for publishing a somewhat different version of Chapter Eighteen, "Theosophy and Gnosticism," and Antoine Faivre and Wouter Hanegraff for publishing an earlier version of Chapter Nineteen, "Alchemy and Theosophy," in *Western Esotericism and the Science of Religion* (Leuven: Peeters, 1998).

Contents

Illustrations

Introduction

This book introduces a religious phenomenon so far almost completely ignored in the English-speaking world: Protestant theosophic mysticism. Although this theosophic tradition—whose most exemplary seventeenth- and eighteenth-century representatives include Jacob Böhme and Johann Georg Gichtel in Germany and Amsterdam, Dr. John Pordage in England, and Johann Kelpius in America—was quite influential on the spiritual lives of countless people and represents an extraordinary historical force, there is only one other book available now in the English language that focuses solely on it, and relatively few books on this subject have been published in this century.[1] Thus, this work represents a pioneering effort, and in it I will offer not only historical information and context concerning this movement, but, more importantly, a way of understanding what theosophy actually meant, or means, for its historical practitioners.

There are precedents for this approach to such a subject. Chief among them is that of Henry Corbin, whose elucidation of Ismaili gnosis and visionary spirituality by "phenomenological" means—that is, by sympathetically revealing the significance of his topic from within it rather than sardonically commenting on it from without—stands as a model of scholarship. Indeed, Corbin's works on Sufism and related esoteric topics were directly influenced by and often refer to precisely the Protestant theosophic school upon which this work focuses, and help us very much to understand the true significance of Protestant mysticism.

Because this is a book intended for an English-speaking audience, and because relatively little attention thus far has been paid to English and American theosophy, I have made sure to include these currents of the tradition. There are numerous European scholars whose work is useful in this field of Western esotericism, most especially Antoine Faivre, the preëminent authority, but also such authors as Karl Frick, Will-Erich Peuckert, Bernard Gorceix, Serge Hutin, Jean-Paul Corsetti, Wouter

Hanegraaff, and Peter Koslowski.[2] I have drawn on these scholars' works where necessary, but as in my book, *American Transcendentalism and Asian Religions*, I have here devoted the majority of my attention to primary works and in particular in this case to previously undiscussed theosophers or aspects of theosophy. This book explores new territory.

As we shall see, our excursion into theosophy—which has nothing whatever to do with the society of Helena Blavatsky that took its name in the late nineteenth century—will be a journey into territory increasingly remarkable and, for most of us, even strange. Nonetheless, we will seek throughout to avoid casting judgment upon our authors from modern viewpoints, and will approach them as objectively as possible, seeking not to explain them away or to denigrate them but to genuinely understand what their work and their lives represent. One may dismiss visions as hallucinations, but such a dismissal rarely aids in our understanding of visions.

In the course of this work I take an empiricist approach, meaning that we will seek to understand these authors as much as possible on their own terms and in historical context.[3] Of course, if we are going to accept our authors on their own terms, we not only will have to suspend our disbelief, but also will have to imaginatively enter into their worldview. If we do not understand something of Böhme's pivotal terminology, and ignore the theosophic cosmology, metaphysics, and iconographic symbolism essential to these authors, then not surprisingly these works shall by and large remain closed to us. Perhaps more than any other school, theosophy requires the use of the imagination not as fantasy, but as inward discipline and visionary means.

Yet if we make this effort, we shall undoubtedly find rewards in proportion to our effort. Many people of European heritage find themselves attracted to Asian religious disciplines, or to Sufism in Islam, or to paganism, or to various modern cults because they find much in modern Christianity lifeless, devoid of spiritual depth. But in fact the Protestant theosophic tradition is also remarkably rich in iconography, cosmology, and metaphysics, offering far more than has previously been recognized in just the kind of spiritual discipline one finds in such traditions as Sufism, Buddhism, Kabbalism, and Hinduism.

No doubt this will come as a surprise to many readers; it certainly has come as a surprise to me. Each step into this theosophic world has startled me with the new horizons that have appeared, with the extent of the material available, and with the remarkable people who wrote and embodied it. Many people may think of Protestantism as a largely historicist, literalist, or fundamentalist faith, grim, puritanical, and devoid of imagination and love. In this work we will find that, for our theosophic authors, these characterizations do not hold true.

Additionally, we will find that even though Protestantism is often depicted as springing up only as a revolt against the institutionalized Roman Catholic church and certain corruptions within it, in fact in theosophy we see not a mere reactionary revolt, but an extremely serious and sustained attempt to return to the very springs of the Christian tradition, incorporating the works not only of Greek Orthodox ascetics like Macarios of Egypt, but also of Catholic mystics like Johannes Tauler, as well as certain aspects of early Christian Gnosticism. Far from historicist fundamentalism, theosophy in fact arguably represents one of the most serious efforts ever of rapprochement between the various Christian traditions, and of return to Christianity's essence.

For these authors, the most important figure in Protestant history was most certainly not Calvin or Luther, but Jacob Böhme, whose influence is found throughout the entire theosophic tradition. Böhme represents not just a commentator on the Gospels, an opponent of institutionalization, or by any means a formulator of a civil code, but in the view of the theosophers, a renewer of the Christian tradition in its essential purity. For them, Böhme—a humble cobbler—was granted a revelation that sums up the whole of the Christian tradition near the end of time. What is more, they affirm that the same realization is accessible to us as well.

Thus, while in this study I will certainly offer some historical context, the primary focus will be on theosophy as a discipline and what that entails, on theosophy as it is explicated by the theosophers themselves. For this reason I will draw extensively on the many letters of Johann Georg Gichtel collected in the massive multivolume *Theosophia Practica*, on the letters and other works of English writers like John Pordage, Francis Lee, Jane Leade, and Edward Hooker, as well as on Johann Kelpius and other members of the American theosophic communities of Pennsylvania.

It is one thing to offer a cold historical account of such authors as these, and quite another to actually look into their world through their letters and narrations. For what we will see—despite the inevitable rifts among some of them—is a remarkably unified understanding, a regimen of spiritual discipline put into practice not just by an isolated practitioner here or there, but by entire communities dedicated to theosophic mysticism, communities found in Germany, Switzerland, the Netherlands, England, and America throughout the late seventeenth, eighteenth, nineteenth, and even twentieth centuries.

This understanding is reflected in many iconographic diagrams or illustrations, and on occasion I will reproduce and comment on some of these as well. For as we shall see, theosophy was a visionary discipline, a practice of the imagination—of images—and of the transcendence of those images. Far from being superfluous, such illustrations are inseparable from the texts and the tradition itself, conveying in an immediate visual way what was by no means a merely intellectual endeavor but a spiritual discipline that meant the soul's transmutation and the illumination of the spirit.

Theosophy has ramifications in many disciplines, including not only religious history but the arts and sciences, and German, Dutch, French, English, and American history, not to mention cosmology and metaphysics. It is not only in the revision of history that this book is revolutionary; in an age when many people have perhaps prematurely given up on Christianity and the richness of its spiritual inheritance, theosophy may restore to them a Christian tradition of striking depth and power.

Admittedly, many of the manuscripts and books from which I quote are extremely rare and inaccessible. But with the publication of this book, and its sequel of primary theosophic texts,[4] it will no longer be necessary for others to transcribe from manuscripts in private libraries by hand, as I have done, and as those drawn to these writings have done since the seventeenth century. For the purpose of this book is nothing less than the revelation of a hitherto almost completely ignored, and yet extraordinarily influential religious movement.

PART ONE

HISTORY

CHAPTER ONE

Böhme

 lthough it is certainly true that in a broad sense, theosophy predated Jacob Böhme (1575–1624)—who can be placed as another in a long lineage of Christian gnosis, stretching from early Christian Gnosticism and orthodox gnostics like St. Dionysius the Areopagite, St. Clement of Alexandria and Origen, through John Scotus Erigena, through Johannes Tauler, Meister Eckhart, and Jan van Ruysbroeck, to Paracelsus—nonetheless, Böhme's life and works represent a decisive moment in Christian history. For Böhme's works are nothing less than a masterful reconstitution of Christian gnosis at the beginning of the modern era, and for this reason any historical account of theosophy must begin with Böhme.

Böhme was born in Görlitz, Germany, during a remarkable era. This was, we will recall, the time of Giordano Bruno and his astonishing, daring attempts to reconstruct a new Egyptian-Hermetic-Cabalistic gnosis for all Europe, the time of William Shakespeare and Sir Philip Sidney, of Dr. John Dee and his conversations with angels, of Rudolph II and his Hermetic court in Prague, an era in short of unprecedented renaissance of Hermeticism and visionary spirituality. Böhme is often viewed outside this context, depicted as a "visionary shoemaker," unlearned and somehow outside the era in which he lived. But in a real sense, Böhme embodies this time, embodies the merging of German mysticism, alchemy, Hermeticism, embodies the new access of "lower classes" to learning, embodies above all the reconstitution of Christian gnosis for a new era.

But we must begin by examining Böhme's life. There are some apocryphal stories about Böhme as a young man that are more important for subsequent theosophers than the mundane details we know. These apocryphal, and we may say, hierohistorical tales, are told by Abraham von Franckenberg, one of Böhme's nobleman friends. According to Franckenberg, as a boy Böhme was wandering in the hills near his home city of Görlitz, and came upon a great treasure hidden in a cave. This discovery, it is said, prefigured his later spiritual revelations, a treasure for all humanity. Franckenberg also tells how Böhme as a young man (an apprentice cobbler) was approached by a stranger with shining eyes who prophesied that he would "amaze the world" and enjoined him to read the Bible and remain pious through coming tribulations.

As Andrew Weeks points out, neither of these tales is improbable: there was an existing tradition of hidden treasure in those very hills, and that a stranger should see great potential in the young Böhme is also entirely plausible.[1] Most important about these stories is how they forecast what was to become a leitmotif for the whole of Böhmean theosophy, what we call "hierohistory," those exact moments of revelation in an individual life when the eternal and the temporal intersect. In a very real sense, these events forecast the great revelation of Böhme's life, that decisive instant when at the age of twenty-five, in 1600, Böhme saw into the luminous center of eternal nature.

For without question the whole of Böhme's lifework centered around this moment of primary revelation when he saw in fifteen minutes more than one could learn in a lifetime of reading books. Böhme's revelation was preceded by a period of deep melancholy, during which he had been in a profound quandary over the existence of evil and suffering in the world—a melancholy that often precedes spiritual awakening not only in Christian mysticism, but in other traditions around the world as well.[2] One day in 1600, Böhme was startled by a gleam of light from a pewter dish, and saw into the *centrum naturae*, so that wandering outdoors, the whole of nature was transformed into luminous meaning, while he was filled with love as if resurrected from death into life eternal.

We need not assume, however, that the whole of Böhme's enormous body of written work derived only from this illumination. It is no doubt much more accurate to say that this revelation was Böhme's "opening," and that the rest of his life consisted in a deepening of this initial spiritual awakening. Such a view would also help to explain why *Aurora*, his first treatise, while full of the prophetical and enigmatic power of his first spiritual illumination, is also somewhat fragmented and not a completed, rounded work, whereas some of his later books, such as *The Three Principles* and *Mysterium Magnum*, are more complete.

We should also note that Böhme's spiritual doctrines ought to be seen in the context of other works written during this time. Too often, his works are viewed in isolation. There are precedents for his revelations within Protestantism of his day. Sebastian Franck, Caspar Schwenckfeld, and Valentin Weigel were all Protestants who emphasized the descent of the Holy Spirit and the indwelling Johannine Logos over institutionalism and legalism. Abraham Behem, influenced by Paracelsus, held that one could understand the waters above the firmament in Genesis 1.6–7 as the glassy seas of the Apocalypse over which reigns the Heavenly Virgin or Celestial Eve.[3] This mystical interpretation has marked parallels with Böhme's own exegesis in *Mysterium Magnum*, and his own doctrine of the Virgin Sophia, so enormously influential in later theosophy.

In other words, Böhme's Sophianic and Hermetic mysticism had direct precedents and parallels. Indeed, Böhme's lifetime in Germany was closely paralleled by that of the Roman Catholic mystic Augustine Baker (1575–1641) in England, who joined the Benedictine order in 1605, was ordained a priest some ten years later, and wrote a book entitled *Sancta Sophia, or Holy Wisdom*, a work much influenced by St. Dionysius the Areopagite and by the fourteenth-century German and English mystical tradition.[4] Baker's book was published posthumously and demonstrates that the mysticism of a Protestant such as Böhme has at least some correlates in Catholicism. Böhme by no means stood completely alone in his time, but in some ways he is the clearest manifestation of mystical and cosmological currents quite independent of him.

Böhme's first treatise, *Aurora*, was written during the first half of 1612, and by late July 1613 Böhme was verbally assaulted by the city magistrates and then by local Lutheran pastor Gregor Richter. According to Böhme, this treatise had been entrusted to a friend who, without his knowledge, circulated it and was responsible for having it copied. Regardless of how this happened, the fact remains that Böhme was publicly censured for having written this unusual, but not especially heretical work. Probably Richter's dislike for Böhme, which at times seemed to know no bounds, came from his viewing as a personal affront Böhme's scorn for those who embraced mere book-learning and the outward church, or "Babel."[5]

Görlitz had become something of a center for heterodox people, or at least people with mystical leanings. And Böhme's own circle eventually included some remarkable people, among whom we should note Balthasar Walter, an extraordinary man who had travelled to the Near East (Arabia, Syria, and Egypt) in search of "Kabbalah, magic, and alchemy" during the late sixteenth century, who came to know Böhme after 1612, and who stayed in Böhme's house for several months during 1619 or 1620. Other prominent, sympathetic members of Böhme's circle include Carl von Ender, a nobleman, Johann Huser, editor of an edition of Paracelsus's works, and Dr. Tobias Kober, who attended Böhme during his final illness.

Böhme refrained from producing any more treatises for some time, but eventually felt compelled by his own inner genius (and was no doubt prompted too by his friends) to continue the work he had begun with *Aurora*. In 1618 he began *The Three Principles of the Divine Essence*, and between 1619 and his death in 1624, he completed an amazing number of treatises and assorted other manuscripts and letters, including *Forty Questions on the Soul*, *The Signature of All Things*, and the massive *Mysterium Magnum*, a commentary on Genesis, as well as numerous other works, some of which were only published by Werner Buddecke in the mid-twentieth century.

This prodigious output of written works during the last years of Böhme's life is all the more remarkable because he was certainly not living a reclusive life, far from it. Having given up his cobbler's shop, he had become a merchant, and was very active in trading, travelling much for business. Additionally, Böhme met informally with those interested in what he had to say about the spiritual life, wrote numerous letters to correspondents seeking guidance or illumination, and in general lived a busy life, not always easily making ends meet. His affairs were complicated by the advent of the Thirty Years War in 1618, and the difficulties this naturally caused.

In the last year of his life, 1624, Böhme saw the publication of *Christosophia: The Way to Christ* by a Görlitz printer, funded by a Dresden nobleman. Arguably the most accessible, and definitely the most devotional of his major works, this book offers a natural introduction to Böhme's Sophianic mysticism and his deep piety. The first book of Böhme's published during his lifetime, *The Way to Christ* incensed Pastor Gregor Richter, who furiously railed against the "enthusiast, or confused phantast" Böhme from the pulpit and in vulgar printed pamphlets. One finds this fury perplexing, given the subdued, simple, and pious nature of the book itself, probably the least difficult of Böhme's major works.

Thus, 1624 was a most trying year for Böhme, who was compelled to leave Görlitz with his family in March. Although he was invited in May to the Court of Dresden, and hoped to find there a sympathetic audience through his patron, in fact he had to return home during the summer, where his family was being persecuted by townspeople whipped up by the snarling pastor. Richter died in August, but he was replaced by another antimystical Lutheran pastor, Nikolaus Thomas. During late summer and autumn of 1624, Böhme travelled through Silesia, meeting with friends and those interested in theosophy.

But all of this travel and the trying nature of his life wore Böhme down, and in early November he returned home to Görlitz for the last time. Already ill, and accompanied by his physician, Tobias Kober, Böhme had to undergo a doctrinal examination by Pastor Thomas before he could receive communion. Even though he passed this examination, when Böhme died on November 17, Thomas initially refused to conduct a funeral service, and did so only when compelled by city officials and Kober. Reportedly, Böhme's last words were, "Now I enter paradise." After his death, Böhme's gravestone was defaced by village rabble, who carried on the hatred that had swirled around him during the last few years of his life, reminiscent perhaps of the reception Christ himself received.

After his death, Böhme's influence of course continued, not least because of his earnest disciples, who had been meeting in Görlitz during the last few years of his life. This group, which held copies of the original manuscripts, made certain that not only were these works preserved, and some of them published, but even more importantly from a theosophic perspective, ensured that practical Sophianic theosophy continued as an actual spiritual discipline. Prominent members of this original theosophic group included Abraham von Franckenberg (1593–1652) and Johann Theodor von Tschech (1595–1649), who helped to keep Böhme's work alive, and to spread it throughout Europe.

We should also mention here that Böhmean theosophy inspired other forms of art, particularly poetry and music, and so the poetic works of Quirinus Kuhlmann (1651–1689) and Johann Scheffler (1624–1677, known as Angelus Silesius, or the "Angel of Silesia") are important bridges between Böhmean mysticism and a broader audience. Kuhlmann, an energetic advocate of theosophy, was burned at the stake in Moscow, and Scheffler converted from Lutheranism to Catholicism. But both authors, and numerous writers of hymns, helped make theosophic premises accessible to other Christians. Others influenced by theosophy include Pierre Poiret (1646–1719) and Antoinette Bourignon (1616–1680), not to mention outright theosophers such as Johann Gichtel, John Pordage, Jane Leade, and Johann Kelpius, all of whom we will discuss in detail shortly.

Having offered this sketch of the seminal theosopher who inspired the entire Protestant cycle of theosophy, we should turn to his works and doctrines, for these form a foundation for all theosophy to follow. By "foundation," however, I do not mean that theosophy entails a doctrinal obedience to Böhme's authoritative revelation. To enjoin doctrinal obedience alone is anathema to theosophy. Theosophers insist above all upon spiritual experience, and many theosophers had already had spiritual experiences before encountering Böhme's works, which acted to confirm and deepen what they had already begun to see for themselves. This scenario is exemplified in Louis Claude de Saint-Martin (1743–1803), who was so delighted by Böhme's writings that he translated some of them into French, also writing theosophic works of his own, much more profound than what he had been writing previously.

Böhme's first treatise, *Aurora*, reveals the scope of Böhme's revelations, which extended far beyond the "seeing into the center of nature" that had represented his first spiritual illumination in 1600. Twelve years later, when Böhme wrote *Aurora*, he had already developed a full terminology that included many alchemical and Paracelsian words. A glance at the chapter subjects is sufficient to demonstrate the breadth of Böhme's visionary doctrines: his topics range from "the creation of the holy angels and the nature of the Trinity" to the angelical kingdom, from "what remains hidden since the beginning of the world" to the nature of hell as wrathfulness, from "God's sport" before time began, to when time will end, from the nature of the mineral, vegetable, and animal kingdoms to the "secret mystery of humanity."

Much has been made of the supposed difficulty of Böhme's works, but in fact his works are not so complicated as to be indecipherable, and many passages are quite straightforward. For instance, in *Aurora* Böhme writes of how nature signifies "how the holy being in the holy Trinity is." He tells us to consider heaven, which is a round globe without beginning or end, "for its beginning and end are everywhere," like God, "who is in and above the heaven, [and] has neither beginning nor end."[6] "And the seven planets signify the seven spirits of God, or the princes of the Angels," while the Sun "is the king and the heart of all things of this world, and so rightly signifies the *Son* of God."[7]

Here Böhme is developing a principle that in fact guides the whole of his work, that nature, human and otherwise, reflects its divine origin. In the planets we see divine qualities that are in turn to be found in mineral, vegetable, animal, and human natures as well. There is, Böhme tells us, a single power that manifests itself in all the myriad stars, and so too "God the Father goeth forth in his deep out of all his powers, and genereateth the splendour, the Heart, or the Son of God in his center."[8] Those were not empty words in Genesis, Böhme tells us, that said God created man in his image.[9]

But just as there is a wrath or fierceness in nature, so too there is a wrath in the human soul. This wrath is the *residuum* inherent in material creation, and "The Holy Ghost does not go into the wrath or fierceness, but reigns in the source of the soul, which is in the light of God, and fights against the wrath or fierceness in the soul."[10] So long as a human being is alive, he cannot attain "any perfect knowledge in this life, till at the end, when light and darkness are separated, and wrath or fierceness is, with the body, consumed in the earth; then the soul sees clearly and perfectly in God its Father."[11]

Even from what we have considered so far, we can see the interconnected, unusual nature of Böhme's writing. His writing is elusively circular, and an assertion about the Trinity thus refers also to the planets, and to human nature. Everything is linked; everything is a sign pointing toward its own divine meaning, and its consequent human implications. Böhme does give some direct doctrinal statements, although the import of his writing is not at all dogmatic, but rather is intended to guide the reader to a way of understanding for himself. This understanding is not of the reason alone, nor is it even possible to fully understand such mysteries in this lifetime. Böhme's spiralling, interlinked method of exposition frustrates rationalistic, categorical thinking—but it is supposed to.

For Böhme's work is intended above all to point us toward our own spiritual rebirth, a process or series of births that continues beyond our present lifetime. Indeed, Böhme writes in *Aurora*, there are three births: there is "the outward birth or geniture, which is the house of death," (fleshly life); there is the astral birth, "wherein love and wrath wrestle the one with the other"; and the third birth "the outward man *neither knows nor comprehends.*" While in the flesh, therefore, man must strive with his soul to "press through the firmament of heaven to God, and live with God." In this way, then, one must unite all three realms—body, soul, and spirit—in this lifetime, pressing beyond the astral to the transcendent spirit.[12]

Thus, the spiritual path Böhme points toward leads through the astral or soul's realm to its spiritual origin. In a sense, Böhme points toward what we might call a Christian shamanism. He writes:

> Some men have many times entered in the sidereal or astral spirit, and have been ravished in an ecstasy, as some call it, and have known the gates of heaven and of hell, and have told, shown, and declared how that many men dwell in hell. . . . Such indeed have been scorned, derided, or laughed at, but with great ignorance and indiscretion, for it is just so as they declare: which I will also describe more at large in its due place, and show in what manner and condition it is with them.[13]

"If your eyes were but open, you would see *wonderful* things," Böhme chides us. "Heaven is *in* a holy man," and hence everywhere that he stands, sits, or lies, there is heaven also.

This insistence, that heaven and hell are present to us now if we can but see them, is a hallmark of all theosophy. As we shall see, Dr. John Pordage's visionary life began with a series of exactly such "openings" of the spiritual worlds as Böhme here refers to, and the history of theosophy after Böhme is very much a history marked by similar visionary revelations in the lives of all our major theosophers. Böhmean theosophy is indeed an experiential visionary tradition, and in fact only direct spiritual revelation can explain the certainty with which Böhme himself, and all subsequent theosophers as well, explain or document spiritual realities such as the nature of the angels.

The magisterial quality of Böhme's prose is itself revealing. Böhme writes with great authority, yet insists that what he writes is not from the reasoning mind alone. Near the end of *Aurora* he asserts:

> This now is the very door of the hidden, secret mystery of the Deity. Concerning which the reader is to conceive that it is not in the power or capacity of any man to discern or to know it, if the dawn of morning-redness does not break forth in the center of the soul. For these things are divine mysteries, which no man can search into by his own reason.[14]

Yet Böhme also maintains his own humility, adding that "I . . . esteem myself most unworthy of such a gift; and besides, I shall have many scorners and mockers against me; for the corrupted nature is horribly ashamed before the light."

Reading *Aurora*, one can see why some religious authorities would take umbrage at Böhme's tone in the book. It is true that Böhme did not intend the book for publication, and indeed even left it incomplete, lacking some "thirty sheets." But at the same time, he did let it circulate among friends, and knew—as we can tell by his references to "scorners and mockers against me" who are made ashamed by the light—that his writings would raise opposition by their very nature. It would appear, in other words, that the magisterial authority of Böhme's voice is despite him; his revelations are in his own view part of his cross to bear in this world.

More than half a decade passed between Böhme's *Aurora* and his *The Three Principles of the Divine Essence*, which he began in January 1618. The numerous subtitles of the book—in the fashion of the time—give some indication of this work's scope. The "Three Principles" are of the "Eternal Dark, Light, and Temporary World," showing "What the Soul, the Image, and the Spirit of the Soul are: As also what Angels, Heaven, and Paradise are" and "What the Wrath of God, Sin, Death, the Devils, and Hell are: How all Things have been, now are, and how they shall be at the last." Here once again we are entering into a work of enormous scope, but what was straightforwardly expressed in *Aurora* is here offered in a much more complicated explication.

Fundamentally, Böhme has a single perspective or way of understanding, which all his works elaborate from different angles, but with *The Three Principles* we are entering into Böhme's most complex exposition, riddled with alchemical terminology and exegesis. A palimpsest, *The Three Principles* is even more circular in its organization than *Aurora*, and it is a profoundly layered book whose multiple levels are all interconnected and reflect one another. At the same time, *The Three Principles* is mature Böhme during what we might call his "middle period" of composition. Consequently, while repeating some of what he wrote earlier, Böhme also does clarify doctrinal points here.

We should begin by examining Böhme's own preface to this work. In it, he begins: "Man can undertake nothing from the beginning of his youth nor in the whole course of his time in this world that is more profitable and necessary for him than to know himself." This admonition recalls the axiom affiliated with Hermes Trismegistus, that we must learn who we are, where we have come from, and whence we go, or the even more primal Delphic admonition: "Know thyself." God has allowed man to "penetrate into the heart of everything, and discern what essence, virtue, and property it has, in creatures, earth, stones, trees, herbs, in all moveable and immoveable things."[15]

Böhme tells us, further, that he has an obligation to set down these words, even though he knows that haughty people will, like swine, root about in his "Garden of Pleasure" and scorn what he has to say. "I cannot well neglect to set this down in writing, because God will require an account of everyone's gifts," and furthermore "as to the children of God, they shall perceive and comprehend this my writing, what it is, for it is a very convincing Testimony." The "children of malignity" will find this book closed to them, but the children of God will find this book to point toward and to confirm revelation for them.

We should recognize, too, that there is a millennialist element within Böhme's writing, which was later amplified in English theosophy especially, and which in turn inspired much of Pennsylvania theosophy as well. Böhme writes: "There is a wonderful time coming. But because it begins in the night, there are many that shall not see it, because of their sleep and great drunkenness; yet the sun will shine to the children at midnight. Thus I commit the reader to the meek love of God. Amen."[16] Since these words introduce us to *The Three Principles*, they place the entire book in a millennialist light, and underscore the pentecostal nature of all subsequent theosophic history as well.

But often this work's mysteries are clothed in alchemical language. For example, Mercurius, Sulphur, and Salt take on multiple, elaborate meanings in *The Three Principles*. Indeed, conveying to the reader what these terms mean accounts for much of this text's difficulty to a reader encountering it for the first time. About Mercurius, for example, Böhme asserts:

> Mark what Mercurius is: it is Harshness, Bitterness, Fire, and Brimstone-water, the most horrible Essence; yet you must understand hereby no *materia*, matter, or comprehensible thing; but all no other than spirit, and the source of the original nature.[17]

Each of these words is broken down into its components, each of which is given additional meanings too: hence, SUL and PHUR signify aspects of Sulphur, MER CU RI and US offer different aspects of Mercurius, and so forth.

With such terms, Böhme denotes different aspects of phenomenal existence. Sulphur represents, in this schema, the "kindling," animating power, or soul of existence, Mercury represents the spirit, and Salt represents the body, or the "cause of comprehensibility." But we must take care not to reduce Böhme's terms to a simple correspondence, for in *The Three Principles*, existence is seen from a supraphysical perspective, as a kind of "wheel" or cycle of elemental reaction and counteraction, of fire "shrieking" against water, for example, that takes place within a "principle."

And in fact, the three principles to which Böhme and subsequent theosophers from Pordage to Saint-Martin make constant reference are not alchemical, but refer to the relationship between God and Man. For God the Father is the First Principle, the Divine Essence; the Second Principle is the Holy Spirit, associated with the "Light-World"; and between these two is the Third Principle, which includes the elemental and sidereal world, where the counterposed powers of Satan and Christ appear. These principles correspond respectively to the "dark-world" or "fire-world," the "light-world" of paradise, and the human world. Living in the Third Principle, the Second Principle is opened unto us, and this opening is in fact the theosophic path.

Böhme's intent is to lead us on this path, to generate an opening in us, not to feed our rational categorizing tendency. The "divine Light" is necessary for real comprehension, but, he writes, "I will represent the high hidden Secret in a creaturely manner, that thereby the reader may come into the depth."[18] For we are invited to enter into this world of visionary physics, if we may so put it. The divine light is necessary for truly comprehending Böhme, meaning that when we try to categorize or rationally schematize Böhme's work we do it a disservice. Ultimately, he tells, we are obligated to become visionaries ourselves, to test out experimentally whether what he writes is true.

From this derives what some perceive as the frustrating nature of the book. The reader is led on a spiralling journey through an ever-deepening cosmic vision while reading Böhme's *The Three Principles*, and although the more systematic exposition of a Pordage is very useful for understanding theosophic principles, we should remember that for Pordage too, and for Böhme above all, theosophy entails not only repeated readings (an immersing in this symbolic cosmos) but eventually an understanding of a different, more profound, and in a sense suprahuman quality. We must immerse ourselves in this symbolic realm until it becomes ours.

"Beloved Reason," Böhme admonishes us, "leave off your thoughts, for with these thoughts and conceits you know not God or Eternity."[19] This is not an admonition that we abandon reason, only that we recognize its limitations. For there are three kingdoms in man, according to Böhme: there is the kingdom of hell, or wrath, there is the kingdom of this earth, the stars and elements, and there is the kingdom of paradise.[20] Now we can understand this through reason, but we participate in these realms with our soul, not with our rationalizing faculty. Reason, in other words, only points us in the right direction, toward paradise, and thus in itself is not enough. Paradise can be attained only by a conversion of the entire being, a movement of the whole soul into light, joy, love.

And so even though Böhme cannot ultimately be systematized, his fundamental message to us in *The Three Principles* is certainly not hard to comprehend. He concludes *The Three Principles* with advice to us that has profound implications for our everyday lives:

> We all in the originality of our life have the source of the Anger, or Fierceness, or else we should not be alive; but we must look to it, and in ourselves go forth out of the source of the fierceness with God, and generate the love in us, and then it stands rightly in the Paradise of God; but if our life stays in the Fierceness, viz. in covetousness, envy, anger, and malice, and goes not forth into another will, then it stands in the anguishing source, as all Devils do, wherein no good thought or will can be, but only mere enmity in itself.[21]

If we let ourselves live in the world of wrath, then to that degree we will be evil incarnate; if, however, we live in meekness, patience, and love, we will indeed be children of God. We grow out of this life like plants, which will in the next life be bathed in the love, joy, and light of the heavenly kingdom.

We will not, here, survey in detail the rest of Böhme's written works, but rather will consider only those aspects of his books that best serve as foundational for the study of later theosophers such as Gichtel, Pordage, and Kelpius. This approach is particularly appropriate because most of Böhme's major works were written in the last six years of his life, and to some degree they do repeat and amplify one another, but it is also appropriate because we do not have space here to consider all of his works and doctrines in detail. A sympathetic and complete discussion of this kind, in English, still awaits us.[22]

There are two works that we should examine here: *De Signatura Rerum,* or *The Signature of All Things*, and *Christosophia: The Way to Christ*. The first of these is Böhme's most complete exposition of the relationships between eternity and time, and between the visible cosmos and its invisible animating powers. The second, *Christosophia*, is Böhme's final and, in a real sense, most practical book, a devotional book that insists upon the spiritual context in which better Böhmean theosophy must be understood. *Christosophia* is a book that can be understood by virtually anyone, and serves as an natural entry into the practice of theosophic discipline that informed many subsequent theosophic communities.

The Signature of All Things elaborates the fundamental Böhmean doctrine that we have seen informing all of his books: that we must experience spiritual truth directly, not through reasoning alone. He begins:

> All whatever is spoken, written, or taught of God, without the knowledge of the signature, is dumb and void of understanding; for it proceeds only from an historical conjecture, from the mouth of another, wherein the spirit without knowledge is dumb, but if the spirit opens to him the signature, then he understands the speech of another.[23]

If we hear someone speak, or read what someone writes about God, that is not sufficient to truly understand him; but "if his sound and spirit out of his signature and similitude enter into my own similitude," "then I may understand him really and fundamentally."

According to Böhme, historical conjecture from the mouth of another does not produce real knowledge: real knowledge comes only from direct inward experience. As we have seen, this principle informs all of Böhme's work from beginning to end, and it is exactly the principle that enrages his outwardly religious critics most. After all, much if not all of Christianity has consisted in affirmations not of spiritual realities, but of historical conjectures. Belief that Jesus Christ was born and died for some takes precedence over whether Christ's presence is a living reality in ourselves—but not for Böhme. For him, inward spiritual verification takes absolute precedence over mere historicism or outward shows of religion.

Furthermore, all real communication, according to Böhme, must take place from an inward union, a meeting of inward "signatures." True communication, therefore, is a union of two beings. For true communication to take place, one spirit must "imprint its own similitude" in another, must participate in the other. This means that in reality communication takes place on an invisible level; and thus we can see why, later in the same century in England, theosopher Thomas Bromley could write that a theosophic circle shares in one another's spiritual joys and sorrows, even at a great distance from one another. For the theosophers all participate in the same paradisical "signature."

But Böhme's doctrine of signatures has ramifications that extend through all levels of the cosmos. For "man has indeed all the forms of all the three worlds lying in him; for he is a complete image of God, or of the Being of all beings."[24] And just as a man's or woman's hidden inward nature or signature is visible through conversations or actions, so too "everything has its mouth to manifestation, and this is the language of nature, whence everything speaks out of its property, and continually manifests . . . its mother."[25] Everything that we see in this world bears signatures that body forth the unseen forces of nature.

These unseen forces or qualities are seen in the seven planets, each of which has traditional associations reflecting its informing nature, and all of which are "midway" between the Divine and Creation. Fiery Mars, with his masculine symbolism, can be seen in animals, herbs, minerals, and man, as can each of the planets. The cosmos is hierarchic and emanatory: "above" are the seven spirits of creation, "intermediate" are the seven planetary qualities, and "below" are all the myriad forms of phenomena, each of which represents unique combinations of these partly hidden inward forces or qualities. Thus, "the whole outward visible world" is "a signature or figure of the inward spiritual world."[26]

De Signatura Rerum is the most Paracelsian of Böhme's works. Like Paracelsus, Böhme considered medicine in terms of spirit, soul, and body; his comments on spagyric medicine are found primarily in the middle chapters of *The Signature of All Things*, and are in the context of spiritual and psychological healing. For spagyric or Paracelsian medicine in Böhme's writing directly reflects his cosmology, and therefore his writing is filled with references to the planets as qualitative powers in the soul's realm, although it is always written with an eye to spiritual significance.

According to Böhme, there are certain herbs, for example, that bear a signature that is visible only to the wise and good. Thus "If . . . Mercury is between Venus and Jupiter, and Mars undermost, then . . . is the universal very sovereign in the thing, be it either a man, or other creature, or an herb of the earth."[27] But "the curse of God hides the eyesight of the wicked," and they cannot even perceive that "with these herbs a man may cure, and heal . . . ; but they are rarely and seldom found, and indeed not one among many sees them, for they are close to paradise." There is also a signature of "witchcraft," which is Mars beside Saturn, Venus under Mars, and Jupiter under Venus, all together under the influence of the Moon, a signature of corruption, poison, and evil. Böhme's spagyric medicine, therefore, exists in a moral context that determines its meaning; it is a medicine of the soul.

The ultimate aim of this medicine is the complete regeneration of humanity, the restoration of a primordial selfless state. This regeneration or resurrection of man takes place through a purification of planetary energies. Everything in this elementary world is "in the curse and anger of God according to the property of the first principle," and indeed without the visible Sun, we would be living in hell.[28] Thus,

> [I]f anything shall be freed from this self-hood, that is, from
> the wrathful death, and be again brought into the universal,
> that is, into the highest perfection, then it must die wholly to
> its self-hood, and enter into the stillness . . . Mars must wholly
> lose the might of fire and wrath, and Mercury also his poison-
> life; Saturn must be a death to himself.[29]

This is, Böhme tells us plainly, the whole of the theosophic work: selfishness must be turned to selflessness, wrath to joy and love.[30] This is the
simple aim of the theosopher: to bring all seven properties into harmony,
to eliminate all diseases and enmities of the soul, to be transmuted into
a "new man born in God."

Indeed, Böhme affirms again and again, in scriptural allusions, that
we must take the childlike selfless path. Love and anger both stir within
us, but if we depart from our selfhood and forsake our own damnation,
and continually cast ourselves "only into God's mercy, that is, into the
suffering and death of Christ, and into his resurrection and restoration,"
and will nothing of ourselves, then God's anger cannot reach us; we live
then as a nothing, in the divine essence wholly, in our "first mother of
eternity" as we were before creation itself.[31] Hence Böhme warns curi-
ous readers that they will "not effect anything in this way" until they
enter into it themselves, and then it will be shown without much seeking, for the "way is childlike, (plain and easy)."[32]

In the end, then, Böhme tells us, he sets before us only "what the
Lord of all beings has given me," a looking glass wherein we may see
what and who we are. His work is "a very clear gate of the mystery of
all beings." Before us is our fundamental choice, between wrath, darkness, and selfhood on the one hand, and joy, light, and selflessness on
the other. It is true that Böhme includes a number of unusual terms in
De Signatura Rerum; his early English translators even offered a brief
glossary. But these terms, like the planetary or other symbolisms here,
are only elaborations or elucidations of his primary affirmation that we
must each ultimately choose our destiny in this world and the next. This
is the "gate of mystery" his work represents.

In his last years, Böhme was more and more intent on revealing the
practical theosophic path, and thus we possess not only various letters
that document his spiritual guidance of various theosophic circles and
individuals, but also dialogues such as "Of the Supersensual Life" or
"Discourse Between Two Souls" that show something of how this spiritual guidance can take place. Naturally, a dialogue between a theosophic master and a spiritually ignorant but eager scholar can only go

so far in suggesting the nature of the theosophic discipline itself, but at the same time, it suggests the unique nature of each spiritual aspirant's path while confirming the general path one must take.

Böhme's *Christosophia: The Way to Christ*, his first book published (1624), and his most accessible and popular work, reflects this practical focus. In it, we see the devotional path Böhme enjoins, and can see why he had such an enormous, if sometimes "underground" impact on religious life across Europe, England, and into America. For *Christosophia* represents a kind of handbook or sourcebook for the theosopher, a compendium of prayers, spiritual advice, dialogues, and brief treatises written on the request of various seekers. Gone from this book are many of the dense alchemical references, the terms of spagyric medicine, and the cosmological explications that characterized the other books we have examined, not rejected, of course, but subordinated to devotional practice.

Christosophia begins with a treatise on repentence, dated 1622, a treatise that emphasizes how a soul must realize "it has become faithless to God," immersed in the earthly, temporal life, and ignorant of divine judgement. Fully realizing its corruption, the soul must turn to God, to the "very precious name JESUS," "in which there is no wrath at all," and "imagine that at this hour and moment it stands in the presence of the Holy Trinity."[33] Böhme begins by emphasizing repentence because if the soul remains convinced of itself, its pride will prevent it from any spiritual revelation at all.

Much of *Christosophia* consists in suggested prayers, imploring God to "teach me what I ought to do so that I might turn to You." "Redirect my will to You. Draw me in Christ to the Father, and help me so that henceforth I might leave sin and vanity and never again enter into them," Böhme writes. These extended prayers are not common in Böhme's earlier works, but Böhme's aim here, in *Christosophia*, is not cosmological exposition so much as teaching us how to redirect our souls, how to orient ourselves toward God, and how to transmute our souls and our lives.

There is also a chivalric aspect to *Christosophia*, particularly where Böhme writes of how the soul "is to strive for the noble, knightly crown; what kind of armor it must wear," and above all, how "if the soul wishes to obtain Christ's conqueror's crown from the noble Virgin Sophia, it must court Her with great love-desire" "in very chaste humility."[34] This "wooing of the noble Virgin Sophia," while certainly present in *Christosophia*, was elaborated and intensified in the works and lives of later theosophers, especially Gichtel, Johann Wilhelm Ueberfeld (who edited the primary [1730] Leiden edition of *Christosophia:The Way to Christ*), John Pordage, Johann Kelpius, and Conrad Beissel.

Indeed, here in *The Way to Christ* we can see the origin of much in the later Sophianic tradition. Sophianic mysticism, of course, does not begin with Böhme, but can be seen in the Old Testament, in the Church Fathers, in medieval Christianity (as in Dante's Beatrice), and in Eastern Orthodoxy. However, when Böhme writes that the "love of Sophia in the growth of the flower of Christ," is "the flower of Sharon, the rose in the valley, of which Solomon [Song of Solomon 2:1] sings and calls his dear beloved, his chaste betrothed, whom he loved as have all the saints before and after him," we see references that were fully developed by Conrad Beissel and the Ephrata colony of Pennsylvania in their female monastic order of the rose of Sharon, and in their Sophianic mysticism generally.

In the many letters of Johann Gichtel—one of the great theosophers after Böhme—collected in the multivolume *Theosophia Practica*, we see elaborated numerous references to the "wooing," the "kisses," the "marriage bed," and the mysterious union with the noble Virgin Sophia. Gichtel takes care to point out that these are not to be understood in a sexual way. Certainly Gichtel's Sophianic mysticism has its origin in such admonitions as this, from *Christosophia*:

> Dear soul, you must always be in earnest, unrelenting. You will obtain the love of a kiss from the noble Sophia in the holy Name JESUS, for she stands immediately before the soul's door and knocks and warns the sinner against godless ways. If he desires Sophia's love she is willing and kisses him with a beam of her sweet love, in which the heart receives joy. But she does not immediately enter into the marriage bed with the soul, nor does she immediately awaken the corrupted heavenly image that was lost in Paradise. This is dangerous for humanity, for since Adam and Lucifer once fell, this may occur again, because man is still tightly caught in vanity.[35]

Böhme's words here are somewhat prophetic, since Gichtel's letters detail numerous cases of those of who wooed the noble Sophia, were restored to Paradise, and fell again.

Later in *Christosophia*, Böhme includes comforting instructions of the Virgin Sophia to the theosopher's soul, and numerous prayers for the morning and for the evening. The comforting instructions of Sophia, coming here, partway through the book, imply that the soul and Sophia are betrothed already, that the initial stage of the journey (repentence) has given way to a nuptial union of Sophia's light and the soul's fire. The prayers Böhme offers in this part of the volume also imply the continuing, intensifying union of the soul and its divine origin at every point of the day, and throughout daily life. This section of *Christosophia* is intended to arm and encourage us in our long struggle to overcome the "bestial man" within us.

But Böhme also includes some stringent warnings on how commonplace Christianity often is "Babel," merely "histories" and "stone churches" without any existential transformation of the soul. He tells us that much of Christianity is but a clinging to the husks, for a man or woman can go to church for twenty or thirty years, hear sermons, partake of the sacraments, be absolved, and yet remain just as bad a "beast of the devil" and of vanity as those who do not go to church at all. Christ's body and blood are in the sacraments, and thus they stand to condemn us if we partake of them without truly participating in them.[36]

We should point out that a primary characteristic of theosophy—a rejection of all sectarianism—has its roots in Böhme's *The Way to Christ* as well. Böhme asserts unambiguously that a Christian "has no sect." A Christian can dwell among sects peacably, even attend their services, but clings to none. "He has only a single knowledge, and that is Christ in him," Böhme tells us. This insistence on complete nonsectarianism recurs throughout theosophy, and its significance is explained in detail by Gichtel in his letters, who held that sectarianism creates an "astral shell" that itself cuts us off from the divine. Even the nonsectarian English Philadelphians were regarded suspiciously as approaching sectarianism by many Continental theosophers. Böhme's admonitions against sects here reverberate through the whole history of theosophy.

The whole focus of Böhmean theosophy is inward, in the manner of Hermeticism and, before it, Orphism and the Mystery traditions stretching back from Greco-Roman and perhaps even Egyptian antiquity. Indeed, some of Böhme's formulations are strikingly Hermetic and Gnostic in flavor, as when he holds that the whole Christian religion consists in this: that we come to know who and what we are, whence we have come, the dire nature of the evil awakened in us, and where we are destined to go after this present life is over.[37] This emphasis on the primacy of the inward life and the soul's destiny represents the essence of Böhme's mission, to unambiguously point us toward actual spiritual transmutation, and away from mere verbal or doctrinal formulations or institutionalized, outward structures.

The final third of *Christosophia: The Way to Christ* consists primarily in dialogues and in an analysis of the "constellations" or psychic constitutions of various people. Both of these sections have similar and complementary purposes: the dialogues help answer questions that theosophic aspirants might have about the nature of their own spiritual discipline and its cosmological foundations, and the analyses of "constellations" help them recognize problems in their own souls, and in the souls of others whom they might be in a position to guide one day. Thus, the final section of *Christosophia*, not surprisingly, is at a much more developed level than the earlier sections of the books; if the earlier prayers and addresses showed the approach to the theosophic path, the later sections of the book show theosophy in all its profundity.

The most extraordinary of the dialogues is that called "Of the Supersensual Life, or a Conversation of a Master and a Student" (1622). In it, the entire conversation takes place at a remarkably straightforward and profound level, as when the student begins by asking how he may come to the supersensual life so as to see God and hear him speak. The master replies that if one could enter for a moment into that place where no creature dwells, one could hear what God speaks. When asked where this is, the master replies: "It is in you. If you could be silent from all willing and thinking for one hour you would hear God's inexpressible words."[38]

At this point comes the most striking moment in the dialogue: the master tells the student that when one experiences God, above nature and creature, one becomes that "which God was before nature and creature," and sees and hears what God himself saw and heard before one was born. This affirmation is very much parallel with the Zen Buddhist *koan* that urges us to realize the face we had before we were born. Our own striving and will to see and hear, to grasp conceptually, keeps us from directly experiencing the supersensual life, our natural inheritance.

We must, in short, enter that *Ungrund* [groundlessness] out of which the world was made. Paradoxically, our desire to achieve or to acquire something—even peace, joy, love, holiness—itself prevents us from realizing that which was before we were born, and will be after we are dead in this world. This, Böhme tells us, is what Christ meant by saying that we must become like little children. We must be like children, who participate directly in reality, rather than being separate from it and intellectually trying to grasp it.[39] This means we must be free from all things, become nothing to all things, just as all things must be nothing to us. Such paradoxes point us toward the inexpressible transcendence of all things, which can only be experienced.

This transcendence of all things is experienced as astonishing brightness, as overwhelming joy and love inexpressible. But as you begin to experience this transcendent love, the world begins to turn against you, Böhme's master tells his student. You must be prepared to truly follow Christ, meaning, to be despised and attacked in this world, and to accept your suffering gladly, something that indeed all our theosophers had to do, since all were publicly assaulted in various ways, as was Böhme himself, and as was Christ. For as long as we live in this world, we must struggle; love and suffering must coexist. It is wrong to look for some blissful state on this earth in which there is no longer suffering, for our life on earth is a trial and a means of redemption, hence a struggle whose resolution can come only when this life is over; we can only taste paradise on earth, we cannot here possess it or be wholly possessed by it.

Yet it is possible for us to taste paradise and hell on earth, for these are states of consciousness. Indeed, Böhme's explanation of how the soul comes to experience heaven or hell after death is extremely interesting. He tells us that if during life a soul schools itself in the discipline of becoming nothing in itself, then through its resignation in Christ it comes to divine rest, and when the body's life ends, divine love and light shine through the purified soul completely. But a godless soul remains caught up in its vanity and selfhood, refusing divine resignation, and continuing to long for the things of this world. Thus, when the godless soul is separated from the body at death, it cannot experience paradise because it is not open; filled with despair and regret, it is also filled with anger, which is hell itself carried in the soul.[40]

Hence, we can see how our spiritual lives on earth bear fruit in the next world—and the same principles hold true for the Last Judgment and the end of time and space. When this material or elemental world ceases to exist, then everything will exist according to its inward or spiritual realm alone, its nature being either the divine love-fire or wrath-fire. The physical body is of course not reanimated—rather, the crystalline, transparent spiritual body will be resurrected, meaning that the soul will meet and unite with its own spiritual being or archetype, "tinctured" with its own good or evil acts and knowledge. The Last Judgment is the revelation of who we really are, in the divine fire, which to some is love and to others, wrath.

In paradise we meet ourselves as we truly are, beyond time and space, our eternal light-body, and in fact, the crystalline spiritual earth will be in us, rather than we being in it. For in question here is not a "location" of a soul "in" paradise, but an existence in a state of consciousness. Paradise must be in us, and for us to experience it after death, we must experience it before death. Our problem is that we think of the afterlife in terms of this earthly life, as a "place" to which we "go," but reality is that the afterlife, be it paradise or hell, is located in us. Here on earth, we are in the world; in paradise, the crystalline spiritual earth is in us.

Böhme's *Christosophia* concludes with descriptions of psychological difficulties that assail souls on the theosophic or mystical path, and focuses particularly on the problem of melancholy. Many mystics have commented on how the soul enters into a "dark night" on the spiritual path, during which time it is tested and strengthened by the withdrawal of spiritual comforts previously granted it. According to Böhme, melancholy, fear, or anguish are temptations that beset the soul, which is as if confined in a dark prison while here on earth, and thus naturally subject to the dark, dry, melancholic, self-consuming humor. The only cure for melancholy is the light of the divine Virgin.

Essentially, Böhme's is a psychology of the imagination, and all ailments of the soul must be cured through the movement or correction of the imagination. For example, if the soul forms an image with a melancholic tenor, and focuses itself on that image, feeding on it, then naturally the soul turns away from God's will; it closes itself off from divine light. The only cure for despair, which is the temptation of the devil, is to turn the imagination back to the Divine. The devil can accomplish man's fall only through the imagination, through suggesting that one's sins are too great for redemption and so forth.

In fact, Böhme offers the kind of lighthearted mockery with which one should greet the devil's insinuations. One should not let one's thoughts descend into disputes, or be caught in rationalizations, or allow oneself either to be flattered or to be frightened. The devil has no power over man save that which man gives him; man always has free will, and as long as he is alive, partakes in the "great tree of all souls," which means God always offers him redemption, however great his sins. Evil does exist, according to Böhme, but it has reality for us only in the degree that we turn away from the divine will, close ourselves off from our own true nature, and let our imaginations dwell in the devil's insinuations and despair.

Of course, not all melancholy comes directly from the devil. Much melancholy derives from the soul's being subject to the melancholic humor, and this can happen to the holiest of souls. The soul's constellation, or astral constitution, may consist of Saturnine and Martial influences or tendencies that make it susceptible to depression, or fear of God's wrath, but the soul must indulge these tendencies. The soul's melancholy, in other words, is a "fantasy," a separation from reality and a movement of the imagination into a circular, uncontrolled "wheel" of tormented thoughts. The devil may take advantage of this fantasy, but it is essentially a self-created delusion.

How does one break this melancholic or fantastic cycle? According to Böhme, one must penetrate into the *centrum naturae*, the principial center of existence, which is beyond the cycles of fantasy to which the soul sometimes subjects itself. This wheel or self-deluding cycle cannot be broken by "self-reason," (by the rational mind), but only by continual profound prayer, by consigning one's entire self to God. It helps, Böhme adds, to live a moderate, simple, solitary life, in an ordinary vocation. But most important of all is prayer, which fundamentally is an openness to the Divine, for without this nothing good can be created in this world.[41]

Böhme's psychology is therefore not aimed, like nineteenth- and twentieth-century psychological models, at merely "balancing" the psyche so that it can function adequately in society. Simply to function in this world is all too often to be subject to the *spiritus mundi*, the worldly spirit about which we will say much more shortly. Böhme insists that "he who lives in the constellation lives like all animals," that there is no constellation so noble that the devil cannot find pleasure in it.[42] Böhme regards the soul's "astral constellation" as often inclined toward evil in itself—those subject to the choleric humor become easily angry, thus allowing into this world wrathful demonic power, melancholics despair and consume themselves, and so forth—and therefore we require divine light and power from *beyond* the astral constellation.

Here we find Böhme's central insight, not only in *The Way to Christ*, but in his many other books, treatises, and letters as well. For while Böhme is most noted for his profound understanding of cosmology, and of the soul's astral constitution and tendencies (his Paracelsian diagnoses of the soul's ailments and medicines), his primary insight is into the necessity that the soul break through this astral "cloud" and hold to its origin in the divine light. Or to put it another way, the soul must cease creating astral fantasies or wheels of imagination, and open itself to the divine will, which alone can bring true transcendent peace, joy, and light.

This fundamental insight of how the soul must transcend the merely astral is depicted beautifully in the frontispiece illustration that accompanied some eighteenth-century German editions of *The Way to Christ*.

In this illustration, we see a globe at the base, above which is a heart encircled by a star-studded serpent and a wrathful dragon. The serpent symbolizes the elemental world, and the dragon the wrathful, demonic powers against which the heart must guard itself. Above the heart is the illuminated but weeping eye, above which are the dark, roiling clouds that separate us from the spiritual realm. Penetrating the clouds is a rope, tied to an anchor caught on a cross, surmounting which is an illuminated eagle.

The illustration depicts the soul's struggle while on earth—its struggle with wrath and with entanglement in the elemental world, and the necessity for holding onto its spiritual anchor in the transcendent divine realm of light, surmounted by the eagle with outstretched wings, the eagle of spiritual sight. For the lower, material and emotional world (the phenomenal world to which the soul reacts) is separated by clouds from the realm of divine light. From below the soul cannot see the divine light directly, save by breaking through the clouds, which represent the soul's astral "shell" or covering.

Thus, the illustration neatly captures Böhme's most essential insight, an insight that proved fundamental to other theosophers as well: the necessity for "penetrating the astral." The implications of this insight are profound and manifold. Above all, it explains why sectarianism is ultimately antispiritual—for to form a sect is to form another astral shell, a carapace of dogma and received beliefs that keeps one from genuine spiritual experience. But it also explains the true danger of "worldliness," which really means remaining caught in the merely astral, in a world of rationality, fantasies, and emotional currents, rather than entering into spiritual reality.

Although Böhme's work has often been denigrated as obscure, in fact, as we have seen, its central implications are quite clear and straightforward. It is true that his cosmology is unfamiliar to us moderns, unaccustomed as we are to thinking about supraphysical principles; his work in this regard requires a shift in the way we think, a suppleness of mind that allows us to use our imaginations as a mode of perception. But fundamentally, Böhme's writing urges us toward spiritual perception on our own; it demonstrates that our afterlives depend upon our present lives, that we must be spiritually awakened now, during this lifetime. This simple message is simultaneously so profound as to take up all the many volumes of Böhme's remarkable treatises.

Here, after all, is why Böhme's life and works had such an enormous impact on subsequent European Christianity generally, and on theosophy particularly, so much so that all modern theosophers are part of the Böhmean tradition. Ordinary people—especially Anabaptists and what are often called "radical pietists," initially a derogatory term for people influenced by Böhmean theosophy—found in Böhme an affirmation of spiritual experience that was apostolic in nature, simple and clear. Subsequent theosophers and visionaries of the seventeenth century onward—Roman Catholic, Protestant, and Eastern Orthodox alike—found in Böhme's work the clearest understanding of visionary Sophianic spirituality, a complete visionary cosmology and spiritual discipline so profound as to be inexhaustible.

No doubt we could continue our explication of Böhme's doctrines almost indefinitely, but I have tried to emphasize only those concepts most critical for understanding our later theosophers, especially Gichtel, Pordage, Leade, Kelpius, and Beissel. All our theosophers were visionaries like Böhme; all used alchemical terminology, and at least some were practicing alchemists; all understood the world through the fundamental concepts of wrath and love; all experienced the visionary mediatrix Virgin Sophia; all were defiantly nonsectarian and warned against being caught in a mere dogmatic "shell." Our theosophers, in short, definitely share a common understanding of the cosmos, and of what it means to be human, and to this day Böhme's writings remain the most important source of this understanding.

Yet each theosopher is unique. For Böhmean theosophy has the remarkable characteristic of being a general understanding within which each individual theosopher develops and, we may say, flowers. This diversity comes, I believe, above all from theosophy's being a discipline, an experiential path that each must walk on his or her own. Thus, Jane Leade and Johann Gichtel can be contemporaries, both with spiritual circles (Leade's Philadelphians and Gichtel's Angelic Brethren), both visionaries with strikingly different views on important questions and wholly independent visionary lives, yet both indisputably part of Böhmean theosophy. For theosophy does not consist, finally, in doctrines to which one must accede, but in a spiritual discipline that each must experience for himself.

The history of theosophy subsequent to Böhme illustrates this point over and over again. We are dealing here with a way of understanding, a spiritual perspective, if you will, that does not depend upon a particular social milieu. Independent of circumstances, theosophy appears in urban Amsterdam and London, in Edinburgh and rustic Germany, in the Pennsylvania wilderness and in revolutionary France. Even during the riots and murders of the French Revolution, the saintly theosopher Saint-Martin went his serene way, carrying on his remarkable correspondence with Baron von Kirchberger, helping others when he could, and studying Böhme. This independence from circumstances characterizes Böhme's own often traumatic life as well, and in our day we may have something yet to learn from it, the legacy of theosophy.

CHAPTER TWO

Johann Georg Gichtel
and His Circle

T o write about the life of Johann Georg Gichtel (1638–1710), after Böhme among the most authoritative of our theosophers, is also to write about his works, for the two are very nearly inseparable. Indeed, the bulk of our information concerning Gichtel comes directly from his own hand, or from the hand of someone very close to him. For Gichtel was author of *Theosophia Practica*, an enormous seven-volume collection of his letters along with his biography—838 letters dated from 1668, when the author was thirty, to 1710, the year of his death, comprising some four thousand pages. If this source of biographical information is somewhat limited and slanted—Gichtel was nothing if not an irascible and polemical writer—its limitations are counterbalanced by the unparalleled glimpse they offer into the life of this theosopher, the "Hermit of Amsterdam."

Gichtel's life began in Ratisbon, Germany, in March 1638, and can be divided into three parts: from 1638 to 1664, when he began to encounter difficulties with the clerical authorities in Ratisbon; from 1665 through 1667, when he moved about, staying for a time with Friedrich Breckling (1629–1711); and from 1668 to his death in 1710, the time during which he lived, wrote, and taught in Amsterdam. Naturally, most of our information about Gichtel (often hagio-graphical) comes from this last period, during which he established his community of the "Brethren of the Angelic Life," the *Engels-brüder*, or the "Angelic Brethren," and became more generally known as a theosopher.

Gichtel's early years were not remarkable; his family was pious, his father a pharmacist, and Gichtel went to study law at Strasburg because he clearly showed scholarly talent. During this time he came to know Knorr von Rosenroth, the Christian Kabbalist, and studied under Johann Schmidt, Heinrich Böckler, and Philipp Jacob Spener, all renowned historians or theologians, particularly Spener. But in 1664, at the age of twenty-six, Gichtel's life changed radically, for he began to realize something of his spiritual calling, and began to become directly involved in the turbulent Protestant reform move-ments of his day.[1]

Gichtel was always a combative sort, as evidenced in countless places in his letters, and certainly this comes through in the biography appended to the letters. There we read the following account of Gich-tel's ouster from Ratisbon: Ratisbon ministers denounced Gichtel, thought he was "a heretic, an enthusiast," that he "came from Holland, and was an Anabaptist," and had him thrown in prison for thirteen weeks, "though he belonged to no sect, nor disputed with anyone."[2] One has to wonder about the latter; Gichtel was somewhat disputatious.

Brought before Johann Heinrich Ursinus—an intransigent man—and his fellow clergymen, Gichtel was tested for his faith, and his biog-rapher gives the following version of these events:

> Ursinus and his so-called clergy and consistories, not thinking as a lawyer he had any knowledge of eastern languages, wanted to drive him into a corner by their learning, but were so well received they became silent as fish, and afterwards warned his brothers and sisters that he had a devil which knew how to handle Scripture, that no one could answer him, whereby they so frightened these, that all his conversation on the Scripture was fruitless, and his own mother told him to leave the ministers alone.[3]

Reading between the lines, one can surmise something of Gichtel's argumentative nature, but one is also reminded of Christ refuting the Pharisees and Sadducees, an allusion evidently intended by the author of the biography.

Although one would think Gichtel's denunciation and imprisonment would have been the low point of his life, in fact it was the turning point, for in prison he had a remarkable vision. Even though his biographer recounts this vision, it is better to offer it in Gichtel's own words:

> In 1664 I lay in prison and was wrestling with Satan. . . . I suddenly fell to earth, and [was] exalted into the spirit, saw a large serpent lying in a three-fold coil around my heart; but in the midst of the circle, it became quite light, and in the light appeared the Lord in the form described by John under the seven candlesticks, who spoke with a deep sigh: If thy mercy, O Lord, were not my comfort, I should perish in my misery.
>
> After these words the serpent was cut up into innumerable pieces, and cast like a flash so sensibly into the darkness of the entrails, that I thought all my insides were broken to bits.
>
> Whereupon I recovered, feeling great strength of faith indeed, but learning that this was merely laying the ground to a bloody struggle, which has indeed continued until this hour, and it would take a book rather than a letter, were I to tell of it.[4]

This experience was really the beginning of Gichtel's subsequent life, for after this serpent vision he was set free, travelled to Switzerland and then to Holland, where he took refuge for the rest of his life—all the while engaged in the spiritual struggle he describes here in its inception in prison.

In the winter of 1666, Gichtel arrived in Schwoll, Switzerland, where he was given shelter by Lutheran minister Friedrich Breckling, who made Gichtel choir leader of Breckling's congregation, appointed him curate of the church, and had him cook, wash, and make beds. During this time Gichtel did preach, but saw that there was little value in mere preaching—ministers, he thought, merely flung words at their congregations.[5] Gichtel's own fortunes followed Breckling, however, for by October 1667, Breckling was being attacked by his fellow Lutheran ministers, and while Gichtel himself tried to defend Breckling (even though Gichtel and Breckling had already had a falling out) in a letter written October 5, 1667, Gichtel's support probably contributed to Breckling's own troubles.

Gichtel himself left Schvoll, ended up in Amsterdam, cold, with no money but two groats, and was approached there by a complete stranger who laid down six silver ducats and left.[6] This kind of miraculous event seemed to happen fairly regularly around Gichtel, whose debts were shortly paid off by a Dutch book dealer who, when he died just after Gichtel met him, left everything to Gichtel, and these books, when sold, paid off Gichtel's debts. In fact, although Gichtel was to reside in Amsterdam for decades to come, he was supported all this time by friends or benefactors—he really did rely upon God to provide through those around him for his own sustenance and that of his colleagues or for the poor whom they helped.

To read Gichtel's biography is to read Protestant hagiography: not for nothing is his biography entitled *The Wonderful and Holy Life of the Chosen Champion and Blessèd Man of God Johann Georg Gichtel.* Readers are advised to check their disbelief in miracles at this work's portals. For Gichtel's life grew more and not less miraculous as time went on, and his biography includes numerous events that defy our expectations or assumptions about this world and its laws. Gichtel himself told the tale to numerous correspondents, and his biographer offers it again, of how he and Breckling and Breckling's wife waxed wroth at one another, so much so that Gichtel was forced to bed for more than a year since "Breckling and his wife with their fiery prayers strove against his [Gichtel's] soul."[7] Eventually, however, an "invisible hand" lifted Gichtel from his bed to the ground, words of forgiveness were spoken, and "Satan's powers were broken."

If Gichtel's friendship with Breckling ended rather nastily, his friendship with Alhart de Raedt ended in, if possible, an equally bad or even worse situation. Raedt was a professor of theology at Harderwijk who had had to leave his chair because of another theological controversy. No doubt introduced to Gichtel by Breckling, Raedt and Gichtel became fast friends in 1682, and in the words of Gichtel's biographer, "they imparted their hearts to each other, and no one that visited them left them unmoved."[8] But this harmonious situation was unfortunately soon to change.

For eventually Gichtel began to suspect that all was not well with Raedt, that indeed a "foreign spirit" had crept into him. In a defining incident, Gichtel and Raedt prayed for a young man who had gone mad, and the more Raedt prayed, the more insane the young man became, until eventually he committed suicide by hanging. In a later incident, a man with whom Raedt lived for a time (after the rift with Gichtel) went quite insane and had to be chained, eventually escaping and coming to Gichtel looking "quite wild and terrible." Through prayer Gichtel was able to help restore the man to sanity again.

But there is more to tell about Raedt's history and motivation. During the spring of 1683, a rival for Raedt had arrived in Gichtel's circle, "the elect man of God," Johann Wilhelm Ueberfeld. Soon Ueberfeld and

Raedt were engaged in bitter dispute, and as Bernard Gorceix notes, "The exact cause of the dispute between Raedt and Ueberfeld is clear: their mutual rivalry for the favor of Gichtel."[9] For Ueberfeld, Raedt was nothing less than "evil personified," the envious envoy of Satan himself.[10] Gichtel himself said that Raedt, like Lucifer, was "seduced by pride and self-love," and "wanted to be the best beloved disciple."

In 1684, Gichtel invited all the Angelic Brethren to sit together at a table, and Raedt sat apart and cried, because of his offenses. Gichtel said three times that they would keep together in love, after which they all went for a walk in the garden, "whereupon Raedt said the words of Christ, 'Whoso is not with us, is against us.'" As they stood in a circle, Gichtel seized the opportunity, saying that since they had made a covenant, the devil would surely try them, and that they must pray for one another, or the great love would be turned into violent wrath, "which by God's impulse he repeated three times also."[11] Thus was their destiny sealed; and Gichtel never was to see Raedt again.

For in 1684 Raedt moved to Warmond, and much later to Utrecht. But more significantly, Raedt denounced Gichtel and his brethren most violently, denunciations that he continued all the way to his death in 1716. Gichtel and his biographer maintain that Raedt turned to alcohol, sought to make gold with the philosopher's stone, and lured a companion of his into drink as well, making drunken attacks upon Gichtel and his fellow theosophers, and giving up the chastity that had been enjoined upon all the Angelic Brethren. Indeed, according to Gichtel's biographer, Raedt went so far as to scoff at all godliness, raging against the truth. How valid these accusations are is, of course, unverifiable.

But it is certain that between this time and Gichtel's death in 1710, his reputation spread not only in Amsterdam, but in Germany as well. Gichtel corresponded with numerous theosophers or aspirants, and knew what was happening in theosophic circles elsewhere in Europe. As the center of the Angelic community in Amsterdam, Gichtel was a spiritual advisor to both men and women, and people not part of this group would also seek him out for advice. Gichtel cannot be accused of not having clear views: he tended to see the world very much in terms of the struggle between evil and good, and this perspective resulted in characterizing people and events more strongly than we might today. But it is no accident that his primary work is his collected letters.

Since we consider the concept of hierohistory in detail in a later chapter, and focus on this aspect of Gichtel's life there, we will only allude to hierohistory here. Essentially, hierohistory refers to the theosophic tendency to record the dates and times of individual spiritual events or revelations. Gichtel's letters and biography exemplify this tendency very well, and one often gets the impression that, for theosophers, hierohistory takes absolute precedence over the progression of linear time that for us moderns constitutes the whole of history. Theosophers' histories—notably Gichtel's four thousand pages of letters and biography—are strikingly absent references to most current events or significant people.

For theosophers generally, and for Gichtel especially, what we moderns call history is of little importance—life should be seen, they insist, in a spiritual light, as a supernatural combat between good and evil, the field for which is human life. Joyous victories and lamentable defeats are chronicled in diaries, letters, or histories—but the relation of this world to the next takes complete precedence over this-worldly history. In a sense, Gichtel's *Theosophia Practica* is simply an extended, even vast hierohistory, the specific cycles of revelation for Gichtel and his circle chronicled both at the beginning and the end of his seven-volume magnum opus of letters.

Gichtel's death is forecast in hagiographical fashion at the end of *Theosophia Practica* by reference to archetypal cycles of time. Sophia appeared to Gichtel in definite temporal cycles during his life, and these cycles culminated forty days before his death, when "the heavenly mother of wisdom revealed herself anew in 1709, December 13." This time of revelation was the greatest, Gichtel said, since the time of Raedt's apostasy, and reached its zenith after Gichtel's physical death early in 1710.[12] The cycle of revelation was renewed in subsequent years among the remaining Angelic community.

Gichtel's primary written work, as we have seen, was his voluminous collection of letters, but he left several other major works behind as well. Among these is a treatise, dated 1696, entitled *Eine kurze Eröffnung und Anweisung der dreyen Principien und Welten Im Menschen*, or, *A Brief Revelation and Instruction on the Three Principles and Worlds in Man*, attributed to Gichtel and Johann Georg Graber and published in 1723. This work—sometimes reprinted under the erroneous title *Theosophia Practica*—includes some very important illustrations on planetary symbolism and the human microcosm, detailing the process of theosophic illumination that is discussed at length in the text.

Gichtel also edited the first major collection of Böhme's writings, entitled *Theosophia Revelata*, published in three successive editions: 1682, 1715, and 1730. Between 1680 and 1682, Gichtel and his colleagues accomplished this remarkable project of collating disparate texts and producing a single, fourteen-volume edition in octavo. This was in fact the primary German edition of Böhme until the work of Werner Buddecke in the twentieth century.[13] These two multivolume series—Böhme's work in *Theosophia Revelata*, and Gichtel's own letters in *Theosophia Practica*—were deliberately complementary, Böhme offering the primary revelational paradigm of theosophy, and Gichtel concentrating on its practical implications through guiding letters.

Although we discuss Gichtel's doctrines at length in our thematic treatment of theosophy, it will no doubt be useful here to sketch some of his primary contributions. But we must recognize that Gichtel saw himself as part of a clear continuity in German theosophy; he was not so much an innovator as a transmitter or exponent of the essential visionary understanding offered by Böhme, a relationship exemplified by the complementary nature of Gichtel's own writings to those of Böhme, and by their linked titles. Nonetheless, Gichtel also offered some definite contributions to theosophy; he was an important figure in his own right.

No one can read Gichtel's letters or biography without recognizing his insistence on celibacy. In this respect, Gichtel went far beyond Böhme, who himself after all was married and did have children. Indeed, some modern authors go so far as to term Gichtel misogynist, a charge not without some basis, but one that ignores Gichtel's writings and reasons for his evident asceticism. We should remember, too, that although Protestantism during this time included a full spectrum of approaches to sexuality, from the wholehearted embrace of sexuality among some, to the communalism of the Eller group, to the radical celibacy of most theosophers in Germany, England, and Pennsylvania during this time. For theosophers both male and female, celibacy was the norm, not the exception. Celibacy—characteristic of Christian monasticism generally, and certainly common among lay people during the early centuries of Christianity—is not a peculiarity of Gichtel, nor is it at all unusual in the context either of Christianity generally, or of theosophy particularly. Dr. John Pordage and his group, Jane Leade and her Philadelphians, Kelpius and his Pennsylvanian community of lay monastics, all enjoined celibacy too, on men and women alike.

When we take the fundamental aim of theosophy—creating apostolic groups oriented to spiritual realization—into account, we can see why Gichtel and most other theosophers enjoined celibacy. For essentially, theosophy means developing in the modern world groups of people whose lives are each completely dedicated to spiritual illumination. Unanimously, mystics and saints throughout the Christian tradition have held that to pursue the spiritual quest wholeheartedly means the renunciation of the earthly Venus, or lust, and the channeling of one's energies toward spiritual realization. The Eastern Orthodox monastic admonitions of the *Philokalia* are exemplary in this regard, and certainly not alone. Gichtel and the other theosophers stand squarely in the Christian tradition here.

But we should point out that there definitely is a transposition of sexual energies onto a different, higher level in theosophy as exemplified in the writings of Gichtel. It is true that Gichtel rejected offers of marriage by wealthy women; it is true that Gichtel remained a celibate bachelor layman all his life. But none of this represents misogyny—it does not reflect a hatred of women, only a rejection of sexual relationships. For we also see in Gichtel's letters a transposition of sexual symbolism into Sophianic mysticism: he speaks of Sophianic kisses, of the Sophianic "marriage bed," and of consummating the love relationship between the soul and Sophia.

In conjoining mysticism and sexual symbolism, of course, theosophers like Gichtel are hardly alone, for in Judeo-Christianity this enterprise goes back to the Song of Songs of Solomon, and appears in the works of Origen and other Christian fathers, as well as in medieval works, including those of Dante, the troubadours, and countless mystics both male and female. It is, it would seem, only natural for Christian mystics to use the language of sexual love to speak of divine love, for after all, what better language do we have to express delight in and union with another?

There is after all a complementary relationship between the "lustful Venus" that Gichtel combats—human desire to satisfy carnal passions— and the celestial Virgin Sophia. If mankind fell through Eve, Franz von Baader was later to write, it is only natural that humanity should also be redeemed through Sophia. For the primal Fall of Adamic man was, in this view, a falling away from the primordial paradise of the Virgin Sophia, and the regeneration of man must therefore be through a return to the Virgin Sophia, who is the feminine aspect of the logos, the Bride of Christ in eternity. Given this perspective, we can see how Gichtel would seek to turn people away from sensual attachment and toward spiritual regeneration in marriage to the Virgin Sophia.

Sophianic mysticism appears throughout Christianity, from Gnosticism through the appearance of Philosophia to the imprisoned Boethius, through the works of Böhme, and Gichtel's primary contribution was elaborating the Sophianic language of theosophic practice. Certainly he did not invent Sophianic mysticism, but Gichtel and his angelic community represent an archetypal form of Sophianic theosophy that was to continue from the seventeenth into the twentieth centuries, and that included both men and women. For an esoteric tradition to continue that long, it has to be based, not just on doctrine, but on spiritual experience; it has to have individual spiritual meaning for those who are attracted to it. Gichtel's Sophianic mysticism is foremost a matter of individual realization, demonstrable not least by Gichtel's letters, which contain far more spiritual advice to individuals than doctrinal formulation.

But inevitably, for Gichtel to be able to offer coherent advice to theosophic aspirants, he had to have a coherent doctrinal understanding that informed all that he said. Naturally, this understanding must be seen in the context of Böhmean theosophy: Gichtel makes occasional reference to such works as Böhme's *Three Principles*, or *The Signature of All Things*, and Böhme's complex cosmology underlies almost all of Gichtel's writings. However, Gichtel does not simply reiterate Böhme, for his work includes definite doctrinal emphases one does not find in Böhme himself. As one might expect, all of these emphases have a practical focus.

In a sense, Gichtel's doctrines are simpler than those of Böhme: he emphasizes how our primary human task is to transmute wrath into love, how we are each ruled by our "astral" "constellation," often in the form of our limited dogmatic Christian beliefs, and how we must penetrate beyond this astral shell to spiritual reality. Böhme is often confusing not only in terminology, but also in formulation, whereas Gichtel is comparatively simple and straightforward. We customarily surround ourselves with an astral shell of wrathful emotionalism and rationality, he tells us, and we must through faith, humility, and prayer let divine power shine through this shell and illuminate us completely.

Although Gichtel's letters comprise some four thousand pages, in fact his central doctrines are not abstruse, and can be elucidated rather easily. Gichtel wrote:

> If any want to strive, let him strive against himself, let him overcome the fiery dragon, viz his own will and self love in himself, then he shall have a reward. My brother's failings must also be mine, we must take them on ourselves, confess them of God, and pray for mercy, that the sin may be forgiven to . . . our brethren.[14]

The origin of sin, Gichtel writes, is simply this, that we no longer "know God's light, viz, Sophia, our heavenly flesh and blood, but look after the light of reason, which can do no more than the other animals, feed and multiply us."[15] We must deny ourselves, Gichtel insists, we must overcome our pride in reason and ourselves.

In fact, it may be useful to see just how telling Gichtel's criticism of ordinary outward religion (which Böhme called "Babel") really could be. In a letter, Gichtel writes that when we live merely according to reason, and are like animals,

> we consider ourselves happy, go to Church and the Lord's Supper, let the parsons take care of our souls; Christ has done everything for us; we stand in the historical clown's faith, and do not want to know anything of the cross of Christ, self denial.[16]

From this quotation alone, we can see how uncompromising Gichtel could be, and how his emphasis on individual spiritual regeneration might well appear threatening to many apparently pious, good Christians. For Gichtel insists that we confront what following Christ really means—and in his view it does not mean acquiescing in a mere "historical faith."

Perhaps this is the best place to conclude our introduction to the life, works, and doctrines of Gichtel. For Gichtel's letters and life stand out as confrontational: they confront us with questions about what we can believe in, about paranormal events, about what Christianity really consists in. Gichtel was known for his confrontations, from his battles in Ratisbon against the theologians when he was in his twenties, all the way to his countless fallings out with various people in the Netherlands, Germany, and elsewhere. He was not, apparently, an easy man to get along with. But was Christ himself? Perhaps more than any other theosopher, Gichtel's work forces us to confront ourselves, who we are, and what religion means. And this is, after all, the fundamental practical challenge of theosophy.

CHAPTER THREE

The Visionary Science
of Dr. John Pordage

O f all those who followed in the visionary path
revealed clearly in the writings of Jacob Böhme, Dr.
John Pordage of England (1608–1681) was without
doubt the most eminent. Richard Baxter, a contemporary
of Pordage's, wrote of him in *Reliquiae Baxterianae*
while discussing those in England who followed the
inward light: the "Behemenists," he observes, "seem to
have attained to greater Meekness and conquest of Passions than any of the rest." "The chiefest of these in England are Dr. Pordage and his Family, who live together in
Community, and pretend to hold visible and sensible
Communion with Angels."[1] Baxter captures well here the
essence of Pordage's personal experiences, which we will discuss in
detail, but those experiences were reflected in Pordage's writings, and on
these we will concentrate, for they are among the most succinct and
lucid of all theosophic writings.

But we must note at the very beginning that Pordage's life and his
writings—like Gichtel's—are nearly indivisible. It is not possible to consider one in isolation from the other, for Pordage's writings directly
reflect his visionary experiences just as do the writings of Jacob Böhme,
the founder of this school. Consequently, even though we will first
examine the records we possess of Pordage's life witnessed by his own

hand and by those who knew him well, and will then look at his writings published both in England and in Germany (a remarkable story in
itself), we should remember that much more than in other cases, each of
these illuminates the other.

Let us begin with Pordage's life—or what we know of it. Son of a
London merchant, Pordage was born in 1608, and entered Pembroke
College, Oxford, in 1623. It is possible that he obtained a diploma of a
doctor of medicine at Oxford in 1640, but some scholars doubt this.[2]
Certainly it is true in any case that he was destined not to practice medicine, but to be a religious. For whatever his other schooling, Pordage
entered into the order of the Anglican Church and was made vicar of the
church of St. Lawrence's at Reading in 1644. Soon, under the auspices
of Elias Ashmole, he was made rector of the rather wealthy parish at
Bradfield, a position he held until 1654.

During his time at Bradfield, Pordage began to have unusual visionary
experiences. At first those experiences came primarily to his wife, Mary
Freeman, an especially pious and spiritual woman whom he married for
that reason.[3] Richard Roach later wrote that the theosophers' group

> had its rise . . . with a fresh conversance and Holy Gale of a
> Divine Life and Power opening first and principally in Mrs
> Pordage . . . [Dr Pordage] married her for the excellent gift of
> God he found in her, which gift he also became in a high
> degree partaker of.[4]

Soon Pordage himself was experiencing remarkable phenomena, including angelic apparitions, and these were witnessed too by others in a
small group of theosophers who gathered around Pordage and his wife
in a prayer group. This group was eventually to include men such as
Thomas Bromley and Edmund Brice—both of whom were educated at
Oxford and themselves wrote theosophic treatises of considerable
import—and women such as Anne Bathurst and Mrs. Joanna Oxenbridge, both women of high society who left records of their spiritual
journeys with the Pordages.

Clearly, company such as this—we might mention too the fifth Earl
of Pembroke, who also left some theosophic, Sophianic treatises—suggests that Pordage moved in fairly high circles in English society during
the mid-seventeenth century. But such people were drawn to Pordage
because he spoke with great authority of spiritual truths that he had
himself witnessed inwardly—and which they too experienced, as their
own treatises and diaries certainly attest. These spiritual experiences

were by no means without controversy, not among the theosophers of course, whatever their social rank (a matter of indifference to Pordage's circle), but among those who heard of such experiences.

Pordage's visionary experiences began in August, 1649, with an "opening" of the visionary worlds that absolutely must be told in Pordage's own words. Pordage writes:

> In August 1649, there appeared in my Bed-chamber about the middle of the night, a spirit in the shape of Everard, with his wearing apparel, Band, Cuffs, Hat, &c., who after the sudden drawing of the Bed-Curtains, seemed to walk once thorow the Chamber very easily, and so disappeared.
>
> That very night there was another appearance of one in the form of a Gyant, with a great sword in his hand, without a scabbard, which he seemed to flourish against me, having the figurative similitude of a great Tree lying by him.
>
> After this had continued the space of a half an hour, it vanished; And there succeeded a third appearance, which was very terrible, being in the shape of a great Dragon, which seemed to take up most part of a large room, appearing with great teeth and open jaws, whence he oft ejected fire against me, which came with such a Magical influence, that it almost took the breath right out of my body, making me fall to the ground. Now you must know that these three were dreadful Apparitions, and very terrible to the sensitive Nature, and might have caused a great distemper to it, had I not been supported in an extraordinary way, by the Ministrations of the Holy Angels.[5]

We might note that one decade later in Germany Johann Georg Gichtel was also to experience an opening of spiritual insight, preceded by the vision of the great serpent that entwined itself around his heart.[6] In any case, such apparitions preceded the equally frightening "opening of the worlds" to Pordage.

For the opening of the worlds was the revelation to Pordage and his family of the good and evil invisible realms that inform this visible world of ours. Pordage writes:

> I say then there were two invisible internal Principles opened and discovered to us, which may be called *Mundi Ideales*, being two spiritual worlds, extending and penetrating throughout this whole visible Creation. . . . Now these two Principles or worlds, seemed very much different from one

> another, as having contrary qualities and operations, by which
> they work on this visible Creation . . . some [creatures in them
> being] poysonful and noxious, others wholsom and harmless.[7]

They had disclosed to them first the evil hierarchies, and then the good, which, for Pordage as for Eckhart and Tauler, are present here on earth in this very moment. Only the Fall prevents us from seeing their presence in our lives.

Judging from Pordage's account, our inability to experience these two principles directly may not be all bad. For the manifestations of the wrathful or evil world in Pordage's case were rather distressing: he witnessed not only the presence of evil hierarchies—in monstrous theriomorphic forms, all "misshapen," with cat's ears and cloven feet and fiery eyes—but their physical manifestations in sulphuric foul odors and even the imprint of their images on the windows, "Cealings," and chimney of the house. This latter series of images, including a remarkable Globe and "a Coach and four horses," "wonderfull exactly done," was so disturbing to Pordage that he and his wife endeavored to "wash them out with wet cloaths, but could not, finding them ingraven in the substance of the Bricks, which indeed might have continued till this day, had not our fear and suspicion of witchcraft and some evil design of the Divel against us in it, caused us to deface and obliterate them with hammers."[8]

As if it were not enough that Pordage and his wife were driven to hammer demonic images from their chimney, they were attacked both in body and in soul by the wrathful beings. Attacked in soul by "strange magical wounds and piercings by the fiery darts of the devil" much as Job must have been, they also felt "material impressions, from the powers of darkness, very noxious in themselves," but "cheerfully born, by invisible support, and quiet submission to the Will of God."[9] Evidently, Pordage and his wife had to undergo this series of apparitions and even torments in order that, like Dante, they be able to pass through the wrathful into the angelical world. We might recall that Dante had to pass through the fire in Purgatory in order to see Beatrice, his angelic guide, and that according to Genesis, those who would reënter Eden must pass the flaming sword.

Like Dante, Pordage also passed through the flames and entered into paradise, which he called *Mundus Luminosus*, or the light world. Here there were "multitudes almost innumerable, of pure Angelical spirits, in figurative bodies, which were clear as the morning-star, and transparent as Christal."[10] Here, they saw the rare beauty of these beings, felt the inexpressible joys and harmonies of heaven, smelled delightful heavenly scents, and heard celestial music. The "tongue can hardly express these Odours of Paradise," and these glorious visions and sounds, Pordage wrote.

These experiences went on for nearly a month, resulting in a kind of inward conflict between the two realms—they were tormented by the demons, then delighted by the angels, subjected to trials, and then offered the grace of spiritual blessings. Apparently people outside the family soon knew that something unusual was going on in their house, and like Gichtel (around whom unusual phenomena also happened with some regularity), Pordage was later, as rumors spread, called a magician or a necromancer. But on his own testimony, he was clearly nothing of the sort: he was, rather, a visionary whose experiences penetrated even into the physical world.

Nonetheless, it was at about this time that Pordage was tried before the local Anglican commission as an heretical minister of the faith. Against him were arrayed a whole range of charges, including provocative statements and immoral conduct. Pordage was able to defend himself well against all these charges: the supposedly provocative or heretical statements imputed to him he proved to have been taken out of context and misinterpreted; the charge that he had kept a mistress in London he demonstrated to be quite false. Thus he was able to exonerate himself from the accusations, and he was allowed to continue as a minister from 1649 to 1654.

During this time, Dr. Pordage and his small group grew to include some of the figures we mentioned before, including Thomas Bromley and Edmund Brice. Richard Roach, a member of Jane Leade's later group, the Philadelphians, wrote of how the group grew in number:

> With the Doctor and his wife were joyned some others and they began to wait together and Exercise the Gifts of Prayer, Exhortations, Singing and under a Living Pr. [presence] and Operation of the Holy Spirit. And not long after were Joynd to 'em two Fellows of All Souls College in Oxford: Mr Thomas Bromley and Mr Edmund Brice, who having heard a sermon Preached in Great Power by Dr. Pordage at St. Maries, the University Church; went together to Discourse with Him, and received Such a Satisfactory Acct. [Account] from him that they Immediate Joynd themselves to this Little Society, and Continued among 'em to their Dying

Day. Also the Earl of Pembroke at that Time being Convinc'd
of the Extraordinary Powers and Operations of the Spirit
among Joyned Himself and waited with 'em.[11]

We may note that two things might be emphasized here: the emphasis
upon "waiting," and the emphasis upon the "Operations of the Spirit."
Both of these suggest the millennialist fervor of Joachim of Fiore, the
medieval monk who wrote of the imminent "age of the spirit" or "third
age." This is not to suggest that the Böhmeans knew or cared about
Joachimite speculation, but to point out the parallels between their independently revealed perspectives.

Certainly it was the visionary "Operations of the Spirit" that drew
together Pordage's little group more than anything else. This is a subject
we will discuss in more depth later—for now, it is sufficient to note that
according to the records of group members, including works such as
Bromley's *The Way to the Sabbath of Rest*, they enjoyed a kind of spiritual communication that allowed them to share in one another's joys
and sorrows even when separated by space and time. It is easy for modern readers, schooled to believe that those who experience unusual phenomena must be psychotic or dysfunctional, to dismiss out of hand such
accounts of theosophers in England, the Netherlands, Germany, America, and elsewhere. But Pordage's group by their own accounts did experience spiritual revelations that resulted in joy and illumination, and we
see no reason to denigrate this, much less to dismiss it.

Still, from the controversy that Pordage and his little group engendered, we can gather some inkling of what went on in their meetings. In
1650 we find that there were numerous enthusiastic villagers who went
to Pordage's prayer meetings and dances—far from being sober affairs,
they were apparently quite a scene. An amazed William Foster went to
gather his wife up from one such event, and found "Mistress Pordich
clothed all in White Lawne, from the crown of the Head to the sole of
the Foot, and a White rod in her hand." Pordage himself came "all in
black Velvet," and group members danced and "made strange noyses,"
villagers addressing Dr. Pordage as "Father Abraham" and Mrs.
Pordage as "Deborah." All continued dancing "expecting when they
shall be taken up to Heaven every hour."[12]

None of this, however, is much more remarkable than traditional
English village Morris dancing given a millennialist cast, nor was it the
only or even the primary form of spiritual practice. More extraordinary
descriptions are to be found in the accounts of Dr. Pordage's second

trial, in 1654, when he was indeed removed from his ministerial position in Bradfield. The accusations in this second trial were refuted by Pordage himself in treatises issued by his colleagues in an effort to reinstate him—from the accusations, and his rebuttal, we can certainly see that some unusual events had become rather commonplace around the Pordage household.

Probably most significant was the constant presence of angels in and around the Pordages' home. Indeed, one of the chief accusations against Pordage was "that he hath very frequent and familiar converse with Angels," that when he was attacked by a dragon in his home, "his Angel stood by him and upheld him." Further, "That Mrs Pordage and Mrs Flavel had their Angels standing by them also, Mrs Pordage singing sweetly, keeping time on her breast, and that his children saw the spirits coming into the house, and said, look there, Father. . . . And the whole roof of the house was full of Spirits."[13]

We noted earlier that one primary characteristic of theosophy is its visionary egalitarianism, and this too is corroborated by testimony in Pordage's treatise *Innocencie Appearing.* Visionary revelation was not the sole province of Dr. Pordage, his wife, and their children: all the theosophers in this circle testified to spiritual illumination, albeit some not in writing. It was said, for example, that

> Mrs Flavel was in a trance, and when she came out of it, spoke many precious things which she had seen in that trance, what was the Philosopher's Stone, that so many learned men had sought after, which she knew to be the Divinity in the humanity, and many other things to similar effect.[14]

One can surmise that such revelations were one thing coming only from an erudite Dr. Pordage, but quite another coming with authority from each member of the theosophic group—and evidently were thus more threatening to authorities, especially in the confused religious climate of the day.

We should recall that Dr. Pordage's two trials took place during a time of religious ferment in England; the establishment of the Anglican Church resulted in the supplanting of Catholic hierarchy with such institutions as the commission for removing ministers, itself part of a more general attempt in England to restore the concept of orthodoxy in the absence of Catholicism. During this time England saw the appearance of numerous, and sometimes extremely radical Protestant movements, including antinomian, libertine Ranters such as Abiezer Coppe, whom Pordage may himself have known personally.

Ranters and other radicals sometimes preached blasphemy, sexual libertinism, and freedom to commit crimes under a specious "liberty of the Holy Spirit," which in turn frightened authorities, and resulted in attempts by bodies like the commission on ministers to establish and protect a new Anglican orthodoxy. Unfortunately, this polarization between Anglican guardians of orthodoxy on the one hand, and religious anarchists like Coppe on the other, produced a situation in which mystics such as Pordage and his colleagues were confused with Ranters and other radicals, publicly reviled, and deprived of their livelihoods and religious freedom.

Some sense of the atmosphere in which Pordage's second trial took place can be gathered from his account of the judge's own behavior. When called before the judge, Pordage protested that the Pharisees of "legal" Christianity were being set upon authentic "spiritual" Christianity. Worse, he said, even a common felon was not tried twice for the same crime, as indeed he was being tried again in 1654. Had they new charges? Pordage writes: "The judge said fiercely: 'You are worse than a felon, for ought I know.' Which language coming from a Judge to the defendent, before tryall, let all sober persons judge of, who are acquainted with the rules of civility, morality, or Christianity."[15] Worse yet, the very act under which he was being tried was itself not instituted until a full year *after* those things with which he was charged had been reputed to take place!

In such an atmosphere, one is hardly surprised to find Dr. Pordage ousted from his pastorate, but his peroration was moving. He wrote:

> And now ye Ministers of *Berks*, my persecutors, tell me, what wrong or injury have I done you; have I lusted to preach in any of your Pulpits? Have I privately gone from parish to parish, or from house to house to get followers, or make proselites of your hearers? Have I publicly or privately railed against you or your Doctrines? Have I not lived privately in my own place, onely holding forth that strict, dying, resigning life, as the way to life eternal[?] Why then am I persecuted with so much fury, and violence, as though I were not worthy to live amongst you? The Lord judge betwixt you and me, and give you to consider and repent of what you have done, in procuring and subscribing the unjust sentence of ejectment, by which as much as in you lies, you have taken away that with which we have cloathed and fed our selves and many others, who have been in want, and so exposed me and mine

to outward cares, and troubles, which are very disagreeable to that life of silence, abstraction, and of continual waiting upon God In which we live, and are called to live. And what is this but like the task-masters of *Egypt*, to force the children of the Covenant, to make Brick without straw? but the Lord is coming to judge himself, who will make all these things work for my good, which others have designed for my hurt.[16]

These are not the words of an antinomian Ranter.

But although he was deprived of his livelihood, and found himself in extremely difficult circumstances for the remainder of his life, these outward difficulties only served to intensify his, and his group's, convictions and inward life. Of course, their persecution did mean that for some years they lived spiritually in the "outer darkness" surrounded by wrath, suffering something akin to what St. John of the Cross called the "dark night of the soul." But eventually they were restored to angelic communications and to the spiritual light. Yet until his death, Dr. Pordage and his small group kept themselves out of public view and therefore beyond the range of censure.

Even when the Restoration took place under Charles II in 1660, and suspended clergymen were allowed to return to their positions, Dr. Pordage did not take this step, but remained quietly with his group of fellow theosophers. As a leader of a small, private, non-Anglican religious group, however, Pordage was constrained to meet with them and to live discreetly, for by 1664 such nonconformist meetings were again outlawed, and their leaders potentially at least subjected to fines and imprisonment. Worse, 1665 and 1666 saw the advent of the Great Plague and the great London fire, seen by many as signs of the Apocalypse (fears intensified by the associations of the number 1666 with the number of the Beast in Revelation). Many people fled London, and Pordage and his group had to return to Bradfield to live, only returning to London in 1668, the year Mrs. Pordage died.

Amid all this outward confusion and danger, then, the secluded and ascetic inward life that the theosophers lived appears all the more remarkable. Of course, it may be that times of outward confusion contribute to the mystical life, since historically it is precisely at such times— early Christianity and the apostolic gnosis; the thirteenth and fourteenth centuries in Europe and such remarkable mystics as Eckhart, Tauler, Merswin, Hadewijch; the seventeenth and eighteenth centuries and the theosophers—that inwardness and spirituality flourish. Outward disruption, though it seem calamitous, may turn one toward inward peace.

This time of outer difficulty also saw the most important affiliation of Pordage's life, in some respects: that between himself and Mrs. Jane Leade, who first felt called to join his group in 1663. She remained a member of his group, and in fact assumed leadership, especially after April 1670, when, after her husband's death, she experienced a vision of the Holy Virgin Sophia, who called her to a virginal life.[17] From this point on, she was to write a large number of extraordinary visionary treatises, and to become a central theosophic figure of her era. In 1674, she moved into Dr. Pordage's own house, at his request, so that together they could form a more powerful spiritual union.

During this time—from the early 1670s until his death in 1681—Dr. Pordage wrote most of his elaborate metaphysical treatises. All these treatises were based wholly and directly on his own spiritual experience, exemplary of which is the treatise *Sophia*, which consists in twenty-two daily journal entries dated from June 21 to July 10, and which contains biographical data from the year 1675. Pordage's magnum opus, *Göttliche und Wahre Metaphysica* [Holy and True Metaphysics], was also written during this time, probably concluded in the year of his death, 1681.

But none of these works were published during his lifetime and, even more surprisingly, only two were published in English after his death. Although all his works had a wide private circulation, and were extremely influential in both England and on the Continent, it remains a strange fact that Pordage's primary works—albeit written in English— were published only in German, and have been accessible only in that language to the present day. How is it that Pordage's writings have not been available in his own language, and that even in German editions his name was changed to Johannes Pordäschens?

There is one primary answer. Pordage and his colleagues, I believe, felt the necessity for his anonymity after the scandalous persecutions of the 1650s and the spiritual and financial difficulties through which they had passed. He earned his keep through his later years, in part, as a medical doctor and herbalist in relative seclusion, and wanted to live an unhindered ascetic spiritual life of prayer. Theosophers, after all, are wholly uninterested in proselytizing, as Pordage pointed out to his persecutors years before; what matters to them is spiritual purity and experience, and since publicity hardly conduces to this, he preferred a public silence and withheld publication.

But this decision produced the anomalous situation in which we find ourselves now: in order to discuss Pordage's works, originally written in English, we must translate most of them back from their German editions. Although this is a somewhat unsatisfactory arrangement, for our purposes it is certainly adequate.[18] In the discussion that follows, we will sketch the outlines of Pordage's major works, and in this way will be able to more clearly understand the lineaments, not of his outward life, but of what he no doubt himself saw as the most important aspect of his life, his visionary life reflected directly in his treatises.

We can begin with the two works published in English: *A Treatise of Eternal Nature with Her Seven Essential Forms* (1681) and *Theologia Mystica, or the Mystic Divinitie of the Aeternal Invisibles, viz, the Archetypous Globe* (1683). Together, these works constitute an introduction to the visionary science that the theosophers practiced, and in a concise, lucid way, take us through Pordage's visionary realizations. Many critics have noted how Germanic mysticism of the Eckhart and Tauler school offers little hint of the path these mystics took to reach their realizations, and one wonders this when reading Böhme himself as well. Böhme's own works definitely reveal a complete visionary understanding, but often seem unordered in expression. Pordage's works reveal Böhmean visionary experiences, but in a scientific order of expression and clarity of images.

The Treatise of Eternal Nature offers a general introduction to the concept of Eternal Nature, the "first original and true ground of all created beings and so of all true knowledge."[19] Outward, physical nature, then, has its origin in an archetypal, pure realm of "Eternal Nature" similar to the Platonic realm of Ideas or Forms. Thus, Divine Nature is "hid in Nature, as a Jewel in a Cabinet"; it is manifested in the Seven Essential Forms, and has its origin in the Abyssal Nothing, which is the "ground of all Essences, and yet no Essence to be seen in it," the "fruitful Mother of all Things."[20] In Pordage's treatise, then, we see a visionary hierarchy or ascent from the natural world to the archetypal, to the Seven Essential Forms (the qualities informing existence), to the Abyssal Nothing of God Himself.

In *Theologia Mystica*, we travel with Pordage on his visionary journey, a journey whose nature is clarified by the preface Jane Leade contributed. Leade writes:

> [S]ince my acquaintance with him *until the Time of his Death*, he was ever more imployed and busied in a internal contemplative Life: the Spirit in him still searching for the deep and hidden Mysteries of the Kingdom. And truly hee was not only a *Seeker*, but a successful *Finder* of that rich Pearl of the Gospel.[21]

She refers, further, to "those wonderful Transportations he had (or rather they had him) for the space of three weeks together. . . . His outward Body lay in passive Stillness in this visible Orb."[22] Pordage offers us "a copie taken out from the Original . . . of all Worlds," which he had seen in visionary trances that sometimes lasted weeks at a time.

In *Theologia Mystica*, we see how, according to Pordage, all the different realms or "worlds," including this "visible Orb" of physical nature, are comprised within the sphere of "Eternal Nature." Eternal Nature includes in its ambit the "Four Elementarie" or "outward visible world" below; the "Dark-fire" or wrath-world of hell on the left; the "Fire-Light," or "Severe World," in the center; and the "Light-Fire World," or Paradise, on the right. Above is the "Angelical, Heaven, or Love-World." Thus, Eternal Nature encompasses all the possible realms of creation, including heavenly, paradisal, hellish, and earthly.

Having established this cosmology, Pordage then takes us through his visionary journey, explaining to us how he perceived the "Globe of Eternity" that encompasses all things and represents also their origin. We can see this "Globe of Eternity" only with the "abyssal Eye of Eternity," concerning which no words are adequate. In this Globe of Eternity we glimpse an "Outward Court," an "Inward Court," and an "Inmost Court," the Holiest place of all.[23] Here we conceive the Trinity in human terms: there is within the Globe an Abyssal Eye, the Heart, and the Breath, a Trinity that has definite parallels in Islamic mysticism as well; we are dealing here with a visionary physiology, hence too with the physiology of the trance or meditative state that allows the visionary to see the Inmost Court and the Globe with spiritual eyes.

Pordage uses these central images—the Globe, the Eye, the Heart, the Breath—to explain visionary spirituality, and the supreme illumination:

> The sight of the Holy Trinity from the opening of the Eye,
> in the inward Court of the Holy Place, is a lively, operative,
> reviving, and yet amazing and surprising sight. . . . No pen can
> decipher it, It is only the Spirit of the Eye that can open it self.[24]

This illumination is essentially a vision of the Archetypes of all things:

> This sight of God's Attributes from the opening of the Eye in
> the Abyssal Globe, is both a ravishing and amazing sight, for
> you do not behold Ideas or Similitudes of things, but the
> things themselves intellectually, which causeth most inex-
> pressible joys, and extasies in the Spirit of the Soul, to which
> nothing in this world can be compared.[25]

This illumination is, even further, beholding God "Face to Face," in the Eye, the Center of the Heart.[26]

Pordage then writes of the Virgin Sophia, who is "co-essential" and "co-eternal" with the Holy Trinity, but not "co-equal" with them, for she is but a passive efflux of the Trinity, its Glory and Mirror. Sophia is "Virgin Purity" because she is "free from all desire, will, and motion of her own"; she is "exalted above all things," a "revealer of the Mysteries and hidden wonders of the Deity . . . she is the Golden Key of the Eternal Eyes by which all the wonders of the Trinity are unlocked." Just as the Holy Ghost creates, so Wisdom manifests and reveals all things.[27]

Finally, Pordage writes of the nature of the angelic spirits, their nature and qualities. The spirits possess a materiality and senses of their own: "These *Spirits* are endued with a Spiritual kind of materiality from the Love-Essence in the Heart of God." Hence, they are "endued with the Spiritual senses of seeing, hearing, smelling, tasting and feeling, whereby they are inabled to discern the object of the still Eternity." They are "refreshed by perceiving the ravishing odors which continually perfume the most holy Place." The spirits have their own language; they have one ear, one eye, one breath (details that underscore their unity) and their "food and drink" is power from the Trinity.[28] Pordage's treatise therefore leads us from the initial vision and cosmology, through the transmuting power of Sophia, into the angelic heavenly realm itself.

In his treatise *Sophia*—which was extremely influential for German theosophers, including Gottfried Arnold, whose own book on the Virgin Sophia was drawn in part from Pordage's—Pordage offers his experiential knowledge of Sophianic revelation in a journal form, dated June 21 to July 10, in twenty-two chapters. Neither the dates nor the number of chapters are accidental. Although I will discuss theosophic astrological symbolism in a chapter on that subject, suffice it here to say that it is no coincidence that the book's first chapter is on the summer solstice, and that the number of chapters corresponds to the number of letters in the Hebrew alphabet, a number sacred in Kabbalist mysticism. In this way Pordage's book is "stamped," so to speak, with spiritual symbolism in its very form, symbolism of the sun (illumination) and of the Logos, or Word.

The contents of *Sophia* deserve a separate study; here I will offer only an overview of the book. Pordage begins by explaining the nature of Sophia, or Divine Wisdom, as well as of the Light World, and the soul's hunger and thirst for spiritual truth. He discusses the meaning of the Biblical references to the creation of a "new heaven and a new earth"; of the harmony of this world below and that above; of the Paradisical Eden in the Soul; and of the Quintessence or Elixir of Life. Pordage explains that the Holy Virgin reveals the New Jerusalem in the heart and soul of the newly reborn man, and he completes his work by discussing knowledge of the light and dark worlds.

This knowledge—of the light and dark worlds—Pordage offers in depth in his *magnum opus*, the three volume *Göttliche und Wahre Metaphysica* (Holy and True Metaphysics). The breadth of this work is quite remarkable; around two thousand pages long, Pordage's *Metaphysica* reveals the realm of eternal nature, the wrathful world, the paradisal realm, and the angelical world in clearly organized sections. About his work he writes: "Dann ich schreibe nicht von Menschen noch aus Büchern noch aus denen Platoniste noch aus Nachforschung der Vernunfft sondern aus Eingebung ewige verstandlicher Geist mit seinem Augen hievon selber vermittels Eröffnung des Englischen Centri gesehen" (I write not as men of book-knowledge, nor like Platonists, nor through the efforts of reason, but rather out of experience, namely out of what my eternal understanding spirit with its eyes has seen revealed of the Angelic centri).[29]

Pordage's first volume discusses the "Spirit of Eternity," and Eternal nature, asserting that God permitted the Fall of his creatures in order to reveal his *barmherzigkeit* (warmheartedness, or compassion). In his second volume, Pordage outlines aspects of the angelical spirits (*Englische geister*), including their undying (*unsterblich*) nature, their possession of a "materiality" different from that of the physical world, which includes an Angelic body (*ein Englischer leib*), their inward unity, their possession of will, senses, and above all, inward freedom. They are powerful (*mächtig*), good, undying, and made in the likeness of God.

We might dwell for a moment on one angelic characteristic Pordage emphasizes: their angelic bodies made from quintessential nature. He writes: "Dieser Englische Leib ist organisch oder hat seine werckzeugliche Glieder: und ist in vielen Dingen dem Menschen [oder Meschlichen Leibe] Gleich oder vielmehr der Mensch ist einiger massen in seiner äusserliche Gestalt nach dem Gleichniß und Bilde der Engel gemacht" (This angelic body is organic or has functional limbs, and is in many things like man, or rather, man is in his outer form made in the image of the angel).[30] He speaks of angelic noses, mouth, ears, eyes, and so forth; and though Pordage refers to the traditional cherubim and seraphim of the Dionysian hierarchy, it is clear that Pordage's knowledge of angels comes not from having read Dionysius, but from having visited with angels, whom he is describing.

At the same time, Pordage tells us, one cannot properly say that the angel is made in the image of God, for God "has no organic or functional body like the angel: rather, the Holy Trinity reveals itself as an eternal Eye that has its continual place in the flaming heart of eternal love, which dwells in the Temple-body of the Holy Spirit, without all form."[31] In other words, although we human beings can perceive through images some aspects of the divine nature, and indeed, this is precisely what happens in visionary revelation, we should not reduce the divine nature to such images, forms, or ideas, but should realize that divine nature can only be understood through visionary experience itself, which cannot be adequately conveyed through language or images. In essence, the visionary revelation through images entails contact (tincture) between two realms, the human and the divine, and the luminous images are the human means of perceiving what in ultimate reality is overwhelmingly beyond conception or expression. The divine is ultimately imageless, but is perceived through images nonetheless.

Pordage's third volume in this work treats of the dark or wrathful world, a topic that reminds us again of why he chose not to have this work published in English. For in it he discusses the nature of demons or fallen angels, *finstern magia* (black magic), sorcery (*von der Zauberen*), the "Hellish Tincture," the devil, "spiritual Babylon," and the spiritual Egypt. Though Pordage was no sorceror, he did not want to risk confusion; at the same time, he could not help but write of what he had seen of hell, as of heaven. He himself wrote that one must pass the wrathful world to enter heaven.

But his third volume does not dwell only on evil and wrath; later in the volume he writes of the "heavenly Tincture," and the Brotherhood of Spirits (*Gemeinshaft der Geister*), topics closely reminiscent of his friend Thomas Bromley's work *The Way to the Sabbath of Rest*. He discusses "eternal nature" and the three courts of the Globe of Eternity we mentioned earlier, as well as the "eternal heart of God" (*Von dem ewigen herzen Gottes*), the Virgin Sophia, or Wisdom, the Seven Forms or Spirits of God, and the Angelical World.

There remain of Pordage's primary works two others, written in the last few years of his life, that we should describe yet: the "Four Tractates" and the "Treatise on the Philosopher's Stone." The "Four Tractates," dated August 3, 1676, discuss the "outer birth and fleshly life of Jesus Christ," the "Mystical and Inner Birth," the Spirit and Degrees of Faith, and, finally, experimental (experiential) discoveries of the union of nature, essences, tinctures, people, and spirits (*Experimentale Ent-*

deckungen von Vereinigung der Naturen/ Essenzen/ Tincture/ Personen und Geister). In this last section on "experimental discoveries" we are introduced to foundations for the "Treatise on the Philosopher's Stone," a very concise alchemical work.

We might remember that Pordage lived during roughly the same time as Thomas Vaughan (1621–1666), arguably the greatest exponent of spiritual alchemy, so called because it did not emphasize laboratory work with actual tinctures and substances, but rather focused on inward spiritual transmutation. Theosophy had traditionally been associated with alchemy even before the advent of Jacob Böhme, in such figures as Paracelsus (1493–1541) and Valentin Weigel (1533–1588). What is more, we know that some theosophers reputedly practiced alchemy in laboratories (including Johannes Kelpius in America), and that Johann Georg Gichtel was intimately familiar with the alchemical work. Of this I shall say more in the chapter on theosophy and alchemy. Here, I only point out that Pordage, in writing on spiritual alchemy, was directly in the theosophic tradition.

The "Treatise on the Philosopher's Stone," only sixteen pages long, is one of the more remarkable works of spiritual alchemy. It illustrates, certainly, how theosophers in general and Pordage in particular drew on alchemical terminology and process to explain theosophic transmutation and revelation. Pordage begins by discussing the "red earth" (*die rothe Erde*) and the "red Tincture of Paradise," the "pure sweet blood of Virginal Humanity." "Tincture" refers to the meeting of two realms, the illumination of the human being by its archetypal essence. He tells us that the fire of the philosophers is the key to the mystery of spiritual transmutation and illumination.[32] This makes sense, of course, because red is the color of fire (and blood), hence of purification that is necessary if the human being is to be fit for revelation.

Essentially, Pordage sketches in this treatise the process by which the human is purified, transmutes his energies from wrath into love, and becomes an illuminated and unified being. Thus, he points out that fallen man is subject to the influences or energies of Mars and Venus, or anger and lust (emotional attraction and repulsion rooted in selfishness).[33] But it is possible to transmute such energies through the union of fire and water, out of which comes the "magical birth" of the "Fire-Tincture." Once one has established this "magical birth," one must pass through further purification in the darkness of God's wrath, which takes place under the signs of Saturn and Mars. This is the stage that, although stringent and difficult, breaks apart the rigid habits and selfishness of the personality.

Out of it comes the harmony of the planetary qualities, Saturn, Mercury, Mars, Venus, and Luna; the process culminates in the "milk and blood of the Virgin," the "Pearl of the Virgin," and ultimately in the unity and harmony of the planetary qualities within the individual, who is suffused with spiritual light.[34] We should note that the alchemical transmutation Pordage outlines is in the order red, black, and white, the three colors that, traditionally, always signify the stages of the alchemical work and that are found in Dante (*Purgatorio*, Canto XXI) with similar symbolism. The treatise ends with the "Pearl of the Virgin," which symbolizes purity and illumination.

Before concluding, we should note that there is an enigmatic poem with commentary called *Mundorum Explicatio; or, The Explanation of an hieroglyphical Figure: wherein are couched the mysteries of the external, internal, and eternal Worlds, shewing the true progress of a Soul from the Court of Bablylon to the City of Jerusalem, from the Adamical fallen state to the Regenerate and Angelical, Being a Sacred Poem* (1661), attributed to S.P., Armig., generally held to be Samuel Pordage, John Pordage's son. *Armig.* is a Latin term for "knight," significant perhaps in that Sophianic literature often refers to the knights of Sophia, her pledged devotees, drawing on the Christian chivalric heritage. Some have argued that because the poem is not in the style of Samuel Pordage's other published poems, his father wrote it. However, after a close study of the poem itself, I believe it most likely that while Samuel Pordage wrote much of the poem, its genesis and definitely some of the abstruse Böhmean marginal commentary attached to the poem are the work of John Pordage.

In the preface, for example, we read: "Religion is not a meer notional knowledge of God, but a practical feeling of him, *non magna loquimur sed vivimir*, let us live well rather than talk well, for knowledge without practice will but encrease our condemnation on that great day, and will but witness against us."[35] And again: "If that my good intention of awakening others to look after those Worlds . . . seriously to consider the immortality of their souls, and of the Eternal felicities or everlasting Torments, they hereafter must enjoy, take effect, I shall think myself happy, if not, I have done my duty, and my peace will be my reward." These words definitely bear the influence of John Pordage. Likewise, the poem itself makes reference to Mars stirring to wrath, to Venus as Lust, to the nature of spirits, and to many other theosophic themes whose content reveals the impress of John Pordage's other visionary works, and whose commentary sounds very much like Pordage himself, as when he writes with authority that "Spirits are not Matter, Form, &c., yet they have Bodies. . . but not as our gross bodies."[36]

All of this underscores, once again, how much theosophy is founded in visionary experience, and how much it forms what amounts to a single discipline. The terminology, the experiences related by theosophers, are essentially unified: there is in theosophy a single process of transmutation that must be encountered individually and experientially. One might object that the terminology and written works as well as the oral tradition of theosophy may produce certain expectations that are then confirmed by experience—but the fact remains that theosophers do independently confirm one another's experiences. It would not surprise me to find that *Mundorum Explicatio* represents Samuel Pordage's independent confirmation of his father's visionary experiences; for all of theosophic literature represents such independent confirmation.

Pordage's works are remarkable because they offer us a lucid, even methodical description of the kind of visionary understanding that the theosophers share. One can tell from the collected letters of Gichtel, for instance, that he had a coherent, unified understanding of the spiritual worlds, but this understanding is in his letters perforce expressed in fragments and with repetition. Pordage, on the other hand, obviously spent many years explaining in clear and relatively simple terms Böhmean theosophy with an almost scientific precision that no other theosopher rivals, including Böhme himself.

It is a great pity, and a historical anomaly, that Pordage's works have not been available in English, the language in which they were written. His influence was far greater on the Continent, and in Germany especially, than in his native England. Perhaps it is finally time that Pordage's significance is recognized in the English-speaking world, and his works are again made available there. But in any case, recognized or not, Pordage remains one of the most remarkable figures in a movement— itself composed of many such people—whose importance remains all out of proportion to its current obscurity.

CHAPTER FOUR

Jane Leade, the Philadelphians, and the Doctrine of Universal Restoration

 fter John Pordage, the most important of the English theosophers was without question Jane Leade (1624–1704), who was responsible not only for the development of the Philadelphians—the group that succeeded Dr. Pordage's circle—but offered the world some remarkable visionary treatises of her own as well. Furthermore, Leade offered her circle and her readers a gentle and compassionate spirituality that, although somewhat controversial at the time, represents a Christian tradition of universal restoration with a long history. We will, in what follows, discuss, first, her life, second, her written works, and third, her doctrines, their reception and import.

Leade was born—according to her own account—to a reasonably wealthy upper-class family in Norfolk, England. She and her family lived a good life, and she received a fine education. When she was fifteen, she was dancing and celebrating on Christmas Eve with her family and friends, and heard a voice that told her, "Cease from this, I have another Dance to lead thee in, for this is Vanity." For three years she lived in melancholy isolation, occasionally reading books and almost always staying apart from people; despite the counsel of her father, Schildknapp Ward, and a chaplain, she felt the sins of the world upon her, and believed that because she had once told a lie, she would stay outside the

57

New Jerusalem. But at the age of eighteen, she "was so richly favoured by her dear and blessed Mediator, as to receive at that time the Seal of her Absolution and Assurance, in a manner very special, there being presented to her in a Vision, the form of a Pardon with a Seal to it."[1]

Soon after this time, she went to London, chiefly in order to find a religious context for and deepening of her visionary experience. But although she attended numerous meetings, she was disappointed until she met Dr. Crisp, a well-known clergyman who had been ousted from his pastorate in Brinkworth in 1642 and had come to London just at the time Leade was there. He was able to resolve all her doubts and to give her a much clearer understanding of what had happened to her; but unfortunately he died in February 1643.

When she became interested in marrying one of her religiously inclined friends in London, who apparently was not of her social class, her parents brought her back to Norfolk in an attempt to marry her off properly, which she refused, since she did not want to marry merely for earthly reasons. Eventually she married William Leade, a merchant, when she was twenty, with whom she lived happily for twenty-seven years. With him she had four daughters, two of whom died, and two of whom reached maturity and themselves were married. Apparently she and her husband shared spiritual concerns.

But in February 1670 her husband died, and the man to whom his money was entrusted absconded with it, leaving Mrs. Leade destitute. What could have been a catastrophe, however, she regarded as in another sense her good fortune, for like Gichtel and many other theosophers, she took this as a sign that she should throw herself wholly on the mercy of God. Thus, she began to live wholly as a member of Pordage's theosophic circle, and slowly assumed leadership of the group, eventually coming to live with the widower Pordage in his house, so that the circle became a true community.

Leade had first met Pordage in 1663, a meeting about which she wrote in her preface to his *Theologia Mystica*:

> Know then, my first Acquaintance with him was in the Year 1663, (the Memory of which shall ever be pretious to mee, because of those great and spiritual Advantages, as to *the Information of my Judgement* about some deep and weighty Points of Divinitie: which none could answer that I could meet with, nor satisfy my searching Mind in those Things, like this holy Man of God, who had profound Abilitie given him in the holy Anointing.[2]

She soon became a member of his circle, but it was not until after her husband's death that she was able to devote herself wholly to theosophy. She and Pordage eventually lived in the same house, along with several others, the better to devote themselves to prayer and mutual religious understanding. During this time Dr. Pordage wrote his most important works.

After Pordage's death in 1681, the responsibility for continuing their theosophic work fell to Mrs. Leade. By 1683, she had had one of his more important treatises published, as well as some of her own, including *The Heavenly Cloud Now Breaking* (1681) and *The Revelation of Revelations* (1683). Upon reading the latter book, a wealthy widow offered Mrs. Leade and her group the use of her home for their meetings, an arrangement that lasted until the widow's death, at which time the group was forced to find another place to meet nearer London. By 1692, however, the theosophic circle had diminished, and it languished until 1694.

During this time, a copy of *The Heavenly Cloud Now Breaking* came into the hands of Baron Kniphausen in Germany, who corresponded with Mrs. Leade for some time, and eventually offered the means to publish her works both in German and English. Baron Kniphausen, who may himself have written a theosophic work published in Amsterdam in 1697 in French, gave a man named Loth Fischer sufficient money to translate Mrs. Leade's works into German, and they were subsequently published in the years 1694 and 1695, causing a considerable stir in German and Dutch theosophic circles.[3]

As Mrs. Leade's name and works began to circulate in Germany and the Netherlands, they reached a brilliant young man, who had been fellow of St. Johns College, Oxford, until all fellows were required to swear allegiance to the new king. He refused, and so had to leave. Born in 1660, his name was Francis Lee. Having left the college, he was at first a tutor to several noblemen, but eventually travelled to Italy, where, in Padua, he took his medical degree, and, in Venice, practiced medicine for two years. Returning to England via the Netherlands, he was given a copy of *The Heavenly Cloud Now Breaking* and, like Baron Kniphausen, was deeply impressed.

Lee explained this situation, and his own reaction, by writing in the third person of himself:

> an ancient devoted matron [Mrs. Leade] having left the world, and retired to end her days in a private cell, finds herself of a sudden much taken notice of without her own country; by the means of a book or two written and printed more

than ten years before, but now first sent over into a neigh-
bouring land, as by a seeming chance, from a merchant to his
correspondent and friend there. Great inquiry is made after
the author . . . [among others by] some men of learning.[4]

At this time, Lee "a young man of good education, travelling homewards,
meets with some of these," "two being doctors of Physic [Dr. Scot at Zol
and Dr. B at the Hague], and the third a Merchant [Mr. Finley at Rotter-
dam]." Lee continues back to England and, with two unnamed "students
of divinity," meets with Mrs. Leade herself, acting as interpreter for the
others. He does not directly say so here, but it is clear that Lee realized
the extraordinary significance of this elderly woman and her "loose
papers" "occasionally penned for her own private memory."[5]

   Mrs. Leade's eyesight was failing during this time, and Lee took upon
himself the transcription of her letters to foreign correspondents and of
her books. As more was published, her writings came to the attention of
those who charged her with supporting "a monastical or eremitical faith"
conducive to Catholicism. We should note here that theosophy has always
attacked "Babel," or mere outward faith without inward transmutation,
and that from a theosophic view Protestantism, in the form of Anglicanism or otherwise, can be as conducive to Babel as Roman Catholicism.
Those who took offense at Mrs. Leade's writings during this time were in
reality distressed by her insistence on inward visionary experience, but
attacked her as having "popish enthusiasm." Lee came to her defense.

   Like Gichtel, and many other theosophers, then, Lee found himself
divested of all his worldly means of support. He had forgone his
appointment at Oxford, "a pretty subsistence that was for life, but also
of all those advantages that he might reap from an academical retire-
ment, on several accounts most dear to him." Additionally, he lost "a
pretty handsome estate" through a legal technicality, and so he was driven into "spiritual retreat" "in a manner almost irresistible." He was
"in effect divested of all he had, was exposed naked to the more immediate care and tuition of . . . providence."[6]

   When Lee had given himself wholly up to divine providence and
cast his lot with Mrs. Leade, he was astounded—just as Gichtel's
acquaintances and friends were astounded at how providence mysteriously provided for him—by how somehow Mrs. Leade was given all
that she needed, and so was he, despite their dire poverty. He wrote:

   The light of God's countenance did seem to [Lee] to shine
   peculiarly upon [Leade], her enemies were made to be at

peace with her, her friends were multiplied on all sides, her low estate was turned as in a dream, and an invisible hand brought in supplies continually, yea abundance, to the great astonishment of [Lee] who could only remember somewhat like it in antiquity.[7]

We are reminded here of the New Testament injunction, "ask, and ye shall receive," and likewise of Gichtel's and Bromley's statements that after a certain stage of spiritual realization is reached, when we ask for sustenance in prayer, it is given us. Gichtel's letters also offer numerous miraculous instances of this principle in action.

From this time on, Leade and her fellow theosophers became increasingly well known, and there came to them other, remarkable people, including Richard Roach, Anne Bathurst, and Joanna Oxenbridge. Each of these was important in his and her own way, and each had individual visionary experiences of considerable significance. Richard Roach had been a fellow of St. Johns, Oxford, like Lee himself, and in 1690 was appointed rector of St. Augustine's Hackney, where he remained until his death forty years later. But he was significant for this group, which came to be known as the Philadelphians, because he published along with Dr. Lee a journal called *Acta Philadelphica: or, The Monthly Memoirs of the Philadelphia Society.*

The name "Philadelphian" came from a reference in the Revelation of St. John to those who are of "the angel of the church in Philadelphia" (Rev. III.7), for whom "I have set before thee an open door" that no man can shut. The Philadelphians are the faithful "remnant" near the end of time who do not abjure Christ for the Whore of Babylon or the Spiritus Mundi; and it is exactly in this light that the Philadelphians saw themselves. They expected the millennium to arrive fairly soon, and like the rest of the theosophers, they were earnestly convinced that they already realized this visionary spiritual reality on earth. And indeed, there are clear connections between theosophic revelations such as those of Mrs. Leade and the book of Revelation that deserve independent study.

Dr. Lee was very important for Mrs. Leade during this time; he served as intermediary between her and the world, saw through to publication her many books, and became like a son to her. In fact, he refers to her on a number of occasions, including his letters to the obstreperous Henry Dodwell, as his mother. She became his mother-in-law when he married Mrs. Leade's daughter, but Lee's relationship with Mrs. Leade went well beyond a merely legal one: like Guillaume Postel in the sixteenth century, who found in a saintly woman named Mother Joanna his spiritual illuminator and mother, Lee found in Mrs. Leade both an earthly and a spiritual mother, in whom he saw the peace that passeth all understanding.

This was a time of great activity for the Philadelphian society, for not only did the society publish its monthly periodical, but Mrs. Leade and Dr. Lee published many of Mrs. Leade's most important works as well. These include *The Enochian Walks with God* (1694), *The Laws of Paradise* (1695), *The Wonders of GOD's Creation Manifested, in the Variety of Eight Worlds* (1695), *A Message to the Philadelphian Society, Withersoever Dispersed over the Whole Earth* (1696), *The Tree of Faith: or, The Tree of Life* (1696), *The Ark of Faith* (1696), and *A Revelation of the Everlasting Gospel-Message* (1697), as well as *The Fountain of Gardens* (1697 et seq.). We will consider the essential content of Mrs. Leade's works shortly.

For now, we should recall that the publication of these works was funded from Germany, and that they were being published and circulated almost simultaneously in Germany, the Netherlands, and England. A number of Dr. Pordage's works were also published in German during this time, under the auspices of the same benefactor. However, these English theosophic works created much more of a stir on the Continent than in England itself. Dr. Lee complained, in fact, that the publications of the Philadelphians met with almost complete indifference in England; while in Germany they were, as we will shortly examine in more detail, the cause of much theological controversy.

Earlier we noted that Richard Roach, a fellow of Dr. Lee's from Oxford, joined the Philadelphians in 1697 and began to publish *Theosophical Transactions* with him. This publication, along with more public meetings of the group—made necessary by new laws—brought the Philadelphians more into the public eye, and exposed them to considerable criticism. Interestingly, the Archbishop of Canterbury met with Roach during this time, and they discussed "the Extraordinary Experiences Consisting in the opening of the Spiritual Senses, visions, voices, transports and which some persons in this Nation were at this time favour'd with all."[8]

Although the Archbishop was sympathetic to Roach and said, "I perceive you are rooted in yr Opinions; however, I will not be a persecutor nor give you or your Friends any Disturbance," he was the exception.[9] For in general, the Philadelphians were publicly attacked both in vindictive pamphlets and in person when they held meetings, exactly in proportion as they came into public view. The earlier policy of the theosophers, to remain in privacy, seems in retrospect to have been the wisest course—but changes in English law requiring public religious meetings forced their hand.

By 1697, the Philadelphian meetings had outgrown their previous quarters at Baldwins Gardens, where in any event Mrs. Bathurst had become "Aged and Sickly," so they moved to new meeting places at Hungerford Market, and at Westmoreland House near Hoxton, where Mrs. Leade lived. The meetings at Hungerford Market met with "great Opposition and Violence from the rude Multitude; and Continued for about Half a Year till, Divisions Growing also among themselves, they were not Able to hold it any longer, and so that Party laid down their Publick Design."[10]

This harsh public reaction to the theosophers' meetings continued both at Hungerford Market, which comprised a group separate from Mrs. Leade and her circle, and at Westmoreland House, where Mrs. Leade's group met. Indeed, it continued even when they moved to more private quarters at Twisters Alley in Bunhill Fields, and in 1699, when they met at Lorimers Hall and drew a very large crowd. The theosophers saw themselves as representatives of the Divine near the end of time and the coming millennium; and they attributed the public attacks to Satan's opposition, who "hath ever been busie to inspire some of his Agents, to raise Tumults against the Publishers of the approaching New Kingdom; and even to curse and blaspheme where we have been met together to bless God."[11]

This public tumult, which apparently at times reached nearly the magnitude of near-riots, is perhaps to be expected when an inherently esoteric religious tradition—requiring a fairly high degree of spiritual development and visionary understanding—is brought before a largely uncomprehending and even hostile audience who are quite likely to confuse it with antinomian Ranters or other alarming and somewhat anarchic sects. Certainly one can see parallels in Islam, where Sufis have been murdered by mobs incited to mayhem by those who identify religion only with dogmatic assertions or external forms, and who are threatened by the kind of visionary spirituality that Mrs. Leade and her circle represented.

The Philadelphians themselves expressed this conflict in a slightly different way:

> It has been the Method of the Philadelphian Society in general, both here and in other Countries, to Enjoy and Communicate what they have received in a more private manner; as two or

three should meet together in Unity: Notwithstanding it hath
pleased God of late to Impel and Constrain some of us, on
account of the near approach of the Kingdom of Christ, to go
forth and Proclaim it openly, which we have done now for
almost these two Years: and lately in a more publick manner;
whereby the Alarm has been sufficiently given and a free offer
made by God of a Renew'd Dispensation of his Grace and
Spirit: which has been generally despised and Rejected, and
the Messengers therof despightfully intreated.[12]

Böhmean theosophy, like ancient Hermetism and, for that matter, like the
Kabbala in Judaism and Sufism in Islam, thrives on intimate conversations
between two or three individuals, or between a master and a disciple. It
cannot be easily transposed onto a public scale without dilution or distortion. Thus, the conflicts that the Philadelphians experienced—which they
likened to casting pearls before swine—are no doubt to be expected, and
we should note that the Philadelphians themselves preferred seclusion.

But we should also note the chiliastic or millennialist import of
theosophy. The Philadelphians came together because they experienced
similar spiritual revelations and mysteries, and they sought to convey
these to those others around them with ears to hear. However one views
the phenomenon, the fact remains that they did certainly experience
some remarkable visions, which were part of a definite spiritual discipline, and which they saw as part of a new Christian dispensation near
the end of time. Although not stridently chiliast—we do not find the
theosophers shouting from streetcorners to warn people about impending doom—implicit in their experiences is the awareness that an unusual
and unexpected grace had been given to them during a particularly turbulent era, lived among uncomprehending people.

We should also note that the Philadelphians lived during an
unprecedented era of sect formation. All around them sects were forming and dissolving, as indeed they were on the Continent. Now, theosophy as a rule does not form sects; as we have seen, and will see in further detail later, theosophers are noncommittal about whether one is
formally Lutheran, Calvinist, Catholic, or Anglican. What matters is
one's spiritual experience, and thus the Philadelphians stressed in their
publications again and again their insistence that they were not a sect,
nor did they wish to establish one. But this insistence rang somewhat
hollow inasmuch as, unlike Pordage himself, Mrs. Leade's group did
indeed form a group with a name and, what is worse in the eyes of some
continental theosophers, a kind of creed and declaration of intent.

Exactly this—the name "Philadelphian," and their creeds and publications—distressed or put off European theosophers who had been initially very much interested in Mrs. Leade's revelations. A case in point is the reaction of Gichtel himself, at first neutral, only later taking a stand against her doctrinal views, for reasons we shall discuss shortly. But the German theosophers generally were put off both by false rumors that had circulated about the Philadelphians, and more importantly, by the tactless behavior of a gentleman by the name of Johann Dittmar von Saltzungen, who acted as an intermediary between the Philadelphians and the German circles.

Dittmar had corresponded with Mrs. Leade in 1702, requesting spiritual guidance, and by the autumn of that year was preparing to arrive in England to meet the Philadelphians. His arrival was preceded by dreams or visions experienced by both Dr. Francis Lee and Richard Roach, and the Philadelphians greeted him as an almost angelic manifestation, not least because they saw that he could form a bond between the German and the English theosophic groups. For this reason, the Philadelphian Society adopted forty-four Articles that were to organize subsidiary or affiliated groups in the future.[13] These articles held primarily that members should try to emulate the original Apostolic Church and that they should negotiate everything in unity and love.

But the very existence of the articles—and of such provisions as the appointment of two officers, one German and one English, to inspect the conduct of respective societies—indicate a move toward organization foreign to earlier theosophy. Dr. Pordage's circle did not proselytize, organized no formal groups, and produced no rules of order; it was a group brought together by visionary spirituality. Mrs. Leade's Philadelphians, on the other hand, did precisely what Dr. Pordage, Gichtel, and German theosophers in general did not: sought to organize into a kind of sect what had previously remained a purely informal group.

However, to be fair, one cannot deny that the Philadelphian articles of confederation come as close as possible to avoiding sectarianism while retaining an authentic group. Articles XX through XXIII in particular affirm strongly that Philadelphians should not judge one another by outward signs or dress; what mattered was one's kindness and visionary realization, the degree to which one was really holy and merciful to others. Such admonitions differentiated the Philadelphians from sects like the Quakers, who wore special forms of dress and held to special forms of address such as "thee" and "thou."

Probably the most important Philadelphian precept was against improper sexual conduct. The Philadelphians were well aware of certain excesses that had taken place in Germany—one thinks of Eva von Butt-lar, originally a Böhmean, whose circle had evidently become libertine—and sought to avoid any temptations in that regard. They forebode the fraternal kiss except if it be completely asexual, and in fact were much inclined toward celibacy, as were virtually all the theosophers. It is true that Mrs. Leade was accused of having an illegitimate child, as was Dr. Pordage before her, but both accusations were ridiculous, and derived from terrible confusion of rumor with fact.[14] The Philadelphians, whatever else one may accuse them of, were not libertines by any stretch of the imagination.

Important, too, was the establishment of *Regulatoren*, or church Elders, to supervise the various circles. We might note that this practice, while found throughout much of Protestantism, does have historical parallels in the Cathari *perfecti*, who were to be celibate and pure. Thus, there were, among the Philadelphians, three degrees of affiliation: the *Regulatoren*, the general society of members, and then those who were sympathetic to Philadelphians, or who were misguided in one or another way, but were not to be shunned or excommunicated. This tolerance marks the whole of theosophy, which might be defined as a pan-Christian mystical community.

Certainly the English theosophers, of whom Mrs. Leade was a central figure, had no intention of forming a separatist sect with formal, institutional structure. As we have seen, this would have been regarded by many other Böhmean theosophers as nothing more than producing another "Babel," another outward church without inward spiritual practice, of which there were altogether too many, in the theosophers' view anyway. But the Philadelphian articles, and the creed that the Philadelphians sought to produce, however carefully worded, was automatically likely to generate suspicion among German theosophers of precisely such an attempt to create a new sect.

No doubt what we possess of the Philadelphian creed offers in itself little with which most Böhmean theosophers would disagree. Compiled soon after the articles of confederacy, the Philadelphian creed affirms essential tenets of Böhmean thought. It affirms that God is above all a transcendent Unity, who reveals himself in the Trinity, but that "beneath" the Trinity in Eternal Nature God reveals himself in two opposing forces, which in turn contain three aspects or powers, between which is a mediating power. Thus, the Trinity is reflected in the subsequent emanations of the Divine "downward" into temporality in these Seven Forms of eternal nature. But only the last of these has a kind of corporeality; and all are part of eternal nature.

Although the Philadelphian creed was never completed—so far as we know—it contains a good general summary of Böhmean theosophic metaphysics. The creed describes the fall of the angel Lucifer through pride, and the establishment of earth and paradise in the place from which he had fallen; it describes the nature of the angels and their mediation between man and the divine. The creed also describes the Holy Virgin Sophia as mediatrix for man, a theme that would have been amply expanded, no doubt, had the creed been finally printed. In the spring of 1703 the Philadelphians were still working on the creed as a publication for all of Christendom, Judaism, and other religions, and they hoped to complete it by that summer or perhaps the following year.[15]

Unfortunately, the seemingly bright future of Philadelphianism as a nonsectarian international theosophic community was virtually obliterated during exactly this time, 1703. The Philadelphians had sent Johann Dittmar to Germany as a more or less formal representative, but he was evidently not the most diplomatic of people. In the previous year, Dittmar had met Johann Georg Gichtel, the sometimes irascible theosoph "hermit of Amsterdam," alienated him by quarreling both with Gichtel and others, and then worsened the situation by sending Gichtel a furious letter. The following year, having alienated the most significant theosopher of the time, Dittmar was sent as a diplomatic representative between England and Germany, a disastrous enterprise.

Already the German and Dutch theosophers harbored suspicions about the Philadelphians—their very name suggested a sect, and some German theosophers including Gichtel disputed some Philadelphian doctrines, most notably Mrs. Leade's belief in universal restoration at the end of time. These suspicions were intensified by inevitable problems in translation, and above all by the inept attempts at diplomatic contact made by Johann Dittmar. For it appears that even though Dr. Lee, Mrs. Leade, and the other Philadelphians took great care to assert that theirs was not a sect, nor did they intend to found one, Dittmar presented the Philadelphian articles and creed as requiring German theosophers' assent, effectively making the Philadelphians appear almost as a formal institution.

To such a group, the German theosophers would not assent. Of course, Dittmar's presentation was quite misleading. Dr. Lee had in fact instructed Dittmar and other Philadelphians to affirm "Universal Peace and Love towards All" and asserted that "though they are deeply sensi-

ble of great Corruptions and Deviations in most, or all, of the Christian
Bodies, or Communities, from the Apostolical Rule, yet do not therefore
formally Dissent, or separate from such a particular Body, Community,
or Church . . . much less do they perswade others to Dissent."[16] This
statement was important not only because of the English theosophers'
precarious position regarding Anglicanism—clearly they did not dissent
from Anglicanism or, for that matter, Catholicism—but also because it
demonstrates that they did not wish to form a separate sect.

However, Dittmar's diplomatic ineptness was not the only reason
that the Philadelphian society failed to expand into the Continent. For
by late 1703, Mrs. Leade was not at all in good health. Her health had
been weak since 1700, when she had already had premonitions of her
impending death.[17] Indeed, in 1702 she wrote "A Living Funeral Testimony," and although by the spring of 1704 she felt somewhat better, she
was stricken again by fever and severe pain, and this continued until her
death. Her painful and protracted death was taken as a sign by Gichtel
and others that some of her doctrines were false, and she was suffering
for them—but however one interprets such difficulties, the fact is she
endured her trial with a patient, graceful, and illuminated countenance.

Mrs. Leade's funeral oration was given by Richard Roach, who
later—after receiving a vision of her appearing from heaven like a globe
of light—assumed leadership of the Philadelphian society itself. But under
Roach's leadership, the society took on a distinctly more private aspect
than such public projects as the journal, the articles of confederation, and
the proposed creed suggested. Indeed, the society returned to essentially
what it had been under Dr. Pordage—a small circle meeting at Baldwin
Gardens, where the Philadelphians had met in 1697 before going public.

It is true that in 1707 the Philadelphians again held a brief public
appearance, when they were inspired by some Camisards, a chiliastic
French sect—expelled into England—of enthusiasts who prophesied the
imminent millennium. The Camisards claimed to be able to prophesy
and even to work miracles. The Philadelphians, albeit now a much more
private circle, met with the French expatriates and, hearing their prophesies about the coming new era, felt that here was another sign that the
millennium was indeed near. The Camisards did not adhere to theosophic teachings, but they did emphasize that one must realize spiritual
truth for oneself, and with this, the Philadelphians agreed (though their
millennialism was not nearly so fervent as the Camisards').

Richard Roach captured something of this moment, writing that in
1707 there was "Actually a Revival and Resurrection of the Philadel-

phian Testimony in Publick, in which several persons, who had been concernd in the First, appeard and bore their Testimony again, yet in such Manner under the Conduct and Protection of the Spirit as not to be expos'd to Injuries and Insults as before."[18] In other words, some Philadelphians appeared in public with the new Camisard prophets, but anonymously, not as Philadelphians per se. Thus, the Philadelphians and the "New Prophets" were "shooting together first on Whit Sunday of that year [1707]," "both animated with peculiar testimonies uttered with great Power and also Effect."[19]

Unfortunately, the Camisards were indeed enthusiasts and, carried away, in 1708 prophesied that one member, Thomas Ewes, would rise from his grave on May 25. This did not happen, and the sect disappeared thereafter, as numerous other millennialist sects both in Christianity and Judaism, in Europe, in Britain, and in America, have dissipated when expected and prophesied events did not take place. So too, albeit more slowly, did the Philadelphians dissipate. The Philadelphians were not simply enthusiasts, but their movement had some things in common with the expatriate French sect, particularly prophesying and millennialism, and that spirit was not sustained beyond their generation.

For, more than the German and Dutch theosophers, the Philadelphians were possessed of a public, prophesying, millennialist, and even sectarian character. Given the aversion of all theosophers to sects, even though the Philadelphians themselves vehemently denied they were founding a sect, Continental theosophers could not help but be suspicious, and such suspicions were intensified not only by Philadelphian attempts to codify articles of confederation and a creed, but by Philadelphian millennialism as well. For their millennialism led them, as the episode with the Camisards demonstrated, to public affiliations and exhortations that theosophers like Gichtel shunned.

This brings us to the doctrinal disputes that the Philadelphians had with European theosophers. Fundamentally, of course, the Philadelphians were in agreement with all theosophers of whatever country, so long as they affirmed Böhmean visionary spirituality. But on certain points the Philadelphians diverged from their Continental counterparts, and in one critical case, were willing to diverge even from Böhme himself. This, the most critical dispute between the English Philadelphians and Continental theosophers, was over the doctrine of universal restoration.

Universal restoration, or *apocatastasis*, was not a doctrine original with the Philadelphians, of course. Among the Church Fathers, Origen upheld this doctrine very early in the Christian era, and such noted Christian writers as John Scotus Erigena in the ninth century A.D. also concluded that universal restoration—the doctrine that ultimately all creatures created by God were destined for spiritual restoration and salvation—was only reasonable. In his *Periphyseon*, he wrote, citing Gregory the Theologian, "Evil is not strong enough to prevail over the power of goodness. . . . [E]vil must have an end . . . [for] nothing evil can endure forever," and indeed, eventually evil will be "entirely done away with."[20]

The doctrine of universal restoration stresses divine compassion over divine judgment; it arises in part from the realization that if man, who is created in the image of God, is able to forgive an enemy, then how much more so is it possible and indeed necessary that God may very well forgive us in the end as well? But the doctrine goes beyond even this, to affirm that God's compassion is so great as to forgive demons and devils, even Satan himself. Thus, universal restoration is rooted in divine benevolence and in a vision of holy forgiveness so powerful that it embraces the whole of creation.

There is a potential problem in this view, however: it can lead to libertinism. For if we are all forgiven in the end, even Satan, why ought we not act as we will in this lifetime? This is precisely the logic imputed to such sects as the medieval Brethren of the Free Spirit, or the Ranters, contemporaneous with the Philadelphians, not to mention the Kabbalistic equivalents in heretical Judaism. But of course. Mrs. Leade, though she affirmed universal restoration, was no libertine and would countenance no such behavior among the Philadelphians. Still, we can see why such theosophers as Gichtel found it necessary to question Mrs. Leade's embrace of *apocatastatic* doctrine.

In Gichtel's letters we find occasional reference to Mrs. Leade, and in these references we can trace Gichtel's reaction to her doctrines, chiefly that of universal restoration. On September 27, 1697, we find Gichtel writing that he had heard of Leade and the controversy over whether the fallen spirits can be raised up and redeemed, and he adds, "I acquiesced, as I do not love a war of words."[21] Gichtel did not want to attack either Leade or her doctrine, not least because he did not know the answer to the question she posed, that of universal redemption. However, Gichtel meditated upon the subject, and perused Böhme as well, concluding in the end that Leade was not right.

In a letter dated January 3, 1708, Gichtel wrote more directly of the matter:

> Though Mrs. Leade wishes to establish this, [the doctrine of apocatastasis], yet she could not maintain her opinion, as may be seen by the treatise of three sheets, called "Everlasting Gospel," which she wrote in answer to my objections. Böhme has treated of this matter in his *Aurora*, and especially in the *177 Questions*, and clearly enough shows the impossibility of the restoration of the devils.[22]

Gichtel was particularly opposed to what he believed Leade's position to be: that the devil could be redeemed by a "verbal remission." But he also held her to be wrong in essence, because she confused the pivotal human state with the unchanging state of spirits. Gichtel wrote:

> Leade indeed imagines that the whole Adamic tree cannot be restored in its integrity without the restoration of the devil, . . . but I see no ground for this. The devil's fall can as little as that of Adam be restored by a verbal remission, for he has lost his angelic light-body and assumed a serpentine one from the darkness; were he to be helped, it must be done by death and resurrection, which is possible with Adam, who fell in the third and inchoative principle.
>
> But how this were possible with the spirits in the unchangeable eternal principle I should like to know in the light of nature. For we are ever ready to mix two principles which can never be mixed, and though they are overcome, one must be subject to the other, as it was in paradise, yet they do not pass away; and thus the dark principle, together with the devil's government, shall eternally remain swallowed up in the light.[23]

Essentially, Gichtel argued, universal restoration is a human confusion of eternal principles.

There was a personal side to the debate as well, however. For during the late 1600s, Loth Fischer—translator of Leade's works into German—sought to convert Gichtel to Leade's cause in Germany. But, Gichtel's biographer writes, "Gichtel saw that she was fantasizing" about *apocatastasis*. Fischer, the biographer continues, said that Baron von Knyphausen would not send them money (he sent Fischer four hundred florins a year to support his translation work), to which Gichtel and Ueberfeld replied that they did not care about money, but about the truth.[24]

Gichtel's biographer continues in a somewhat typically acerbic fashion:

> LF [Loth Fischer] now feels what it is to play with spirits— he has made himself a devil and enkindled the innocent Mrs.

Leade with his venom and caused her to blaspheme with him, of which she knew nothing before. Wherefore also her lamp was extinguished, because her spirit reached into the tincture of Sol only, wherefore at the end of her life she had to pass through the fire. And her society in England has since perished.[25]

To this passage in the manuscript translation is pencilled in the following notation: "True—see Freher, *Anti-restoration.*" It is the case, as we saw earlier, that Mrs. Leade suffered at the end of her life; but whether one can attribute this to her doctrine is another matter. In any event, it seems evident that Mrs. Leade's doctrine of universal restoration came directly from her own visionary experience and nowhere else; Gichtel's and his biographer's attacks on Leade here do not hold up well under scrutiny.

Initially, Mrs. Leade did not even countenance the doctrine of universal restoration: in her *A Revelation of the Everlasting Gospel Message,* she wrote that "albeit I had heard of such a Notion, I did altogether disregard it; and would not entertain any belief concerning such a latitude as this, that should extend so far, as to recover the whole lapsed Creation, till I had an apparent Vision opened unto me."[26] Even after her vision was granted her, she had trouble reconciling it with the work of Jacob Böhme for, as Gichtel pointed out, Böhme himself did not embrace *apocatastasis.*

But eventually Mrs. Leade came to terms with Böhme by recognizing that her own revelation represented a gift of grace special to her own era:

And whereas some highly illuminated, who have great Veneration for Jacob Behmen's Writings do object, That he in his Principles seems to contradict this Universality as to the apostatiz'd Angels: I must own, that Jacob Behmen did open a deep Foundation of the Eternal Principles, and was a worthy Instrument in his Day. But it was not given to him, neither was it the Time for the unsealing of this Deep. God has in every Age something still to bring forth of his Secrets, to some one Gift, to some another, as the Age and Time grows ripe for it.[27]

This concept of continuing revelation—similar to the Buddhist recognition that there are certain revelations hidden and only discovered or revealed when the era is ripe—is entirely consistent with the theosophic revelation itself. For if Böhme's revelation, and any mystical revelation within the Christian tradition, is recognized as a natural continuation or growth of the tradition, then it is not sensible to expect that Leade's own revelations should be excluded, unless they be proven false.

But as we have seen, Leade's visionary revelation of universal restoration has respected predecessors in the Christian tradition and, although not a generally accepted doctrine, is at least a legitimate possibility within the total spectrum of Christian doctrines. It seems altogether too easy to deprecate her visionary revelation as heretical without considering that the term *heretical* is itself quite problematic within the broader context of Christian history. After all, virtually all Protestant sects have been deemed heretical at one time or another, just as even hesychasm, the central spiritual praxis of Eastern Orthodoxy, has been deemed heretical by some within that tradition, and just as the great Roman Catholic mystic, Meister Eckhart, was attacked as heretical. Of course, if the test of heresy is whether a given author's work or life conduced to authentic inward spiritual virtuous transmutation, then Leade, like the hesychasts and Meister Eckhart, was not heretical.

In fact, Leade's doctrine of *apocatastasis* seems to derive from a very powerful illumination and an overwhelming sense of divine compassion. It is as though the experience of light she had was so strong that in it there was no longer any place for evil or demons. In *The Enochian Walks with God* (1694) she wrote:

> Oh my Friends! What more joyful tidings can come to our ears than this one Everlasting-Age that shall swallow up all those ages wherein sin and death have reigned, with all those miserable effects that have been ever since the creation of this world? . . . Behold, saith the Lord, '*I will make all things new, the End shall return to its original-primary-being, let none grudge that the grace of God of this latitude is, as to make a complete restoration; for as there was neither sin, nor centre to it, so it must be again, when the hour of God's judgment shall come, to pass a final sentence thereupon, to cast all into that lake and bottomless pit where all of sin, and death, sorrow and curse, shall become a non-entity: then nothing of diabolical spirits (any more God's offenders, and his creature disturbers, or tormentors) shall be; all this in the prophecy of eternity will be known, and everlastingly rejoiced in, as forerunner of this blissful Jubilee Trumpet of the Everlasting Gospel of love, peace, and reconciliation to every creature capable thereof, in flesh, and out of flesh, that are not yet fully redeemed.*'[28]

The doctrine of *apocatastasis* does have a mathematical precision in its equivalence of the prior harmony and unity in God "before" creation, with the restoration *after* time of the fundamental harmony that the Fall of man rent asunder.

Leade's vision does not say that a given individual will be freed after death from the consequences of his actions during life. By no means does she deny the sufferings of those in hell or purgatory. But she does affirm that the "finishing of this Great Mystery" will be "when all souls will have passed through their purgation in their several degrees."[29] In fact, Leade's emphasis on purgation after death is not at all far from Gichtel's own views: central to Gichtel's own spiritual life was his experience of praying for three years for the salvation of a friend who had died by suicide, and Gichtel's ultimate success in seeing that friend's posthumous "movement" from purgative suffering to spiritual rest.

There is admittedly a significant difference between Gichtel's prayerful intercession for a friend's suffering soul, and Leade's affirmation that ultimately all beings will be freed from suffering—but this is a matter of degree. Gichtel was careful to emphasize that it was not his own efforts that liberated his friend from suffering, it was Christ working through Gichtel's prayers or meditation. And if Christ can liberate from suffering Gichtel's friend, can he not also liberate others so suffering? Indeed, is this not the meaning of Christ's harrowing of hell, that he came to liberate souls in torment who turned to him?

But this is the essential objection to Leade's doctrine of universal restoration: that there are malevolent spirits, demons, and devils who will not heed Christ's call. These are beings who have made their choice, not for good but for evil and, obdurate, continue in their selfish, destructive, dissonant path. How can such beings be saved? To this one cannot offer a clear answer; this is a mystery, the "great mystery" according to Leade and others who affirm universal restoration. But we will recall that Leade's *Everlasting Gospel* does give us part of the answer, for after the final judgment, demons will be "*cast all into that lake and bottomless pit where all of sin, and death, sorrow and curse, shall become a non-entity.*"[30]

Whatever else one may say about her, one cannot accuse Leade of being dogmatic; she simply offers her readers what she was given in vision and enjoined to tell others about. She writes:

> Thus I have given you a true and single account of what in my spiritual travels I have seen, known, and understood, by being admitted into that Heavenly Court *at certain times and seasons*; and shall leave this living testimony to the spiritual-minded, hereof to judge; for no other can receive or fathom this wisdom of God.[31]

She is certainly willing to accept criticism [from Gichtel] gracefully:

> [H]aving met since with some pretty deep Arguments from an
> Illuminated Behmist, that thinks he has such strong Argu-
> ments from Nature and Scripture, as might overturn the final
> restitution of the fallen Angels, this I take no offence at, so far
> as I find any searching out for the Fundamental Truth.[32]

This is a remarkably open statement, coming from someone whose primary spiritual revelation was under attack, and perhaps if more Christians approached one another in such a spirit, the history of Christianity, reflected in such lamentable institutions as the Inquisition, would
have been less violent.

Certainly Leade was not alone in holding this view of universal
restoration: others among the Philadelphians also held to it. Chief
among these was Richard Roach, who also held to a millennialism long
after the Philadelphian society proper had run its course. His millennialism is visible in the titles he published: *The Great Crisis, or the Mystery of the Times and Seasons Unfolded* (1725), and *The Imperial Standard of Messiah Triumphant; coming now in the Power and Kingdom
of his Father, to Reign with his saints on Earth* (1727). So too Roach's
defense of universal restoration is evident in *The Imperial Standard*,
wherein he has a chapter entitled "A Confirmation of the Doctrine of
the Universal Redemption."[33]

Essentially, the Philadelphian society differed from its Continental
neighbors in three central ways, then. First, it was, or attempted to be, a
defined group with articles of confederation, a creed, and a public identity
that theosophy in general did not tend to embrace. Second, the Philadelphians tended to be millennialist or chiliast in doctrine, and their expectation of New Jerusalem's imminent revelation often separated them from
their European counterparts. Thirdly, the Philadelphians in general
embraced the doctrine of universal restoration as part of their millennialism, a view unacceptable for German and Dutch Böhmeans who held to
a somewhat stricter interpretation of the Bible and of Böhme.

Without question, the Philadelphian revelations related by Jane
Leade and the other Philadelphians had little historical impact. Indeed,
although there have been several small circles that continued the English
theosophic tradition—including a circle in Glasgow, Scotland, that during the late nineteenth century published small manuscript reproduc-
tions of Leade's major works—the Philadelphians have not been well
known or influential in Christianity, Protestant or otherwise. But this is

perhaps not surprising, since theosophers generally are nonsectarian and uninterested in founding an external tradition that would carry on regardless of whether its members realized inwardly the spiritual truths of their tradition.

Yet one has to wonder nonetheless whether the significance of the Philadelphians and of theosophy generally is not all out of proportion to its apparent historical influence. For theosophy represents an emphasis on direct spiritual experience and on a visionary spiritual discipline within Protestantism that has its parallels in Kabbalism within Judaism and Sufism within Islam. And the Philadelphians represent one point in a Christian theosophic spectrum, just as Isaac Luria or Abraham Abulafia represent points in the Kabbalist spectrum, or as Ibn Arabi or Suhrawardi represent points in the Sufi spectrum. In this realm, historical influence is not nearly so important as the illumination that a given individual manifests. Here, it is not a matter of founding a sect, but of bringing forth in oneself a spiritual possibility.

There is a real principle at work within Protestantism, just as within Roman Catholicism, and within Eastern Orthodoxy. This principle is none other than individual spiritual realization, the flowering of the individual in relation to his God. Mrs. Leade and her society represent a spiritual possibility in the same way that Lurianic Kabbalism represents a spiritual possibility within Judaism. If we were to ignore it, or remove it from our spectrum of spiritual possibilities, we would be the poorer for it. This is not to say that we must agree with it, only that we should recognize the perspective that Leade and her circle represent.

One has to wonder whether the Philadelphians and the visions of Mrs. Leade do not correspond in some respects to the unfolding of some later schools in Buddhism. Hinayana Buddhism gave birth to Mahayana Buddhism, all-inclusive Buddhism that held as its central tenet the universal liberation of all beings, and the vow to further this liberation characterizes the *bodhisattva*. An impartial observer could not denigrate the concept of the *bodhisattva* as a degradation of the Buddhist tradition, but must recognize it as a legitimate unfolding of the tradition, an opening out to embrace all beings—even those suffering in hell—in universal compassion. Perhaps Mrs. Leade may best be seen in this light.

Mrs. Leade once said that the angels of judgment are many, but the angels of healing are few. Certainly she was more an angel of healing than an angel of judgment, more an embodiment of visionary grace and mercy than of severity or judgment, as Gichtel often seemed to be. It may be that this difference corresponds to possibilities inherent in what it means to be a woman or a man, to be feminine or masculine, as shown in the archetypes of the Virgin Mary interceding, or the Virgin Sophia bestowing grace, or Christ coming to judge the quick and the dead. But in any case, Mrs. Leade is an irreplaceable, unique figure in the history of theosophic spirituality.

CHAPTER FIVE

Dionysius Andreas Freher,
Allen Leppington,
and William Law

Although we can establish with certainty that theosophy continued in England after the death of Mrs. Leade in 1704 and the dissolution of the Philadelphian society proper, it is impossible to know the details of this continuation. Whereas for the Philadelphian society we possess records—including the journal *Acta Philadelphica* and various other sources including the works of Leade, Bromley, and others—for the years following the dissolution of that organization, our information is exceedingly sketchy. But it is entirely possible to trace the lives of the primary theosophers in England during the eighteenth century, even if we do not possess details.

Any account of theosophy in eighteenth-century England must take into consideration the works of Dionysius Andreas Freher (1649–1728). Freher was, after Pordage, the most important British exponent of Böhmean theosophy. Author of numerous commentaries and illustrations that amplify much that was previously obscure in Böhme's own works, Freher was without question a valuable explicator of abstruse theosophic points. But Freher is also important because, like all the other theosophers, his theosophic inspiration was his own, and the light he sheds on Böhme's works comes from his own experience of what Böhme

79

had also realized. Freher, above all a commentator, was also a significant author in his own right.

But of Freher's life we know little. A native German, he was born in Nürnberg on September 12, 1649, moved to England in the late seventeenth century, developed a faithful circle of fellow theosophers that included the illustrator J. D. Leuchter and the merchant Allen Leppington, and finally died on December 5, 1728 (November 24, 1728, according to the Old Style calendar). During this time, Freher never published any of his writings, nor were his works published in their entirety throughout the nineteenth and twentieth centuries.[1] Freher's influence remains primarily on his own and later theosophic circles, for whom his works were extremely important.

But we can reconstruct some elements of Freher's life from his works and other sources. C. A. Muses points out that Freher's family in Nürnberg was prominent, and included numerous jurists, theologians, and doctors.[2] That Freher came from an upper-class family can be surmised from his writing as well, for he liberally sprinkles through his work Greek and Latin phrases or quotations, common to those with a classical education. How he made his living while in London is uncertain, but without question he devoted an enormous amount of time to the study of Böhme both in England and in Germany, and spent even more time writing his treatises and composing illustrations.

Freher, like virtually all theosophers, developed a small, loyal circle of theosophers around him, and these helped him in the work of copying manuscripts and creating or duplicating illustrations. In his inner circle Freher included five close friends: John Berry, Allen Leppington, Jeremias Daniel Leuchter, and two men, named Lorentz and Carlshoff. The first three were native Britons, and the latter two were, like Freher himself, emigrants from Germany. Leuchter and Leppington were Freher's faithful amanuenses, copying his manuscripts with good hands, and creating his remarkable, complex Böhmean illustrations, whose significance is rivalled only by the illustrations accompanying Gichtel's edition of Böhme's complete works.

We can infer from their lifelong loyalty to Freher, and from the exceptional labor that their copying certainly entailed, that Freher's closest friends were not simply his secretaries but were theosophers in their own rights. For as we have seen, theosophy has always engendered small groups or communities whose primary focus is theosophic practice. Indeed, in letters to the Bow Lane Church, a congregation devoted to reading Böhme, Freher indicts them for not embodying Böhme's principles in their lives, and for not being what they read. From this alone, we can conclude that Freher's own group was more inclined to actual theosophic discipline. That Freher was inclined this way is attested to also by his extraordinary humility, the fact that he sought no public notice and published no books.

The exact nature of Freher's circle and his relation to it can be further elucidated by considering briefly some of his writings, to which we shall return in more detail. Freher was given to a dialogue form, and a number of his works take the form of master-disciple conversations. One such treatise was his "Three Conferences between a German Theosopher and an English Divine," occasioned by Freher's conversations with the Reverend Edward Waple of St. Sepulchre's, Skinner Street, London. Waple was evidently a close friend of Freher's, who in fact lived in Waple's house until his death in 1712. From this relationship—Waple was a keen student of Böhme—we can see that far from being fictional, Freher's "Conferences" undoubtedly reflected actual conversations.

Like Gichtel, the Hermit of Amsterdam, Freher was a somewhat reclusive, spiritual, ascetic, and deeply respected theosopher figure, more or less a master in his circle. He stayed as a guest in various homes, and was valued above all for his spiritual insight; his life, like that of Gichtel, resembles the lives of countless Sufi shaykhs in Islam. He was devoted to spiritual discipline and to conveying his understanding to others; like Gichtel, Freher probably relied wholly upon Sophia-Christ to provide food and the other necessities of life through whatever channels might prove necessary, usually the gifts of friends and admirers. Like Gichtel, and like Böhme himself in later life, Freher lived on faith.

But faith provided through worldly means, and so Freher was given the support of various wealthy citizens, not least of whom was Allan Leppington (1686?–1769). Leppington was a significant member of Freher's circle, but he also carried on his father's legacy as the head of a fairly prosperous drysalter's company in London. (We might note that the term *drysalter* is an English term for merchants who deal in foods preserved in salt, including tinned meats and pickles, and also for merchants who deal in dyed goods.)[3] Lemuel Leppington had three sons, the oldest of whom was Lemuel Jr., but it fell to his two younger sons, Allen and John, and especially Allen, to run the Salters Company for nearly fifty years until Allen Leppington's own death.

Allen Leppington's deep interest in Böhmean theosophy developed after the Philadelphian society had ceased public activity in 1703, and began with the Bow Lane Church, a group that met not far from Bread

Street, where Allen Leppington lived. The Bow Lane Church, whose precise location is unclear, succeeded the Philadelphian group as a center of theosophic activity, particularly from 1706 onward. Freher was introduced to the Bow Lane Church in about 1712, and between 1712 and 1715 he wrote four letters to the congregation, chiefly admonishing it to abandon mere intellectualism and to experience theosophy for themselves. These four letters were copied out by Allen Leppington, and are preserved in the Walton collection of Dr. Williams's Library in London.

Indeed, Leppington's chief contribution to theosophy—in addition to the financial support he provided some theosophers—lay in his devoted hand-copying of virtually all Freher's extensive works. Leppington copied Freher's "Conferences," and along with Leuchter (whose hand is responsible for the extraordinary Böhmean illustrations accompanying Freher's works), must have known Freher very well, and worked with him not only as a copyist, but as a fellow theosopher. According to oral tradition in the Skilbeck family, whose Salters' Company Allen Leppington headed, there were numerous other theosophic manuscripts kept within the family until the mid-nineteenth century, when Alice Skilbeck saw fit to destroy them out of some misguided sense of "orthodoxy."[4]

Freher died in his eightieth year, in 1728, and his place in the theosophic circle to which Leppington belonged was subsequently taken by William Law, who actually learned German in order to read the works of Böhme. It is likely that Law came to know Freher's writings between 1732 and 1736 by way of Allen Leppington, and as C. A. Muses argues, it is also likely that Freher was an unacknowledged but very profound influence on Law.[5] Many of Leppington's theosopher friends died before him, and Law himself died in 1761, eight years before Leppington. So Leppington remains most important as a background figure, a remarkable merchant linking together several major figures of English theosophy, without having left works of his own that have survived to our own day; he remains, like so many others, a devoted, little-known theosopher.

No doubt the best-known writer among our British theosophers who succeeded the Philadelphian society during the eighteenth century was William Law (1686–1761), Leppington's friend. About Law we know considerably more than about Freher and Leppington, partly because Law was much better known than the others. Unlike Freher, whose works Law copied out by hand himself, and unlike Leppington, his friend, Law published numerous books during his lifetime, and was widely regarded as an important religious figure in England. But Law was rather careful to downplay the extent of his indebtedness to Freher, the Philadelphians, Pordage, and Böhme.

Law was born in King's Cliffe, Northamptonshire, and was educated at Emmanuel College, Cambridge, of which he became a fellow in 1711. His personal history is interestingly parallel to that of Dr. John Pordage. For, like Pordage, Law refused to take the oath of allegiance to, in Law's case, King George I in 1714, making him a Nonjuror, forcing him to resign his college position and disallowing him other public positions as well. Law then lived in Putney, near London, at the home of Edward Gibbon from 1727 to 1737, where he tutored the historian Gibbon's father. In about 1740, Law moved back to King's Cliffe, where he lived a celibate and quiet life shared with Hester Gibbon, the historian's aunt, and Mrs. Hutcheson, a rich, pious widow, until his death in 1761. His later years, like Pordage's, were spent studying Böhme and writing in relative seclusion.

In many respects, then, Law followed exactly the pattern set in the previous century in England by Dr. John Pordage, attracting a kind of Protestant monastic community of lay people around himself. This community, at King's Cliffe, was renowned for its generous charity. Law and an anonymous patron established a poorhouse for young girls, teaching them to read, knit, sew, study the Bible, and attend church; they gave clothes, money, and food to the poor through almshouses they established. Mrs. Hutcheson had a substantial income, but she and Law gave away all but a tenth of their income to the poor. They all led an abstemious life, with prayers morning, noon, and night, Law himself arising at five A.M. and spending much of his day reading in his large library of mystical authors, writing, and praying.

Law's personal library is revealing because it demonstrates again how much Law shared the theosophic tradition. As we have noted, theosophy is marked by an indebtedness to St. Dionysius the Areopagite, the Desert Fathers, St. Macarius of Egypt, and the German mystics, including Ruysbroeck, Tauler, and the *Theologica Germanica*, all of whom are represented in Law's library. Above all, though, in later life, Law studied the manuscripts of Freher—which he copied by hand—and the works of, in his words, "our Behmen, the illuminated instrument of God" through whom the birth, development, and meaning of all things is "in eternity" opened.[6] Thus, Law recapitulated in his own library the historical influences on theosophy and their culminating authors, particularly Böhme and Freher.

Law discovered Böhme between 1733 and 1736, and had studied Freher's works from 1737 onward, but, as C. A. Muses points out, he did not give much credit to either, particularly to Freher. Muses notes:

> It is generally held, and repeated from one critic to the other,
> that William Law's works are the most competent exposition
> we have of Boehme. But it is not generally known that the
> principal and uncredited source for Law's expoundings were
> the writings of Dionysius Freher.[7]

As Muses points out, most scholars have ignored the influence of Freher on Law, including Stephen Hobhouse, in whose anthology of Law's selected writings Freher's name does not even appear in the index. But Law himself did not ever cite Freher, and probably would not have cited Böhme himself openly (even though some of his works are chiefly paraphrasings of Böhme's works) except that he was publicly accused of plagiarism by a Dr. Trap. Only after this charge did Law openly refer to Böhme.

Some critics have wondered why Law did not make more overt references to Böhme in his own writings. However, when we consider that Pordage, the greatest English theosopher, had his works published only in German and after his death, when we consider that in England there was considerable sentiment against the Böhmean "enthusiasts" because of their insistence on spiritual experience, and when we recognize that even objective recent assessments affirm that Law's "later writing, in all of which he expressed his admiration for and indebtedness to Boehme, alienated him from former admirers like John Wesley . . . and Dr. Samuel Johnson," we can see that, and why, Law paid a price for publicly affirming Böhme as much as he did.

But there is another reason that Law did not constantly cite Böhme or Freher: the primary tenet of theosophy that one must understand for oneself the spiritual realities of which other theosophers write. Theosophers refer to, but do not rely wholly upon, the writings of other theosophers, even Böhme himself. When we read the voluminous works of Pordage in German, when we read the works of Leade or even those of Gichtel, we do not find a constant citation of Böhme there either. Clearly all these authors are steeped in Böhmean tradition, clearly they embody theosophy, but their works are each unique manifestations of it, not merely parrotings of Böhme. So too Law's works represent his own personality and understanding of theosophy.

It is commonly repeated by scholars that Law represents England's greatest interpreter of Böhme, but the fact is, Law is simply England's best-known, if not most profound, Böhmean author. Without doubt, Britain's most profound and encyclopedic theosopher is Pordage, whose work far surpasses that of Law in breadth and insight. But Law is a fine stylist, whose devotional writings are at once eloquent and simple. Of course,

Böhme himself had an eloquent and simple devotional side, manifested in such works as *Christosophia: The Way to Christ*. Yet, as anyone knows who has tried to make his way through some of Böhme's more cosmological works, his work can be extraordinarily dense and difficult. These deeper aspects of theosophy are by and large missing from Law's work.

Still, if one comes to Law's later writings with the entire theosophic tradition in mind, one can see just how much Law was influenced by theosophy. Freher and Böhme were given on occasion to the dialogue form, whose antecedents are found in works such as those of Giordano Bruno, earlier in John Scotus Erigena, earlier still in the *Corpus Hermeticum*, and earlier still in the works of Plato. So too in his most Böhmean later works, such as *The Spirit of Love*, Law uses the dialogue, developing his theses through conversations between Theophilus, a master theosopher, Theogones, and Eusebius. It is in these dialogues that we find references to "Behmen" as the "chosen instrument of God."

Indeed, virtually the whole of *The Spirit of Love* consists in explication of theosophic premises. In it, Law through the mouth of Theophilus explains the seven spirits of God, the nature of wrath, evil, the Fall of man and Lucifer, redemption, and numerous other topics all of which are wholly Böhmean, some passages being almost paraphrases of Böhme, whose work, along with Freher's, Law had studied very extensively for many years, until he had absorbed it so that it could flow naturally from his own pen. Although occasionally somewhat stilted, and never possessing the scope of Pordage's works, Law's dialogues attest to just how closely he had studied theosophy.

His later works also demonstrate Law's indebtedness to the Philadelphians. For although Law did not want to be identified with the "enthusiasts," and did not allude even to Freher, much less to Leade, he has much in common with Jane Leade, Richard Roach, and the other Philadelphians who preached universal restoration. We have seen how Mrs. Leade taught the absolute precedence of love over wrath, even to the point of affirming, as Origen did, the doctrine that even demons will ultimately be redeemed. Law—who was cautious—never went quite so far as Leade in such affirmations. But he definitely asserted the absolute precedence of love over wrath.

On this central and defining question among theosophers, Law stands somewhere near the middle of the spectrum; while he does not quite directly teach the doctrine of *apocatastasis* like Leade, Law does insist that in God himself, there is no wrath nor any anger at all. God is pure, boundless love. Wrath only came to be when Lucifer fell and created nature fell into materiality; and so "God can no more begin to have any wrath, rage, or anger in Himself after nature and creature are in a fallen state than He could have been infinite wrath and boundless rage everywhere and from all eternity."[8] Wrath is simply a result of fallen creatures being separated from the Divine will to love. Thus—and this point is critical—all creation, good or evil, exists "to turn temporal evil into eternal good," for through creation *the supernatural Deity wills and seeks the restoration of fallen nature and creature to their first perfection.*"[9]

Thus, Law tacitly is indebted to the Philadelphians, and in fact his mission is rather close to theirs—like them, and like the Pennsylvania theosophers, he restates Böhmean premises in ways that are much more readily understood than Böhme's own complex terminology and circuitous treatises allowed. In this task, Law was preceded by Pordage, of course, whose organized, lucid treatises served a similar purpose. In fact, at times we can find what may be Pordage himself appearing in Law's prose, as when in *The Spirit of Love* Law writes that

> In eternal nature, the three contrary properties of desire, answering exactly to the three contrary motions of material attraction, are in themselves only resistance, rage, and darkness . . . till the supernatural Deity kindles its fire of light and love in them; and then all their raging contrarieties are changed into never-ceasing sensibilities of unity, joy, and happiness.[10]

This is certainly very close to Pordage's writing on eternal nature, and at the very least suggests that Law and Pordage were much more akin than Law would publicly acknowledge.

We will recall that Pordage, in his defense against the attempts to have him removed from the ministry, explained how he and his family had had revealed to them on earth the mysteries of hell and of paradise. Law writes of exactly the same truths, placing in the words of Theogenes, one of his characters, the exclamation:

> Oh Theophilus, you quite surprise me by thus showing with so much certainty how the powers of eternity work in the things of time. Nothing is done on earth but by the unchangeable workings of the same spiritual powers which work after the same manner, both in Heaven and in Hell.[11]

Hence, he adds, "I now sufficiently see how man stands in the midst of Heaven and Hell under an absolute necessity of belonging wholly to the one, or wholly to the other, as soon as this cover of materiality is taken off from him."[12]

Matter is simply a partition apparently separating us from eternity, and Law, like Pordage, affirms that both heaven and hell surround us now. But Pordage's visionary affirmations, like those of Leade, are much stronger than Law's. Law only goes so far as to assert the principles informing visionary theosophy; unlike the Philadelphians, he never goes the next step, to affirm like Pordage and Leade that not only do heaven and hell surround us in principle, they can be directly witnessed, experienced at this very moment on earth. Law was a far more subdued and merely intellectual theosopher than the Philadelphians to whom he was indebted.

Precisely this difference between Law and his visionary predecessors accounts for their respective public receptions. Law was a Böhmean theosopher, to be sure, but his theosophy was so refined, and so shorn of references to its antecedents, that it was not nearly as threatening to a modernist worldview as the extraordinary revelations of Pordage or Leade. Thus, it is not surprising to find that although in essence Law's writings are in the same theosophic stream as the other works we are here examining, Charles Williams could write of Law's works that they form "perhaps one of the best statements of the pure Christian religion that have ever been issued," and Rufus Jones could term Law a "saint" and a "prophet."[13] One is hard pressed to find acclamation like this for Pordage or Leade.

This is the central paradox of Law's most important works: Law's mystical Böhmean cosmology alienated some readers, yet this cosmology and the theosophic inspiration it reflected was the very source of Law's writings. Thus, his later works perched between a broader audience and the theosophy he was interpreting to that audience. Law's treatises form an introduction to the theosophic tradition, and if they do not reflect the visionary insights of a Pordage, or the revelations of a Leade, or the practical theosophy of a Gichtel, or the extraordinary breadth of Böhme's books, still his aphoristic gift and his ability to make theosophic insights accessible to many earn him a lasting place in the history of theosophy.

CHAPTER SIX

Johannes Kelpius and
Pennsylvania Theosophy

We have considered theosophic groups or communities in Germany, the Netherlands, and England, and now turn to the emigration to Pennsylvania of a theosophic community that, in a very real sense, links all of these other groups. The leader of the first Pennsylvanian group of theosophers was Johannes Kelpius, a remarkable, learned young man who led a group of German theosophers to England and then to Pennsylvania, where he headed the first theosophic community in the New World for fourteen years until his death in 1706. Often romanticized, and held by some to be a Rosicrucian, Kelpius was in fact a theosopher in the classical Böhmean tradition, whose life and primary works are well worth documenting here.

Kelpius was born in Denndorf, Germany, in 1670, and after studying at the Gymnasium, in 1687 went to the University at Tübingen, then to Leipzig, and finally to Altdorf (now the University at Helmstadt) studying theology. Because his father died when he was young, Kelpius was sent to the university by family friends. Important among others in his life were the renowned Professor Fabricius, Philipp Jakob Spener, and the Christian Kabbalist scholar Knorr von Rosenroth; Kelpius corresponded with his old preceptor Dr. Fabricius from a distance even as an expatriate.

Kelpius was evidently a brilliant student who had mastered classical learning, astrology, and other esoteric disciplines as well.[1] He was possessed of a profound religious genius, and even though Kelpius did not leave behind a vast collection of letters, like Gichtel, or clear, organized theosophic treatises like Dr. Pordage, his remaining journal, letters, hymnbook, and treatise on prayer, as well as his reputation carried on in later Pennsylvania theosophic manuscripts, all attest to his deeply pious religious nature. He published in 1689—at the age of sixteen—his doctoral thesis on *Theologiæ Naturalis*, and at the age of seventeen published two books, one on the royal road between Scylla and Charybdis (with chapters on Tertullian, Gregory Thaumaturgus, Arius, Augustine, and Pelagius), the other on Aristotelian ethics.[2]

About Kelpius's learning we also have much evidence. The Reverend Peter Miller, the successor to Conrad Beissel, leader of the Ephrata Community in Pennsylvania, which succeeded Kelpius's community, wrote that

> Kelpius, educated in one of the most distinguished Universities in Europe, and having had advantage of the best resources for the acquirement of knowledge, was calculated to edify and enlighten those who resorted to him for information. [He knew well] works of the Rabbins, Heathen and Stoic philosophers, the Fathers of the Christian Church . . .[3]

But, Miller continued, Kelpius's main precept was that inscribed over the entrance to the temple at Delphia, "Know Thyself," followed by the injunction of Marcus Aurelius, "Look within, for within is the fountain of good." These precepts fit well with the works of Jacob Böhme and Paracelsus, whom Kelpius studied very deeply.

As the epigraph to his journal chronicling his journey to the New World, Kelpius included the following from Seneca, quoted in full:

> I cannot go beyond my country; it is the one of all; no one can be banished outside of this. My country is not forbidden to me, but only a locality. Into whatever land I come, I come into my own: none is exile, but only another country. My country is wherever it is well; for if one is wise he is a traveller; if foolish an exile. The great principle of virtue is, as he said, a mind gradually trained first to barter visible and transitory things, that it may afterward be able to give them up. He is delicate to whom his country is sweet; but he is strong to whom every single thing is his country; indeed he is perfect to whom the world is exile.[4]

Kelpius chose a quotation from Seneca exemplifying an idea common to theosophy generally, that our lives in this world are exile from our true home, paradise. But this quotation also underscores the difficulty Kelpius and his fellow theosophers felt in making their decision to leave Germany and come to Pennsylvania.

During the late seventeenth century, Europe was embroiled in religious turmoil, as the persecution of Gichtel in Germany, and of other theosophers in Germany and England, demonstrates. Some theosophers grew tired of this persecution, and decided it would be best to travel to America, where they would live in the wilderness but would at least be free to worship as they pleased. Gichtel, of course, refused this option; living in Amsterdam, he said that one faces the devil wherever one goes, and travelling to Pennsylvania would not change one's essential spiritual task. But Johann Zimmermann (1634–1694) and Johann Kelpius, living in Germany, decided otherwise, and along with a small contingent of like-minded theosophers, set out for England and, from there, for Pennsylvania.

We might note that Zimmermann was a learned mathematician, astronomer, and theosopher in his own right, a man with a profoundly millennialist bent. He had written several treatises from a Böhmean perspective on the "Europäische Babel" and the imminent return of Christ to earth, and so had much in common with the more millennialist wing of the English Philadelphian theosophers.[5] Zimmermann and his group left behind what they saw as decadent Europe for the New World because they expected the apocalypse, and wished to await, in the wilderness of Pennsylvania, the millennium prophesied in the Johannine Revelation.[6] This explains the peculiar name given by other settlers to this band of theosophers once in Pennsylvania: the "woman in the wilderness" community. Kelpius's group saw themselves as the devotees of the "woman in the wilderness" prophesied in Revelation to go forth and await the second coming of Christ, the woman in the wilderness being interpreted as the Virgin Sophia.

Zimmermann's little band included, besides Kelpius (second in command at the age of twenty), Heinrich Bernard Cöster, Daniel Falkner, Daniel Lutke, Johann Seelig, and Ludwig Biedermann, among a group of forty or more, both men and women. They arrived in England midway through 1693, and stayed with English Böhmeans—the Philadelphian group of Jane Leade (Pordage had been dead more than ten years by this time)—for half a year. This was in most respects a congenial meeting, for not only were there German emigrant theosophers already in the Philadelphian community (who tried to maintain contacts with

theosophers in Germany), but some Philadelphians were of a millennialist bent that must have confirmed that of Zimmermann's community.

On January 7, 1694, after Zimmermann's untimely death, Kelpius
and his group resolved to take passage to America, and on February 7,
1694, they booked the ship *Sarah Maria*, captained by John Tanner.
Kelpius's diary tells of their difficulties in passage even before leaving the
vicinity of England:

> My apprehensive mind presaged evils with a fortunate out-
> come. Falkner said the same of himself. We were visited first
> by the impress-gang of the kind. Then we were driven
> towards the sand-banks by a contrary and turbulent wind;
> wishing to escape these, we sought safety in our anchor,
> whereby we should have perished if not Divine providence
> had made it, that the great weight of the metal, which, under
> our ship, would have perforated the same had not the anchor
> been broken itself. Our anchor being lost in this manner, we
> were at length borne upon the sand-banks by the whirl. All,
> saving a few, feared the end was at hand. The Captain having
> fired off four cannon, called those [ships] who were near to
> the rescue, but [none] took pity on us. We furled the sails and
> committed the vessel to the turbulent billows, whilst the
> sailors were despairing.[7]

Despite the sailors' despair, Kelpius and his fellow theosophers continued
praying, and their ship was in fact saved from destruction—which salvation they attributed to the power of their unified prayer. While awaiting
and after receiving a new anchor, they encountered further difficulties, but
survived them all, and finally were able to truly set sail for Pennsylvania.

Kelpius's diary kept during the voyage is perhaps most interesting
for its marginal notations. Along the margins of the journal he placed
the astrological symbol that reigned for a given hour of the day—and
so a typical entry might read "An auspicious wind. A north-wind
drove us from our place. In consequence of the wind changing to west,
we were tossed about all night." Aligned vertically beside this entry
are the symbols for Jupiter and Venus, followed by the signs for the
Sun and then for the Moon.[8] This notation is continued for the entire
journey—an astrological log running alongside Kelpius's patient
remarks on the weather and sailing conditions. Such careful calculations as this notation belies suggest that Kelpius was carrying on
exactly the traditions begun by his predecessor and friend, Johann
Zimmermann, astrologer and mathematician.

Astrology played an important role in the lives of the Kelpius group, not only on a daily basis and in the manner found among all the theosophers, as constituting the foundation of theosophic psychology, but in a new way as well—as marking the inception of the millennium. Kelpius kept track of the daily position of planets—as his journal reveals—but he did so not only to see how daily events corresponded to planetary governance, but also to see the signs on the sky that would mark the beginning of the apocalypse. Kelpius certainly understood the planetary symbolism used psychologically in theosophy—Venus equated with lust, Mars with anger—but he looked also to the stars and planets to reveal the spiritual cycles unveiled in time.

In this respect, Kelpius's theosophy differs even from the restoration theology of Jane Leade, for he and his group looked forward to the imminent apocalypse and millennium revealed within the first years of their lives in the New World. Thus, we can see a spectrum of theosophers' views on this critical question. Gichtel did not live his life based in expectation of imminent apocalypse, and opposed the Philadelphians; Leade and some Philadelphians looked forward to the restoration of all fallen spirits in an *apocatastasis*; and Kelpius's group looked forward to the prophesied end of time within but a few years, according to Zimmermann, in the fall of 1694. Kelpius's millennialism, and his preoccupation with astrological revelation of time cycles, reflects a long European Christian tradition that includes such figures as Joachim of Fiore and Simon Studion, with his careful calculations of time cycles and of the imminent apocalypse in his *Naometria*.

Our little band of theosophers arrived in Philadelphia on June 23, 1694, and literally kissed the earth, after ten weeks of arduous voyaging. They made their way to Germantown, and built a settlement along the Wissahickon river, their settlement designed more or less along monastic lines, with an anchorite cell carved into the hillside for Magister Kelpius. Indeed, that they were organized along monastic lines is evident, too, from the names that they had for one another: Kelpius was *Philologus*, Seelig was *Pudens*, Falkner was *Gajus*, and the Reverend A. H. Francke was *Stephanus*.[9] Unlike some of the Puritans, the theosopher settlers looked favorably upon the indigenous tribes as possessing wisdom, and offered them medical and other services for free.

The Kelpius settlement took no name, and said that they belonged to no denomination. But because their sermons or exhortations often referred to Revelation 12.1–6, they became known by other settlers,

German or otherwise, as "the woman in the wilderness" community on
the Wissahickon. A later work of the Ephrata colony (which succeeded
the Kelpius group) explained their unnamed way of life as follows:

> While giving up their souls to their Creator, and devoting
> their whole lives to a preparation of their hearts for the glori-
> ous inheritance prepared for the faithful, they mutually
> instructed each other, and cemented a bond of brotherly love
> and holy affection. They professed love and charity toward
> all denominations, but desired to live without name or sect.
> 'The Contented of the God-loving Soul' was the only name
> they acknowledged.[10]

This account suggests not only how they lived, but underscores their
refusal to participate in sectarianism, a refusal characteristic of all
theosophers. But like Böhme and Gichtel, Kelpius was at times very
much inclined to criticize those who merely gave lip service to Christianity. For Kelpius and the other theosophers, religion was a matter of
the heart's illumination, not of adherence to a name.

As is generally the case among theosophers, although we possess
some letters and publications of Kelpius's group, it is difficult to tell
exactly how they lived their daily lives. We know that they held services
morning and night, to which those of any denomination were invited;
we know that they sang many hymns composed by Kelpius or brought
over from Germany; and we know that the community emphasized
chastity and prayer. We also know that they celebrated their landing in
Pennsylvania annually on St. John's Eve, and of these celebrations the
most renowned was on the seventh year after their arrival.

On St. John's Eve, the seventh year after their arrival, the Wissahickon community lit fires at night,

> When they observed . . . a white, obscure, moving body in the
> air [that] attracted their attention, which, as it approached,
> assumed the form and mien of an angel. It receded into the
> shadows of the forest, and appeared again immediately before
> them as the fairest of the lovely. . . . They fell upon their knees
> to welcome the harbinger of good tidings, but alas, the spirit
> vanished while the devoted brethren were praising God for
> the deliverance at hand.[11]

The angelic apparition did not reappear that night, although they continued their prayers until morning. For the next three nights, they continued
prayer vigils, and on the third night it reappeared, but then vanished, which

they attributed to impurity among one of them, a member who confessed he had committed a crime in Europe before coming to America.[12]

It is, of course, difficult to know what to make of such an apparition. Certainly these events—especially with their parallels in Gichtel's letters, Pordage's treatises, and elsewhere in theosophic literature, as well as their numerical symbolism—are characteristic of theosophy, which is a visionary discipline. Most theosophic visions, however, are individual, not a group affair. When Gichtel talks about visions seen by groups, it is often to point out their dubious nature, since each person tends to see something different in accordance with his own "astral constellation." And one could certainly dismiss the angelic apparitions to the Kelpius group as something of a mass hallucination. But one has to wonder, for the apparition did appear according to an archetypal number cycle characteristic of theosophic hierohistories, and it appeared to all alike.

Probably the best indication of Kelpius's own religious views is to be found in a letter he wrote to Stephen Mumford (1639–1701) of Long (Rhode) Island, dated December 11, 1699. In it he writes:

> Dear Friend and Brother,
>   In fellow-fighting in that Free and Royal Spirit which strives for the Prize of the first Resurrection when in this Midnight the Cry of the Bridegroom's coming is sounded forth among the Virgin waiters for the Preparation of the Temple Body, wherein the King of Glory and Father of the coming Eternity is to enter.[13]

He writes, further, of how,

> since that glorious Primitive Church of Christ Jesus the Apostacy hath run in a continual current till this very day, and though this Stream hath divided itself in many smaller Rivulets, under several Names of more reformed Purity, yet you are not ignorant how they derive their Emanation from one Spring and . . . to the same end, viz, that the Woman in the Wilderness might be carried away by the Flood.[14]

Nonetheless, he continues,

> Therefore you, as a Remnant of her seed, long for to see your Mother and groan for the Manifestation of her children. No wonder then, if your continual Gazing upon this Supercaelestial Orb and Sphier from whence with her Children, causeth you to observe every new Phœnomena, Meteors, Stars, and various Colours of the Skei, if peradventure you may behold

at last an Harbinger as an Evidence of that great Jubelee or
Restitation of all things and glorious Sabbath-ismos, or the
continual days of Rest without intervening or succeeding
Nights, whereof God hath spoken by the mouth of all his
Prophets since the world began.[15]

From these excerpts we can see revealed in Kelpius's own words
how he had sympathizes with the "restitution of all things" expected by
the Philadelphians, and how he and other Pietists have seen "such
Miraculous Powers and operations" as have not appeared since Biblical
times. They have seen

Ectases, Revelations, Inspirations, Illuminations, Inspeakings,
Prophesies, Apparitions, Changings of Minds, Transfigura-
tions, Translations of their Bodys, wonderful Fastings for 11,
14, 27, 37 days, Paradysical Representations by Voices,
Melodies, and Sensations to the very perceptibility of the
Spectators who was about such persons.[16]

These people have been baptized "with such energical drops out of that
supercaleistial Pillar of Cloud by Gifts and miraculous Manifestations of
the Powers from on high." Given these observations about the Pietists
by Kelpius, we can more clearly see the context in which the Virgin
appeared in the wilderness.

Kelpius concludes his letter to Mumford—founder of the Seventh-
Day Adventist sect—by calling attention to their living in the end-times,
the apocalypse being imminent. In the sunset of human history, one can
well expect such events as apparitions and ecstasies, according to
Kelpius, for the approach of the millennium and the descent of the spirit
upon humanity must necessarily leave its imprint upon people more and
more clearly. Kelpius's letter reveals the fervor of his community's millennialism, and the profound connections between this millennialism
and the visionary phenomena that they experienced during what they
regarded as the end-time of humanity.

As this letter suggests, Kelpius was in contact with many people,
both spiritual leaders and ordinary folk, throughout the east coast of
America. In fact, he was held in great esteem throughout the provinces,
and as Sachse notes:

[T]he fame of Johann Kelpius's piety and learning . . .
extended to other parts of the country, and his correspondence must, for that day, have been quite extensive, and it

included various conditions of people. An instance of this is
shown by his letter of 8 October 1704, to Mary Elizabeth
Gerber of Virginia.[17]

In this very extensive letter to Gerber, Kelpius offers his assessment of
the Quakers and other sects, noting that even the ways of the apostles
themselves could become a cloak for hypocrisy. One has to remain humble and still, he admonishes. Other letters remain as well, including letters to Johannes Fabricius in Germany, Heinrich Deichman of England,
and Hester Palmer of Long Island, New York.[18]

Kelpius and his congenial community got on well with the Indians.
In a letter to Dr. Fabricius, Kelpius recounted how William Penn and his
fellow Quakers had met with Indians who patiently listened to their pro-
fessions of faith and then said that Quakers spoke of God but did not
act or live based on their words. Kelpius noted that the Father's house
has many dwellings—meaning that the Indians had a spirituality too.
The problem of sectarianism or exclusivism among Christians much
occupied Kelpius in his various letters, and his attitude toward Native
Americans is emblematic of his own refusal to judge others.

By 1706, the year of Kelpius's death, his little community had seen
a number of changes. Already other settlers had begun to move into
their vicinity on the Wissahickon, already some members had been married (beginning with Biedermann), and their millennialism had been
somewhat tempered by circumstances. At the same time, the community
on the Wissahickon had become reasonably well established and generally respected in the area. They had even developed a kind of "wilderness theology," according to which living in the wilderness was interpreted as taking place in three stages, the first being spiritual Egypt, the
second the leaving of this Egypt, and the third being a special high state
reserved for those of "extraordinary Qualifications and Endowments."[19]

But Kelpius had never been in good health, and by July 1706 he
had been seized by a "great cold" (i.e., consumption); he grew more ill
in the following year, and in 1708 he died, after fourteen years in the
wilderness, at the age of thirty-five.[20] Reputedly an alchemical practitioner who hoped that he would be translated bodily at his death into
a spiritual state, Kelpius died like an ordinary mortal, and at a relatively young age, though he had certainly accomplished a great deal in
his short life, having held together his little community and maintained
intact the theosophic practices and knowledge he had brought with him
from the old country.

Although Kelpius left behind only a few writings (particularly a hymnbook that includes invocations of Sophia), and certainly no extensive works on the order of Pordage's treatises on metaphysics, he did leave a sterling reputation, a treatise on prayer and contemplation, and a noble little community. As to his reputation, Sachse wrote the following encomium:

> By reason of his scholarly attainments, devout life, independent bearing, and, it may be said, broad humanity, together with his repeated refusals of worldly honors and civil power that were at various times thrust upon him, the Magister on the Wissahickon stands out in bold relief as a prominent example of piety and disinterestedness.[21]

Given Kelpius's continuing reputation—he is to this day cited by some as a Rosicrucian and master alchemist—we can conclude at least that he was certainly a remarkable personality.

Kelpius's treatise on prayer is a model of economy, and demonstrates quite clearly the profound parallels between his Protestant mysticism, the German Catholic mysticism that preceded the theosophers, and the Greek Orthodox mysticism that influenced them. For Kelpius affirms the different forms of prayer, and holds—like the mystics of other faiths—that

> Forasmuch as internal prayer is so weighty a point that one may call it the only means to attain perfection in this life and to kindle the pure and disinterested love in our hearts, and as all Christians . . . are called to this state of pure love and perfection, and will, by the power of this call, have the necessary grace offered to them to attain such a state: so this inward prayer suits all persons, even the most simple and ignorant, who are also capable of performing this order or manner of prayer.[22]

All Christians are called to the same inward form of prayer, the unceasing prayer of the heart.

This prayer of the heart—which is found in Eastern Orthodox and Roman Catholic traditions too—is not a matter of petitioning God, nor even of using discourse or reason at all. Indeed, this prayer is not even, exactly, a matter of the heart's intention, since

> All that the soul is and what is in her prays through and in Jesus Christ: and being not intent upon her own will, nor thinking discerningly on what she prays for, she receives at

once what she has need of. O what a power has prayer with God! But what prayer? The inward prayer of silence, the inclination of the heart to God, without thoughts, words, or images: where we expect and wait for all from the power and mercy of God. Those who perform this prayer obtain therein so much strength that they are not only comforted themselves but they also comfort others who are oppressed.[23]

Here is the most critical point: Kelpius enjoins "the inward prayer of silence, the inclination of the heart to God, without thoughts, words, or images."

The ultimate prayer of the heart, according to Kelpius, is a prayer that takes place "unceasingly," which can only happen in a mysterious way through God's grace. Such prayer of the heart is not a matter of contemplation, or meditation, or even direct intention, as much as it is a constant reciprocal union with God. For after all, it is not possible in human life to dispose oneself constantly to contemplative prayer, even in the ascetic hermit's life. Thus, if we are to be in unceasing prayer, it must be through a constant union with God's will, taking place through the union of our will with God's in a mysterious way.

So far Kelpius was comparatively orthodox, but there are some unorthodox stories told about his death. He was cared for from the winter of 1705–1706 onward by Christiana Warmer of Germantown and by Dr. Christopher Witt, who prescribed herb-decoctions (*hausmittel*) for Kelpius, unfortunately to little ultimate effect. This reveals nothing strange. But according to the Reverend Heinrich Melchior Mühlenberg, who arrived in Pennsylvania in 1742, he was given the following account of Kelpius's death by Daniel Geissler, Kelpius's confidant and assistant. Kelpius thought that he would be bodily transfigured at death, like Elijah and Enoch. He struggled three days and nights, praying, but on the third day ceased, and said to Daniel that it was not to be, for "it is ordained that I shall die like all the children of Adam."[24]

This, however, is not the strangest tale surrounding Kelpius's death. For Kelpius supposedly gave Geissler a sealed casket, and told him to cast it into the deep water of the Schuylkill River. Geissler took it to the river and hid it, thinking to possess its contents after Kelpius's death. But Kelpius, upon Geissler's return, raised himself up and said accusingly that Geissler had not done what he had asked, but had hidden the casket on shore. Geissler, now convinced of Kelpius's powers, hurried to the river and tossed in the *arcanum*, whereupon it exploded and for a time lightning and thunder came out of the water. Geissler returned, and Kelpius said that the job was well done, and died.[25]

This tale is not, however embellished, is not entirely improbable, because Kelpius was known to practice alchemy, as did some other elders of the Wissahickon community, and he was reputed to have a laboratory and alchemical library. He and the other elders were said to practice the Hermetic science on certain nights when the stars and planets were in proper alignment, which again, given the planetary notations on his ship log, is not improbable. As to the contents of the sealed casket exploding upon contact with water, we might note that there are chemicals that explode under those circumstances, and that practical alchemy does involve experiments with such chemicals.

Kelpius was succeeded by Johannes Seelig as leader of the Wissahickon group, but Seelig did not care for the responsibilities of acting as shepherd to such a group, and so retreated to his hermitage. Conrad Matthew led the group after Seelig retired, but by this time the group had split into two general categories: the ascetic hermits living in the wilderness, and those who married. It was about ten years after Kelpius's death that a new group of emigrants arrived from Germany, led by another remarkable man, Johann Conrad Beissel, and they established a new settlement, which meant a theosophic community once again would sink its roots in America.

Beissel's history was very much parallel to that of Johann Gichtel, save that whereas Gichtel stayed in Amsterdam, Beissel emigrated to Pennsylvania. Beissel was born in April 1690, near Baden, Germany, and his father died two months before his son's birth; Beissel's mother died when he was eight. His father had been a journeyman baker, and young Beissel had to travel from town to town working as an apprentice baker, until he returned home with his *wanderbuch* and baked a master's bread. Eventually he met a man named Johann Adam Haller, a friend and correspondent of Gichtel's, who introduced him to theosophy.

We should note that Böhmean theosophy was closely allied to Rosicrucianism in Germany during the seventeenth and eighteenth centuries, and that it is often difficult or even impossible to separate them. Essentially, both movements have as their basis a very similar Hermetic science, and indeed, share so much symbolism and terminology as to be at times identical. For example, the planetary progressions and linkings that we find emphasized by Böhme and Gichtel are reiterated by numerous Rosicrucian manuscripts of the seventeenth and eighteenth centuries.

Thus, it is not surprising to find that Haller and Beissel are linked by some not only with theosophy, but with Rosicrucianism as well. It is very difficult to tell what the exact relationship was between theosophers and the brethren of the Rosy Cross, but because the two are so similar, and draw upon similar sources—and because many of the secret orders that sprang up in Germany and Eastern Europe during the eighteenth century included numerous theosophic elements—it is not surprising to find some historians claiming Beissel and Haller (and Kelpius) to be Rosicrucians. Julius Sachse writes rather romantically of the Rosicrucian fraternity of which he claims Beissel was a member:

> Through [Haller] Beissel obtained an introduction to, or was initiated in, the local Rosicrucian chapter held under the name of a Pietist conventicle, which organization counted many of the most learned and distinguished men in the community among its members. But being under the ban of the secular as well as the religious authorities, they were forced to hold their meetings in secrecy.[26]

Historian Jeffrey Bach calls into question, I think rightfully, Beissel's "Rosicrucianism" in Sachse's account, but it is also true that later Rosicrucian treatises are deeply indebted to Böhmean Theosophy.[27]

When Beissel's association with this group came to the attention of a master baker, he presumably had Beissel's *wanderbuch* confiscated, which in turn forced Beissel to wander like Gichtel after his banning, from job to job, destitute. Thus, in the summer of 1720, at the age of thirty, Beissel set sail for Pennsylvania, albeit with the disapproval of many friends, including Dr. Johann Samuel Carl (1676–1757). Beissel found Pennsylvania much as Gichtel would have predicted, had he still been alive—not so holy, certainly not Edenic. Working as a weaver in the New World, Beissel observed his fellow Germans, and was less than impressed: "the great freedom of this land was one cause of their being thus sold under the *spiritus mundi*, through which all godly influence has been lost, and each one depended upon himself."[28]

On November 12, 1724, came a critical moment: Beissel was baptized by Peter Becker in the Wissahickon river. As the *Chronicon Ephratense* has it, "It was thus that Wisdom brought him into her net: he received the seed of his heavenly virginity at his first awakening; but now a field was prepared for him in America into which he might sow this seed again."[29] Eventually, Beissel gathered a small community around him, and built a "monastery on the Cocalico river," separated into male and female sections, and ordered on a more or less medieval model, complete with Capuchin robes.

It is worth pointing out, to emphasize the diversity of Pennsylvania settlements, that a nearby German community in the Conestoga valley held to some fascinating beliefs inherited from the old country. Led by one Johannes Zimmermann, this community only held worship on days of an increasing moon, of which the most important was the first day of a full moon, upon which they would play music (see Numbers 10.10). This community taught that after death, souls were carried up in a "bark" of the New Moon, whereas the evil souls were carried downward. Bearing some parallels to certain Egyptian beliefs, this tradition of a "bark of souls" may reflect pre-Christian folk German beliefs.[30] It is surprising how such folk traditions were carried on orally within German tradition through Christianity even to Pennsylvania.

Although the Ephrata community of which Beissel became the leader did not practice around the lunar cycles with quite the intensity of the Zimmermann group, one finds that, as theosophers, their community did conform to the same kind of hierohistorical patterns that we find in Pordage, Gichtel, and other theosophic communities. To take a single example: one Stephen Koch was upset by the death of an original theosopher hermit, Heinrich Traut, on January 4, 1733. He had lapsed, married, like so many of Kelpius's group, so "His Virgin [Sophia] left him and he fell into earthly ways until finally, after many tears of penitence, she again took him up."[31] Traut's death put Koch into a deep funk. But on May 3, 1733, after much distress, Koch was restored to joy and peace on a full moon night after sobbing to God. In 1736 he "saw in a vision a beautiful Virgin come into the meeting of the devout brethren, who preached wonderfully concerning sanctification and a life of virginity."[32] Thus, Koch and Traut both continued the hierohistorical Sophianic pattern we saw in Gichtel's life.

Beissel became the leader of the Ephrata colony, and developed some forms of spiritual practice that had been characteristic of the previous Wissahickon group, particularly regarding diet and music. Indeed, there is a distinctly Pythagorean pattern to Beissel's way of life. Like the ancient Greek master, Beissel enjoined a special diet, according to which milk causes "heaviness," eggs cause "extraordinary desires," potatoes and roots are "useful," and "beans carry a weight with them, and satiate too much, and create an unclean desire." Uncooked pure water is best for drinking, and diet as a whole is the preparation of the body for spiritual discipline, hence "the royal art."[33] Proper diet prepares the body to hear the celestial angelic harmonies that in turn can be expressed in music, another primary characteristic of Pythagoreanism as well.

Beissel was eloquent in expressing exactly why diet and music were necessary for the soul's purification. He writes:

> It is required of both scholar and master to know how, in addition to all other circumstances, it is requisite that one seek upon every occasion to make oneself agreeable and acceptable to the Spirit of this high and divine Virtue. As he, according to our experience and knowledge, has within himself the purest and cleanest spirit of the everlasting celestial virginity requires a compliance with the demands of an angelic and heavenly life. In the meantime the wants of this body are to be restrained, and attention given so that the voice becomes angelic, heavenly, pure and clear and not become strong and harsh, by a coarseness of food, and become valueless.[34]

Like Gichtel, Beissel advises living an "angelic and heavenly life" on this earth in order to realize fully "the purest and cleanest spirit of the everlasting celestial virginity." Music helps harmonize the soul that is pure through diet and practice of the virtues; it is also the soul's expression.

From these aspects of the Ephrata community life, we can see that their whole lives were devoted to spiritual practice. At the Fall of Adam, they believed, Sophia departed from man, and so the purpose of the new angelic brethren was to unite souls with Sophia, to regenerate man in the Virgin. The purpose of the sisterhood at Ephrata was likewise to unite with the heavenly bridegroom, so there was a complementary relationship between men and Sophia, women and Christ. Every aspect of daily life was related to this quest for harmonization of the soul and unification with Sophia.

In these doctrines, Beissel and his group were deeply influenced by Gottfried Arnold (whose primary works were written between 1696 and 1700, the year he was married), particularly his observations on the nature and character of the married and the unmarried life. So influential was Arnold that the "Observations of Arnold" were circulated as late as 1850 in Pennsylvania.[35] Thomas Bromley's *The Way to the Sabbath of Eternal Rest,* the manual of theosophic practice by this friend of Pordage, was also very important for the Ephrata group, whose printer Christopher Sauer (Sower) published a new version for the community.

Like Gichtel, Beissel himself was at one time or another estranged from nearly everyone, but he always sought reconciliation. Christopher Sauer, the Ephrata printer, was estranged from Beissel because he "lured" Sauer's wife into celibacy, but Beissel also had disputes with Conrad Matthäi, Peter Becker, Conrad Weiser, and numerous others. These disputes, like those of Gichtel, were often acrimonious, but unlike Gichtel, Beissel seems not to have generated lifelong hate-filled enemies quite on the order of Raedt and Breckling, although he certainly came close at times. Perhaps this is because Beissel was more willing to be reconciled with those who disagreed with him on one or another point.[36]

One such disagreement was particularly important: the conflict between Beissel and another powerful personality, Israel Eckerling. During the late 1730s and early 1740s, Beissel's influence over the Ephrata community waned, and during the same time Eckerling gained authority. Eckerling was much more interested in prosperity than Beissel, and as Prior of the community he established a lumber mill, new houses of worship, a tannery, a sawmill, paper manufacture, printing, a quarry, and a farm, as well as instituting a much more elaborate ritual tradition. Beissel opposed these changes but endured them, and when, in autumn 1745, Eckerling left Ephrata, Beissel curtailed most of these new operations, seeing them as a betrayal of their original spiritual discipline.[37]

This conflict between Eckerling and Beissel reveals an underlying conflict inherent in Ephrata's history generally—the struggle between the celibate or monastic groups and the householders. Naturally, this dynamic in the community drew on an even more fundamental division inherent in the group as a whole, the division between the outside world and Ephrata, marked by its struggle against the *spiritus mundi* and the life of this world that most people outside Ephrata led. For the householders, and Eckerling's circle especially, had much contact with outward society through business affiliations, while Beissel and the celibates remained aloof. This internal struggle in the community was never finally resolved, and in fact it is common among all religious communities that include celibates and householders both.

There can be no doubt, however, that Beissel's conflicts derived also from his own autocratic ways. He ran Ephrata, and the combination of spiritual authority and temporal power in one man led to problems. Although Beissel took the name "Friedsam Gottrecht" for himself (as it was the custom among the brethren to assume new names to mark their new birth in Christ), some of the brethren wanted to address him not only as "brother" or "Friedsam," but as "Father" as well, which others held to be suitable for God alone. This struggle came to a head when the printer Christopher Sauer found that some members held Beissel to be virtually equal to Christ—Sauer, enraged, then attacked Beissel as the anti-Christ.[38]

Although we will shortly discuss alchemy and theosophy both generally and in relation to the Wissahickon and Ephrata communities, we should note here that about 1762, Jacob Martin, a "High Philosopher," arrived at Ephrata, a follower of Michael Sendivogius (1566–1646) who practiced physical or laboratory alchemy.[39] He brought with him many alchemical manuscripts and processes, and built a laboratory near the Ephrata community, seeking the "red tincture" of Sendivogius, with which Sendivogius had reputedly transmuted lead into 120,000 thalers of gold and created the *lapis philosophorum*, or "philosopher's stone." It is unclear what Beissel's own views on physical alchemy were, although as the cases of Gichtel, Pordage, and Kelpius show, most likely Beissel was not averse to it, only to the greed and foolishness it sometimes engendered.

As we have seen in every theosophic group we have considered, individual hierohistory is exceedingly important, and Beissel's community is no exception. The *Chronicon Ephratense*, the historical record of the Ephrata group, details a number of such spiritual revelations, but the most sensational and well known was certainly that of Catharine Hummer. Her own words are recorded in the *Chronicon*, and in the following account we will draw on them. Hummer's revelations are important because they demonstrate that hierohistory was in Ephrata, as in Pordage's, Leade's, and even Gichtel's circle, as much the province of women as of men, and indeed it seems at times that revelation comes more easily to women than men. (We will recall that Mrs. Pordage's revelations preceded those of John Pordage, for instance.)

Catharine Hummer's revelations began while she was "sitting in the kitchen near the fire on the night of October 3d, 1762, between ten and eleven o'clock."[40] She heard someone knock at the door, but upon answering the knock, found no one there, nor a second time, but the third time she found an angel standing on her right, who told her that it was nigh unto midnight, and he sang with a thunderous sound. He announced to her that the Ephrata people should follow a spiritual path, not worldly ways, and after the revelation she "lay in a trance for the greater part of seven days and nights, so that my spirit was separated from the body."[41]

During this trance state, Hummer was, like Pordage, "led through strange conditions and dwelling places of spirits, and I saw such wonderful things that I greatly hesitate to reveal them." After this revelation, she customarily could speak with angels, and could ascend to the heavenly realms, wandering through indescribable habitations of the blessed, feeling inexpressible joy. On November 12, 1762, she again ascended "up into invisible eternity," and this time saw all the prophets and apostles, saints, and patriarchs. These visions continued until April 1765, and her father, a Baptist preacher, spread the word far and wide, so that many were baptized by him, and during services they held it is said that angels sang hymns.

Foreknowing what might happen, Beissel wrote Hummer a letter, urging her to remain celibate and not marry, "for the Virgin never deceives, because she is the mother of the eternal Wisdom, through which all things were created." If, however, the fallen angels gain the upper hand for a time being, nonetheless in the end their power would be abolished. Despite his admonitions, however, Hummer married, "the spirit retired into its chamber again, and the whole work stopped and fell into decay, which is usually the case with all angelic visions and revelations."[42] In Beissel's view, corroborated by circumstances, the virginal life is necessary for such wonders to take place.

The circumstances of Beissel's death are poignant. By the mid-1760s, Beissel had become somewhat estranged both from Prioress Maria, the head of the sisterhood, and from the brotherhood as well. He was accused by some of wine drinking, was involved in other controversies, and held that "I am now the same that I was when first exposed to the *spiritus mundi*, namely, an orphan." Like Kelpius, he expected bodily translation at death like that of Enoch in great antiquity, and was disappointed to find that this was not to be. His last words were said to be, "O woe! O woe! O wonder! O wonder!" He died on July 6, 1768. Like Gichtel's, Beissel's death was followed by posthumous appearances, Beissel's from two days onward. Two sisters, Catherine Knodel and Barbara Höfly, died the same day, which was regarded by the community as their accompanying him to paradise.

As to those of Beissel's writings that remain to us, we possess far more than we do of Kelpius's, and in fact many of Beissel's works are available in English translation.[43] Most revealing for our purposes are Beissel's sermons, from which we will draw shortly in sketching his theosophic perspective. But there also remain to us Beissel's hymns—Ephrata was famous for its musical performances, which were apparently quite ethereal and not unlike Eastern Orthodox, medieval Catholic, or even Tibetan music for their exotic resonant beauty.[44] And we have the

Chronicon Ephratense, the record of the Ephrata community, as well as Beissel's *Theosophical Epistles* and assorted other works.

Beissel's letters, like Gichtel's, are exhortatory and not sources of historical information. But this tendency is of course aligned with the theosophic tradition generally, for theosophers are not particularly concerned with daily events save within a spiritual context. What matters for them above all is hierohistory, the events of spiritual revelation, and upon these—upon how one attains and sustains revelation—Beissel, like Gichtel and our other theosophers, focuses almost exclusively. He writes of himself as "a non-entity in this world," as a "stranger and pilgrim in this world," and his letters are in keeping with these descriptions: he is not concerned with wordly events so much as with the revelation of the otherworld.

In one epistle Beissel offers this prayer for his correspondent: "May the spiritual life force and Jesus Christ, the spirit of love, greatly flourish in your soul so that you may live, and may the healing power, acquired through the blood of Christ, be what you desire. Amen." This is a remarkably simple and evocative prayer, an invocation of the "spiritual life force" and the "spirit of love." We are enjoined to live "a guilt-free, unmaterialistic, chaste, and sober way of life" so that the enemy may not claim any part of us. "I could add more," Beissel continues, "but I am not permitted to elaborate in writing or orally so that I do not lose my strength."[45] Like Kelpius, Beissel in his letters looks forward to the "advent of a new world" and the "Philadelphian period of our church."[46]

During the last several decades of Beissel's life at Ephrata, both the male and female monastic orders developed as independent, related entities. *Die Rose*, a rule for the Sisterhood of S(h)aron, was published in 1745, its translated title in full being *The Rose; or the acceptable flower for S[h]aron's Spiritual betrothal with their celestial Bridegroom, whom they have espoused as their King, Ruler, Spouse, Lord, and Bridegroom unto all Eternity*. The Sisterhood took as its emblem the Rosicrucian motif of a pelican feeding its young with the blood of its own breast. We can see, here, how the Ephrata community was really the incorporation of Christian esotericism into daily life.

Several years before, in 1743, the press of Christopher Sauer brought into print one of the first Bibles published in America, and in addition to *The Rose*, 1745 saw the publication of several books by Beissel, including *Mystische Abhandlung über die Schopfung und von des Menschen Fall und Wiederbringungen durch des Weibes Samen . . .* (*Mystical Treatise on the Creation, Fall, and Restoration of Man through the Woman's Seed*), and *Die Hohe Zeugnüsse* (*The High Testi-*

monies), and *Die Weiderstellung Der Reinen Paradisischen Menschheit, oder des Jungfräulichen Ebenbildes Gottes . . . in einer Sammlung geistliche und Theosophischer Episteln (The Restoration of the Pure Paradisical Humanity, or the Virginal Image of God . . . in a Collection of Spiritual and Theosophic Letters*), which includes thirty-seven meditations and sixty-seven letters on theosophic topics. Ephrata also published a book on comets during this fertile time.[47]

But most important for our purposes—understanding what Beissel actually taught, and what drew and kept the Ephrata community together—are Beissel's *Dissertation on Man's Fall* and his sermons. These works give us a remarkable impression of how Beissel came to his understanding, the struggles he went through, his realizations, and above all the part that "divine femininity" played in his spiritual perspective. For Beissel's work reveals a definitely Böhmean theosophic understanding, one not nearly so concerned with cosmological elaboration as Böhme himself, but more practical.[48] Beissel, like Gichtel, was concerned above all to communicate to others the theosophic path he himself walked.

Without question, the most revealing work is Beissel's *Dissertation on Man's Fall*, in which Beissel not only explains the spiritual crises that eventuated in Ephrata itself, but lucidly sets forth the essence of the theosophic path as he sees it. He begins by pointing out that "A profound concern of my spirit moved me to put down this wondrous writing," which he saw as an indescribable gift. He writes:

> In the days of my godly youth, I sincerely believed that it would be sufficient if I made every effort to reach the utmost purity in a life of sacred love and enlightenment. But this caused so many severe and dificult conflicts within me that I was often frightened and horrified.[49]

He found that the more he strove for good, the more evil raised its head. His essential problem: his "heavenly magia" was faded, and "the heavenly femininity could not manifest herself because of the fall of Lucifer."[50]

Here is the heart of Beissel's spirituality: more even than Gichtel, Beissel simplified Böhme's complex spiritual vision and theosophic path to terms accessible to many hearers. Beissel recognizes "the true nature of my fiery masculinity," which "is totally opposed to the attraction of my holy amorousness by the holy Virgin."[51] Ultimately, after years of miserable struggle, Beissel realized that there could be no uniting of the old Adam and the Virgin in him: like Jesus, he had to be nailed to the cross.

In the old covenant, the high priest married a virgin; in the new covenant, the Virgin will marry no one but a priest of the order of Melchizedek.

Thus, one's self-will and "fiery masculinity" has to be put to the cross, for only "thus the fountain of mercy flows out into the whole world to bring salvation."[52] Beissel proclaims: "Here begins the restoration of all things." This is perhaps the most revealing statement in the whole of the sermon, for it clearly links Beissel with the millennialist tendencies of many theosophers in England and on the Continent. Like Leade, Beissel affirms universal restoration, but he emphasizes its beginning in the regeneration of the individual. The purpose of each human being is to enter into a spiritual inward marriage, to restore inward paradisal harmony, and any more expansive doctrine of universal restoration has to be seen first in light of individual spiritual experience.

Not surprisingly, Beissel's version of the Fall and regeneration of man is considerably simpler than Böhme's, but at times takes surprising turns. Beissel asserts that Adam became spiritually blind when he "desired to be sexually separated like the animals," and that the whole of creation was divided into male and female, femininity subordinated to the masculine. If Eve had not succumbed to the serpent in the Garden, if she had remained in her virginal state, then Lucifer would have been bound, and the whole earth "would have been filled with innocent childlike people."[53] Eventually God would have led out of the wilderness his femininity, lovely as the sunshine and terrible as a host of war with banners, the Virgin would have absorbed "all the awakened male will," and so "the restoration of all things would have come."

These speculations have a practical foundation: if man fell through Eve and lust, then it is not only possible, but logical and necessary to "reverse" the Fall and ascend through the Virgin, or "heavenly femininity," to attain a "body of light in paradise" once again. This is done through celibacy, through overcoming lust and being clothed by "raiments of light." Men are to liberate themselves from their fiery nature through the Virgin; and women too, addressed as themselves virgins, must "hasten to the source, the Mother of eternity, whose femininity has remained immaculate."[54] Thus, both men and women on earth are fallen, sexual "tinctures," which, rather than mixing profligately with one another, ought to be restored to their primordial purity in the Virgin through spiritual discipline.

For both men and women, therefore, Beissel advocates union with the feminine "raiment of light." Masculine self-will rules this fallen world, to be sure, but it is only by becoming feminine in relation to divine power that men and women can be saved. Beissel exclaims: "O how much does the eternal Mother, or heavenly femininity long to be in us, in order to reduce and abolish our ascending will, and to put on us once again the female raiment of light."[55] The Godmanhood of Jesus expiates the sundering that the Fall of Adam and Eve caused—but it does so by restoring heavenly femininity!

Beissel sees human teleology in precisely this context. Each of us is enjoined to make our lives trajectories toward a restored, paradisal state. He writes of Everyman that "If during his life he has much of the heavenly femininity, constantly mortifying his fiery masculinity, he will awake in the resurrection in a male and female body of light according to his achievements."[56] Thus, Beissel's mysticism sees daily life as a constant struggle, as a crucifixion of the masculine fiery nature, and as a continuous striving toward the Virgin Sophia, and by no means as a static condition that, once achieved, is not to be relinquished. "As often as my industry brings forth a flower of paradise, a sword is drawn against me, as if I had committed the greatest crime," Beissel writes.[57] And so it continues for each of us unto death.

Beissel's writings as a whole reveal a profoundly spiritual man, who like St. Theresa of Avila saw himself as a "nobody," and whose cosmology is very much in the traditions of Gichtel, Pordage, and our other theosophers. Böhmean theosophy elaborates their worldview, to be sure, but each has has own, slightly different, and always practical perspective. Beissel offered his correspondents, readers, and fellow theosophers an entirely practical way of life that has some striking parallels with some early Christian Gnostics, with the medieval Cathars, and with the high German mysticism of Tauler and Ruysbroeck. But Beissel's views are his own, an independent and sometimes rather unusual confirmation of Böhme's visionary Sophianic mysticism, perhaps more stringently Sophianic than any of the other theosophers we have considered.

Beissel's Sophianic mysticism is certainly intense. His hymns, his writings, apocryphal stories about him all bespeak Sophianic mysticism as his central contribution to theosophy. Beissel, in the New World, condensed the theosophic path into a schema that could be understood and practiced by all in his monastic community, laypeople and celibates alike. Of course, one has to suspect that what we see reflected in Beissel's Sophianic mysticism is to be found in more popular theosophy that remains less documented, but that existed in Pennsylvania, in England, and on the Continent. Beissel's gift was to express this somewhat more popular theosophy in clear, succinct terms. Only in this way could theosophy be made accessible to a broader community such as Ephrata.

This remains the most remarkable characteristic of Pennsylvanian theosophy: here, in the wilderness of eighteenth-century America, the German settlers were free to live both extremes, as theosopher hermits and as members of theosophic communities. In Europe and England, theosophers tended to live as members of ordinary society, while practicing theosophy in what amounted to lay orders such as the Philadelphians. But in Pennsylvania, theosophers could live in near-complete anchoritic isolation, or as members of experimental theosophic communites such as Ephrata—or as both. In America, theosophers could live as hermits and follow the path to the complete exclusion of worldly life, or in a community wholly dedicated to the same spiritual aims.

Given this freedom, it is hardly surprising that Kelpius, Beissel, and the other theosophers of Pennsylvania should have seen their passages to the New World as the dawning of a new time cycle, as the advent of the Holy Spirit's descent much like that prophesied by Joachim of Fiore. It is true that the millennium did not dawn on the whole of mankind in 1694, or 1700, or 1761. But in a sense, we can see how a new time cycle was dawning for the theosophers themselves during this remarkable time in Pennsylvania. Free of religious intolerance and worldly persecution common in Europe, the Pennsylvania theosophers were indeed living in a new sacred space and time, their whole world now able to reflect and embody their individual spiritual quests.

The Pennsylvania theosophers, then, offer a wholly different aspect of American history than that generally acknowledged. We are taught about Calvinist views of wilderness, worldly success, and the European inheritance, and these worldviews are often presented as characteristic of all early America. However, the Pennsylvania theosophers represent a strikingly different form of Protestantism, one with a developed wilderness theology, one that incorporated many elements of medieval Catholicism with its magic and mysticism, and one that was certainly not inclined to embrace worldly success as a sign of spirituality. At the very least, the Pennsylvania theosophic communities reveal the range of religious perspectives in early America, and at most, they suggest a path that American culture at one time might have taken.

CHAPTER SEVEN

Christopher Walton and
His Theosophic College

The history of theosophy has always been the history of remarkable individuals, and certainly one of the most noteworthy in this chronicle is Christopher Walton, a Methodist minister who made it his life's work to continue theosophy in mid-nineteenth-century London. Walton was himself a theosopher, as is evident from the illustrations he developed for his extraordinary *Memorial of Law: Notes and Materials For a . . . Biography of William Law.* But he was a theosopher with a grand vision for the future of theosophy: he planned not only to publish a thirty volume series of books suitable for a complete course in theosophic study (including the works of Böhme, Freher, and many other authors), but also to establish a theosophic college, and to create a great Hermetic library. If he was not entirely successful in these endeavors, nonetheless Walton's vision is still well worth looking at today.

In the notes to his *An Introduction to Theosophy, or the Science of the Mystery of Christ*(1854)—the bulk of which is simply a republication of several works by William Law—Walton outlined his grand plan for an entire course of theosophic books, in order that

> this *science* of the *ground and mystery of things*—of all nature and grace, which may be termed *the gospel of the last*

113

days, will be found to be fundamentally opened and fully established in the series of writings composing the present publications, when completed.[1]

Walton was here claiming no more for theosophy than was claimed in any other theosophic writings, for Böhmean theosophers in general tend to follow Böhme in affirming the universality of theosophic insights, held to comprehend the totality of possible human knowledge.

But Walton did enter theosophy into the broader dialogue with other religions that was well underway in the mid-nineteenth century.[2] In fact, he went farther than simply entering theosophy into dialogue with other religions—he held theosophy to be the key to all religious traditions. He wrote:

> What the world now wants, and is prepared for; what all religions want,—the Christian in all its divisions and sub-divisions, orthodoxy and heterodox, serious and formal, or rationalistic, the Mahomedan, the Jewish, the Oriental in all its phases and diversities,—in order to the Unity of the faith, the embrace of the Truth, is, a *perfect system of philosophy and theology*, or in other words, the Science of the *ground and mystery of things*.[3]

This theosophy alone could provide, through its special apprehension of the "birth and constitution of Nature, how all is magical, or the working and effect of Will; and then of Man, as to soul, spirit and body."[4] Theosophy, for Walton, was nothing less than the universal key to religious understanding.

This key to all spiritual understanding, Walton believed, was being offered to all humanity through the writings of authors like Böhme, Freher, and Law, and through theosophic discipline. Thus, there was a millennialist element to Walton's writings in the mid-nineteenth century that strongly echoed the millennialism of the Philadelphians during the early eighteenth century. Walton asserted our era to be "these last ages," theosophy to be "the gospel of the last days," and, following Böhme and Jane Leade, saw approaching or upon us the "Enochian age . . . the *time of lilies and roses*, (the efflorescence and fruitage of the varieties of the paradisical or regenerate human life and intellect,) and . . . the *downfall of Babel*."[5] Like Leade and Böhme before him, Walton assigned the word *Enochian* to the age of regenerated humanity, but gave a special significance to the discoveries of modern science in the coming new era when, like Enoch, humans would walk spiritually with angels.

For Walton saw the modern science of his day as moving toward the ancient wisdom of the alchemists and magi. In his *An Introduction to Theosophy* he was particularly effusive about the discoveries of "animal magnetism" and "vital energy" in all creatures, which he believed would shortly open out into a merging of science and religion, so that scientific and religious experimentation would be along precisely the same lines. He hoped a *"divine horticultural art"* would appear out of this merger, "under the combined direction and manipulation of the qualified professors of a *Theosophic College*, spiritually regenerated men."[6]

This theosophic college needed a curriculum, and so Walton published first his *Introduction to Theosophy*, but in it included a list of the other books necessary for the college. Among these we find that the works of William Law and the church fathers predominate, along with John Tauler, Gottfried Arnold, Peter Poiret, the complete works of Böhme and Freher, with "*Diagrams* and *Symbolic Illustrations*," the works of Platonists Ralph Cudworth and Thomas Taylor, and of course the works of Gichtel and of Louis-Claude de Saint-Martin, the *Theologia Mystica* of Pordage, the *Theosophic Transactions* of the Philadelphians, the works of Jane Leade, and those of Thomas Tryon. Here, in short, is a catalogue of theosophic books, the only odd portion of which is the inclusion of a section on "Popular Experimental Transcendentalism, or Animal Magnetism."[7] Undoubtedly, with this one exception, this is a thoroughly theosophic curriculum.

But Walton's vision of this curriculum naturally led toward establishing an actual theosophic college. This college, Walton envisaged, would be "located in some peaceful, secluded, rural retreat,—the primary object of whose association, [would be] the cultivation of the germ or principle of the divine life and knowledge, in themselves and their selected pupils . . . by the appliances of sublime magian science and art."[8] For after all, theosophy was most difficult for "a simple individual, without scholarship, and of very imperfect devotion, dwelling in the heart of the metropolis, and daily immersed in the grovelling, distracting concerns of the world." Walton hoped to found a true college like those of antiquity, a place devoted not merely to the accumulation of data, but to spiritual illumination.

Naturally, his grand scheme was doomed in nineteenth-century mercantile London, but this did not prevent him from publishing, appended to *Introduction to Theosophy*, a clarion call for an *Academia Cœlestis*. In this advertisement he calls for

> Any Lady or Gentleman, or number of individuals, whom
> it may have pleased the Lord of all, to honor with the free
> dispensation of such an amount of money, and to inspire
> with the wisdom and piety, to devote it to so noble, and
> *divinely philanthropic* a purpose . . . may place [one hun-
> dred thousand pounds] *to his* [the editor's] *Account at
> Messrs. Glyn & Co., Bankers*, London, designating it, "For
> Theosophic College."[9]

Although his call to the wise and enlightened of his time apparently fell
largely on deaf ears, Walton's forthright call for financial support
included also an overview of how his school would function.

Of course, Walton's sketch of the college in its infancy was hardly
likely to inspire most mid-nineteenth-century British merchants or
other possible financiers, not least because "the community at first,
shall consist of not more than three or four individuals; possessed of
gifts and endowments corresponding to, or being an immediate reflection of, the *spirit* and *principles* distinguishing the present Work."[10] In
Walton's view, to assemble two or three remarkable individuals would
be much more important than gathering together a mob of unsuita-
bles; he held that only those with a "high and peculiar degree of eru-
dition," combined with a thorough knowledge of design, medicine,
chemistry, electricity, or botany would be adequate. Novices would
then be tested, and conducted through "a course of perfect inward
and outward Purification," the goal being an "angelical simplicity,
purity, and holiness."[11]

Although Walton is somewhat coy about such matters, and hardly
systematic, he does at times allude to what we might call paranormal
aspects of the spiritual life. When discussing the relationship between
the theosophic masters of his proposed college and their students, for
example, Walton calls the "enlightened superiors" "true divine *clair-
voyants* (Matt. 5.8), and writes that this new college would follow the
practices of the "ancient *theurgic, and *pure philosophic* schools" to produce "modern sublime discoveries of *magian science* and *art.*"[12] This
magian science is clearly alchemical, and Walton goes so far as to suggest that graduates of the college might function as "highly graduated
magi—free handlers of the tincture" who could "act as all-potent
medici, for the healing not only of the sickness of the body, but for the
purification and exaltation of the moral nature of the soul! and again,
of the *intellectual powers!*"[13]

Walton defines what "tincture" means. He writes:

[T]he abyss of nature and creature, wherein the soul that has died to itself, and become all divine, is found . . . is the pregnant womb of Goodness, Light, and Truth. Which is especially said to be a *magia*, and to have a WILL—unoriginate, unsearchable, and . . . incomprehensible by any creaturely imagination . . . [and] whose nothing-and-*all power* of Light, being a *superintellectual* fire, oil, and water of life . . . is designated by the *alchymic* name of *tinctura*, or *tinctura suprema*.[14]

"Tincture," in other words, refers to (here Walton quotes Dionysius Freher) "a thing which *separates*, educing the pure and clear from the impure, and which *brings the life of all sorts of spirits, or all sorts of essences, into their highest degree of exaltation*." The alchemical tincture is the cause of the "shine, or lustre" in all creatures, indeed, the "cause that all creatures see and live," albeit stronger in some than in others, and hidden from the unworthy.[15]

Here, Walton touches upon a theme characteristic of all theosophy—alchemy, the science of life. This accounts for Walton's fascination with "vital magnetism" or "natural magnetism," the "laying on of hands" and transferring of vital energy from the well to the sick, commonplace in science of his day. Walton saw vital magnetism as a variation on alchemy, and alchemy in his view was the science of life's power, one might even go so far as to say that it was the science making miracles possible. Although Walton is careful in what he writes, evidently he sees theosophers following in Christ's path by being able to heal the sick and to attain the exaltation of life's power through alchemical illumination of the soul. His college would be an institution dedicated to this purpose.

But the college would also serve secular purposes, Walton affirms. In his vision, the theosophic college would restore a cultural center to Europe, indeed to the whole world. Its members, basing themselves on kabbalistic knowledge, would be able to reform the English language into a pure form that could express properly the divine Word. This new language would in turn give birth to a new poetry and to celestial music, as well as to other forms of art. In fact, all aspects of human culture would be renovated—architecture, all the designs of artifacts with which we live, our means of entertainment, every aspect of human life would be simplified, purified, and made a reflection of its spiritual purpose.

With this grandiose vision of humanity's complete renovation, Walton ends his advertisement for an *academia cœlestis* or theosophic college. While we might smile a bit at his plan, the fact is that Walton's vision of what a college ought truly be is much closer to the traditional

Pythagorean or Platonic academies of antiquity than any modern college. Furthermore, Walton was much more open to scientific knowledge and experimentation than one might expect; like some recent physicists, Walton saw in theosophy a possible union of religion and science that would allow both to break free from historicist or materialist petrification.[16]

Although Walton was not able to see his theosophic college become a formal reality, he did have a small circle of theosopher friends that, in effect, amounted to the same thing. After all, even in his formal proposal for a college, he thought it should start with only three or four remarkable people, and these he found in Edward Burton Penny and his wife Judith Penny, who along with Walton formed the nucleus of British theosophy from the 1850s through the 1870s. Penny and his wife were responsible for translating and seeing to publication some of the works of Louis-Claude de Saint-Martin, the great French theosopher—and, we will recall, Saint-Martin's works were part of Walton's proposed curriculum.

In fact, the Pennys' translations of Saint-Martin had appended to them a revised formal proposal for the publication of all subsequent volumes in Walton's theosophic series of books, revised to include by the 1860s such works as Franz Molitor's books on Christian Kabbalism, the works of Franz von Baader, and of course all the other theosophers we would expect, including Gichtel, Leade, and Saint-Martin.[17] By this time, Walton's constant publication of proposals and advertisements to gain funding for his series of books and his college had also drawn the attention of the American Transcendentalist Bronson Alcott (1799–1888), friend of Emerson.

That Alcott was intensely drawn to Böhmenist mysticism we can see not only in his search for books by such authors as Law and Pordage while in England in 1842, and in references in his books to Böhme, but also in his later attempts to forge connections between the American Transcendentalist movement and British Böhmenist disciples Walton and Penny. However, despite their common love for Böhme's works, Alcott and the British mystics made only a sporadic alliance. In 1867, Alcott wrote to Christopher Walton, warmly proposing that Walton contribute to the New England Transcendentalist publications and organizations such as the Free Religious Association. Alcott wrote:

> My studies for many years have lain in the direction of the Mystic authors, Jacob Behmen being a favorite, and, as I judge, the master mind of these last centuries. I was fortunate, when in England in 1842, to find not only his works in Laws' edition, but most of the works of his disciples; Taylor, Pordage, Frances Lee, Law, and others.[18]

Walton replied with an extensive letter, but it was a year before Alcott responded.

Alcott's belated reply revealed how much he was interested in Böhme and in the publications Walton and Penny were bringing out in England. Alcott had been able to read copies of the English Böhmenists' translations and other works through the Harvard library and elsewhere; he had, he wrote Walton, read them all.[19] This intensive reading "deepened" Alcott's "conviction" "of the exceeding importance of giving to the world full accounts of the lives of Behmen's illustrious desciples."[20] "I hope nothing will defeat your purpose of doing this," Alcott wrote, for "it is a kind of thought with which our advanced thinkers should be familiar in order to justify any claims to a real knowledge of spiritual things." "I wish I could add that any considerable number of our advanced thinkers had penetrated the core of the Mystery."[21]

Alcott did what he could to cement connections between W. T. Harris's *Journal of Speculative Philosophy*, a chiefly Hegelian organ of St. Louis Transcendentalism with which Alcott was affiliated, and the British Böhmenists, coaxing Penny or Walton to write articles on Böhme for it. "You will see by his table of contents how comprehensive his [Harris's] range is, and yet that without Boehme it is not inclusive," Alcott wrote. But by 1873, Alcott was still writing Walton, trying to coax him to write an article on Böhme for Harris's journal. And although Alcott took the liberty of having Harris publish a letter from Walton as a sort of advertisement for him—and even sent Walton copies of the journal, as well as of Alcott's latest book, the bonds between American Transcendentalism and British mysticism never really materialized, save in Alcott himself.

But Walton continued to expand his circle, to publish advertisements, notices, and above all to carry on his grand project for a theosophic library of publications. During the late 1860s, Walton published an advertisement for the services of a young erudite gentleman, conversant in theosophy, who could translate some major theosophic works from the German into English. This advertisement brought to Walton a man named Charles William Heckethorn, who between 1868 and 1869 transcribed in a neat hand into leather-bound books the four thousand pages and seven volumes of Gichtel's *Theosophia Practica*. Although the translation was not published, it was read by those in Walton's circle, as demonstrated by the marginal annotations.

Heckethorn went on to write a two-volume compendium, *The Secret Societies of All Ages and Countries* (1875), republished in 1897 as *A Comprehensive Account of Upwards of One Hundred Sixty Secret Organisations*, evidence that Heckethorne's interest in esotericism went beyond his translating endeavors. Here he wrote of Walton himself:

> [T]he hierophant that initiated me into the mysteries of the German theosopher [Böhme] was undoubtedly the most learned Böhmite in this or any other country; in fact, the only man who understood him thoroughly. . . . But whoso is not convinced [of Böhme's greatness] by Böhme's demonstration of the seven properties cannot be convinced by any argument.[22]

This is high praise indeed from Heckethorn, who elsewhere in the same book proves himself highly skeptical of esoterists and occultists in general. Not a theosopher himself, Heckethorn remained highly respectful of Walton and of Böhmean theosophy generally.

At this time in his life, it must have been clear to Walton that his years of labor in bringing theosophy before the public, his grand publishing project, and his vision for a college were not to come to fruition. But he had accumulated the greatest library of English theosophic manuscripts in the world by this time, including the works of Dionysius Andreas Freher, Leade, and numerous other remarkable theosophic works that remain unpublished to this day. This collection currently resides in Dr. Williams's Library in London and, along with Walton's books, is his primary theosophic legacy, an invaluable mine of theosophy.

But Walton also left behind a book entitled *Memorial of Law: Notes and Materials For a . . . Biography of William Law*, an extraordinary and in many ways a frustrating work that exemplifies Walton's strengths and weaknesses as an author. *Notes and Materials* includes a wealth of information on British theosophy totally unavailable elsewhere, including the only works of Freher ever published, and much on Jane Leade, Francis Lee, and the other Philadelphians. At the same time, *Notes and Materials*—dedicated, as the title suggests, chiefly to William Law's relationship to theosophy—is surely among the most disorganized works one could imagine. Footnotes consisting in extracts from Freher's works stretch on for countless pages, marching on and on in incredibly tiny type. In brief, though *Notes and Materials* is invaluable for the study of British theosophy, it requires much perusal.

Undoubtedly one of the most striking features of *Notes and Materials* is a foldout illustration attached to the inside front cover that demonstrates Walton was unequivocally a theosopher in his own right, following exactly in the tradition of Gichtel and Freher, both of whom were also responsible for generating remarkable theosophic illustrations. As we have already seen, symbolic illustrations are very much a part of theosophy as a concise way of revealing theosophic cosmological principles. Certainly among the greatest responsible for theosophic illustrations was Dionysius Andreas Freher, and Walton followed directly in Freher's tracks, being among the only people in the nineteenth century to have even seen Freher's many extraordinary illustrations, much less to have spent years studying them, as Walton did.

This series of illustrations with commentary, Walton wrote, were "Designed by the Editor of the Introduction to Theosophy as the First of Three Series of Symbols to Illustrate the Principles and Scope of the Work, and as a Key to the Philosophy of Böhme, Freher, and Law." Like virtually all theosophic subtitles or headings, Walton's have scope: these illustrations taken together form

> A Serial Consideration of the One Instant, Eternal, Universal Act, Of the Generation and Evolution Of The Ineffable Unity, or Magic Will of Light, in Trinity and Wisdom, or Conceived Word of Understanding, and of the Coeternal Manifestation or Corporisation of Itself, in and by the Essential Sound or Fluid Element of Nature, with its Seven Fountain Spirits, Properties or Qualities, Two Equipoised Principles, and Three Constituent Parts.[23]

Although Walton's description of his illustrations' scope may seem overblown, in fact it is accurate. Like Freher's illustrations, Walton's repay long study; they do in fact illustrate the basic cosmological principles of theosophy in a very condensed and lucid way.

In an unusual endnote pasted into the back cover of a copy I consulted—Walton was forever pasting notes and addenda into various copies of his two major books, and in some cases writing out such addenda in a neat longhand in the blank pages—Walton wrote that he held his work back from publication for several months, making sure that his own words rang true in living experience, and he challenged readers to disprove a word of it, not by quoting scriptures or the opinions of others, but by living experience.[24] This theosophic experience is reflected in all of Walton's writings, and especially in his theosophic illustrations.

In a summary illustration that includes all ten circular figures comprising the "true principles of all things," Walton shows the complex arrangement of all spheres in the process of creation, beginning with nothingness and moving in a spiralling way through stages or spheres arranged in the form of a cross within a circle. In the center of many circles is an eye, in others—and in the center of the entire diagram—is a heart aflame. This symbolism can be seen in the illustrations and works of Dr. John Pordage, and is characteristic of all theosophy. In fact, these illustrations, like all theosophic works, consist in a unique combination of symbols common to all theosophers. One could say that theosophic illustrations all speak the same symbolic language, but in individual ways.

The tenth of Walton's illustrations, showing the macrocosmos, is especially interesting. He writes that it reveals

> The Eye or Mirror of Deity, With Its Imaged Magic Evolutions, Showing the Ground and Relations of Temporal Nature, Its Matter and Powers, (Or of Place, Time and Space,) To the Abyssal, Spiritual, Mental, Eternal Nature, Of Light and Dark, Life and Death Powers.[25]

This figure has in its center an eye in a flaming heart, around it the superimposed triangles of the seal of Solomon, around which are the six planets (the Moon and Saturn, Jupiter and Mercury, Venus and Mars), then day and night, and the physical earth in an inverted circle around the sun in its center. All creation, then, has at its heart the eye and heart of God, and is surrounded by the "Abyss, Magia, or Nothing," which has "no quality or property of being."[26]

Most noteworthy about this illustration is how it graphically demonstrates the shift in perspective that theosophy requires. Ordinary understanding has the earth as a globe, orbiting the sun; but Walton's illustration shows how our world has at its center the "seven fountain spirits" symbolized by the six planets and the sun, and at its heart and surrounding it, God. The physical world is seen "inside out," so to speak. One could hardly think of a better way to illustrate the radical shift in understanding that theosophy as a spiritual discipline represents. In order to understand what Walton means to say with this illustration, we have to let go of our old way of seeing the world—another way of expressing what theosophers call being "regenerated."

In *Notes and Materials*, Walton includes two epigraphs that convincingly demonstrate his view of theosophy as the final Christian dispensation. "The time is born for Enoch to speak, and Elias to work again" refers to the Enochian mysteries of Christianity—the prophetic mysteries of communication between angels and men that theosophy represents. The other epigraph reads:

> The manifestation of the "mystery of Christ"—of Deity, Nature, and all things (and universal refinement of philosophy and theology) was the *Elias* mision of Behmen, Freher, and Law, and God's last dispensation to mankind.[27]

Although Walton writes more than a century and a half after the Philadelphians and long after the Pennsylvania theosophers, like them he sees Böhmean theosophy as the final divine revelation to humanity, the means through which eternity's mysteries are opened to us now.

Following theosophic tradition, Walton writes that theosophy means an opening into miracles and wonders, which are certainly not confined to antiquity. Walton concurs with Gichtel's editor, who writes:

> [I]n the life of extraordinary persons, such as Gichtel was . . . if some things appear too wonderful, we ought to remember we are here in the *dominion of inward wonders*, where, he that is experienced, may measure and understand according to his experience, but cannot, and must not exceed it. . . . He who has never traveled in the *inward way*, in which all wisdom leaders her true disciples, he who lives not *entirely* from faith, as did Gichtel, but yet is governed by worldly prudence and self-love, will see nothing, and probably will not hesitate to affirm that there is nothing herein but refined enthusiasm and "error." Such individuals however, had better not read Gichtel's life at all: it was not lived for them, neither was it written for them.[28]

For Walton, as for theosophers in general, paranormal phenomena, including miraculous healing and visionary revelation, can happen today.

However, not all theosophic visions are the same. Of Böhme Walton tells us "Behmen was a perfect clairvoyant," albeit not just in "astral" "phantasaic" nature like Swedenborg or even Jane Leade, but in the true ground found by regeneration in Christ, for "then all is natural to us."[29] Leade—like Emmanuel Swedenborg—Walton condemns as having "become subject to be turned as to *an end*, to the non-essentials of visions and revelations."[30] Thus, Leade's visions were extraordinary, but also extravagant; "however profound may have been her experiences, her works can only be received of *enlightened* Christians of the present day, as a medley of unprofitable, yea hurtful, and yet, in some points, most interesting curiosities."[31] Yet theosophy can lead to more complete spiritual vision, as Böhme's revelations attest.

Chiefly, though, Walton's *Notes and Materials*, as its title suggests, is a compendium of much previously unpublished or very rare theosophic manuscript materials. It includes, for instance, the poem "Solomon's Porch; or, the Beautiful Gate of Wisdom's Temple. A Poem, Introductory to the Philadelphian Age," probably by Francis Lee, added to Leade's *A Fountain of Gardens* (1696–1700).[32] It also includes Lee's 1703 manuscript "Proposal for the raising a Stock to print Books of Mystical Divinity" or "heathen mystics" and "cabala," a plan that Walton's own massive publishing proposal echoed a century and a half later.[33] And Walton includes in his book such nuggets of information as the fact that Francis Lee possessed a much longer version of Pordage's *Mystica Theologia*, written "in the doctor's own hand," than that published in the 1680s.[34]

But much space is also devoted to the life of William Law, who historically bridged the gap between the Philadelphians of the early eighteenth century and the later British theosophers of the nineteenth century. Walton saw Law as his spiritual mentor and as the central English theosopher, so he took care to describe in detail Law's abstemious way of life, his rising for prayer at five in the morning, his cell, holding the works of Freher, Böhme, and Lee, looking out on the garden, his spiritual entry "in[to] abyssal silence before the interior central throne of the divine revelation" (words that directly reflect Pordage's writings).[35]

Walton also includes some previously unpublished letters by another theosophic figure historically intermediate between the Philadelphians and himself: one Mary Pratt, a humble "woman, a mother." These letters, dated September 16, 1792, and October 14, 1792, reveal a woman deeply immersed in theosophy. Pratt tells her correspondent:

> I wrote not from books, but from my own heartfelt experience and I sincerely wish you may die daily to rise into celestial pleasure. Every place to me and every state is heaven. . . . Oh, dear friend, I cannot pray for your case, but I pray for your extreme fires to begin, that from those burning furnaces, the resplendent gold may be brought forth.[36]

Like many mystics, she was intensely ascetic:

> My soul exults in the prospect of a separation from the polluted hell I live in, namely the body. No other hell to them who have passed over the first death, over them the second death has no power. This foul body is like a *beast*. . . . Oh, that every soul who is seeking this inestimable *pearl*, may soon find it.[37]

Clearly, Pratt stands directly in the line of theosophers from Böhme and Gichtel, Pordage, Leade, and Law, one of no doubt many theosophers of whom we have almost no historical trace.

Walton, like his predecessor theosophers, was very private, and we cannot tell from his writings precisely the way he lived, but we can extract some details. Certainly he shared his theosophic understanding with a small circle of friends that included the Pennys, and certainly he practiced theosophic discipline himself. He alludes at times to a science of the breath, and refers often to "vital magnetism," which leads one to believe that he followed some kind of meditative discipline that led on the one hand to a stilling of the mind, and on the other to an arising of vital power. Like Pordage and Leade, Walton undoubtedly practiced meditative prayer that led to and perhaps beyond trance states.

Although there are no doubt some modern theosophers—and some Russian authors of the early twentieth century, including Vladimir Solovyov, Nicholas Berdyaev, and Sergei Bulgakov, who were clearly influenced by Böhmean theosophy and carried this into Russian Orthodoxy to establish an Eastern Orthodox Sophianic mysticism—I am ending this historical sketch of major theosophers and their communities with Walton. It is interesting to read of Solovyov in the British Library, poring over theosophic works of Pordage and others, in a kabbalistic enthusiasm. But none of these Russian authors exemplified pure theosophy in the way that Walton did.

The theosophers and their communities that we have examined in this historical study are the major figures in the theosophic movement, stretching from Germany into the Netherlands, England, and America. Although like Walton many of them are little known, each offers a unique interpretation of theosophy, and when we consider the movement as a whole, each theosopher seems like a voice in a choral arrangement, woven into a harmonious work. Perhaps the most remarkable element of theosophy—its diversity within unity—remains at once its strongest and weakest point. For the theosophic insistence upon direct spiritual experience—years of spiritual practice—means that the discipline will always be, in the end, esoteric. There are not many theosophers—yet each one (including near-forgotten people like Mary Pratt) adds a unique voice to this extraordinary movement.

PART TWO

THE CYCLE OF
FOUNDATIONAL
DOCTRINES

Introduction

Perhaps it seems strange to speak of a cycle of foundational doctrines in theosophy, rather than of a system. But theosophy requires a different way of understanding than simple linear or categorical exposition. No one who has read the major works of theosophy will come away without recognizing that this is a perspective requiring a spiralling growth of knowledge, more or less in layers. This is not to say that it is impossible to categorize the basic doctrines of theosophy. Indeed, arguably the greatest of English theosophers, Dr. John Pordage, did precisely that in his *Göttliche und Wahre Metaphysica* (*Divine and True Metaphysics*). However, reading Pordage's works, like reading Böhme's, still requires a deepening understanding, and this deepening is the cyclical foundation of theosophy.

It is common for scholars of Böhme to try and schematize his works, and this is true of his earliest English translators, as when Edward Taylor presented his audience with a glossary and tables, or when more recent explicators have presented readers with many brief quotations from Böhme organized along categorical lines. These approaches have their merits, to be sure—particularly Taylor's 1691 glossary. But Böhme wrote as he did to a purpose, and ultimately all students of theosophy will have to confront his seminal books and treatises directly. This confrontation and assimilation is different than that required by most reading.

For reading Böhme from a theosophic perspective requires not just the assimilation of information or terminology, but also an actual reorientation of one's being. This is why his books and treatises approach subjects from myriad angles, and repeat themselves with slight variations, time and again. Böhme's purpose in writing was not just to convey rationally assimilated information, but to effect changes in one's soul. Doing this requires repetition, which is common in sacred texts around the world. Coming to understand Böhme is an existential, not just intellectual process.

The foundation of Böhme's works is a single principle, succinctly expressed in a dialogue in *Christosophia*:

> The student said: "Does the soul not go into heaven or hell just as a man goes into a house or as a man goes through a hole into another world?" The master replied: "No, there is no entrance in such a way, for heaven and hell are present everywhere. There is only the changing of the will either into God's love or into wrath. This takes place in the time of the body—as Saint Paul says, Our walk is in heaven (Philippians 3.20)."[1]

There is only the changing of the will, in this life, either into God's love or into wrath. Love is selflessness, the giving up of the bestial ego-will to the divine will; wrath is individualism, self-will. Love is light, and paradise; wrath is darkness, and hell. We enter these while we are alive in the body, and reap the consequences in the afterlife.

This simplicity is why Böhme and Christian theosophy had such an impact on the spiritual lives of ordinary people across Europe, England, and into America. It is all too common, especially for modern scholars, to ignore Böhme's most fundamental principle and to emphasize the complexity of his cosmological doctrines. Admittedly, some theosophic terminology requires definition, and as we shall see, it is important to elaborate such central doctrines as the emanation of worlds, the nature of the cosmos, and the human purpose. But we must keep in mind, while discussing these topics, that theosophy's primary impact was on religious life and only secondarily on theology, philosophy, and literature, primarily practical and only secondarily theoretical.

CHAPTER EIGHT

The Divine Nature

I n his efforts to explain the nature of God, Böhme was forced to resort to various analogies, just as was St. Dionysius the Areopagite more than ten centuries before him. Like St. Dionysius the Areopagite, Böhme had to speak in similitudes because human nature requires symbols as intermediate between us and reality, which otherwise would remain incomprehensible to us. Indeed, this is why spiritual literature of all kinds, far from being mere fantasy, is so powerful, for it mediates between transcendent reality and the temporophysical world. To speak of God's nature is, of course, the most profound form of literature possible.

In *Aurora*, Böhme tells us that God resembles a wheel, within which are seven other wheels, each of which can swivel within one another. He writes: "Suppose a Wheel standing before you, with seven wheels, one so made in the other that it could go on all sides, forward, backward, and cross ways, without need of any turning back or stopping."[1] The seven wheels remain always one, and this one generates all seven, for the seven wheels are the seven spirits of God, the unity always generating all the others. The seven spirits of God the Father—the wheels—have at their common center a nave, which is the Son or Heart of God, to which they are all connected by spokes, which are the Holy Spirit.[2]

These images—this symbolic unity—allow us to understand something of the Holy Trinity's nature. Through the image of the wheels, with their naves, spokes, and fellies, we see the timeless nature of the Divine, and we are given to understand something of how the Father (felly), the Son (nave), and the Holy Spirit (spokes) relate to one another in unity, within this threefoldness a sevenfold nature, the Seven Spirits who are generated images of the Trinity. Naturally, the Trinity is ultimately beyond human comprehension, but symbols such as the wheel give us at least some means of perceiving its nature, which is in turn reflected in the cosmos and in man.

For as we have seen, the cosmos and human beings reflect the three-fold nature of God. There are three worlds: the dark fire world below, the elemental world in the middle, and the paradisal world above. These three worlds appear in man as well, and correspond to the Father (and his anger), the Son (as incarnate Word, and love), and the Holy Spirit (as light and creative power), respectively. Hence, both macrocosm (the three worlds) and microcosm (humans) are really elaborations or manifestations of the Trinity. Conceived as a hierarchy, this triune arrangement suggests the transmutation of the soul in its return to a paradisal state: encountering the fiery anger of the sword that guards paradise (the Father), incarnating the Word (Son), and realizing the paradisal light (the Holy Spirit).

In a real sense, therefore, divine nature is known by human beings through the transmutation of our own souls, and through correspondences—the way the cosmos and humans reflect their divine origin. For example, God is a unity, generated within which is the Trinity, generated within which are the Seven Creative Spirits. Just as the Trinity is reflected in the three worlds—in wrath, materiality, and love—so too the Seven Spirits are reflected in the seven planetary qualities, which are found throughout the cosmos. The seven planets embody in the realms of soul and body qualities that become progressively "denser" as one "descends" from soul to body, just as by "ascending" from body to animating soul to serene spirit, one would encounter ultimately the emanating Seven Spirits of God—the fountains of creation, Böhme calls them.

About divine nature, Böhme writes in "On the Divine Intuition" (1622) that in himself, God has nothing, nor gives himself anything.[3] The divine nature is *Ungrund*, or groundless and transcendent, the near side of which is God:

> God is the eternal One, or the greatest stillness, so far as he exists in himself independently of his motion and manifestation. But in his motion he is called a God in trinity. . . . This

is the precious and supreme ground, and thus to be considered: the divine will shuts itself in a place to selfhood, and becomes active in itself; but also by its activity goes forth, and makes for itself an object, that is, Wisdom, through which the ground and origin of all things has arisen.[4]

Wisdom (Sophia) is therefore "intermediate" between creation and God; she is the matrix through which God "objectifies" himself in creation, through which his activity takes place. Obviously, she is not a member of the Trinity, but in a sense, through her the Trinity is made known in the "objective" realm of creation, and so man returns to God through her as well.

But we should remember that conceptual schemata like this do not in themselves do justice to the divine nature. Even to speak of "ascending" from body to soul is inappropriate, since who or what is it that "ascends"? Who comprehends? We can say "the soul," but what does this really mean? Ultimately, God comprehends himself through man. The mystery of divine nature is, finally, the mystery of human nature as well. We can speak in symbols and even categorically of divine nature, but such schemata do not at all adequately convey the reality, in fact themselves present a barrier to actual understanding.

At the same time, symbols such as those used by Böhme are very important for us. They give us a conceptual framework, a way of understanding and assimilating ourselves to the spiritual path. This is why so many theosophers subsequent to Böhme were delighted to discover his writings, not because those writings themselves offered experience of the Divine, but because they help one to understand such experiences in a coherent context, and indeed point one toward a further deepening of one's knowledge. Probably the classic exemplar of this contextualization is the eighteenth-century French author Louis-Claude de Saint-Martin, whose discovery of Böhme, he tells us, immeasurably deepened his understanding.

If we were to condense Böhme's writing on the divine nature into its most concise form, we would probably have to say that everything in the elemental world and every human being bears the stamp of the Divine. The divine nature can be known, therefore, by analogy through its stamp on all things, but most of all through its imprint on human nature. For the human being is indeed made in the image of the Divine, meaning that each of us reflects within our very nature divine wrath, the elemental world, and the world of paradisal light, manifestations of the Trinity. Each of us also bears within us at our very center the divine stillness, the still point of the turning worlds that, in the end, is all that truly is.

CHAPTER NINE

The Divine Emanation
of Worlds

 lthough we have discussed this subject earlier, in the
chapter on Böhme's writings, it is important to con-
sider the divine emanation of the worlds in greater detail
here because it is basic to all of practical theosophy, especially in theosophic communities such as those of Gichtel,
Leade, Kelpius, and Beissel. By "worlds" here, I mean only
what Böhme meant primarily by this term, the "three
worlds" found in all of theosophy: the dark or wrath
world, the light world of paradise, and the elemental world
in which we exist. These three worlds are always present to
us, but in theosophy they are presented in a particular order
and are related in ways that demand explanation.

It is true that in Kabbalism, in Gnosticism, and in theosophy we
do find occasional allusions to realms previous to our present physical world, destroyed in long-forgotten conflagrations, only traces of
which remain in our collective memory and in allusions such as the
"kingdom of Edom" in the Old Testament.[1] According to this doctrine, there were, in previous time cycles, realms in which previous
humanities lived, but in which they destroyed themselves. There are
some parallels between these allusions in Kabbalism and Christian
theosophy, regarding human beings "emerging" into successive
worlds, meaning successive time cycles. Interesting though these ref-

erences are, they need not concern us here, since they do not concern
our theosophers.

For the three primary worlds—the wrath world, the love world, and
the elemental world—exist in us. Thus Böhme writes:

> So also are we to consider man: He stands and lives in three
> worlds. The first is the eternal dark-world, the *centrum* of eter-
> nal nature, which begets the fire, the source of suffering; the
> second is the eternal light-world, which begets eternal joy and
> is the divine dwelling place in which the spirit of God dwells,
> in which the spirit of Christ takes on human being, and drives
> out the darkness so that it must be a cause of joy in the spirit
> of Christ to be in the light; the third world is the external vis-
> ible world, the four elements and visible stars. Each element
> has a star according to its own characteristic in itself out of
> which desire and characteristic rise, just as in a mind.[2]

These three worlds are described here in the order of creation, which is
a continuous, universally present process, not simply an "event."

It is useful to consider the Neoplatonic concept of emanation here,
even though there are fundamental differences between Neoplatonism
and Böhmean theosophy. According to Plotinus and Proclus, for example, the entire cosmos is the crystallization or condensation of higher
states of existence, which in turn reflect yet higher, purer states, themselves emanations of absolute Being itself. Thus, the archetypes of this
world are not only purer, but more real than what we see here below.
Absolute Being contains the essences of all beings, who manifest themselves in successively more material, hence temporal and spatial realms.
But Böhme uses the term *Ungrund*, or groundlessness, to describe the
nature of the God-head, not Platonist terms like "Absolute Being."

Still, something of the same understanding of emanation applies in
Böhmean theosophy. According to Böhme, all creation, from highest to
lowest, is inspired by a single "breath of God," a "magical fire's breath"
and a "source-spirit of the light, out of the great fiery love's desire."[3] In
other words, creation "begins" with divine wrath, or fire, affiliated with
God the Father as a jealous, angry God. But creation also has a loving,
merciful side, and this is the luminous aspect of God's breath. The third
aspect of creation is the elemental world, with its congelation into time
and space. Temporality is born out of eternity, which in a sense surrounds it; all three worlds are part of a single divine breath.

Originally, all three worlds or aspects of the divine breath were balanced, and this balanced unity was the original paradise. But this har-

mony was rent asunder by two "meta-events": first, the fall of Lucifer and his legions of angels, and second, by the consequent Fall of man in Adam and Eve. These "falls" refer to an improper mixture of realms originally harmoniously separate: Lucifer, through pride and self-will, "fell" from the light world into the world of wrath and darkness; and then brought this world of wrathful darkness "up" into the elemental world through the temptation and "fall" of Adam and Eve. All of this is to be understood as spiritual symbolism for events with real consequences, not as history: hence the term "meta-events."

Now, the corruption of the elemental world by darkness and wrath meant the appearance of time or history, and so of death. At precisely this point, humanity forgot its paradisal, luminous nature, which, fading, was replaced by the external, "hardened," physical world, much as, according to Plotinus and the Neoplatonists (drawing on the Egyptian Mystery tradition), humanity is in exile from its luminous, archetypal home. According to theosophy, human beings had awakened in them their fiery, wrathful, fallen nature, and so became part demonic and part bestial. This is the condition in which we live today.

But it is not the end of the drama—for just as there is a fall into temporality, death, and ignorance, so too is there an ascent out of suffering, a return to paradisal unity. This resurrection from temporality, hence from our exile here below (which amounts to death), takes place through Christ. God becomes man in order to redeem all creation, to change hell and its wrath into love, darkness into light. We are enjoined to open ourselves to the divine transmuting power while alive here on earth, because this is the decisive moment for us. Here alone can we participate in the determinative reharmonizing of the worlds, transmuting wrath into love, so that in us the original paradisal harmony of the three realms can be restored.

For eventually this drama will be entirely played out—eventually, eternity will blast time asunder. Everything will return to its original condition prior to creation, and this will entail the re-separation of the worlds. No longer will the elemental world be subject to time or death; only the pure, celestial elements will exist in their archetypal, paradisal forms. Wrath and darkness will be "closed away"; this re-separation is called the "last judgment," meaning the separation of all light and all darkness. This ultimate reseparation, which is in fact a redemption, takes place through Christ, the celestial principle illuminating all the realms, and taking back to himself all that is his own, all that is of the light in the whole of the three realms.

But this celestial drama takes place in miniature in each of us, at each moment. In other words, all three realms are also to be found in each human being, and the process of redemption can therefore take place in us, if we turn our will into love from wrath. If, however, we turn our will into the wrath, then we accomplish the Fall within ourselves, and to the degree that we do this we will be in hell after death. Thus, following Christ really means realizing paradise in ourselves during this lifetime, so that when eternity is finally revealed throughout all creation, we are already in paradise.

Eternity is present at every moment, surrounds and permeates creation, even though, caught in the illusory river of temporo-spatiality, we do not ordinarily perceive it. Thus, the entire celestial drama of emanation, fall, and redemption takes place around us and in us constantly. It is not at all a matter of something having happened in the distant past, or happening in the far-off future, for because of the nature of divine emanation, all realms of existence are here around us at this very instant. According to theosophy, this is why Böhme, Pordage, Gichtel, Leade and the other theosophers could see angels and demons while on earth, for we human beings live at the matrix of all worlds.

If we were to point out the one fundamental divergence between theosophy and the Neoplatonic worldview, it is this: theosophy takes account of evil. For while in Neoplatonism evil is generally regarded as illusory, as we have seen, in theosophy, evil, and the wrath world, is very real. Its power is only the power to sway or to infect, but nonetheless, it possesses a realm of its own, and can invade the human sphere, indeed, longs to do so. Theosophy is not ultimately dualistic, inasmuch as everything appears in ternaries, including of course the Holy Trinity—and from its perspective, its cosmology and metaphysics is therefore comprehensive in illuminating the nature of not only this world but all worlds.

CHAPTER TEN

The Fall of Lucifer,
Humanity, and Nature

Christian doctrines regarding the fall of Lucifer, the Fall of Adam, and the consequent inheritance of original sin by humanity often today are largely ignored. The tendency of modern theology has definitely been away from concentrating on sin or evil; indeed, some contemporary liberal theology seems inclined to do away with these concepts altogether. But in theosophy, these doctrines take on a special significance, not because theosophy is pessimistic, but because theosophers hold that recognizing the nature of evil is critical to understanding ourselves and our cosmos. Theosophy does not so much add new doctrines to European Christianity as amplify and shed new light on traditional theology, particularly as regards the question of evil.

According to Böhme, existence comes into being through a "terror" or a fierce anguish through the Father. From this terror is generated a "wheel of anguish" or a "wheel of fierceness," which is the fire or dark world. But there arises another will, which is the transformation of the fire or dark world into the gentleness and joy of the light world. This transformation from the fire world into the light world takes place through the Holy Spirit. Thus, "in the terror Nature divides into two beings, as mentioned above, one through the Father's will into fire or into the fire-world; and one through the Father's other will that is drawn or generated in Himself into the majestic light-world."[1]

From this fundamental divine economy of creation we can see that the dark or wrath world is essential to existence, and that in fact the dark world exists in order to give birth to the light. In a sense, we could say that the dark world exists like a shell or limit of creation, allowing "space" for creation to take place between it and the unutterable light of paradise. Consequently, Böhme tells us outright, "The dark world is therefore the ground and origin of the light world; and the terrible evil must be a cause of the good, and all is God's."[2] The dark world could only be the origin of the light world if wrath could be converted into love and light.

For from the perspective of the divine light itself, only the light exists. Hence, "in God's kingdom, viz in the light-world, no more than one principle is truly known. For the Light rules, and the other sources and properties all exist hiddenly as a mystery, for they must all serve the Light, and give their will to the Light."[3] It is a matter of perception: what in the light world gives joy and life, in the dark world causes enmity and dissension. What in the light world gives delight, in the dark world gives pain. But from the perspective of the light world, there nonetheless is only light and joy.

Intermediate between the light world and the fire world is the principle called "God's wrath," and those who awaken this principle (be they demons or human beings), then are abandoned by the light and enter completely into the dark world. Awakening this principle of wrath means allowing it to enter into one's soul; it means entering into dualism, hence into rage, fear, and anguish. These are all founded in separation or isolation, and the fall of demons or people is therefore a fall into further isolation. Facing and transcending our own sinful nature means confronting exactly these things within ourselves, passing through and transcending dualistic states of suffering. Ascent takes place through love.

The Fall of man or other beings, on the other hand, takes place through division or, to use other words, through pride or egotism. For the Fall of man essentially duplicates the fall of Lucifer himself. Lucifer, once an angel, fell from the state of angelic serenity and joy into rage and duplicity, and having done so, seeks to bring humans into the same conditions. Böhme explains this in a 1624 dialogue between a devil and a poor soul lost in the kingdom of this world. The devil tells the soul that if it eats that out of which creatures are good and evil, it will be like God Himself; the devil advises the soul to turn its attention from God to the things of this world, to wish to become Lord over all things on earth. In other words, the devil teaches self-reliance in place of reliance on the divine.[4]

The devil tells the soul that it is high and mighty, rich, dominant, respected in all the world, but does so by insinuating himself into the soul's own reason. The soul believes that it is guiding itself and, so believing, continues on in a path leading to damnation. But when the "spark of divine light" of Christ is revealed in the soul, the soul sees itself as it really is, as a specter, indeed, a monster in God's sight, wholly distorted by pride, wrath, envy, and lust—all of which consist in clinging to or rejecting oneself and the things of this world. Then the soul realizes its true state and tries desperately to regain the divine, but cannot, and falls into misery and depression.

Here is a critical point in the soul's path, for then the devil in the soul argues that Christ has already paid for the sins of all men, that the soul need only remember Christ's suffering, take comfort in it, and forget about coming to know the divine directly in this lifetime. Live in this world now, the devil says, and in old age you can repent; the spiritual life requires no struggle like that the soul feels in longing for God while on earth. Hence, the soul is deflected from the spiritual path by the devil's insinuations told itself by itself. Yet the soul also feels hope even in its self-doubts. Christ exists even in the soul's hell. Indeed, the revelation of divine power always entails the soul's seeing itself as the wormish, tortured, hideous countenance it bears through its own errors. Christ's revelation and the soul's transmutation always entail passing through suffering; according to theosophy, true Christianity is by no means simply remembering Christ's sacrifice several millennia ago.

But at the same time, theosophy emphasizes that the soul must never rely upon itself or its own efforts. The soul's only valid spiritual effort is to rely wholly upon divine grace, to overcome the self-will that deforms the soul into a hideous monstrosity. Only when divine grace enters into and surrounds the soul, is revealed as the soul's essence, radiating light, can the soul be truly saved. Salvation consists in mirroring the divine will, which is the will to reveal its own joy, delight, and harmony. Paradise must grow in the soul like a plant, transforming hell into heaven, growing upward toward the light naturally as a plant seeks the light, rising out of dirt.

However, since according to theosophy the human world is subject to Lucifer, anyone who begins this process of transformation must realize that this world will scorn him, revile him, so that Christ's true way will remain hidden. Böhme warns us that Lucifer—the principle of self-will or pride (including intellectual pride foremost)—will incite whomever he can to attack the soul that has travelled far enough along this spiritual path.[5] And in fact the history of theosophy shows time and again that the fiercest enemies of theosophers are proudly orthodox religious people such as Richter, who attacked Böhme himself relentlessly, or the Anglican committees who attacked Pordage and his circle, enraged at theosophy's denial that belief in a historical Christ was adequate for salvation.

Although theosophy does not assert Lucifer's domination over the entire cosmos (making of Lucifer a kind of Gnostic demiurge), as we have seen, theosophy does hold that the physical cosmos came about, in part, through the fall of the angels, that the whole of nature is marked by this fall. And indeed, this view does explain how nature can embody such a round of suffering as is visible in illnesses and wounds, in parasitic and predatory creatures—precisely while also embodying glimmers of paradisal harmony and beauty. Our cosmos bears the marks both of evil and of good, both of paradise and of hell, both of joyous delight and of suffering. Our cosmos is intermediate between hell and paradise, and bodies forth both at once. The theosophic path is to transmute the principle of hell into that of paradise through overcoming self-will—the path of spiritual regeneration.

CHAPTER ELEVEN

Spiritual Regeneration

If it is true that the whole of nature and all human beings are marked by the Fall of Lucifer, and of primordial man, it is also true that all bear within them the possibility for spiritual resurrection. For even though our present world came into being through a disruption in primordial harmony—through the creation of the elemental world, and the irruption of the wrath world "upward" into it— our world is the intersection of all three realms, and hence bears within it also paradise. In a sense, we may say that our world is shot through with both paradise and hell, permeated with them, and our task as human beings is to be restored to the paradisal state.

For exactly this reason Louis-Claude de Saint-Martin spoke of Christ as "the Repairer." By this he meant that, to use a formulation embraced in Eastern Orthodox theology and found also in Böhme, that in Christ God became man in order that man could become God. Indeed, some Eastern Orthodox theologians have used the term "God-manhood" to describe the nature of Christ. But in any case, Christ as "Repairer" refers to the necessity for the spiritual regeneration or rebirth of human beings; through Christ the disruptions in the primordial harmony of the worlds are repaired, and through his nature we are restored to our original paradisal state.

Thus, in *Six Theosophic Points*, Böhme writes that "our whole teaching is nothing else than how man should kindle in himself God's light-world."[1] This kindling of God's light world is possible through Christ. Böhme continues: "For if this be kindled, so that God's light shines in the soul's spirit, then the whole body has light, as Christ says: If the eye be light, then is the whole body light (Matthew 6.22,23)." We must each turn a close eye upon ourselves and our own inner nature to see whether wrath, envy, falsehood, and lewdness have power over us, for if these are not like poison to us then we are only human in outward form, but demonic inwardly, meaning that the fiery wrath world alone is kindled in us.

There are, in other words, according to theosophy certain signs by which one can tell the degree to which one is regenerated. One who has "a constant desire after God" so strong that one can "break and transform into gentleness the evil essences," who "can let all go that shines and glitters in this world," who "can do good for evil," who can give all his worldly goods to the needy, "for him the divine power flows, so that he may kindle the light of the kingdom of joy therein; he tastes what God is."[2] Christ is born of the Virgin in such a one, who even while alive in the body has realized the "heavenly essence in himself."

We should keep in mind, however, the archetypal truth of Christ's persecution on earth. For although one may be regenerated in this life, this paradisal restoration does not extend to the wrathfulness still extant in the world and in other people; in fact, it incites wrath against one. Because the *homo novus* (new man) "dwells not in this world," the devil remains "hostile to his essence, which contains the inward center," and therefore "he incites the evil animal-men against him, to vex and persecute him, so that the true humanity remains concealed." So long as we are alive on this earth, we are in a realm of struggle and of long-suffering, for we remain intermediate between wrath and love even if we have become love and light incarnate, as much as this is possible.

From this we can understand better the persecution of Böhme himself in his own home town, as well as the persecution of numerous subsequent theosophers. Böhme had good reason to consider in depth this most paradoxical of life's aspects, the persecution of clearly spiritual people as exemplified in the crucifixion of Christ himself. He concluded that while it is true that someone who has taken the path of the Repairer—and whose purpose is to restore the original paradisal harmony in himself and in all beings—has kindled the light of paradise within, this does not at all mean a freedom from the existential struggle so long as one is alive, a mystery crystallized in the words of Christ: "Father, why hast thou forsaken me?" Bodily life is inherently a partial exile from paradise.

Fundamentally, then, spiritual regeneration is a reorientation of one's being from selfishness to selflessness. Selfishness, in Böhme's perspective, means a bestial life subject to wrath, hence an unconscious life pulled and pushed by emotional tides; selflessness on the other hand means a conscious life lived in the light of the Divine. A selfless life is a life anchored in the Divine, for only in the transcendent Divine do we find a center freed from the winds of action and reaction. Ordinary man is bestial because he lives solely beneath the astral shell, subject to envy, anger, and deceitfulness, an animal-like creature who possesses reason.

This perspective is illustrated in the frontispiece to several German editions of *The Way to Christ*, which shows a heart beset by a serpent and a dragon, above which is the weeping sun, and then clouds separating what is below from divine light above. The heart, beset by bestial forces, is anchored by a rope penetrating the clouds to a cross in dazzling light above, surmounted by an eagle. The illustration shows how the heart must maintain faith, must remain centered upon the divine light and the cross during all its earthly tribulations. For only this will sustain the soul during the struggle of earthly life, separated as it is from the Divine by its own astral clouds, by its emotional currents and rationalism and conceptualizations.

According to Böhme, spiritual regeneration is a function of the soul's imagination. The soul has the capacity through its imaginal faculty to perceive earthliness or the "dark world's kingdom" on the one hand, or the paradisal light world of God on the other. The soul's imaginal faculty is like a mirror, and the mirror can be shut up in darkness or can reflect the light. "As long as it imaginates after God's Spirit, it receives God's power and light, and knows God," Böhme writes.[3] But if the soul's mirror reflects earthliness or wrath, it must be spiritually regenerated, born anew—turned to reflect the light again.

Thus, spiritual regeneration, in theosophy, has both an active and a passive quality. The soul must struggle against wrath and bestiality; this is the chivalric, active aspect of the soul's transmutation in relation to the outward world. The ultimate symbol of the soul's struggle in this world is the suffering of Christ. But at the same time, the soul has a passive relationship to the realm of spirit and light, symbolized by the imaginal mirror. For however much it must struggle in relation to wrath and the temptations of this world, the soul must be a mirror to the dazzling luminosity of paradise.

Gichtel elaborated on the practical nature of this theosophic rebirth within us in his letters, as when he wrote:

> By the earnest imagination of the soul into God's loving paternal heart, the love is made substantial in us, and the wrath or the anxious driving of nature is softened, or subdued. It is the same with the innermost birth of our hearts as with the imagination of man and wife, by whose strong impression a living soul is infused into the seed, and a form is produced for, or communicated to the birth according to the strongest imagination of the two, whence the children are formed after either the father or the mother.[4]

The strength of the willed imagination within ourselves communicates to the heart the serene, luminous imprint of Christ. Or to put it another way, the willed imagination draws Christ into our souls, "For the new birth in us is Christ only, who there formed himself into the humanity, to bring it with him to the Father."[5]

The new birth or spiritual regeneration is therefore at once a turning of the soul toward God, or *metanoia*, and as a result of that willed imagination, an opening that allows Christ to manifest himself in us. Those who live in the historical faith do not open themselves to God, and so when death comes they have no comfort in the afterlife, for the wrath seizes them. According to Böhme, Gichtel, and the other theosophers, we must give up our self-will (which theosophers say is really a hell-life) and let Christ's love manifest itself in us. This is the straightforward, simple heart of the theosophic message.

CHAPTER TWELVE

Angelology and Paradise

There are some scholars who emphasize the unique nature of Böhme's revelations, occasionally ignoring the degree of his indebtedness to previous Judeo-Christian theological tradition. While Böhme's visionary cosmology and metaphysics is unique for its comprehensiveness and lucidity, however, it is also remarkable for the degree to which it incorporates so much of the existing Judeo-Christian theology, from currents as disparate as Jewish and Christian Kabbalism, alchemy, and German medieval mysticism. Nowhere is this unity of disparate theological currents with visionary understanding more evident than in Böhme's exposition of angels and paradise.

We can see this unified theological perspective from the earliest of Böhme's works—*Aurora*—onward. In *Aurora*, Böhme discusses the origin and nature of the angels and paradise, beginning with the matter-of-fact "*Verbum domini*, The Word of the Lord, by the *Fiat* (that is, the saying, Let there be angels) comprised the qualifying or fountain spirits into a will; and that is the creation of the angels."[1] There are seven spirits of God, in the center of which is their heart, the Son of God; thus all embody one will. All the manifold angelical hierarchies emerge out of this central will, and yet even though the hierarchies all partake in the central seven spirits of God, different powers or tendencies predominate in each.

In his exposition of the angelic hierarchies and natures, Böhme is apparently drawing on his own visionary experiences. He writes that just as "the flowers in the meadows" each receive their colors from their essential qualities, so too the angels differ. Thus, some angels have a "brownish" or purple quality, others a translucent, watery nature, others "are like a green precious stone, which sparkles like a flash of lightning," others still are "yellowish and reddish," and those "strongest in the quality of love" are "very light and *bright*; and when the light shineth on them, they look like *light blue*, of a pleasant gloss, glance, or lustre."[2] All these observations give one the definite sense that they come from Böhme's own journey through angelic ranks.

But he also uses the inherited terms of Judeo-Christian angelology. Hence, when explaining how just as the sun is the king of the planets, so is the cherubim a "king of angels," Böhme uses the inherited Hebrew word traditional in Christianity at least since the angelological treatises of St. Dionysius the Areopagite. Böhme does not systematically elaborate the angelic hierarchies in the way that Dionysius did, but he does employ some of the traditional language and names, including sections on the angels Michael, Lucifer, and Uriel. When reading Böhme, we often feel, more than in the work of perhaps any other author, that we have entered into a vast cosmos incorporating all previous traditional Judeo-Christian language and understanding, and that Böhme is drawing our attention only to main points of reference.

In *Aurora*, Böhme explains the nature of the angelical realms, and this description is echoed in numerous subsequent theosophic works in different languages. Böhme writes that the seventh fountain spirit is the ground of the angelical nature, being "very lightsome and solid as a cloud, but very *transparent* and shining, like a chrystalline sea, so that a man can see through and through it all."[3] Angels have "compacted" bodies composed of a brightness out of nature, and are as swift as the divine power itself, some swifter than others, and though they have no wings, they do have hands and feet like men. Indeed, after the day of resurrection, there will be no difference between men and angels.[4] Similar descriptions of angels can be found in the works of Pordage, Leade, and the other English theosophers, all evidently independent visionary confirmation of what Böhme wrote.

Hence, Edward Hooker, one of the London Philadelphian circle, wrote in his *The Triple Crown of Glory* under the name Philochristotheus that "God is an Invisible Spiritual Substance, who Filleth all things and is everywhere present," for

> Hee doth continually manifest His Spirit of Life, Love, and
> Wisdom . . . sent in the highest or third Heaven with inex-
> pressible Glorie and Brightness, which doth surround His
> own Bodily Substance of the Angelick Heaven with perpetual
> light; and with which Heavenly Body Hee doth surround this
> world, with Glauncing a Spark of its Glorie thro' the Sun, for
> the Light of the World.[5]

Angels, Hooker writes, partake in the spiritual substance of God, and
have their being in the "third heaven," which is light and joy, transparent to the overwhelming luminosity of God.

Böhme, Pordage, Gichtel, and all the other theosophers insist on the
point Hooker makes here—that the "Bodily Substance of the Angelick
Heaven" surrounds us here in this present world, although we do not
see it. We are enjoined to realize this "Bodily Substance" while alive, and
its nature is love. Gichtel writes: "For the life of eternity is nothing but
love, and if we wish to enter into that paradisal life, we must also be
nothing else but love, so that one equality may comprehend and hold the
other."[6] The angels exist bathed in love and radiating love, for it is their
nature. This love is the emotional content, if we can so put it, of the light
that completely surrounds and permeates our opaque world.

What prevents us from realizing this angelic state of light and
love? According to the theosophers: our self-will. In a dialogue
included in Böhme's *The Way to Christ*, the master tells his student
that "He who finds love finds nothing and everything." This means
that "he finds a supernatural, supersensual abyss that has no place as
its dwelling," and "nothing that can be compared to it," yet is "the
ground out of which all things proceed," so "you will be in it a king
over all the works of God." When the student in turn asks where this
Ungrund or abyss dwells in man, the master replies "Where a man
does not dwell, there it has its place in man."[7] By this he means that
when a soul dies to its own self-will, it opens itself to the divine will,
and realizes its angelic nature.

This is an absolutely critical point. When a soul conceptualizes the
divine nature—the supersensual abyss or *Ungrund* that emanates love
and all beings—when it seeks to grasp this nothingness, then the nothingness will flee or evade it. But when the soul gives itself up to the nothingness, then it becomes dead to its own will, and the nothing, pure
God's will, makes the soul alive according to its own nature. To echo the
words of St. Paul, it is not I, but Christ in me. The soul can realize the
angelic nature or realm only when it ceases to look outside itself, ceases

to externalize the divine as "something" that it can possess, and instead opens itself to divine love.

When this happens, Böhme tells us, the soul is lit by a fiery love that continually burns up the "I," and were the soul to enter into hell, this fiery love would "break hell for its sake." This fiery love is the angelic nature—heaven itself—and determines one's posthumous state. For the last judgment is simply the removing of materiality to reveal the hidden natures of all beings, who are resolved then into either wrath and self-will, or love and selflessness. Thus, those in whom the angelic fiery love is burning will find this fire burning after death in even more purity, and after the last judgment, everything in the cosmos will be restored to its primordial condition, wrath wholly separated again from love.

Hence the angelic realm or paradise is not at all like a house into which a soul enters after death. Such concepts are intellectual constructs that do not bear much relation to reality. Rather, the angels dwell in the love and light of God, which is omnipresent even if veiled from us by our own self-will and by exactly such rational constructs. According to the theosophers, we must relinquish this desire to seek after and possess spiritual reality for ourselves and turn inward, opening ourselves to the divine will, and only then will we be be able to see the angelic realm of light that is our inheritance.

In the marginal notes to a poem called *Mundorum Explicatio* (1661), attributed to Samuel Pordage, the notes probably by John Pordage, his father, we find the following:

> Spirits are not of Matter, Form, &c. yet they have Bodies which are distinct from them, but not as our gross bodies, subject to our outward sences, but to our inward: For had they not bodies they could not be visible to our internal eyes which pierce into their Kingdoms and habitations. . . . Their Bodies likewise are of a spiritual substance made out of Sulphur, Mercury, and Sal, in the inward ground of Eternal Nature, the bodies both of Angels and Devils being of the same Matter, but that those are Harmoniz'd by the property of the Light or second Principle, these harmoniz'd by that of the dark or first principle.[8]

Each human being possesses such a spiritual body, and when the corporeal body dies, then this subtle body "in the inward ground of Eternal Nature" is consumed either in wrath or in love, depending on which of these it has lived in before death.

As long as we possess a corporeal body, however, we are somewhat opaque, and not immersed completely in the wrath or in love. We feel the effects of the wrath in ourselves as the tweakings of our conscience, and can experience it sometimes more directly—just as it is possible to be possessed by love, to become luminous even while on earth. There are, after all, numerous cases of saints who while praying became light. We also can, the theosophers tell us, see with our "inward eyes" the angelical kingdom, just as we can sometimes see the demonic realm. From such seeing came the works of Böhme, Pordage, and the other theosophers. But only when we have died, and only when the last judgment is complete, can we truly know the angelical realm.

It is true that theosophy does unite a number of theological traditions, including foremost the celestial hierarchy of St. Dionysius the Areopagite with the German mysticism of Tauler, along with some influences of Jewish Kabbalism. In fact, it would be possible to make close comparisons, and show the exact parallels of these traditions with theosophy. But such a comparison does not seem warranted here, because theosophy is based fundamentally in direct spiritual knowledge.[9] Böhme's, Pordage's, Gichtel's, and the many other theosophers' angelologies, they affirm, come directly out of their own visionary experiences, and if there are parallels with these previous traditions, the parallels are confirmatory rather than solely influential.

Conclusion

In this general discussion of theosophy's fundamental doctrines, I have emphasized what I believe to be the most critical aspects of the theosophers' theological understanding. Certainly there are some divergences among the theosophers, primarily differences in emphasis, but these are not fundamental to theosophic doctrine. The theosophers as a whole share a common way of understanding the cosmos, its origin, purpose, nature, and dissolution. For despite their diversity and their occasional disputes, theosophers represent a single lived discipline and a single general perspective, whose residue remains in their writings.

The doctrinal form of this discipline and vision I have called a "cycle" because each doctrinal aspect is intimately linked to all the others. One cannot, for example, fully understand the theosophers' views of angels or paradise without also considering human nature, the nature of the cosmos—and the dissolution of the cosmos. This cyclical nature of theosophic doctrine is reflected in the peculiarly spiralling quality of many theosophic writings, especially those of Böhme. But theosophic doctrine, even in the scientific, categorical form of John Pordage's treatises, exists, from the theosophers' perspective, only to introduce us to a way of understanding for ourselves.

Although theosophic doctrine is often labelled abstruse by modern commentators, in fact, as we have seen, its essential points are strikingly simple. Most fundamental of these is the differentiation of love and wrath, or light and darkness, or union and separation. The most basic concepts of theosophy, these are also the most profound and the most helpful for understanding how we are to live. For to the theosophers, theosophy in the end is not a matter of doctrines. Theosophy is more an invitation into a way of seeing and understanding ourselves and nature; it is a discipline of living, and asks us only to verify for ourselves if its fundamental doctrinal cycle is true.

PART THREE

THE ART
OF THE SOUL'S
TRANSMUTATION

CHAPTER THIRTEEN

The Science of Imagination

In virtually all popular and most literary depictions, as in scholarly representations, Protestantism is nothing less than the abolition of Roman Catholic iconography and the rich fund of images and icons that belong to the Christian tradition as a whole. Indeed, if we were to believe the literary creations of Nathaniel Hawthorne, for example, Puritanism in particular, consists in mainly grim, repressed, somber people who occasionally persecute outspoken or egregious women and even men. However, such near-caricatures of Protestantism do not begin to account for the richness of the tradition as a whole: for as we shall see, the theosophers were far indeed from being opposed to the world of the imagination.

But to discuss the imagination here requires that we begin by defining our terms. By imagination, the theosophers do not refer to "fantasy." Fantasy is daydreaming; fantasy has no discipline about it; fantasy is letting the mind follow its own meanderings, and in the spiritual realm this can be dangerous or even fatal, for it can lead to delusion and even to a complete disconnection from reality. By contrast, imagination refers to the science of images, to visionary inspiration by means of images. Imagination, in short, is not a matter of human creation, but of human perception.

For imagination is the faculty by which human beings can perceive and represent to others who do not themselves perceive, the archetypal worlds of which this world is a reflection. As we will recall, according to Böhmean theosophy, this physical world is only one of numerous worlds that interpenetrate this one. There is a wrathful, dark, demonic world, a fiery world, a light and love world, and a paradisal angelical world above all of these. All of these worlds are perceptible here on earth for those who have developed their imaginative faculty, their capacity to see not with earthly, but with spiritual eyes.

Within this context, we can see how theosophic visions are not mere fantasy, nor fanciful hallucinations, but entail an actual visionary science. Theosophic visionaries have themselves passed beyond what Böhme and Gichtel called the *spiritus mundi,* or spirit of this world, the astral shell that surrounds us and keeps us from realizing our true archetypal home and purpose. The theosophers have entered into our archetypal, paradisal home from which we have wandered, and to which we are enjoined to return. Böhme writes: "Look well to it . . . turn instantly, and consider where you are lodged, in how hard a house of bondage your soul lies imprisoned; seek your native country, from which your soul has wandered, and where it ought to return again."[1]

This metaphor of exile and return homeward is, of course, profoundly Gnostic in its resonances. According to it, we human beings are exiled far from our native world of paradisal light and freedom from suffering. But our home is accessible to us while we are here on earth; here on earth is the decisive moment for all eternity. Böhme and later theosophers urge us again and again to break through our astral shell, to turn away from merely brutish, even demonic urges or inclinations, and to enter into the spiritual joy and rest that the Virgin Sophia offers us. To do this is to return to our paradisal home while on earth, a return that lasts for all eternity.

According to Böhme, people already bear within their souls certain images—people use their imaginative faculty inadvertently. We are all servants, he writes, if not to sin and darkness, then, through spiritual discipline, to the light. For if we give ourselves up to a bestial life, to gluttony, drunkenness, lechery, lying, and deceit, then "the eternal Mind figures him also in such an Image of an Adder, Serpent, and Beast, hidden therein, which will be manifested at the [Deceasing] of the Body."[2] When we live in sin, we inadvertently create inward bestial self-images that are revealed after death: a covetous man after death lives in a hell of covetous need that can no longer be fulfilled.

Thus, every man and woman already use the imaginative faculty inadvertently, through daily actions and thoughts, developing images in the soul that continue on after death. Indeed, according to Böhme this is the nature of hell: that the individual soul configures itself in a given distorted, bestial image that continues on, and is revealed fully, after death. For this reason we are obligated to change ourselves while alive on earth: we are enjoined to turn our imaginative faculty toward chastity, purity, transcendence of all earthly things, because in this state of purity we are able to conform our soul's imagination to the pure and archetypal world.

Böhme leaves no room for doubt about our posthumous state. He warns man to give "himself up to the Obedience of God, and yield his Mind up into God, to strive against malice and wickedness, and the lusts and desires of the flesh, also against all unrighteousness of life and conversation, in humility under the Cross," so that the "eternal Mind figures him in the Image of an Angel, who is pure, chaste, and virtuous, and he keeps this Image in the Breaking of the Body, and hereafter he will be married with the precious Virgin, the eternal Wisdom, Chastity, and paradisical Purity."[3]

We live on earth daily between hell and the kingdom of this world, and our soul's original noble image constantly suffers while on earth, because while on earth we cannot free ourselves wholly from our bestial and hellish wrathful aspect. But we can turn our imaginative faculty toward purity, chastity, humility, and light. For "to whatsoever the mind inclines and gives up itself, in that is the spirit of the soul figured by the eternal *fiat*."[4] Böhme insists upon this point again and again: we create in this lifetime the image that our soul will bear for all eternity. However we discipline our mind by continual concentration, our soul will bear that image after death, for eternity. If we turn our minds toward the virginal angelic light, we bear that image; if we turn toward the wrath, or toward the bestial, we bear that image.

Böhme could not be more explicit:

> Now behold, child of man, (seeing you are an eternal spirit) you have this to expect after the death of your body; you will be either an Angel of God in Paradise, or a hellish ugly diabolical Worm, Beast, or Dragon; all according as you have been inclined here in this Life; that Image which you have borne here in your Mind, with that you shall appear; for no other image can go forth out of your body at death but that which you have borne here—that shall appear in Eternity.[5]

Thus, we must turn our wills toward the divine, and seek to realize our original, angelic, luminous natures, inclining our imaginations into the paradisal realm and striving against our bestial nature until we become restored to the angelic realm while alive, insofar as this is possible.

What is the angelical nature like? It consists in the unity of the angelic imagination and the will of God. Böhme describes the angelic paradise:

> Thus it is with those Angels that continued in the Kingdom of Heaven in the true Paradise: they stand in the first Principle in the indissoluble Band, and their Food is the divine Power; in their Imagination . . . is the Will of the Holy Trinity in the Deity; the Confirmation of their Life, Will, and Doings, is the Power of the Holy Ghost. . . . All they do is an Increasing of the heavenly Joy, and a Delight and Pleasure to the Heart of God, a holy Sport in Paradise . . . to this End their God created them, that he might be manifested, and rejoice in his Creatures . . . so that there might be an eternal Sport of Love, in the Center of the Multiplying (or eternal Nature) in the indissoluble eternal Band.[6]

In other words, God created the angels in order that he might delight in them, and in them know himself, a formulation with direct parallels both in Kabbalism and Sufism. This mysterious participation of the angels in God takes place through their imagination—the faculty by which they know God and his joy, the sport of his love.

Now, every human being possesses this faculty as well. In most of us, however, this imaginative faculty lies dormant, and in its place are earthly preoccupations with venery, acquisition, jealousy, anger, and other confusions. Theosophic discipline, therefore, consists in turning one's mind toward its original, angelic, paradisal image in God. Gichtel, in a letter dated May 24, 1698, wrote of exactly this imaginative discipline in medicinal terms, as expelling poison from the body: "He that wants to drive a poison or disease out of his body, must use a counterpoison, or medicine. Thus he that wants to overcome the wrath in flesh and blood, must by imagination and desire introduce the love into the wrath."[7] Our imagination and desire, in fallen man turned outward toward this world and caught in wrath, must be turned rather toward paradise, so that while alive we live in paradisal love.

Hence Gichtel distinguishes between astral man and the spirit. Man must strive to resist the earthly stimuli that lure the soul and keep man in his astral shell; we must "set our imagination on Christ."[8] Gichtel further explains his school's praxis: "We have . . . received a medicine in the inward man, viz Christ's substantiality, which Böhme calls Sophia, wherein we can set our imagination [and] we can in ourselves comprehend ourselves in Sophia and drive away the devil's poison in body and soul."[9] This poison assails astral man; it cannot touch the angelic or spiritual essence of man, but can obscure or distort it.

Gichtel elaborated on this Sophianic discipline of the imagination, explaining exactly how the imagination can be made to work:

> As soon as in our soul or body the devil moves himself or assails the inward man, the imagination runs to the most sensible place, searching out what the enemy intends . . . calling on the virgin in the heart for assistance.
>
> That takes place either by the evil conjunction and influence of the constellation, or the strife of the elements in the body, in the stomach or other members . . . or by false images or thoughts in the soul or mind.
>
> As soon as we feel this, we curse it, draw our imagination inwards, and set it on Sophia, who immediately enters into the imagination, tinctures the painful spot in the body, and casteth out the devil's poison.
>
> [Though the devil opposes the tincture-fire of the virgin] we do not allow the imagination to go out of Sophia, until the enemy is put to flight and the pains have disappeared.
>
> And if the imagination become too weak, we add prayer and sighs, so that the devil may be arrested, but we must be in earnest.
>
> With this sword we have hitherto, by the strength of Jesus, barely resisted and driven away many an evil influence.[10]

For Gichtel, the imagination is the faculty that perceives Sophia, but it is also the central battleground for the soul, since the imagination must be kept properly focused. Spiritual practice is the constant invocation of Sophia into the imagination in order to drive out poison wherever it occurs, in body or soul.

As in Eastern Orthodoxy—including Russian Orthodoxy—and in Buddhist, Hindu, and Taoist spiritual disciplines, so too in theosophy: spiritual practice is a matter of training the inconstant mind to become focused and constant. What Patanjali said in his famous aphorisms—when mind's activity is controlled, illumination results—Gichtel and the other theosophers also affirmed.[11] For the theosophers, the doctrine of imagination is essentially the science of controlling or focusing the mind, meaning a concentration of the will.

In fact, Gichtel said outright that Adam's Fall came about not through any physical action, but through the imagination. In a letter commenting on Genesis, much in the tradition of Böhme, Gichtel writes "Now Adam did not eat thereof [the fruit of knowledge of good and evil] with his mouth, but with his imagination, and was overcome."[12] Imagination is the soul's capacity to conform to the divine will, or to a perverse, Luciferic will, to unify and ascend, or to divide and to fall. And since Adam fell through imagination, it makes sense that through the same faculty can man rise again from the condition of spiritual death in which he finds himself. This is why Gichtel and his fellow theosophers insist that we must each realize the harrowing of hell and the resurrection into life eternal of Christ—in ourselves. This is an act of imagination, of conforming the soul to its divine archetype in Christ.

Our own resurrection from the dead—our own spiritual rebirth—is accomplished through the holy Virgin Wisdom of God, whose longing for our rebirth is greater than our own. Gichtel affirms this forcefully:

> Our heavenly Virgin is so enamoured of our *limbus* that no man can believe it; but our fickle mind and inconstant will and heart prevent her influence.
>
> And if you are minded to woo her, as indeed I perceive the tinder to be kindled in you, earnestly seize in prayer, praying for a steadfast mind and will, and for the teaching and guidance of the Holy Spirit, because wonderful incidents open themselves, surpassing all reason; never shrink back . . . but let God's word be your comfort and inheritance.
>
> For the Virgin desires to have body, soul, and spirit for her own, to nourish and provide for it herself.[13]

Thus the imagination's discipline is ultimately a matter of concentration sufficient to allow the Virgin Sophia to accomplish the transmutation she longs to accomplish in us. If we never shrink back, but remain steadfast in prayer, we will be spiritually nourished and provided for.

Theosophic discipline of the imagination, therefore, is at heart a matter of holding the mind steady, of remaining faithful to Sophia, who then will accomplish her work in us. This explains the nature of theosophic illustrations such as those accompanying Gichtel's *Eine kurze eröffnung* (*A Brief Opening*) or the complete edition of Böhme's works edited by Gichtel, or, for that matter, the illustrations accompanying Dr.

John Pordage's treatises. All of these illustrations or diagrams reveal simple, archetypal images—the heart, the eye, rays of light through darkness—that "open up" in the soul when concentrated upon.

In Tantric Buddhism, the aspirant visualizes an entire mandala or geometrically organized set of images, or a deity whom he intends to invoke or transform himself into—but this is not exactly the way that the theosophic science of the imagination works. The theosophers, like tantric practitioners, do work on focusing the mind through "prayer without ceasing," similar to Hindu or Buddhist *mantras*, or invocations. However, theosophic illustrations serve not as iconographic images to be perfectly visualized so much as maps of the country to be traversed, or as indications of the stages to pass through.

Moreover, it is not insignificant that while Christ is likened to a sun in the heart-center, and while the Holy Spirit is affiliated with the head, and Sophia with the throat, in theosophic praxis, there are generally no images affiliated with these centers. Disciplining the imagination can make the aspirant a vessel pure enough to house the Virgin Sophia, but she, like the Holy Spirit, and Christ, is generally represented in theosophic diagrams as pure illumination. Images help us in the struggle to overcome attachment to earthly things, but ultimately they must lead us to imagelessness, to transcendence of all things, most of all of the conceptualizations to which we human beings so relentlessly cling.

This is why Gichtel—in some ways our best source because his voluminous letters were written precisely to guide others along the practical path of theosophic discipline—insisted that once the will and the mind become constant and faithful to Sophia, she will accomplish the spiritual transmutation within us. Sophia represents the natural, pristine, primordial Virgin state of our mind before its fall into and attachment to passions and the outward world, its subjugation to astral forces and attractions. This primordial, original state is imageless, above the astral realm and astral man; it is luminous and full of joy; it is divine delight in itself, experienced through its creatures.

Consequently, even though our theosophers use terms of gradual transformation and illumination, what the science of the imagination ultimately reveals is not spiritual power added onto the soul, nor knowledge given to one from without, but the original, luminous state before creation itself. This is our "inheritance," our "birthright," as Gichtel says. It is the esoteric meaning of Christ's parable of the prodigal son, for though it appeared he had lost everything in wandering away in exile, nonetheless he remained a full inheritor of the Kingdom, if only he returned to realize it.

At this point we must consider the nature of the imaginative faculty within theosophy more generally as the means of spiritual revelation. The imagination exists between the archetypal realm of spiritual Forms or Ideas and this earthly world that is but a reflection of the archetypes. The imagination encompasses therefore the field intermediate between the realm of pure luminosity and the physical realm, the "plastic" or "subtle" realm of shifting images, the astral realm. In this realm the soul's purification and transmutation through illumination of the spirit takes place. The imagination cannot be ignored in spiritual discipline; it is precisely the site of our spiritual battles.

When the imagination sets itself on Christ-Sophia, then, it acts as a conduit for spiritual illumination of the astral body, the soul. If the imagination, on the other hand, does not move beyond the astral realm of shifting images and fantasies or influences, then there is no true spiritual discipline, and indeed the soul can become wholly Luciferian, meaning misdirected, perverse. But if the imagination can focus wholly on the transcendent luminous and mysterious power of Sophia, and through this the Holy Spirit can illuminate the astral body, this body, slowly but surely, becomes a vehicle for that spiritual luminosity.

Thus imagination, in theosophy, only has meaning insofar as the imagination breaks beyond the merely astral and serves as a conduit for transcendent illumination, what Dante in "Paradiso" called "rivers of light." It is entirely possible for the imagination to fashion images of Sophia or of divine things, to invest them with a false luminosity, and to bow down and worship what in essence is itself. This is a subtle but profound distinction, and extremely important. For it is one thing to realize that one's spiritual center is a creation of the Divine in order to know himself in himself, and another to create visionary phantoms of the imagination, deceiving oneself by believing in those phenomena as divine manifestations.

But the theosopher must work through the imagination, for just as all creation comes into being "downward" from God through magia (the magical creative power that informs all nature), so man must "ascend" upward through magia again. This is exactly the reversal of the Fall of man. Adam fell through the "will of his desire," and we must be reborn and ascend through the will of our desire for the Divine. This will, write Böhme, Gichtel, and Baader, is magia, the divine creative power, the "original state of Nature" before manifestation in the substantial world. Magia "makes each being according to its will," and thus can appear as good or evil.[14]

According to Edward Taylor, in his *Theosophick Philosophy Unfolded* (1691), "there are two magia's, one of the Unity, the other of the Multiplicity, or Astral Powers. And two Magi in Man, the Spirit of God, and Reason, into the latter the Devil easily insinuates."[15] The astral magia is but the reflection in the subtle world of the divine magia; the soul is naturally inclined to listen to the astral magia, the earthly rational capacity in man, at the expense of the suprarational divine magia, or inspiration. The divine magia is the divine creative power whose matrix is Sophia, divine wisdom. The illuminated theosopher therefore directly sees and in a sense participates in divine creation.

This is why Dr. John Pordage wrote that wisdom "is a revealer of the Mysteries and hidden wonders of the Deity," the images that inform all creation. "As *the office of the Holy Ghost is to effect and create all things*, so the office of Wisdom is to manifest and reveal all things," he continues.[16] The theosophers' penetration beyond astral reason into the divine wisdom means that they see the divine images or "Figures," which "*are not Shadows* and Empty representations, but Reall and Substantial." They are "not only figures of Heavenly things, *but* the Heavenly things themselves."[17] These images are filled by the "fullness of the Living God" with "Life and Spirit and Power."

Consequently, to return to our Gnostic theme of returning homeward, we can see how exactly it is that Böhme and the other theosophers could write with such authority of what will happen after death to the individual, and after Judgment Day to all creation. According to them, they had penetrated beyond the astral into the angelic and timeless realm and had perceived it in their imaginative faculty, had seen it with the eyes of the spirit, heard it with spiritual ears, felt it with all their spiritual senses, through a spiritual body. For the theosophers, as for the early Christian Gnostics, this world is a kind of exile, and all creation itself "groans in travail" in exile from its joyous, eternal spiritual archetypes in heaven.

Böhme is very specific about this. In his *Of the Supersensual Life*, he writes that after individual death, as after Judgment Day, "the gross earth" and the "gross flesh of man shall perish" and only "spiritual flesh and blood" will remain. The "good virtue of the mortal body shall come again and live forever in a kind of transparent crystalline material property," "as shall return also the good virtue of the earth, for the earth likewise shall become crystalline, and the divine light shine in everything that has a being, essence, or substance."[18] In short:

> When the visible world perishes, then all that has come out of it, and has been external, shall perish with it. There shall remain of the world only the heavenly crystalline nature and form, and of man also only the spiritual earth; for man shall be then wholly like the spiritual world, which as yet is hidden.[19]

This hidden spiritual world the theosopher knows intimately through spiritual imagination.

We need to note here one central characteristic of the spiritual world according to theosophy: in the present world we can speak of man in the world; but in the spiritual world we must speak of that world *in man*. The spiritual world exists within angelic man, so his "outward" surroundings reflect his inward nature. This is partly what Böhme means when he writes that "man shall be then wholly like the spiritual world." These "spiritual landscapes" that conform to one's inward nature are eternal by comparison to fleeting earthly life; in them manifest our spiritual works during our lifetime, our spiritual condition.

According to theosophy, then, selfhood and selfishness are like a shell we build around ourselves, separating ourselves from the divine will. To do this is the nature of fallen man; we wish to preserve and augment ourselves at all costs. Spiritual practice consists at first in striving to gain something; we look outside ourselves and fantasize that divine power exists elsewhere; we look for God without, and seek for some special experience that marks a wholly new self. All this only increases our selfishness, however. Only when, Johannes Kelpius wrote in *A Method of Prayer*, we are able to give up all outward searching and let ourselves sink inward toward the divine will, do we begin on the spiritual path in earnest.

According to theosophy, when we have truly begun to see the illusion of selfhood, and recognized that we are already living in hell—in the anguish of dividedness and confusion—we can begin to overcome our selfishness and our spiritual imagination begin to perceive the archetypal realm of its paradise. Jacob Böhme explains this in the form of a dialogue between a distressed soul, who longs for God, and an enlightened soul. The enlightened soul tells the other that "you bear the monstrous shape of the devil, and are clothed therewith." You are, he says, already in hell. To break free, "you shall do nothing at all but forsake your own will, that is, that which you call I."[20]

The soul must give up selfishness and sink its own will into God. Only then shall the soul begin to lose the demonic creatures that cling to it, its devilish "covering," and its evil inclinations begin to wither away.

This happens by a gradual illumination, the slow penetration of the soul by light, in which the creatures of darkness cannot survive. When the soul depends wholly upon God for its sustenance, it arrives at length "to a high state or degree of grace; and the gates of the divine revelation, and the kingdom of heaven, are opened to and manifested in it."[21] The kingdom of heaven is manifested in the soul—the soul does not "enter" heaven so much as heaven is manifested in the soul via its imagination.

So let us sum up what we have said on the theosophic doctrine of imagination. Contrary to the meaning the word *imagination* has generally taken on, for theosophers imagination refers both to the soul's capacity to generate images or concepts, (astral reason) and to the soul's capacity to perceive spiritual reality. According to the theosophers, spiritual discipline means breaking through the astral shell that our selfishness creates around us and penetrating into the transcendent light of spiritual reality. Here the soul perceives within itself through spiritual imagination the spiritual world, the celestial earth of its own nature. This is eternal paradise, and Böhme warns us we must realize it in this lifetime. As we have seen, then, theosophic spirituality is indeed a discipline of the imagination, in a very particular sense. According to the Böhmean tradition, what matters in religion is not outward forms of religion, but inward experience. This inward experience comes via the imagination, our faculty for perceiving spiritual reality within, for overcoming our fallen nature and becoming illuminated. In short, in theosophy we find discipline that speaks directly to the heart by way of our innate imaginative faculty, our eye in the heart.

CHAPTER FOURTEEN

The Eye
in the Heart

I was first directly confronted with the image of the eye in the heart when reading through Dr. John Pordage's treatise entitled *Theologia Mystica* (1683), a wonderful introduction to the spiritual path of eighteenth-century theosophers or followers in the path of Jacob Böhme. This image, simply drawn, shows an eye in a heart aflame, and its purity is very powerful. The image has remained with me ever since, and although I have subsequently seen the image in many illustrations and works, this first glimpse remained the most hauntingly evocative, perhaps because of its sheer simplicity. In fact this image of the eye and the heart recurs throughout Böhmean mysticism, and is a key to the entire theosophic tradition, particularly the seventeenth-century English school.

Of course, the image of the heart is characteristic of Christianity in general, and plays an important role in devotional traditions such as the "cult of the sacred heart" in Roman Catholicism. I would hardly argue that the image of the eye in the heart is unique to the Protestant theosophic movement of the seventeenth and eighteenth centuries. Indeed, its power comes in part precisely because it is archetypal. Found or implicit in Roman Catholic and Eastern Orthodox iconography and writings, this image resonates very deeply within us—Orthodox images of the Virgin, for instance, often show the Christ child with his head and eyes precisely at the level of the Virgin's heart, while she is clad in a crimson robe.

This iconography appears in Dante's work too. In his *La Vita Nuova*, the collection of poetry and narrative in which Dante tells of his relationship to the angelic woman Beatrice, the images of eyes and heart recur in different combinations time and time again. Indeed, after one pays close attention to the ways the images of eyes and heart reappear in this poem, one eventually begins to suspect that the work as a whole is nothing less than a visionary recital of Dante's spiritual transmutation revealed in exactly the way the eyes and the heart are referred to by the poet, as in the sonnet "The eyes that weep for pity of the heart" (XXXII). Interestingly, like the Virgin, Beatrice wears a crimson robe when first Dante sees her, and again when he sees her in vision after her death (XL).[1]

During the seventeenth and eighteenth centuries, the image of the heart became extremely prominent in both Catholic and Protestant iconography. However, it is sometimes hard to tell to what tradition a given series of engravings featuring the heart belongs. One finds that some series of engravings showing the heart in various stages of transmutation (being swept out and purified, aflame, being crowned, for examples) appeared in both Catholic and Protestant books with different sets of commentary or verses. And how does one categorize the *Herzensspiegel* (*Mirror of the Heart*), a work attributed to fourteenth-century mystic Johannes Tauler, who, although he was certainly himself Catholic, was enormously influential for the Protestant theosophic movement?[2] Although today we might like to make firm boundaries between Catholic and Protestant spiritual works and art, in reality such boundaries during the seventeenth and eighteenth century were by no means clear.

For example, Lutheran Divine Daniel Cramer published in his *Emblemata sacra* (1624) a series of fifty emblems in which the heart underwent various trials, being weighed on scales, crowned with thorns, lit with a torch, and so forth.[3] In 1629 Father B. van Haeften published his *Schola Cordis* in Antwerp, a work which was based on Cramer and added the figures of Anima and Love. And in 1645, Francesco Pona published his *Cardiomorphoseos* in Verona, Italy, comprising one hundred cardiomorphic emblems.[4] There are in fact countless examples of such emblematic series featuring the heart during this time, almost indifferently Catholic or Protestant.

But there are some emblematic cardiomorphic series that are definitely of the theosophic school of Jacob Böhme. One of these, already mentioned, is the *Hellerleuchtender Herzensspiegel* (*Illuminated Heart's*

Mirror) (Amsterdam, 1680), with a commentary attributed to Johannes Tauler and illustrations by Nicholas Häublin. The connection to Tauler here as in other manuscripts and books of the time firmly links the seventeenth-century German Protestant mysticism of Jacob Böhme's school with its Catholic fourteenth-century predecessors.[5] However, the *Herzensspiegel*'s primary significance lies in how it embodies in illustrations a process of spiritual revelation through images.

The *Herzensspiegel* begins by showing the conflict between wrath and love—the fundamental forces of darkness and light central to the Böhmean cosmology—and by showing the heart being bound in darkness. But the heart is soon illumined by eyes, and though later in the series of images the heart is shown in dominion over all things, it is still separated into an upper and a lower heart, still in a process of purification. In Figure XI, we see a figure kneeling and praying, his eyes connected to Christ before him by a simple line, another line connecting his mouth to the house, the animals, the plow, a nearby ship, food and drink—in short, we see the praying man blessing everything in his world through Christ. Although in subsequent illustrations the heart is attacked by the devil and wrath, this wrath is eventually integrated, and the final illustration shows a serpent below a lamb with a book and seven candles, all within a heart.

The process we see in this series of illustrations—the commentary to which is attributed by some to friends of Jacob Böhme himself, perhaps Paul Kaym or Abraham Franckenberg—is a visual representation of what we find in the written theosophic works of the time.[6] For theosophy is nothing less than the transmutation of the individual soul, its purification and illumination. This process is not merely an intellectual game, but an actual inward process that entails much struggle and suffering, as we see in Gichtel's letters, collected in the massive seven-volume series *Theosophica Practica* (Leiden: 1722, 3rd. ed.).

In fact, very specific aspects of the heart-images were reflected in the lives of the theosophers, particularly the images showing wrath and the devil's attacks. For nearly every one of the theosophers passed through the wrath of public attack by irate clergy or lay people. Böhme himself was relentlessly attacked for his mysticism by Gregorius Richter, the local Lutheran pastor, and after Böhme's death his gravestone was defiled; likewise, Johann Georg Gichtel was driven from his native Germany by clergy; Dr. John Pordage was driven from his church position in 1654; and so forth. The conflict between wrath and love, the spiritual struggle depicted in these illustrations, was part of daily life.

Similar patterns can be seen in the lives of those who produced other books of illustrations. In 1736, Christian Hoburgh published his *Levendige Herts-theologie* (*Living Heart-theology*), a series of emblems showing the heart's purification and illumination by Christ. Emblematic titles include "Here Jesus sings in the heart," and "Here Jesus wounds the heart," or "Here Jesus crowns the heart." Hoburgh (1607–1675) constantly attacked "Babel," the Böhmean word for external or outward religion, and, driven from one clerical position to another, lived mainly in abject poverty. *Levendige Herts-theologie* reveals the difficult path that apparently Hoburgh himself sought to follow.

Many of the diagrams and illustrations that accompany primary theosophic writings such as those of Jacob Böhme or Thomas Bromley, however, are not in a series, but rather include an entire process and cosmology in a single work. For example, the illustration accompanying the only work Jacob Böhme ever himself saw into print, *Christosophia: The Way to Christ*, shows a heart rooted in the earth, around which are entwined a dragon and a serpent, and above which is a weeping eye in a flaming sun that in turn is anchored to an illuminating cross, topped by an eagle with wings outstretched. The illustration cites Joel 2.12, 13, which urges turning your heart toward the divine kindness.[7]

In this illustration, we see the stage of separation and purification, of spiritual struggle, which is after all the subject of *Christosophia*. The heart and the eye in the flaming sun are not united, the eye is weeping, and the lower sphere of the heart is held to the cross by a rope and anchor, all of which implies that one should hold to the transcendent light and penetrate the clouds that separate us from it. The verse from Matthew refers to taking heaven by force, which has been done from the days of John the Baptist until now. Spiritual work is difficult, this illustration suggests.

Probably the most beautiful, and certainly my favorite of these illustrations is that which accompanied Thomas Bromley's *The Way to the Sabbath of Rest* (1678/1710). Bromley, like his friend and fellow theosopher Dr. John Pordage, was a working theosopher whose writings came out of personal experience.[8] Pordage's treatises—only two of which are available in English—are among the most accessible of all Böhmean theosophic writing. Lucid and straightforward, with almost no exotic terminology, Pordage's treatises offer keys into theosophic visionary or imaginal work. And Bromley's work continues this tradition, *The Way to the Sabbath of Rest* later becoming quite influential for American theosophic communities.

We are definitely here considering a visionary discipline of the imagination. Bromley and Pordage were part of a circle of theosophic practitioners who lived in or near London from the mid-1600s through the early
1700s—Pordage died in 1681, Bromley in 1698, but their circle continued
for some time after. This group, some members of which later became
known as the Philadelphians, were adamantly nonsectarian Christians
who strove to lead extremely pure lives, and who practiced a science of the
imagination that led not only to visionary experiences, but also to spiritual transmutation and illumination as seen in the many writings of Jacob
Böhme, who may be considered as the founder of this school.

The Way to the Sabbath of Rest takes us along the theosophic path,
which is in no small part also a visionary path involving the training of
the imagination. Bromley tells us that we are "strictly to watch over the
Phantasie, which may easily err in this particular [being drawn to pleasant images]." It must "as much as possible [be] reduced in Subjection to
the illuminated Understanding." Eventually one transcends images and
is able to "cease from all Imagination," although Bromley warns that
this is only for those who have attained "constant intellectual Sight and
Apprehension of God," else this ceasing of thought and image will be
but a "fall into a Kind of Stupidity."[9]
Eventually,

> Imagination being now overcome, and the animal Man mor-
> tified, the Soul cannot but clearly discover its Growth in the
> Image of God, and the Resurrection of the angelical Man,
> which now evidently perceives itself springing up in a new
> Principle, above the Spirit of the World and its mixt Laws.[10]

In this new principle, the laws of time and distance are transcended,
Bromley tells us, and we join a spiritual community in which we can feel
the sufferings and joys of others from afar. Like Christ's disciples, those
in this community feel "their Hearts to burn within them" and "reach
those that are far absent; because it is not corporeal, nor subject to the
Laws of Place or Time."[11]
This struggle is not easy. Bromley writes: "We must know, that in
our Progress, we may many Times be cast into Terror and Anguish; yea
feel Hell awakened in us, and afterwards be delivered by some influence
of Christ's Spirit, and infusions of his Love."[12] Nonetheless, the soul
"turns its Eyes from Nature" to Eternity, and it begins to smell the Paradisal "delightful Odours," which infuse themselves into the Tincture of
the Heart. And eventually, "The Soul being brought thus far in the

Heart-work by the Power of Jesus," the will is "constantly drawn toward the Heart of God."[13]

Bromley distinguishes between the "Head-work" and the "Heart-work," which refer to stages of spiritual awakening seen in the illustration. He writes that in "Openings in the Head," the "inward senses of hearing and seeing are resident," while in a heart-opening one directly experiences what one sees, for

> whatever in a divine Sight (Eternity opening in the Head) we clearly and distinctly view and behold, the same (in a Heart-Opening) we really feel and handle in a spiritual Way; for in it we come experimentally to know and percieve the Motions and administering Influences of Angels.[14]

This process of transmutation appears to be: one first sees the eternal with the inward eyes, and then actually experiences the eternal with the heart.

Exactly this transmutative process appears in the illustration that accompanies Bromley's book. The illustration shows three spheres: the dark sphere of "Sathan," the astral realm including sun, moon, and constellations, and the illuminated sphere of Sophia, above. Within these spheres are three crosses: below is a dark cross, in the center of which is the seed of a stalk, around which is a spiral. Here begins the work, rising up toward the light. In the middle is a cross with an eye in its center, symbolizing the intermediate stage of "Head-work" in which one sees Eternity but does not inwardly experience it. Above is the white cross within which is the eye in the heart, the experiential culmination of the theosophic work, topped by the head of what may be wheat in the blinding light of Sophia, Virgin of Wisdom.

We may regard these treatises, and the illustrations that accompany them, as so many clues to the actual science that Pordage, Bromley, and their circle practiced. In this light, Pordage's treatise *Theologia Mystica*—published posthumously in 1683 by Jane Leade, Edward Hooker, and other members of the circle—particularly helps us understand what these theosophers meant by the symbolism of the eye in the heart. For in *Theologia Mystica*, Pordage leads us through a particular series of images in what he calls the "Globe of Eternity." He speaks, for example, of an "Outward Court," an "Inward Court," and an "Inmost Court," the "Holiest place of all."[15]

Pordage, like Bromley, speaks of the opening of the inner eye. He writes: "Now the Eye opening divides it self into three parts, the first of which is the Abyssal Eye, the second is the Heart, and the third is the outflowing Breath."[16] The mysterious unity in trinity of these three reflects the mysterious unity in trinity of God Himself. And when this eye opens,

> This sight of God's attributes . . . in the Abyssal Globe, is both a ravishing and amazing sight, for you do not behold Ideas or Similitudes of things, but the things themselves intellectually, which causeth most inexpressible joys and extasies in the Spirit of the Soul, to which nothing in this world can be compared.[17]

To see, here, is to experience; there is a unity between seer and the vision here that manifests in joy.

It is clear that Bromley and Pordage are describing the same process of illumination, but their accounts focus on different aspects of it. In fact, reading the letters, manuscripts, and books that remain of this school—for, alas, many have apparently been destroyed or lost—one realizes that each one of these authors has gone through a similar process in a very individual way.[18] Leade, Pordage, Bromley, Hooker, each speaks in similar language, using the same symbols—but the angle of approach is slightly different in each case. Apparently there is a process or series of experiences of something greater than each individual, which each person can approach and experience uniquely.

Above all, this image of the eye in the heart reminds us that under consideration here is not abstract intellectual speculation, but direct experience. The theosophers wrote about what each had directly witnessed, not just with the eyes, but with the heart as well. These potent symbols are universal and simple, reflecting the theosophers' desire to return to Christian origins, and their refusal, in many cases, of any sectarian affiliation whatever. In the end, perhaps the symbol of the eye in the heart can best be described as clear vision in love.

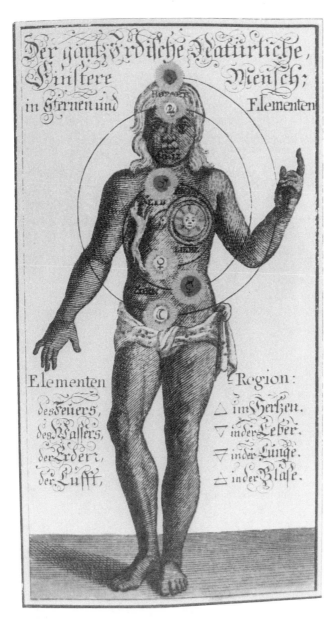

PLATE 1. "Earthly, Darkened Man," from Johann Georg
Gichtel, *Eine kurze Eröffnung und Anwesung der drei Prinzipien und Welten im Menschen* (Leipzig: 1696). Here we see the
planetary energies in fallen humanity, manifesting as anger,
envy, and so forth.

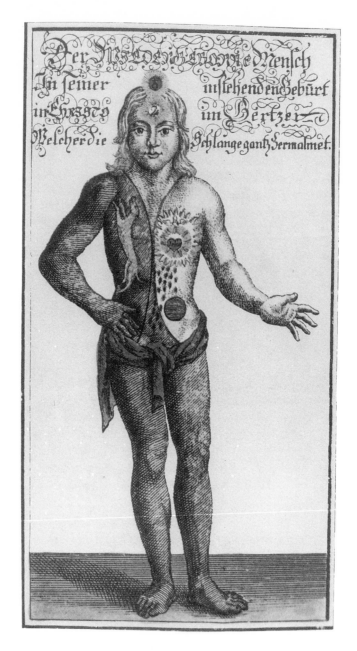

PLATE 2. "Awakening Man," from Gichtel, *Eine kurze Eröffnung*, 1696. An individual on the spiritual path, engaged in spiritual struggle.

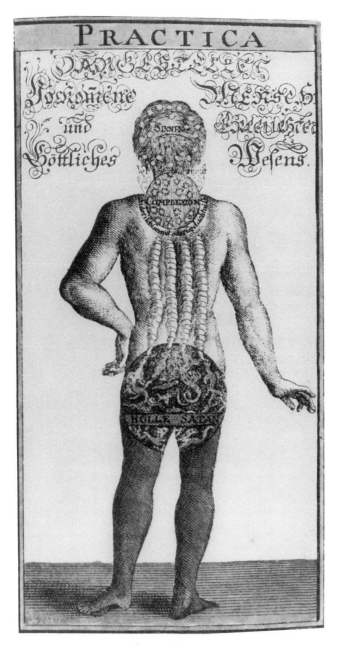

PLATE 3. "Theosophic Man," rear view, from Gichtel, *Eine kurze Eröffnung*, 1696. In this image, we see the process of transforming fallen energies.

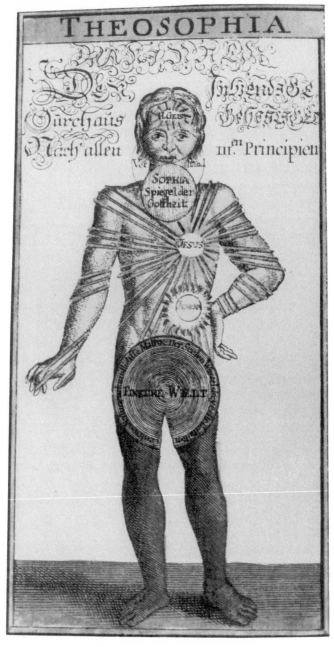

PLATE 4. "Theosophic Man," front view, from Gichtel, *Eine kurze Eröffnung*, 1696. Illuminated humanity.

PLATE 5. Frontispiece illustration from Thomas Bromley, *The Way to the Sabbath of Rest* (London: 1650; Germantown, Pa.: C. Sower, 1759). Notice the eye in the heart at top.

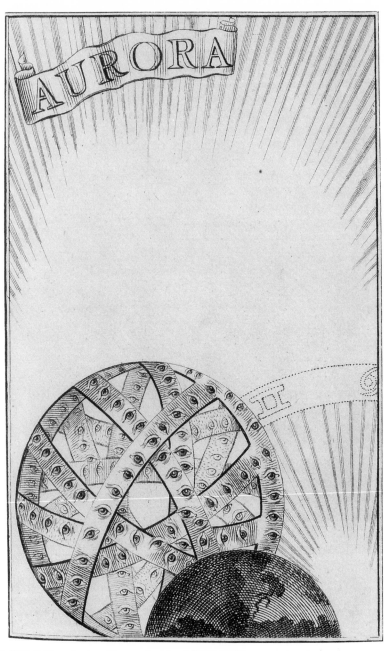

PLATE 6. Frontispiece illustration from Jacob Böhme, *Aurora*, from *Theosophia Revelata*, edited by Johann Georg Gichtel, 1730.

PLATE 7. Frontispiece illustration from Jacob Böhme, *The Way to Christ*, from *Theosophia Revelata*, edited by Johann Georg Gichtel, 1730. Notice the proximity, but not yet union, of the eye and the heart.

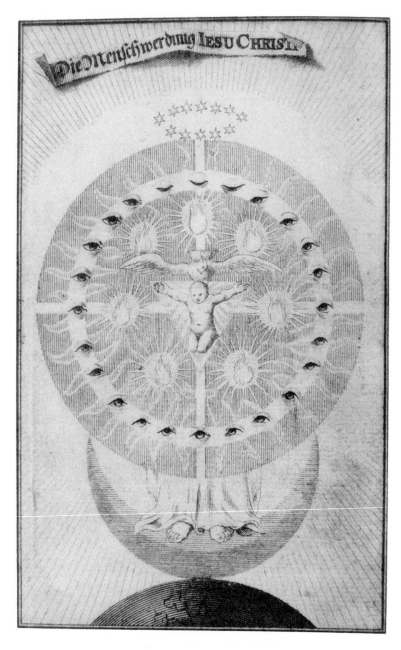

PLATE 8. The frontispiece for Jacob Böhme's *Menschwerdung Jesu Christi*, or *The Becoming-Human of Christ*, from *Theosophia Revelata*, edited by Johann Georg Gichtel, 1730.

CHAPTER FIFTEEN

The Physiology
of the Soul

Many readers will have heard of *chakras*, the Sanskrit word for energy centers in the body, awakened during certain yogic practices. Some will have heard, too, of how the *sephira* in the Tree of Life in Jewish Kabbalism correspond in some ways to the symbolism of the *chakras* of Tantric disciplines. A few may have run across references to the subtle physiology recognized in Islam, particularly in Ismaili Sufism. But almost no one, one could wager, will have heard of esoteric physiology within Christianity, still less of such an understanding in, of all places, Protestant Christianity during the eighteenth century in Europe. But in fact, as we shall see, theosophy too has its subtle and spiritual physiology.

Perhaps we should begin by pointing out the fundamental differences between the traditional Christian understanding of how the body, the soul, and spirit are interrelated, and the modern perspective. Modern science is interested in physiology as mechanism—extremely complex mechanism, perhaps, but ultimately as mechanism. Modern medicine works chiefly on the body; one finds occasional recent attempts at medical psychology, but on the whole modern physiological sciences have been chiefly concerned with physical chemistry and other ultimately reductionist analytical methods. By contrast, traditional Chris-

tianity—by which I mean Christianity that holds to a tripartite understanding of the human being as microcosm—inverts this hierarchy: most
important is spirit, then soul, and the body is a vehicle.

Traditionally, both in Western and Eastern Christianity, we can discern an emphasis upon the tripartite human nature, and on the necessity
for subordinating the demands of the body to the proper ordering of
pacified soul and illuminated spirit. This is the essential ascetic struggle,
not to reject the body but to use it, to live fully through it, and not only
to live virtuously but, even more, to realize while in the body the soul's
pacification and the spirit's illumination in love. Modern people tend to
value the body more than the soul, and soul more than spirit; the ascetic
reverses this order, placing the body last—not neglecting it, or abusing
it, but not indulging it either.

Böhmean theosophy, as we have seen time and again, consists in an
intention to return to the apostolic church in its purity as a circle of spiritual friends. The theosophers enjoined chastity and control of the body
not because they despised or abused the body, but because they felt that
only in this way could the body be a proper, nonobtrusive vehicle for
spiritual realization on earth. One who is caught in the cycle of desire is
therefore unable to focus on spiritual illumination; this is why ascetics
in general, and theosophers as well, often go into retreat. When one is
no longer bombarded by the demands of a society bent on encouraging
accumulation and on intensifying desires, one is freed to focus wholeheartedly on spirituality, often among others who have also so dedicated
themselves, like the apostles.

When we look to the *Philokalia*, the collection of Eastern Orthodox
writings on asceticism and spiritual praxis, we find what amounts to a
handbook of spiritual psychology. St. Maximos the Confessor, for
instance, writes that it is important to cut off the passions by "appropriate detachment from those things by which they are roused." One
cuts off attachment to wealth by frugality, to fame by inward practice of
the virtues—but "only he who has renounced the impassioned conceptual images of these things had made a monk of the inner self, the intellect." What matters most is to be "completely freed from impassioned,
conceptual images."[1] Thus, "cleanse your intellect from anger, rancour,
and shameful thoughts, and you will be able to perceive the indwelling
of Christ."[2] Spiritual psychology is more important than asceticism,
which "has only a limited use."[3]

Similar advice is found among the great medieval Roman Catholic
mystics Meister Eckhart and Johannes Tauler, who were very influential

for the Protestant theosophers. Meister Eckhart begins his 22nd Sermon by saying "When I preach it is my wont to speak about detachment and how man should rid himself of self and all things."[4] Indeed, Eckhart spends most of his time discussing exactly how one enters and maintains a state of detachment and overcomes the passions. Likewise, Johannes Tauler—Eckhart's near-contemporary—wrote that because of the Fall, the soul is inclined outward toward time and transitory things, away from eternity. Thus, "We can see now that a reversal must necessarily take place if . . . a birth is to occur. There must be a definite introversion, a gathering up, an inward collection of faculties without any dispersal, for in unity lies strength. . . . And this is the introversion we are speaking of." We must meet God "in complete abandonment of self."[5]

It is no surprise that among the manuscripts circulated in theosophic groups in Germany, the Netherlands, and England were works attributed to Johannes Tauler. Indeed, German Roman Catholic mysticism and Eastern Orthodox mysticism were deeply influential for the Protestant theosophers, who often appended to their own works references or quotations from the Eastern desert fathers, and from German mystics such as Tauler. Appended to some of Dionysius Andreas Freher's manuscripts, for instance, we find "The Life and Doctrine of Brother Nicolaus the Hermite," and "A Short Dialogue Between a Learned Divine and a Beggar," attributed to Tauler.[6]

These are remarkable documents, above all for what they reveal the theosophers thought important. Brother Nicolaus the Hermite was a medieval ascetic who miraculously lived for many years without eating; he lived, rather as many Tibetan Buddhist ascetics reputedly have, on prayer and meditation. His asceticism was not starvation, but complete transcendence of the body while alive. The short dialogue between the beggar and the divine, who "if we may believe the ancient Copies was John Taulerus himself," tells the story of how a medieval divine was "inflamed with a most vehement desire" to experience God, going many nights without sleep, lost in prayer, and finally was told by heaven to go to his church doors, where he met a beggar.

The beggar was a more realized spiritual person than the divine, and told the divine that whatever happened to him, whatever the beggar suffered, "agreeable or otherwise, sweet or bitter, I gladly received it at [God's] hands as the best." Thus, like Eckhart and Tauler, the beggar preached detachment and humility, the fruit of which is peace and power. Further, the beggar tells the divine, "I can now, and do by his power in me, so govern and command all my inward and outward senses, that all the affections and powers of the old man in my soul are conquered and are in subjection to me; Which Kingdom no man can doubt but is better than all the Kingdoms and Glories of this World." "What hath brought thee to this perfection?" asked the divine. "My silence, sublime Meditation, and union with the ever-blessed God of peace and rest," the beggar replies.[7]

That such works, drawing on medieval Catholic spirituality, were circulating among the theosophers shows that they drew from earlier Christian mystical traditions their essence, the emphasis on transcendence of the body and on inward detachment. We see this emphasis reflected in theosophic treatises and especially in their practices, which included frequent and prolonged prayer, retreats, and extended meditation as requisite for visionary revelations, even though visions themselves came as unanticipated gifts. I draw attention to these practices, and the doctrines of detachment that inform them, because all of these entail a profound, detailed spiritual psychology.

But we will focus here on a central aspect of that psychology, meaning the symbolism of the planets and their affiliation with particular bodily centers. Planetary symbolism has traditionally had implications not only for the macrocosm, including herbs, animals, and minerals, but for the microcosm, for the human being. According to the doctrine of signatures, everything in creation reflects planetary symbolism or qualities: fiery, red things reflect the symbolism of Mars, silvery, watery things reflect lunar symbolism, and so forth. This is also true of the human body.

In fact, the only Christian illustrations of which I am aware that depict both the planetary symbolism of the human body and its relationship to the entire process of spiritual transmutation are found accompanying a treatise published by Johann Georg Gichtel in 1696. The first of these illustrations shows the unregenerate *finstere mensch*, or "dark man," who is wholly subject to his earthly nature. In this illustration we see a spiral extending inward from the top of the head (Saturn), down through the hand and arm to the lower abdomen (the moon), up through the forehead (Jupiter), down to the umbilical region (Mercury), up to the upper chest (Mars), down to the solar plexus (Venus), and finally around to the heart (the sun). In the abdomen is anger, in the chest is jealousy, in the head is ambition or greed, and in the heart is love. Opposite the heart in the chest is a dog, symbolizing desire, the animal self.

This illustration shows man in the unregenerate state, meaning that in it we see the spiral forces of emotions; man is subject to his elemental self. The heart is associated with fire, the liver is linked with water, earth is related to the lungs, and air to the bladder. These are the seats of elemental man, and the planetary symbolism of the body also has an elemental significance. The moon is below, related to the generative organs, which are traditionally affiliated with water; the heart is affiliated with the sun, and is traditionally the body's center, associated also with love. But we will note that in unregenerate man, the heart is encircled by a serpent; the sun-heart is naturally golden and illuminating, dry and warm, but it is surrounded in unregenerate man by the cold and damp serpent. Unregenerate man is prisoner to emotional reactions, to desire, jealousy, and anger.

We should note, too, that the planetary symbolism is linked in a particular order; it follows a spiral path that moves from the sun (masculine) to Venus (feminine) to Mars (masculine), and so forth, following the spiral outward. Thus, the spiral path follows a natural polarity both inward and outward, an astrological polarity that corresponds, not incidentally, to the zodiacal polarity that also moves, in general, from masculine to feminine to masculine as one circles the zodiac. We also should point out that this "dark man" bears love in his breast; he is capable of love, but has not yet realized this potential in himself. To realize it, he must turn anger into love; he must transmute negative emotions into positive ones.

Finally, we should recognize that the seven planets, here, correspond to the seven forms or emanations of eternal nature. Man can only realize or comprehend the seven forms of eternal nature because he possesses in himself their reflection in the planetary qualities, just as the seven planets themselves are their reflection in the cosmos. Thus, fallen or unregenerate man possesses *in potentia* spiritual reality within himself. But the clouds of emotional reaction and desire obscure this in him; and he must strive to realize actually what is only virtual in him. The four illustrations depict this striving.

The second of the illustrations shows man in a partially regenerated state. His body is now only partly subject to the *finstere welt*, or "dark world." The dog, representing his animal nature, is now turned outward, away from the heart, and the serpent no longer encircles the sun-heart, which now drops blood downward. The heart, inscribed "Jesus," shows an eagle or phoenix (or, most likely, a dove, representing the Holy Spirit) rising out of its luminescence, and below the heart the only planet visible is Mercury, which receives the blood. Above we can see Jupiter in the forehead, and, at the crown, Saturn, represented by a cross upon a globe, a traditional Hermetic symbol for wisdom. In the illustration as a whole we see man striving toward spiritual illumination.

The final two illustrations in this series depict illuminated, regenerated man front and back. So we can say that although there are four illustrations, the third and fourth form aspects of one illustration, meaning that there are only three stages. We might add that this numerical relationship corresponds to the Trinity plus Sophia, who complements Christ and does not actually make a fourth to the Trinity. The illustration showing regenerated man from behind has below, in the generative region, hell and Satan. Thus, man is never wholly freed from the dark region's influences, as shown by lines of smoke that reach up from below. But above we see three circles near the head: below is "*Complexion*," in the middle is "*Vernunft*," or "reason," and above is "*Sinne*," or "intellectual sense." The head itself is dotted with stars; here, man is no longer subject only to the planetary influences, or "astral region," but has broken beyond this limitation.

The most important of all these illustrations is the third, which shows illuminated man from the front. Here the sun-heart (Jesus) has illuminated the whole being; his rays penetrate the entire being. Where before was Mercury, now is Jehova, and above, where before were Jupiter and Saturn, is the Holy Spirit. In the region of the throat is Sophia, the play of the Godhead. The dark region still exists, but it is constrained to the generative region, and the process of transmutation has gone as far as it can while one is alive and has a body with its inherent demands. Here the planetary symbolism is transposed into a wholly religious meaning; what before was negative, now is illuminated and positive.

Thus, these illustrations do not show the exact equivalent of *chakras*, by any means, nor is it especially useful to think of them in that way. Comparative religion only goes so far. Much more useful is to stay within the Christian tradition itself, perhaps with sidelong glances toward Islamic and Jewish esotericism where these can help illuminate our given subject. There is some danger of distorting particular spiritual disciplines and cosmologies if we approach them with, for example, kundalini yoga in mind when nothing of the sort applies in the actual tradition at which we are looking. Theosophy is not a tantric discipline, nor is tantrism especially helpful in explaining Gichtel's illustrations here.

More useful is the cosmology manifested in earlier Christian works like the *Divine Comedy* of Dante. Now the *Divine Comedy* is clearly a visionary recital that has direct parallels in Islam: it is Dante's recital of his visionary journey through the entire cosmos, an individual vision, to be sure, and an individual journey among people whom Dante would recognize, and with guides that are especially suited to Dante himself, but nonetheless through terrain that each of us could traverse, from hell through purgatory to paradise. This visionary journey is marked by precise astrological and planetary symbolism, so that each level of his ascent is affiliated with a particular planetary quality. This make sense when we consider that the outward journey of Dante is really an inward journey reflected outward in visionary terrain, for the planets represent qualities or states within each of us.

When we look at the text accompanying Gichtel's illustrations, we find that the illustrations are indeed meant to depict aspects of a spiritual awakening within a Christian context, and that although Gichtel definitely does not offer us a visionary recital like that of Dante, he is nonetheless insistent that we must undertake an inward journey and process of spiritual realization. Thus, Gichtel writes at the beginning of his chapter on "natural man":

> When the wisdom-loving reader seeks God in his wonders, and wishes to see his hidden Trinity in himself, he must contemplate all things in himself, must learn to experience in himself the threefold birth and life; he must come to know God's eternal likeness and image is in himself, according to the dark, fire, and light-worlds.[8]

Gichtel, like all the theosophers, emphasizes the inward nature of the spiritual journey much more than, say, a Muslim theosopher such as Ibn Sina, or an earlier Christian theosopher such as Dante, for whom the inward journey takes on an outward, dreamlike form.

But we should recognize that Gichtel's inward journey is not solipsistic; he affirms that we must see the dark, fire, and light realms in ourselves, but those worlds are not the creation of the theosopher's fantasy. Rather—and I suspect this is the result of historical necessity—the Christian theosophers of the modern era like Gichtel are well aware that because the modern age is intrinsically different than the medieval traditional world, man experiences spiritual realities in a more "psychological" way. In the medieval era Dante traversed the whole of the Catholic Christian cosmology in a visionary journey, but in a modern world of scientistic materialism, spiritual realities are recognized more as inward visions.

This recognition is made emblematic in our illustrations here, which are after all of an individual. The theosophic journey—and this is as true of Dante's visionary recital as of the many Muslim and Christian visionary recitals—is always individual, always unique, while being also part of a larger tradition. This continuity in experience is indeed what makes a tradition, and because of it we can speak of a theosophic tradition, which is a particular spiritual discipline. Thus, anyone who enters theosophy will experience certain general realities, but in a unique or individualized way. Dante saw in hell those he knew; it was hell, but it was his hell and their hells he traversed, just as it was his paradise and their paradises.

And so the theosophic journey entails revelations of subtle physiology unique for each individual, while conforming to certain general patterns. Each individual is governed, according to theosophy, by a particular astral "constellation" or combination of astrological influences. Thus a given individual may be inclined toward rage, while another is very much inclined toward luxury and venereal excess. Such tendencies are in fact reflections of particular planetary combinations, and so it is necessary to understand such astral constellations in order to "diagnose" other people, but even more important in order to understand oneself. One has to understand how to counterbalance a given tendency with its "antidote."

The great Renaissance Platonist physician and magus Marsilio Ficino explained this "planetary medicine" at great length in his treatises and letters, and practiced it both in his own life and as a spiritual advisor to others. Ficino practiced a kind of sympathetic magic found throughout history and in countless cultures, according to which when a given planetary tendency grew too powerful—say, Saturn, with its tendency toward melancholy and darkness—he would counter it with the golden light of the sun, with golden jewelry and flowers, with light clothing and walks out of doors.

Gichtel, like Ficino, used to play music in the evening because the audible harmonies helped restore the soul's harmony and gave him joy. The harmonies of the strings reflect and invoke the harmonies of the spheres; music has always been recognized as being invocation too, as, in the Greek tradition, Pythagoras and Orpheus attest. Thus, Gichtel wrote that "The sensual music, dear Mr. B., bringeth me to the supersensual, though apprehensible to few," so "from my youth upwards I have had a great liking for music."[9] As early as 1676 Gichtel wrote, "For I am all day like a string stretched on the bow, and shared in strife with

Satan and his hosts; then in the evening I devote one hour to music," implying that music transcends earthly strife and even death.[10]

Ficino and Gichtel also shared a particular emphasis upon understanding the influence of Saturn, that planet, we will recall, identified with the crown of the head, with intellect, and also with melancholy, the philosopher's illness. About Saturn, Gichtel wrote:

> There is in the cold Saturn an influence of the heavenly efflux, and all the colours, even more than in the sun, wherein there is death and life, light and darkness, poison and medicine, and a deep harmony of all the seven spirits of nature.[11]

The theosopher's goal is to transmute the potentially negative influence of Saturnine intellectualism into the radiant light of the transcendent intellect infused by the Holy Spirit's power. What might be poison—intellectualism, false and dogmatic concepts—can also be medicine, what might be death can be light and life through spiritual illumination.

But what distinguishes theosophy from Ficino and his sympathetic magic? Essentially this: for the theosophers, as for Ficino, the soul's constellation must be understood and balanced, but the theosophers did not stop with such harmonization. Rather, subjugation to the astral constellation characterized the "dark man," and the theosophic path consisted not in working only on the harmonies of the soul, or psyche, but in transmuting the whole being through prayer and spiritual illumination. It is necessary to harmonize the astral soul just as it is necessary for an instrument to be in tune and played well; but truly beautiful music is far more than simple tuning and skill, it is transcendence of self. So too with the theosophic path.

In theosophy we see this illustrated in countless ways, but most explicitly in the illustrations upon which we have focused so far. For, we will recall, these illustrations show the planetary spiral and influences of the unregenerate man, then the partly regenerate man whose sun-heart is illuminating him, particularly Mercury. We will note that in the partly regenerate man, there are four planets visible: Saturn, the intellect at the head's crown; Jupiter, the regal king at the forehead; the sun-heart, from which drops of blood fall; and Mercury in the abdomen, onto which the drops fall. Mercury, of course, is associated with the word, and communication; Saturn is associated with the highest intellect, and Jupiter with reason—the process of regeneration, in short, does not entail the denial, but the incorporation and transcendence of the word, reason, and intellect.

However, the illustration showing regenerate man most clearly reveals how the goal of theosophy is not simply the harmony of the planets, but their transmutation or revelation as spiritual illumination through the sun-heart that is Christ. The soul is a constellation of planetary influences, but our purpose as human beings is not only to harmonize those influences—we must break beyond the merely astral to the transcendent spiritual power that is "buried" within them. This is where subtle physiology, the soul's physiology, becomes in essence a spiritual physiology.

The culmination of theosophic discipline and prayer is the illumination of the whole being through the heart-sun that is Jesus Christ, his actualization in us. Traditionally, in Christianity as in many other religious traditions (including aboriginal traditions), the heart is recognized as the center of the human being. The heart is far from being a mere organ, or even, in the subtle physiology we have seen elaborated so far, the reflection of the sun in the human constitution. Rather, the heart-sun is, in spiritual physiology, the point at which spiritual reality bursts through into human experience with supernal light and inexpressible joy. This we see in the culminating illustration in Gichtel's series.

The heart is central to all Christian mysticism, but particularly to Eastern Orthodoxy hesychasm, in which the central spiritual practice is the "prayer of the heart," the invocation of Christ in the heart of one's being. St. Isaiah the Solitary, for instance, wrote, "Guard your heart, and do not grow listless," as the center of his advice to the hesychastic practitioner and, citing numerous scriptural references to the heart, warns against allowing evil thoughts into the heart.[12] Likewise, St. Peter of Damaskos entitled the final chapter in his discourses "Conscious Awareness in the Heart," urging us to leave behind all things and offer to Intelligence our intelligence, and St. Makarios of Egypt also emphasizes contrition in the heart, likening the heart to a tomb, in which Christ must be resurrected.[13]

Some of our theosophers had read the Eastern fathers, especially St. Makarios of Egypt—Gichtel's massive collection of letters does contain the following "Sayings of the Ancients suitable to be added to this *Theosophia Practica*": extracts from Makarios's homilies, Chrysostom, John Climacus, *Scala Paradisi*, as well as from Tauler and St. Bernard of Clairveaux.[14] Ernst Benz has pointed out that St. Makarios of Egypt was available in a translation from the Greek in Paris in 1559, and in 1594 an edition of his homilies was published in Frankfurt. Gottfried Arnold's edition—Arnold was, of course, an erstwhile friend of Gichtel's and wrote more or less from a theosophic perspective—was published in 1716 as *Denckmal des Alten Christenthums*, or "Memorial of Ancient Christendom."[15]

But it is not necessary to attribute eighteenth-century German, Dutch, English, and American theosophers' heart symbolism to their contact with Eastern Fathers. That is not how the theosophers worked. Theosophy is a spiritual discipline in itself, and its adherents incorporated extracts from Makarios of Egypt, John Tauler, or other writers because those authors' works corroborated the theosophers' own experience and understanding. The theosophers incorporated readings from both Eastern and Western mystics because they recognized the authenticity of those writings through their own experiences, and because those writings helped place theosophy in a larger historical context.

Thus, to return to the final illustration in Gichtel's *Eine kurze eröffnung*, we see here not a subtle, but a spiritual physiology primarily. The heart is the place of central illumination in the human being; through prayer, the heart reveals Christ to us. The word "Jehova" marks the place in the abdomen where Mercury was, but here is revealed as a sun like the heart. The throat—really from the mouth to the chest just above the heart—is marked as the realm of Sophia, "Mirror of the Godhead," and the upper part of the head, earlier the realm of Jupiter and Saturn, is here become the realm of the Holy Spirit. The "dark world" remains below; Satan threatens man as long as he remains alive.

The theosophic process of illumination reveals first the subtle powers governing man, then reveals "behind" or in those forces their spiritual origin in Father, Son, and Holy Spirit, reflected in Sophia. The Holy Spirit is in the upper region of the head because the Holy Spirit inspires the divine intellect in man. Sophia is in the throat because through prayer, fasting, and invocation man comes to realize Christ—thus, like the "heart-line" in some Native American petroglyphs, Sophia's realm extends from the mouth almost to the heart, Christ. Sophia is associated with the word, and with breath, through which man lives, and through which he can return to a state of spiritual realization and unity like that enjoyed by Adam before the fall. The Father is represented in the abdomen—formerly the realm of anger—because human anger is like a distorted reflection of divine wrath, which belongs to the Father. Thus Jehovah is just above the dark world, which is divine wrath incarnate.

In this way we can see that the human being is indeed an image, not only of the cosmos with its planetary influences, but even of the eternal, which includes the Trinity and Sophia above, and the infernal world and

Satan below. With this realization we begin to understand just how important our human life is for the Böhmean tradition of Gichtel. If we human beings are indeed created in the divine image—possessing the divine intrinsically within us, however soiled by sin and ignorance it may be—we also have within ourselves the wrathful or dark world of sin and ignorance. How we live determines which of these worlds gains dominion, not only during the existence of the body, but after death as well. To practice theosophy is to move toward illumination and joy; to live for the body and for this world is to move toward darkness and wrath.

But the theosophic illustrations depicting the physiology of the soul and spirit do not represent a discarnate spirituality: rather, we see here a spiritual discipline firmly grounded in the body. Like St. Peter of Damaskos, Böhme and Gichtel affirm that we should by no means reject the body, but should realize spiritual truth while alive on earth, recognizing our body as an opportunity for spiritual realization. Spiritual realization can be likened to an ascent into consciousness through the body: the groundless will is identical with the Father, increasing consciousness of the heart is identical with the Son, and the head—full consciousness, the entire process—is identified with the Holy Spirit.[16] Thus, man's body is created in the image of God indeed, and is meant to reveal that image even in its very form.

Earlier we spoke of the unanimity with which Christian mystics both Eastern and Western emphasize detachment of the intellect from all created things, and its reunion with the Divine. We also spoke of how the Bible, the Church fathers, and numerous mystics including the hesychasts all affirm the prayer of the heart, and the centrality of the human heart in Christian spirituality. We are enjoined to purify our heart of evil thoughts, to purify our heart until we realize its inherent reflection of divine perfection. What distinguishes the Böhmean theosophic path from the paths of these other mystics in Christianity? Above all: the more elaborately developed use of images in depicting subtle and spiritual physiology.

For although Gichtel's illustrations upon which we have been focusing refer directly to subtle and spiritual physiology, in fact many of the more abstract Böhmean illustrations reveal very much the same symbolism. Consider, for instance, the frontispiece illustration to Thomas Bromley's *The Way to the Sabbath of Rest*, arguably the clearest single guide to Sophianic mysticism in practice. This book, by the friend of Dr. John Pordage, discusses exactly what is revealed more abstractly in the frontispiece: the progressive revelation of spiritual truth.

There are three crosses in this diagram, each at the center of a circle or sphere, but the process the illustration depicts begins below, in darkness. The bottom cross is dark, and is located at the center of the wrathful, or dark, world whose circumference reaches exactly to the base of the top, pure white, cross. Yet the center of the dark cross is the seed of a plant whose head is above, in the light. Around this seed in the darkness is the concentric spiral of existence—exactly like the spiral we see around "planetary," or dark, unregenerate man in the first of Gichtel's illustrations.

The second cross is not wholly dark, but intermediate, and it is surrounded by the sun, moon, stars, and zodiac, symbolized by the twelve numbers, which symbolize also time in general. Here, in the center of the cross, is an eye—this is the stage of awakening, of the spiritual eye opening, of a human being beginning to realize his divine origin and meaning. Here too we see the stalk arising from the seed down below in the dark center; and the leaf emerges just below the eye in the diagram. This intermediate cross corresponds to the Gichtel illustration in which the human being is part dark and part light.

The third and highest cross is pure white, symbolizing pure light and freedom from darkness, wrath, and confusion. The sphere of which this cross is the center reaches down only to the top of the wrathful spiral below; it does not participate in the wrathful, demonic world. In the center of this pure white cross is a heart, within which is an eye; the heart, as is generally the case in theosophic illustrations, resembles a flask, out of which arises the head of wheat, symbolizing spiritual fruition. This symbol, the eye in the heart, reveals the union of the head and the heart, of the Holy Spirit and the Son, of spiritual vision and the very center of man.

This illustration as a whole reveals the individual spiritual meaning of dying unto oneself and one's selfishness in order to be born anew into a life of spiritual freedom. This we see in New Testament verses such as John 12.24, "Verily, verily, I say unto you, Except a corn of wheat fall into the ground and die, it abideth alone: but if it die, it bringeth forth much fruit." Or again, St. Paul writes in 1 Corinthians 15.35 ff., "But some man will say, How are the dead raised up? and with what body do they come? Thou fool, that which thou sowest is not quickened, except it die: . . . So also is the resurrection of the dead. It is sown in corruption; it is raised in incorruption: . . . It is sown a natural body; it is raised a spiritual body."

All the images in this illustration—like all the images in the Gichtel illustrations—come from the natural world and from natural processes.

But they are employed to illuminate spiritual transmutation; birth, divine motherhood, the immaculate virgin Sophia, the symbolism of darkness and light, the symbolism of the eye and the heart, the symbolism of seeds dying in order to be born a plant and bear fruit, all these images are here transparent, and refer to a process of spiritual rebirth at the center of theosophy. Nature here reveals the transcendence of nature.

What is more, all these images derive completely from the Christian tradition. None are foreign to it. It is the use of images themselves that distinguishes the theosophic path from other forms of Christian mysticism. For theosophy does not have an iconography—itself a science of images—found in both Roman Catholic and Eastern Orthodox traditions. Rather, theosophy uses images designed to reveal the transcendence of images; the illustrations we have been examining do not depict saints, or Christ, or Sophia—they depict instead the spiritual path one follows in order to realize spiritual realities in oneself, in one's own body.

Where Eastern Orthodoxy and Roman Catholicism emphasize the intercession of the saints and spiritual beings on our behalf, theosophy—incontestably a modern tradition—takes a different perspective. For the theosophers, images are not presented to be worshipped, or as part of a ritual—no one would think of worshipping the illustrations we have been looking at here. Rather, the theosophers regard illustrations as a constellation of images depicting the mystical process itself; where iconography depends upon a relationship between spiritual powers and us, theosophic illustrations are like a mirror, reflecting back at us our own spiritual transmutation.

For this reason, theosophy is an inherently esoteric tradition. About iconography one can certainly say that it possesses an outward form, calling the pious toward faith, and an inward meaning that speaks only to those with eyes to see. But theosophic imagery speaks only to those with eyes to see; it mandates the inward transmutation that it represents. Without reference to this inward call, theosophic imagery is without meaning.

To achieve spiritual awakening, the theosophers developed a definite spiritual discipline, and occasionally we catch glimpses of this discipline's full complexity in Gichtel's letters. In 1697 Gichtel wrote:

> For the light arises in the heart, the fifth form (the second principle) and the Holy Spirit goes forth into the head (viz., into the sensibility of the third principle), the sixth form, and openeth the seventh in the mind, viz Sophia, or the temperature. Reason cannot apprehend it, for it requires an inturned spirit and long practice.[17]

In other words, the theosophers had developed an extensive terminology for discussing spiritual awakening via subtle and spiritual physiology, a terminology that in turn was reflected directly in the images we have been examining.

Earlier, we pointed out a fundamental agreement among Christian mystics both Eastern and Western regarding how the mystical path consisted—certainly from St. Dionysius the Areopagite onward—in ascending beyond all created things to a state of detachment, of transcendence. This transcendent state is ultimately imageless, but as St. Dionysius the Areopagite points out, the spiritual aspirant moves through images to a state of imagelessness. Animal images or other symbols, including wings, point us toward certain aspects of divine reality; they are not themselves that reality, but human beings require these symbols or images in order to perceive aspects of divine reality that would otherwise be overwhelming.

Theosophy, which developed in a chiefly Protestant ambience, is nonetheless directly in this larger Christian mystical tradition. Admittedly, the theosophers' use of imagery in their illustrations is not iconographic, nor could it be so at all within Protestantism. But seen in context of the Dionysian understanding of images as reflections of a greater spiritual reality, theosophic illustrations represent simply another manifestation of exactly what St. Dionysius affirmed: sacred revelation, he writes, proceeds "naturally through sacred images in which like represents like, while also using formations which are dissimilar and even . . . ridiculous," "for the Deity is far beyond every manifestation of being and of life . . . [of which] every . . . intelligence falls short."[18]

But theosophic illustrations are more explicit than iconographic symbolism. When in Greek Orthodox iconography we see the Theotokos, or Mother of God, holding Christ around whose head is a halo, the Theotokos holds him so that his head is exactly at the level of her heart. This is not an accidental symbolism: it conveys a spiritual symbolism similar to what we see in theosophic illustrations showing the heart as an illuminating Jesus-sun. But in iconography this symbolism is implicit: we see first of all the Theotokos and the Christ child, images instilling faith in Christ and in the Virgin Mary, and the inner meaning of those images is hidden, not to say secondary. In theosophic illustrations such implications are explicit and cannot be missed.

Indeed, the theosophic path is distinguished by precisely this paradox made explicit: the theosophy details one's movement through images to imagelessness, through the subtle or astral body to the "body of power" or the spiritual body. Theosophy details its cosmological doctrines far more than other forms of Christian mysticism, precisely because theosophy developed in the modern era. Theosophy, then, stands directly in the traditional current of Christian mysticism, but it incorporates into its literature and art the precise stages through which the spiritual aspirant must pass. Central to theosophy, therefore, is both cosmology—understanding nature—and microcosmology, the science of subtle and spiritual physiology in individual human beings. For to understand the outward world, man must realize his own true nature in its various levels, as body, as soul, and as spirit. This progressive revelation is really the unveiling of the forces that govern him as an unregenerate creature, and then the unveiling of his more and more transcendent essential, luminous being. This essential, luminous nature is man's original, unfallen "spiritual body."

Thus, for theosophy spiritual realization is ultimately a process of revealing what Gichtel calls man's original luminous spiritual "body of power."[19] We are not here talking about the astral body, the constellation of planetary tendencies or forces that make up an individual personality. Rather, when an individual encounters the "tincture" of the Virgin Sophia, she brings into the soul a "dowry" or spiritual power that reveals the soul's intrinsic spiritual nature, and it is this revelation that makes man a "priest of the order of Melchizadek," that is, makes him a truly responsible human being, responsible again as a truly free spiritual being of power, not subject in the same way to emotional forces.

For this reason Gichtel wrote of spiritual seeing, spiritual hearing, spiritual tasting, spiritual touching and spiritual smelling: theosophic mysticism leads to entry into a visionary world, and to inhabit that world, one has a spiritual body, a pure, luminous, visionary body. Here lies a great mystery, about which Gichtel was writing at the end of his life, on December 7, 1708, to a friend: "may you also be immersed in the glassy sea of love and baptized with fire, for the spiritual feeling, seeing, hearing and smelling cannot be expressed by words, nor compared to anything, but must be tasted."[20]

Of course, we are here in very dangerous territory, for Christian mystics are unanimous in saying that visions cannot be trusted; man is in constant danger of being deceived, deluded. St. Theresa of Avila constantly tried to test her visionary experiences to see if they were of God, as did many other visionary mystics. The theosophers are no exception to this rule. In fact, this is exactly why they speak, and depict in illustrations, subtle and spiritual physiology. Their visions are simply part of a complete process of spiritual transmutation, and thus theosophers emphasize that visions alone are not to be accepted, save if they conform to scripture and are accompanied by the other signs of spiritual trans-mutation that form so large a part in theosophic literature and art.

In fact, Gichtel was among the most discerning of theosophers in this regard, and did not pay much credence to the visions even of other theosophers such as Leade or Pordage, much less to those of unschooled people. Gichtel writes on August 12, 1692: "There is a great distinction between visions, requiring a clear understanding . . . we are chiefly ruled by the constellation, and therefore it has its working in us, and not all the seeing ones see into the third heaven, nor into the second like the prophets, but only into the outward."[21] To mistake astral shades or images for authentic spiritual realities is to be deceived. Gichtel goes on to write that "three or four years ago" "many well meaning people about here saw fiery flames falling from the air, others saw angels, and other again devils—and this at the same hour and place. Whereby one and the other were puffed up; one wanted to drive the devil out of one possessed, but became himself possessed, and died in that state."[22] Judg-ing from the history of the Inquisition, this last is an all too familiar tale.

But the fact remains, there are authentic visions, recognized in Catholicism by the official church, in Orthodoxy, and in theosophy. About these Gichtel writes: "Heaven indeed teacheth something from a good man, wherein it rejoiceth, and manifests its joy by visions." Nonetheless, "they are not powers of God, but visions only, which are magical, and have an issue very different from man's conceptions." Speaking of himself in the third person after the fashion of St. Paul, Gichtel adds that "Twenty eight years ago I knew a man who had been caught up to the third heaven . . . but whether he had been there in the body, he knew not. . . . He said, that to taste, feel, and receive the pow-ers of God, was more than having visions every day."[23] Gichtel had him-self wrestled with the hellish spirits; and "the blessed angels have played with me during the day like children." But "all this is but a paradisal prelude, and whoso would seek for it, would be deceived."[24]

Although many theosophers were visionaries, including Gichtel and Böhme himself, they are not united by this fact alone. Indeed, as we have seen in the case of Jane Leade, her visionary revelations in the end separated her from her fellow theosophers in Germany and Hol-land, especially from Gichtel himself. Theosophy is characterized, not by visions alone, but by its very particular cosmology and meta-physics, intrinsic to which is its subtle and spiritual physiology. To

realize one's subtle and spiritual nature inwardly is also to see outwardly the visionary complement to a given inward state: this is the
theosophic corollary to the traditional aphorism that the microcosm,
man, reflects the macrocosm.

For theosophers, visionary revelations crown or culminate a complete transmutation of the human being; one develops a "spiritual
body" capable of living in the divine realm, and this in turn constitutes
one's visionary experiences: visions are experiences in supra- or
infrahuman realms. Of course, this "spiritual body" is not an accre-
tion really "developed" outside oneself—it is oneself, oneself as before
creation, oneself as an angelic being. But as fallen beings, humans have
to begin in a sinful state and struggle back toward recovery of their
luminous, free, original nature—and this luminous, free, original
nature is precisely one's spiritual body, ultimately free from all images
and created things, but comprehensible to us, through the head, the
eye, and the heart.

It remains to discuss fruitful parallels in other traditions with the
doctrines of our Christian theosophers, beginning with Sufism. In Islam,
one finds a direct parallel to our Protestant theosophers among the
many Sufi theosophers translated or cited by the remarkable French
scholar Henry Corbin. Corbin's work on Sufism and Ismaili gnosis is
deeply indebted to the doctrines of Paracelsus, Böhme, and Baader, and
thus his explications of and translations of Islamic doctrines take on a
special significance for us. Most useful here are his translations of Sufi
works in the selection entitled *Spiritual Body and Celestial Earth: From
Mazdean Iran to Shi'ite Iran.*[25]

In *Spiritual Body and Celestial Earth* we find an excellent introduction to the concept of "interworlds," meaning *barzakhs*, or realms
of ever more intense luminosity and delight "above" the earthly. These
interworlds are inhabited by angelic beings and angelic "landscapes"
very much akin to what we find described by our Christian theosophers. Indeed, Shaikh 'Abd al-Karīm Jīlī describes in detail the "six categories" of ranked "Adamites" or spiritual beings connected to our
earth, ranging from the invisible Perfect Ones to the "pillars of the
earth" who take "pure apparitional forms" to the "Angels of inspiration" to the "men of wild lands" to, finally, those who "resemble sudden inspiration."[26] Such categories do not discriminate even between
Islamic and non-Islamic, or between heretical and orthodox: in question for these Sufi mystics, as for the Christian theosophers, is a visionary spirituality solely addressed to those who have eyes to see, nothing

less than direct contact with the angelic realms, in regards to which human conceptualization cannot suffice.

The importance of works such as those cited by or translated by Henry Corbin and found in various forms of Sufism and Ismaili Gnosticism lies not in any imagined "influence" on Christian theosophers—for demonstrably there was none—but precisely in the absence of such influence. It would make a profoundly interesting study to compare Christian, Islamic, and Jewish theosophers in terms of their visionary parallels and mutually illuminating commentaries and disciplines. Sufism, too, has its "prayer of the heart"; and while comparative religion has its limits, at the very least such parallels should corroborate for us the importance of certain spiritual modes or perceptions within the Judeo-Christian and Islamic spheres.

In Judaism there are likewise parallels with the theosophers' visionary physiology, if we may so put it. These parallels are found in Kabbalism, the greatest scholar of which during the twentieth century was certainly Gershom Scholem, who was a member of the Eranos circle to which Corbin also belonged. There can be no doubt, as Scholem himself affirms, that Böhme and the theosophic school was directly and indirectly influenced by Kabbalist mysticism, and that central to Kabbalist as to Christian theosophy is the premise that, as Scholem put it, "a man's ascent to higher worlds . . . involves no motion on his part, for 'where you stand, there stand all the worlds.'"[27] In Kabbalism, particularly that of Moses Cordovero (1522–1570) and Isaac Luria (1534–1572), the doctrine of emanated and of human inward correlates to them takes on perhaps its most elaborate forms.

But although there is more than a question of influence on Böhmean theosophy by Kabbalism—there is no doubt of it—the fact remains that we are here discussing particular visionary spiritualities whose practitioners insist time and again that one must realize these doctrines within oneself. Given this, while we can certainly trace the direct and indirect influences of Kabbalism on theosophy, such doctrines as those of subtle and spiritual physiology do not require a Kabbalist influence—these doctrines come, the theosophers themselves say, and we have no reason to doubt it, out of their direct experience and realizations.

For in the end, theosophic doctrines of subtle and spiritual physiology bring us directly back to the individual, and the individual body, soul, and spirit, precisely as they are intended to do. There is without question much work to be done in this field, particularly in tracing the intricate relations and parallels between Christian, Jewish, and Muslim theosophies. But such considerations should not obscure from us the fundamental message of the theosophers: that we human beings are enjoined to realize for ourselves, directly, by the transmutation and illumination of our own bodies and souls, the spiritual realities that may be conveyed or seen in images, but that are ultimately imageless and full of joy.

CHAPTER SIXTEEN

Turning Wrath
into Love

Throughout its history, theosophy has incited the wrath of those who belong to what Jacob Böhme called "Babel," meaning the "outward church," those who are concerned not with spiritual discipline but with appearances, not with the state of the soul but with historically based faith. One can well imagine the reaction of those who, believing themselves good Christians, are told that Christianity is not merely attending church, or professing faith, but a very difficult spiritual discipline. Indeed, at times it would appear that Christianity's true history is a perpetual recapitulation of the story of Jesus himself, who met with nothing if not wrathful indignation from the scribes, pharisees, and rulers. How an individual deals with this wrath is the crucial question, one which the theosophers answered in a very straightforward way, with a single voice: turn wrath into love.

But before we turn to how, exactly, the theosophers went about this, we should first discuss Böhmean cosmology. According to Böhme, we can understand the cosmos in terms of "worlds" or "realms." These realms are not separate from our present world, but rather interpenetrate with it, although we ordinarily cannot see them. For instance, there is a wrath world, whose element is fire and discord and anger—separation—and it is accessible to us right now, present in us if we are angry.

Likewise, there is a realm of love, and this too is accessible at this moment, if we love and are kind to others. But these realms also have an existence more or less independent from us, which we may term demonic and angelic respectively.

The idea that there are actual realms of demons and angels may appear to us as antiquated or medieval. However, the fact remains that for Böhmean theosophy such realms are recognized as real, not on the basis of hearsay, but out of direct personal experience. We discussed earlier how John Pordage underwent a strange series of visionary experiences beginning in 1648, and how during this series of experiences he and his family saw the wrath world "open" before them. So powerful was this visionary experience, which lasted for days on end, that it manifested itself in the smell of brimstone and sulphur, and in the imprinting of demonic images on the windows, walls, and ceiling of his house, images he and his wife eventually had to chip off or erase.

It is easy for us today—conditioned as we are by psychological explanations—to dismiss the visionary experiences of a Pordage or a Böhme as hallucinations. But it is somewhat harder to dismiss them as such when there are even physical manifestations, and when numerous people witness such events. In any case, our own practice here is not to dismiss visionary experiences or events out of hand because they do not fit our preconceptions of how the world should be, but rather to try and understand those experiences in the context of our authors' own understanding. And in fact, when we look at these visionary experiences in the context of Böhmean theosophy, they fit cleanly into that context.

According to Böhme, Pordage, and Gichtel, in the sphere of eternal nature there exist simultaneously numerous worlds that are condensations of the essential ternary Mercury, Salt, and Sulphur. Each of these has characteristic qualities: Mercury is fluid, Salt crystalline, Sulphur dry and burning. Naturally, the wrath world partakes primarily of the sulphuric. But there are also the "Angelical-heaven, or Love-world," the "Light-fire world, or Paradise," and the "Four Elementarie, or outward visible world." Now the four elements—fire, earth, air, and water—exist in all these worlds, but in different forms. Only in this physical world are the four elements visible as we know them. In the wrath world, these elements exist only in chaos or discord; in the paradisal world, these elements exist only in a rarified form, and in the Angelical world they exist too, but in an even more spiritualized form.

All of these realms or worlds are accessible to us as human beings, but most of us never see them in inward vision, not because we cannot, but because we are inclined to recognize only, as Plato said, that which can be grasped with the hands. Nonetheless, we see in various human emotions and mental states the reflections of these various worlds. Certainly we all know well enough the manifestations of the wrath world, with its fiery anger, and the fear it can generate—both fear and anger reflecting separation, division, and discord. At times, too, we know the joy and light that belong to the paradisal world, just as at times we feel despite ourselves the loving kindness characteristic of the angelical world. We human beings, in the theosophic view, are like the theater or the players for these forces.

Böhme, Pordage, Bromley, Leade, or Gichtel all believed that they saw with inward eyes the principles or forces governing us. But what is more, they claimed to have experienced these principles in a more direct way than most of us do. That is: according to Böhmean theosophy to see with inward eyes is not all; it is also possible to actually experience these worlds inwardly. This inward experiencing Bromley calls conjoining the eye and the heart, and it is one of the last stages in the process of trans-mutation he describes in *The Way to the Sabbath of Rest.*

Bromley writes in his treatise—which was definitely produced with the approval of both Pordage and Leade, with whom he worked—that the process of spiritual transmutation is truly underway when the practitioner begins to experience spiritual communion with others following the same path. When, Bromley writes, "the Soul begins to draw near the eternal World," the "blessed Tincture of Jesus" "flows into the Soul like a River of Oyl mixed with Fire, which affords that unutterable Delight, which cannot be conceived by those that know it not experimentally."[1] Here, the Soul begins to take on "holy Commerce in pure Love," and sees its own likeness in the saints, who delight in one another.

When this "holy Commerce in pure Love" begins, it is as if those who share this communion are linked in a remarkable and hidden way, virtually as if a new inner organ had blossomed: the heart is opened. "Here we bear one another's Burdens, and so fulfil the royal Law of Love," writes Bromley. Indeed, so intimately linked are the communi-cants, they cannot help but inwardly share all their joys and sorrows. Earlier in his treatise, Bromley had said that those in this path at a cer-tain point realize a communion among themselves not subject to distance or time; here this royal Law of Love is taken to a new and celestial degree, and their realization is of communion with the saints and angels.[2]

I have spoken of this communion elsewhere at greater length; here I want only to note that this inward "opening" of sensitivity appears to produce a corollary sensitivity—to wrath. Apparently, in other words, the opening of the inward vision penetrating eternal nature allows one to see and experience heavenly joys, but this same opening entails a correlate opening of the wrath world. This of course makes sense, and indeed as Edward Hooker wrote, one must pass through the flaming sword to reenter Eden. Pordage's first illumination was of the wrath world, and demons; only later did he experience paradisal and heavenly delights.

This correlativity is suggestive. Most of all, it suggests responsibility. One who sees heaven also sees into hell; one who has risen high enough to experience paradise also, like Lucifer, may potentially fall very far indeed, and in any case may be exposed to the wrath world in a way most of us are not. At the very least, it would seem, our visionary theosophers, in realizing the light, are also more sensitive to darkness. This sensitivity to the wrath world reappears several times in the lives of our theosophers, preeminently in the lives of the most profound of them, Pordage and Gichtel.

Pordage encountered the wrath in his life not only in his first visionary experience, which he recounted in the treatise *Innocency Appearing* in 1654, but in fact for several years continuously after his having been censured by the Berks Commissioners. Pordage wrote in his treatise "On the Dark World,"

> In the year of our Lord one thousand six hundred and fifty-three or fifty-four, I heard the Spirit of Eternity say that, being an unprofitable servant, I should be cast into the outer darkness where there is weeping and gnashing of teeth. As soon as these words had been uttered, I was also drawn into the dark Center, and circled about there for five years until I was released therefrom.[3]

Now, there are several ways one could read this statement. One could say that, having been publicly stripped of his livelihood, and libelled severely in the process, Pordage then attributed this dark time later to the curse of the Spirit of Eternity. Or one could say that Pordage was spiritually cast into the outer darkness, and this was only reflected in his outward circumstances—wherein he received public vituperation, definitely entering physically into the world of wrath.

But in either case, the effect was phenomenologically the same: outwardly, he was scorned, and inwardly, he was circling in the "outer darkness." One can attribute the latter to the former if one wishes, but the fact remains: his inward and outward circumstances corresponded.

This suggests that Pordage experienced the wrath in a more acute way than many people might; it is as if the public censure created an atmosphere around him and his fellow theosophers. For it was not Pordage alone who was affected.

In a collection of historical documents in Germany called the *Apparatus ad historiam ecclesiasticam novam* we find that when in 1652 Pordage began holding theosophic meetings in his home, a person was admitted who did not sincerely live a pure and virginal life as the theosophers demanded. After the group excluded him, he raged against them, and Mrs. Leade remarks that there was a time when the small group had to pray day and night to protect themselves from the assaults of the dark wrath world.[4] It was during this time that Dr. Pordage was called before the Commission for ejecting Scandalous, Ignorant, and Insufficient Ministers.

In other words, it appears as though, when this one member of the group "fell," and was ejected, this "opened up" the wrath world, so that the entire group felt they were under attack and had to pray day and night. Something of this can be explained by the fact that when someone is excluded from a group and in turn rages against the group, it is difficult for the group itself not to respond in anger too. Thus, the prayer might be seen as controlling the anger of the group. But from their own perspective, this little group of theosophers was deliberately absorbing the wrath that was directed against them—precisely as Christ absorbed wrath through accepting the cross.

If this situation we have described were peculiar to the English Böhmeans, we could perhaps dismiss it as singular—but in fact in the late seventeenth and early eighteenth century we find almost exactly the same pattern appearing among the German theosophers, especially Gichtel. As we have seen, we are fortunate in that Gichtel left some four thousand pages of letters documenting his spiritual life and practices. And in these letters we find admonitions that the heart of spiritual praxis is in fact to bear others' burdens spiritually, to turn wrath into love.

While considering someone who accused him of heresy, Gichtel wrote, for example, that we must share others' burdens:

> My brother's failings must also be mine, we must take them on ourselves, confess them of God, and pray for mercy, that the sin may be forgiven to . . . our brethren. Love seeth no evil, as you may learn from the parable of the prodigal son. . . . But the angry brother can do nothing but thunder, tell lies, be angry, and exalt his I-hood. . . . May the most high forgive our transgressions and sins! We bless all that curse us.[5]

In another letter, Gichtel wrote of Christ adding ever "to our souls his flesh and blood—clothing our naked soul, that it can stand in the fire, and this He doeth until the soul can live with our suffering in the fire of God's wrath; there by the love it overcometh the wrath."⁶ This, he wrote, is what it truly means to be a priest of the order of Melchizadek, bringing expiatory sacrifices for the sins of the people.

But there are two instances from Gichtel's life more telling than any of these others in this question of turning wrath into love. Although Gichtel himself referred to these stories in his letters, in his biography we find the fullest history of Gichtel's unusual relationship to the erstwhile Lutheran pastor Friedrich Breckling and to Dr. Alhart de Raedt. According to the biography, before Gichtel was accused of heresy, banished from his home town, and stripped of his livelihood, he was given refuge by Breckling. Gichtel and Breckling became close; Gichtel worked for his church, and after Gichtel left Breckling was banished to Holland, where the Angelic brethren began to group around him, and where Gichtel defended Breckling against public attacks.

But as evidently happened with some frequency around Gichtel, he and Breckling became bitter enemies, and according to Gichtel, Breckling—as Mark Twain might have said—was a good hater. In fact, Breckling was so good a hater that his

> wrath-prayer or word, called pestilence in Hebrew (Psalms XCI.6), crept on in darkness, until in 1680, it approached the tabernacle of our champion's [Gichtel's] body, and threw him on a bed of sickness, which lasted a whole year, with a quartain fever, which devoured all his bodily powers, so that the illness was exceedingly painful because Breckling and his wife with their fiery prayers strove against his soul.⁷

Breckling and his wife also became sick and bedridden like Gichtel, and only when "the words of forgiveness" were spoken was Gichtel freed from the wrath, lifted out of bed as by an invisible hand, whereupon "Satan's powers were broken."

Nor is this the only such incident. An even more remarkable story is told by Gichtel and the anonymous biographer of Dr. Alhart de Raedt. In 1682, while living in Amsterdam, Gichtel and Raedt had become fast companions, so much so that

> not one among his co-combatants . . . understood the deep ground of the union between Gichtel and Raedt, so that they often spoke with great marvelling and praise of God of their

acquaintance; and there was such an intense love between the
two, that they would have imparted their hearts to each other
and no one that visited them left them unmoved . . . the virginal tincture infused itself into all their conversations.[8]

But this extraordinary relationship, which resembles that between Rumi
and Shems-i-tabriz in Sufism, was not to last.

Eventually, Gichtel began to recognize that something was amiss in
Raedt; he had become "self-willed." A signal instance of this came when
Gichtel and Raedt prayed together for a young man who had gone mad.
Gichtel "perceived a foreign spirit in Raedt, and therefore asked: 'On
what foundation shall I pray with you?'" Nonetheless, Gichtel and
Raedt began to pray, but

> the more he penetrated into God, the worse the patient
> became, until at last he was found dead in his room, having
> strangled himself, and shortly after Raedt's secession [from
> the brethren] became apparent. Hence it is seen what a per-
> verse constellation Raedt had become, and what harm he did
> by admitting Satan.[9]

After Raedt had left the brethren and was living in Leyden, a man with
whom he lived went quite mad, and came to Gichtel looking "wild and
terrible." Gichtel prayed, and then "in one instant he appeared to
become quite another man."[10] According to Gichtel, Raedt himself
turned to drinking, blasphemy, and unchastity, and on the brethren
poured forth his "bitter zeal."

It is difficult to know what to make of this account—Gichtel did
have a history of altercations with almost everyone, at one point or
another. But clearly, when one of the brethren allowed the wrath world,
or a "foreign spirit" into himself, the results were evidently not good.
We might note that Raedt was deeply jealous of Ueberfeld, the editor of
Gichtel's collected letters, and that Gichtel's biographer makes the following remark:

> The first attack of wrath was made on Ueberfeld in the
> year 1691, about the autumnal equinox, which has always
> been fatal to the brethren; the wrath devoured his life in one
> instant. But by the introversion of the spirit into the love, and
> exit out of the wrath, the love also entered into the wrath and
> devoured it. When the wrath tested the love, it was frightened
> and let go the body, so that in ten or twelve days Ueberfeld
> rose again. Dying in Christ had been great gain for him . . .[11]

This account helps explain a great deal.

From Gichtel's viewpoint, Raedt was not able to withstand the onslaught of the dark world, but succumbed; Ueberfeld, on the other hand, was able to exit wrath and enter the love world, whereupon the love vanquished the wrath. In this way Ueberfeld, like Gichtel, and like Christ, "rose from the dead." We will recall that Gichtel was under assault from Breckling and his wife for more than a year, and that Pordage circled in the outer darkness for four or five years; but eventually the practitioners were given a reillumination.

It seems unnecessary to adduce more examples here of this same principle; more useful perhaps to now suggest its implications. Certainly these stories—from very similar theosophic circles in Germany, Holland, and England, whose members sometimes only vaguely knew of one another's existence—strongly suggest that the same principles and methods produce remarkably similar results in theosophy as in other fields or disciplines. But the implications of these hagiographical tales of wrath and love go beyond just theosophic circles.

As we have seen, the theosophers saw themselves not as belonging to Protestant, Catholic, or other denominations, but as purely and simply Christian. Now, nothing seems more essentially Christian than to return love for wrath and persecution. Indeed, as we suggested at the beginning of this discussion, this is after all the essence of Christ's own fate at the hands of the scribes, pharisees, and Romans—one could think of no better illustration of what Böhme meant by the conflict between "Babel," or outward religion, and inward spiritual realization.

But there are further implications still. When someone sows discord and hatred in the name of religion, he is manifesting the dark or wrath world, allowing it an opening. Certainly one could ascribe to the Inquisition, for instance, an origin along these lines, inasmuch as the Inquisition represents murdering and torturing in the name of Christ. Yet we might remember that the wrath is also a manifestation of God, and that in theosophic tradition it is said that our soul must learn to clothe itself with Christ's robe and learn to withstand the fiery wrath of God before death, or it shall have to suffer after death.

Consequently, even though it is our individual task to transform wrath into love, wrath has its place in the scheme of things; without it one could not be tested, nor could one transmute it into love through spiritual alchemy. There is here a definite parallel with Tibetan Buddhist traditions that include in their pantheon wrathful deities; here, too, rather than striving to separate oneself from wrath, one embraces it, absorbs it, and transmutes it into love. For wrath and the wrath world has a necessary place in the cosmos, and this place is one of purification.

After all, each of us has sown discord, made mistakes, sinned. If we agree with the premise that divine mercy and divine wrath are in an ultimate sense one, the difference being in the perception of the individual soul, then perhaps we can see how to be tested and purified in the divine wrath is, finally, to be invested with the robe of glory and peace. The theosophers sometimes express this as passing the flaming sword back into paradise; but whatever the terms, the reality being expressed seems the same. We must not only pass through the wrath and be purified, we must, if we are to fulfil our role as part of the priesthood of Melchizadek, finally accept the wrath of others as our own burden, and reply with love.

This is a mysterious process. Gichtel tells the story of how he once prayed that he could take on himself the burden of one of his acquaintances, and for days he was surrounded by what amounted to a cloud of wrath; he felt its fiery impulses time and again, but slowly it faded away and the peace and joy of Sophia returned again—and his acquaintance was freed from the wrath. We might be inclined to criticize Gichtel himself for being a bit testy with many of his own colleagues, friends, and acquaintances—but in the light of such anecdotes, perhaps this testiness takes on a slightly different implication.

Whatever we may think of such anecdotes, of which there are many instances in *Theosophica Practica*, no one could deny that the principle here is a noble one and bears a special relationship to the very heart of Christianity itself. In fact, it throws light on the whole of Christian history, and strongly implies that, in the end, true Christianity is not a matter of defending orthodoxy against heresy, or of upholding dogmatic convictions, but of the soul's purification, pacification, and enlightenment.

CHAPTER SEVENTEEN

Penetrating the
Merely Astral

 M any aspects of theosophy seem at first somewhat foreign, particularly if the theosophers use the terms peculiar to Jacob Böhme's work. But while this is true of the more technical Böhmean works, it is not true of the practical theosophers, including such authors as Johann Georg Gichtel, Edward Hooker, Thomas Bromley, or John Pordage. For these authors are much more inclined to discuss theosophy not in elaborate cosmological terms (though they may draw on such terminology on occasion) but in straightforward practical terms, using examples from daily life. To understand some of these examples, particularly those of Gichtel, we must understand what is meant by penetrating the astral realm in spiritual practice.

For the theosophers, "astral" or "sidereal" refers to an intermediate realm between the spirit and the physical worlds. This intermediate sphere, that of the soul, is at once within us as our psyche, and, without us, reflected in the form of the planets and stars. In other words, the individual soul is a microcosmic reflection of the macrocosm. One may say, too, that the sphere of the stars and planets is rather like a boundary between the physical and the spiritual realms, so that through the canopy of stars and planets shines the supernal light of the transcendent, almost like pinpricks in a dark cloth.

These planets and stars condition the light, refract it. Thus, the light of the sun, or of the twelve zodiacal signs, or of any of the planets, although in an ultimate sense the same light, differs when refracted through the quality of Venus, or Mars, for example. This "conditioning" of the refracted light is astrological, and in a broad sense makes up what we experience as emotional or mental tendencies. Mars, for instance, is associated with redness and with anger, while Venus is associated with green, beauty, luxury, sensuality, attraction.

For this reason, many followers of theosophy have created elaborate charts showing the qualities informing both people and the cosmos. One set of such charts was published in London in 1654 by H. Blunden, and is entitled *Four Tables of Divine Revelation*. This work bears a certain debt to many earlier such tables found in works by, for example, Henry Cornelius Agrippa on natural magic. Essentially, Böhmean theosophy continues or incorporates the worldviews affiliated with medieval alchemy, Hermeticism, the Platonism of Ficino and Pico della Mirandola, and Jewish Kabbala as well as natural magic, all of which share a comprehensive understanding of the entire natural world as reflecting spiritual qualities or principles. Thus, the *Four Tables of Divine Revelation* may be seen as a culmination of all these traditions, a synthetic and complete cosmology and metaphysics.

But the cosmology and metaphysics reflected in the *Four Tables* and in many other Böhmean or Rosicrucian documents of the seventeenth and eighteenth centuries was not dissociated from daily experience and from the sects and people that the theosophers knew. Rather, such a cosmological understanding was directly reflected in the way that our theosophers saw their world. Not only natural phenomena but also the human world could be understood in terms of "signatures," meaning sidereal or astrological configurations. In fact, we can even go beyond this, and say that this cosmology and metaphysics was central to the lives of the theosophers and to the spiritual disciplines that they practiced.

Central to this perspective was the fluid concept of the astral. The astral refers to what we may call the realm of the collective psyche—which is not to say unconscious, since it is precisely consciousness under consideration. The astral is the collective or individual psychic atmosphere in which people live. Thus, an individual may have a tendency toward melancholy, or toward lust, for instance. These tendencies are "phantasies," meaning obsessive thoughts that develop in a spiral around us in our mental atmosphere or ambit.[1] The same tendencies also produce societal institutions or sects, which are essentially collective versions of what also governs individuals.

From this concept of the astral we can begin to understand why it was that our theosophers consistently—whether in Germany, the Netherlands, England, or America—refused to develop sectarianism or institutions. Of course, there were some institutional necessities in such communities as Ephrata in America; one had leaders and rules. But even these communities often refused to give names to themselves, so that titles had to be applied from without, as in the case of the "woman in the wilderness" Böhmean community in Pennsylvania.[2] This refusal to be named came directly from the theosophers' adamant rejection of forming just another "astral" sect.

In other words: the theosophers held that to create another sect is to create another set of doctrines and phantasies to which people can cling, instead of directly experiencing religious truth in themselves. Francis Lee, one of the most learned of the theosophers,wrote of the Philadelphians,

> They are a Religious Society for the Reformation of Manners, for the Advancement of an Heroical Christian Piety, and Universal Peace and Love towards All: who though they are deeply sensible of great Corruptions and Deviations in most, or all, of the Christian Bodies, or Communities, from the Apostolical Rule; yet do not therefore formally Dissent, or separate from such a particular Body, Community, or Church in which they have before liv'd according to the best of their Light, and Understanding: much less do they perswade others to Dissent from that Communion, which they are Previously obliged to Adhere to.[3]

The theosophers did not want to encourage people to cling to new doctrines of a newly created sect—for that would be only piling one error atop another in a vain attempt to correct it. Rather, they felt that one could remain Lutheran, or Catholic, or a part of whatever sect one held to—and experience true Christianity in oneself.

The theosophers held that to create a sect, or any kind of individual phantasy, was to create a kind of astral "covering" that in itself prevented seeing reality. The canopy of the heavens provides the best analogy: for the theosophers, as for some of the ancient Gnostics, the heavenly spheres represent celestial qualities that are reflected in minerals, plants, animals, and people. But the stars and planets spread out on the night sky also represent a canopy through which shines an unconditioned transcendent light, like pinpricks through a dark cloth. The theosophers insist that one must not mistake the refracted light of, for instance, Venus, for the unmediated pure light of liberty.

Thus, Gichtel wrote of the Quakers that they are in "an astrum of Venus" that "has its wheel above the obstinate Mars," but

> since this sidereal spirit is nearest to the sun, it is grounded in the light of the sun. [Yet it] is only an astrum, and seeks again an astral host, viz., a sect. And I know that if they were to overcome this astral host, and press with their will-spirits into the liberty, they would drop their sect, since in the most inward ground they taste Christ.[4]

Indeed, Gichtel elsewhere writes, the *spiritus mundi*, or spirit of this world, is constantly trying to lead us into the "Venus heaven" of this world's comforts.[5] If one wishes to attain true religious certainty and insight, one must penetrate beyond this tendency.

Yet on the other hand, the astral atmosphere that one creates and clings to in order to reinforce selfhood is also a protection. To break through the astral without the spiritual armor of Christ is to invite disaster for oneself. Thus, Gichtel observes that "Whoso has not put on Christ, and is not armed, let him remain still in his *astrum*, for mighty gods and spirits are not to be trifled with."[6] One must keep in mind here that Gichtel is not talking about abstract things here, but the actual lives of people he knew. Gichtel's letters are replete with references to people who became alcoholics, committed suicide, violently attacked Gichtel and his brethren and sisters, or went insane. We can no doubt attribute much of this to the dangers of breaking through the astral without spiritual protection.

Yet on the other hand, those of exoteric or historical religious faith—who regard Christ in an outward way, rather than striving to realize the state of Christ in themselves—are simultaneously protected and imprisoned by that faith. This is why the theosophers did not advise people to leave behind the Christian sect to which they belong; rather, they held that one should transcend that sect or form. In a letter dated October 6, 1696, Gichtel wrote:

> As regards Mr. N——, I have indeed found him to be a fine mind, but observed that it is mightily imprisoned under the yoke of the astral heavens, and that without the divine anguish-fire, it will hardly break through.
>
> And our present Christendom is universally enchained under this dominion, so that it no little grieves an enlightened

> mind, when yet it cannot help, for faith is so dead under reli-
> gious opinion that without the true spiritual new birth it can-
> not be roused and wakened, as I have experienced in myself.[7]

According to Gichtel, we must pass through the anguish-fire, and the relinquishing of all that we cling to, in order to experience the divine liberty of the true spiritual new birth. We must suffer the fire to enter the light, pass the angel of the flaming sword to enter the garden.

Essentially, Gichtel suggests in his letters, we must go beyond religious dogma and the concepts we cling to, relinquish astral phantasies that surround us, and, through prayer without ceasing, penetrate into the uncreated light that brings joy in the heart. If we do not do this, we remain caught in the belief that

> if we are baptized and have an historical knowledge of Christ,
> which is called faith, diligently attend church and the Lord's
> Supper, that then we shall be saved. And we forget the denial
> of self, the mortification of the flesh, the death of selfhood,
> together with the renewal of the Holy Spirit, . . . it follows
> that when the soul must leave the earthly body, it finds itself
> naked and bare without a new body, wherein it could share
> in the wrath of God, and is seized with great fear. [Thus our
> souls must] afterward bathe in the fire, while all impurity is
> burnt away, and the small spark at last attains strength, and
> passes from the anguish of the fire into rest.[8]

We are purified either here on earth or after death: one way or another, we must pass through the wrath.

It is particularly interesting that Gichtel observes we need after death "a new body, wherein [we] could share in the wrath of God." Biblically, Gichtel's comments are grounded on I Corinthians 15.4: "There is a natural body, and there is a spiritual body." But from the way Gichtel writes, we can tell that he is speaking not as an exegete; this is someone who, as he himself tells us time and again, has seen with his own inward eyes and heard with inward ears the truth, including what happens to us after death. Furthermore, what Gichtel says makes logical sense as well: if we have not shared before death in the wrath of God, we will experience it as something coming from without us and engendering great fear, after death.

In essence, Gichtel is advising an imaginative process by which wrath and fear can be transformed into love. This process of transmutation requires that one distinguish between the call or stimuli of "astral man" and the spirit, that one "set the imagination on Christ."[9] Gichtel writes: "He that wants to drive a poison or disease out of his body, must use a counter-poison, or medicine. Thus he that wants to overcome the wrath in flesh and blood, must by imagination and desire introduce love into the wrath."[10] This transmutation penetrates into or encompasses every aspect of one's life; to penetrate beyond the "outward church" is to purify one's daily activities, and one's soul, or astral man.

This is a difficult struggle, for to break free of one's conceptual, often sectarian attachments is not possible until one has first broken free from one's personal, "astral" attachments. Of this truth we have some striking examples in Gichtel's letters. In one such example—which we have discussed already in a different context—Gichtel met a young woman obsessed by jewelry and fine things. He prayed that he might take this burden on himself, and consequently was sorely troubled for some days afterward by this phantasy, which surrounded him with the lure of jewels. But he unceasingly prayed, and the phantasy slowly left him—while the young woman had been wholly freed from it. Gichtel through prayer took upon himself the astral phantasies of this woman, and so freed her for spiritual practice.[11]

In another such instance, a woman had been troubled for ten years by the ghost of her dead husband, who followed her, ever asking for her prayers. She asked many people about this, and all those she questioned said that the soul was really the devil—"but the woman knew her husband, and could not get rid of the dream [apparition] until Gichtel opened to her the ground of her soul, whereupon she attained peace."[12] Here again—as in another case, in which Gichtel took upon himself the virulent anger of a man he knew—Gichtel acted to free someone from mental attachments.

In all these cases, our theosopher helped free people from the things their soul was clinging to, in order that they could in freedom realize spiritual peace. Such peace is not possible so long as one's mind is clinging to any created thing, so long as around oneself are woven the veils of phantasy. Emotional problems such as great wrath, or attachment to jewelry, or attachment to one's deceased husband, all encapsulate the soul and prevent its illumination; they are like astral shields. In this respect, we can certainly view Gichtel as a practicing psychologist.

But we should remember that, according to Gichtel and the other theosophers, religious practice and doctrine can itself also form a subtle veil against realizing the inward meaning of these practices and doctrines. From the theosophic perspective, this inward meaning and actual, existential transmutation of the soul takes absolute precedence over all outward forms of religion. Thus Gichtel said once in a letter that inward, unceasing prayer in the heart is absolutely necessary, and that he can hardly bring himself to say even the Lord's Prayer outwardly, for what truly matters is within.

Here we begin to see why the theosophers could easily be misunderstood and attacked, particularly by those powerfully attracted to orthodoxy. Concepts of orthodoxy, while necessary for the maintenance and definition of a tradition, themselves can become ways of asserting selfhood and inflating pride. One learns through the ratiocinative mind and feels that through this accumulation of knowledge one has mastered the truth, when in reality one is more prey to pride than ever. Such a person would no doubt be terribly threatened by a Gichtel or a Pordage, who insist that such knowledge and concepts are hollow facsimiles of the one thing needful, which is actual transmutation of the soul.

Yet as we have seen, the theosophers took care not to denigrate the sacraments or spiritual practices of the "outward church," of whatever denomination. Indeed, even the Philadelphian society—as close to a sect as any theosophic group came—directly asserted that one should not leave one's own sect or tradition, much less denigrate it and, in joining the Philadelphians, create a new sect and astral barrier to spiritual realization. Rather, one should remain Catholic, or Lutheran, or in whatever denomination outwardly, while inwardly working in the spiritual struggle through prayer toward liberation.

It is true, of course, that wherever one finds mysticism founded on the transcendence of forms, there is a danger of libertinism. The mysticism of Eckhart and Tauler was accompanied by the excesses of the Brethren of the Free Spirit, against whom the German mystics warned their hearers. So too the later German and English mystics had some followers who, having heard the Böhmean admonition to transcend formal religion and realize inwardly the truth that shall set one free, understood this freedom to be freedom from conventional morality. Certainly this error is to be found among the so-called Ranters, the seventeenth-century English sect that preached blasphemy, sexual license, and the use of alcohol.

Probably the most notorious of the Böhmeans in this regard was Eva von Buttlar, who from 1687 to 1697 lived in the circle of the court of Eisenach, having married a dancing instructor and court steward. In 1697, however, she underwent a religious conversion, and was dismissed from the court circle as a result. Returning to her home town of Eschwege, she encountered the writings of Dr. Pordage and other Böhmeans, and she became an adherent of Sophianic mysticism, generating a small circle of adherents. But apparently Eva von Buttlar and her circle greatly misunderstood the principles of Sophianic mysticism, chiefly the necessity of chastity constantly affirmed by Gichtel and other Böhmeans on the Continent, and by Pordage, Leade, and the other English Böhmeans as well.

For Eva von Buttlar, basing herself on a personal revelation, apparently believed that she was an incarnation of Sophia, and the "second Eve," and that she therefore ought to unite with as many men as possible. She and two of her circle—men named Winter and Appenfeller—also held themselves to be incarnations of Joseph, Mary, and Jesus, or Father, Son, and Holy Spirit. In her circle, it was charged, all things were held in common, including rights of sexual union. Of course, we cannot tell today whether these charges are accurate—certainly, as the case of Dr. Pordage himself shows, there were many false charges levelled against Böhmeans. But whether true or not, the case of Eva von Buttlar does illustrate what might happen if one assumes liberty from the *spiritus mundi*, the astral realm, and the influence of Venus while in fact being wholly subject to them.[13]

No doubt Pordage himself, like Gichtel, would have been horrified by such a result of Böhmean theosophy. But there are enough examples of such cases in German and English history—one thinks of the Ellers in Germany, whose group held that they were Joseph and Mary, their son actually Jesus himself, or of Abiezer Coppe in England, who apparently shouted blasphemies while preaching, sometimes naked, and held that the dispensation of the new age allowed for unlimited copulation—to suggest that when misunderstood, the theosophic concept of penetrating the astral and of transcending religious forms can have disastrous results.

Of course such examples cannot be ascribed to Böhme or his fellow theosophers, whose ascetic way of life was well known and acknowledged even by those who in general very much disliked the school. As a rule, theosophers insist that one remain within the church or denomination to which one already belongs; never do they suggest that man has received a dispensation to libertine freedom. In terms of theosophic psychology, however, we can certainly understand why such confusion can come about. Failing to understand the nature of phantasy, the libertine mistakes his own veil of concupiscient illusions to be spiritual in origin; he takes literally what must be understood spiritually, and so in a strange way, makes of theosophy an aberrant kind of fundamentalism. He holds that an individual literally becomes Christ, or a member of the Trinity, that Sophianic mysticism entails a literal, not spiritual but carnal, union. Far from achieving spiritual liberty by penetrating the astral, he is in fact, from a theosophic worldview, ever more deeply enslaved by it.

Curiously, precisely the same poles—libertinism on the one hand, and asceticism on the other—were attributed to some Christian Gnostics of the second and third centuries A.D. One cannot help but wonder if Böhmean theosophy is not in essence a manifestation of the same spiritual perspective one finds in ancient Gnosticism. More than one modern scholar has suggested this, and in fact, theosophic scholars themselves, including Gottfried Arnold in his *Unpartyesche Kirchen-und Ketzerhistorie (Impartial Church and Heretic History)* (1700), held to a thesis along these lines.[14] To the relationship between theosophy and Gnosticism, and its ramifications regarding "penetrating the astral," we now turn.

PART FOUR

CONTEXTS

CHAPTER EIGHTEEN

Theosophy and Gnosticism

M ost people today are probably more familiar
with early Christian Gnosticism of the second
and third centuries A.D. than with Böhmean theosophy
of the eighteenth century A.D. This is, of course, somewhat paradoxical, since historically early Christian
Gnosticism is certainly more distant from us. But modern religious scholarship has uncovered and focused on
Gnosticism in depth—we have numerous remarkable,
comprehensive, and comparatively neutral studies of
Gnosticism, the most prominent of which is that of German scholar Kurt Rudolph—while theosophy has been
given almost no attention at all, especially in the English-speaking world. Those few modern scholars who have focused on
theosophy have often noted the striking parallels between Gnosticism
and theosophy, but no one has closely examined this topic phenomenologically. Thus, our effort here will be to suggest both lines of
enquiry and the central points of convergence between these two
apparently disparate historical movements.

But first we need to consider how much Böhmean theosophy was
directly influenced by early Christian Gnosticism. Naturally, there is little reason to posit some kind of historical continuity between theosophy
and early Christian gnosis; while there are certainly numerous historical

enigmas involved here (the resemblance between some forms of Jewish Kabbala, Mazdaean, Manichaean, and Gnostic Christian religions has been noted before), it seems unnecessary and conspiratorial to posit a grand historical "initiatory transmission" when it should be obvious that in question is not historical transmission, but the rediscovery of essentially the same religion of light in different cultural contexts.

Certainly there is ample proof that some of the later theosophers, who had a scholarly bent, recognized the congruence between Gnosticism, particularly Valentinian Gnosticism, and Böhmean theosophy. In Germany, of course, this affinity was recognized by Gottfried Arnold in his *Unpartyesche Kirchen-und Ketzerhistorie* (*Impartial Church and Heretic History*) (1700), as it was by Ferdinand Christian Baur later in the same century. But this affinity is not to be taken as an endorsement; the theosophic scholars recognized that theosophy was not identical to Gnosticism.

Although to my knowledge this has not before been recognized, the later English theosophers of the early eighteenth century came to the same conclusions. In Dionysius Andreas Freher's "The Substance of a Conversation betwixt a German Theosophist and an English Divine, Mr. W. and Mr. J." we find in a question and answer format that the subject of ancient Gnosticism soon arises. The "Gnosticks," it is asserted, "derived from Eastern Theology," and "held that there was an Abyss, or State of Silence in God, long before the production of the Logos, or Word; which I find your Masters contradict in asserting the Eternity of the Logos."[1] The connection between theosophy and Eastern Orthodoxy we will discuss elsewhere; for now we should note the subtlety of the theological question here.

The questioner offers a possible compromise position as well, noting that some assert "the Eternal Logos to be the Son of God, but also [affirm] the necessity of a Super-Angelical Nature, or a Created Son of God, which opinon some Orthodox Persons have thought not to be all-together hæretical."[2] The theosopher's answer apparently does not directly oppose this position, but emphasizes the inward nature of the theosophic revelation, for he replies, "Our Masters assert the Eternal Inward Speaking word to be the Son of God, but they also say that somewhat is to be spoken forth by the word in the Godhead."

Here the English questioner broaches the subject of Sophia, divine wisdom, the feminine counterpart to the logos, a divine "Emanation distinct from the Logos." "Our Masters," the German theosopher tells the English divine, "seem to me to assert such an Emanation, which they call

Divine Wisdom, and conceive to be subordinate to the Trinity, and to be Eternally Spoken, and breathed forth in the Godhead by the Word and Spirit."[3] The English interrogator replies:

> Sophia, or Wisdom, is a celebrated Emanation amongst the ÆONS of the Gnosticks, and one of the Sephirôth of the Jewish Cabbalists, and is also described by some as a kind of a most subtle spirit, Quintessence, or anima mundi, the Chief of the Created Beings of this world, and pervading all of them.[4]

While the Sophia of the "Gnosticks" is not here said to be identical to the Sophia of the theosophers, clearly our theosophers themselves recognize the parallels between their school and its antecedents in Kabbala and in ancient Gnosticism. We will return to Sophia again shortly.

We should note here that the theosophers are not inclined to stigmatize Kabbala or Gnosticism as heretical because theirs is a school of experience more than of received doctrine. Freher's "Conversation" does represent an oral transmission of theosophic concepts from Germany to England—and very likely has its origin in actual contact between German and English theosophic circles—but we should be aware that while the "Conversation" is primarily engaged in transmitting essential Böhmean cosmology, this cosmology contextualizes and supports theosophic practice and visionary spirituality; it is not simply "dogma" to which one accedes. The essential concepts of Böhmean theosophic cosmology provide one with a way of *seeing* the cosmos in an ever more profound sense; if there are historical parallels to this, all the better. Thus, although the theosophers were aware of Gnosticism, they were not inspired by it.

But we should note the form that Freher's "Conversation" takes: it is, precisely, a "Conversation," questions and answers, a dialogue, the same form that we find in many early Christian Gnostic texts, as also in the *Corpus Hermeticum*. A conversation or dialogue presumes that there are only two people, a master and a student, although in this case the student is extremely learned and not merely a foil for the master as in some dialectic expositions, for instance John Erigena's masterpiece *Periphyseon*. Here we have two highly developed intelligences, almost equals, one of whom is more experienced in the school of the German "masters" than the other. But Freher's "Conversation" is definitely in the tradition of individualized Hermetic revelation dialogues with direct parallels in Kabbalistic, Gnostic, Platonic, and Hermetic texts.

There is much more to be said about Freher's "Conversation" and Gnosticism. But most important is the general nature of the exposition, which shows an extremely high level of theosophic understanding in both parties; the English questioner in certain respects seems to know more than, or certainly as much as, his German partner. Thus the dialogue assumes the form of mutual affirmation: each demonstrates or tests his understanding against the other, and both against our "German masters." As in Hermeticism generally, here it is not a matter of an ignoramus going to an idealized, exaggerated master for illumination, but rather two highly developed intelligences working together in the same spiritual method and understanding, testing and deepening their experience in dialectic. This is a very important point.

We will not be surprised, then, to find the following exposition attributed not to the German theosopher's answer, but to the English theosopher's question:

> And I think that it may be accordingly safely asserted, that God who is an Infinite mind or understanding, may be consider'd first as Seeing or knowing Himself as One in his own Central All-sufficiency; Next, as seeing or knowing himself, in Distinction as his Son, who is his Express Image, and Generated Wisdom, and then, as Seeing or knowing all possible beings actually in their Ideas, or Forms, in his eternal Logos (Himself as generated) as in an infinite Omniform Mirror, which some call the Ideal Wisdom or Ideal World; and take [it] not to be any thing really distinct from God, but to be the Essence of God as understood by Himself.[5]

This understanding of the Divine knowing himself through the archetypes of all creation as in a mirror is essential to English theosophy, and central to John Pordage's treatise *Theologia Mystica* (1683), which details exactly our entry into this understanding in terms of visionary revelation. Without doubt, Freher was working in the same tradition as Pordage here.

The German theosopher confirms this understanding of the profound relationship between God and his knowledge of himself in the ideas or archetypal forms of all things contained in the Logos. God knows himself through the Logos "as in an infinite Omniform Mirror" of the ideal world of archetypes. What is more, his masters consider the Trinity as an "Eternal Diffusion, Opening, or Manifestation" of the "Eternal Infinite Abyss of Being and Perfection" contained in divine unity by an "Eternal willing, Living (or Operating, Working) Delight in itself."[6]

This understanding of the Divine as realizing itself in creation is found throughout Christian mysticism, including the Eastern Orthodox church fathers. But this insight has a correlative implication: if God is to realize himself fully in this world, it can only be through those who, as earthly creatures, unite the three worlds of body, soul, and spirit—it can only be through mankind, of whom Christ-Sophia is the archetype of perfection. Hence, the purpose of human beings is not to simply believe in an historical Christ who saved them vicariously, but to realize in themselves the fullness of human possibility through spiritual knowledge, gnosis, spiritual insight, the purest exemplar of which is Christ-Sophia, the Logos-Sophia.

For Christ, as the incarnate Logos, is therefore intermediary between the transcendence of God and the phenomena of creation, for he contains the archetypal or ideal world within which are the forms or ideas, the archetypes of all things in creation. In order for a human being to realize the Logos in himself, he must allow the Logos to be born in him, which implies that he must realize a new form of seeing, a new inward vision. This vision is born through Sophia, or Divine Wisdom, who is the "Mother of the Logos," imaged in the Virgin Mary who gave birth to Christ.

Thus, the theosophers use some of the same terms as the Christian Gnostics of the early Christian era, particularly Logos and Sophia. And the theosophers' insistence on inward realization of truth through gnosis is similar to Gnosticism. But the theosophers do not interpret Gnostic terms mythologically, as oftentimes the Gnostics did. Thus for many Gnostic sects, Sophia meant the female archetype of divine wisdom, but was imaged as a fallen mythological being who needed to be restored to her original purity. The theosophers do not work with mythology, which was much more accessible to the early Gnostics in the wake of the Greco-Roman mystery religions.

Rather, the theosophers are essentially spiritual psychologists, if we may put it that way; their emphasis is quite clearly on inward vision alone. This is not to say that the early Gnostics did not realize the mythological Sophia as an inward experience—no doubt they did, just as in Apuleius's *The Golden Ass* Isis is revealed as an overwhelming experience in the mystery religion. But the theosophers lived in a modern "demythologized" and scientific world, and in such a world mythological realities are primarily accessible only as spiritual or visionary psychology.

Nonetheless, there are other fundamental parallels between Gnosticism and Böhmean theosophy, perhaps most important of which is the place of the seven planets or seven spirits, in Gnosticism sometimes called the "hebdomad." Both in ancient Gnosticism and in theosophy—as in antiquity generally, and in traditional medieval Catholicism—the seven planets are seen not merely as bodies revolving in orbit, but as qualities that can be found throughout the natural world. Thus one can speak of a "Martial" person who is fiery, angry, violent, or of a "Jovial" scene, or of a beautiful scene that partakes of Venus, her green, luxuriant nature. Such qualities can be seen in minerals, plants, animals, and people.

But there is more to the hebdomad than astrological correspondences or signatures, both in Gnosticism and in theosophy. In both, the seven planets are also seen as reflecting cosmological principles, called in Gnosticism "archons," and in theosophy the "seven spirits" or "seven forms." The Gnostic archons and the theosophers' spirits are anterior to the planets; they are anterior to creation itself. The archons, however, assume a maleficent quality; they represent—for Gnosticism as generally depicted in contemporary scholarship—the cosmos as "imprisonment" for the spiritual being. This is not so in theosophy—here the seven spirits represent the principles informing creation, emanations of the Divine. The cosmos, for theosophers, is not exactly imprisonment, nor are the seven spirits like archons, who apparently oppose human spiritual development.

Kurt Rudolph elaborates on the "penal" significance of the seven planets in Mandean religion:

> A common conception in Mandean literature is that of the release of the soul from the charge of the evil forces, i.e., the "Seven" [planets], by an act of force on the part of the "helper" or messenger of light. Not only does the idea of the wall of the firmament, which has to be breached, play a role here, but also that of the super-terrestrial penal stations, on which the sinful are detained; they can be redeemed only by a feat of the world of light (assisted in no small measure by the prayers and ceremonies of the earthly community!).[7]

The luminous spirit, who belongs intrinsically to the world of light beyond the astral realm, is constrained by these seven forces personified in the form of beings, and can in Mandean tradition only be saved by the world of light and its intrinsic grace.

So too, in many early Christian Gnostic traditions—as in late antiquity generally—fate or *heimarmene* entraps human beings within the astral sphere of the seven planets, the hebdomad. Only beyond the sphere of Saturn is there paradise, in the "eighth realm"; the pleroma, or transcendent realm of inconceivable light is beyond this eighth realm in the "ninth."[8] We might note, however, that the only distinction to be made between this cosmology and precisely the same cosmology as it appears in the poetry of Dante more than ten centuries later, is the interpretation of the cosmos as "wicked" or in opposition to human illumination. In both cases earth is at the center, around it are the successive planetary spheres, and around these are the inconceivable pleroma of divine light.

Exactly the same cosmology appears in Böhmean theosophy with, what is more, a historical awareness of its antecedents. In Freher's "Conversation" we read the following exchange:

> Q: I remember I have read somewhat of what you have said in the writings of the Hermetick Philosophers and of those who have delivered down the Traditions of the Chaldaick and Egyptian Philosophers. But from whence do they suppose all the mixt things of this world to arise, as from their first Root or Principle?
>
> A: From Seven chief invisible active Beings, which they call Spirits, Forms, and Qualities, answering in outward Temporal Nature, to the Seven Spirits of Eternal Nature, which are supposed by them to be in every thing in this world.[9]

Thus, the seven spirits are the "First Root, Sperm, Spiritual prima materia of all things," and the seven planets are their reflection. The theosophers are aware of how their cosmology has its parallels in the cosmology inherited from late antiquity, seen too in medieval Catholicism. But nowhere in this cosmology does one find the apparently uniformly maleficent planetary symbolism attributed to Gnosticism or to Mandean religion.

This is not to say that for the theosophers, the planets could not take on a malevolent symbolism. Everything depended upon the individual psyche or attitude. For example, Gichtel wrote often of those who were under the domination of Mars, were wrathful, fiery, or of the blandishments of the "Venusian" love of luxury and venery. These influences were always to be opposed, overcome. But these planetary powers were essentially seen in terms of the individual or collective psyche. Whole groups might be dominated by such powers or qualities, as can be seen in the hatred and frenzies whipped up by war, for example, yet among the theosophers these powers are not externalized in the form of specific planetary demons, mythological beings to be opposed.

At the same time, we do not know precisely what the maleficent "hebdomad" really signified for the psyche of the individual Gnostic in late antiquity. It may well be that the "maleficent" planetary demons are simply representations in mythological form of the same inward experiences one finds again in eighteenth-century theosophy. After all, there is a direct continuity of tradition in this sense: Christianity embraced among its many forms in antiquity some movements called Gnostic, and therefore it is not that surprising if a similar movement were to reëmerge in the Christian tradition many centuries later, simply because it corresponds to real possibilities inherent in the tradition itself.

But some theosophers did more or less distinguish themselves from Gnosticism conceived as heresy. For example, when Henry Dodwell wrote Dr. Francis Lee (the Oxford Orientalist scholar, who had married the daughter of theosopher visionary Jane Leade and was a member of the Philadelphians) one of Dodwell's accusations against Leade was precisely that she was nothing more than a Gnostic heretic in new clothing. Lee, whose writing style is nothing if not pedantically long-winded, defends his mother-in-law carefully: "There are three points which you take notice of, and call *antiquated heresies*, which I shall say nothing to vindicate in this place, but only set them in their true light; whether it be heresy or truth, new or old."[10] Lee does not deny an affinity to Gnosticism; he is concerned with what is true, and if the truths Leade espoused are found in Gnosticism, so be it.

The central charge Lee answers is "of Gnosticism, from the seeming to introduce a female personality into the Deity."[11] The "female personality" is Sophia, the feminine personification of Divine Wisdom, and Lee affirms that Leade's visionary spirituality only continues the ancient tradition from Solomon through the New Testament and the Church Fathers of referring to Sophia or Wisdom in this way. Lee writes: "She useth to speak of Wisdom in the same manner as doth Solomon in his Proverbs, and the author of the Book of Wisdom: yea, as Christ himself doth, Matt. xi.19." Thus: "She means not to assert any diversity of sex in the Deity, as the Gentiles and Gnostics did."[12]

And indeed, Sophia or Wisdom for the theosophers is essentially different from the Sophia of the Gnostics. For Valentinian Gnosticism, Sophia is a mythological being, the drama of whose fall, repentence, and redemption is a central theme in the "Apocryphon of John." "The Apocryphon of John" tells the myth of how Sophia created without the help of the higher God, and so was born the monstrous demiurge Yaldaboath, from whom in turn mankind was created, whose task it is to be redeemed like Sophia.[13] This essentially negative symbolism is not found among the theosophers: just as the theosophers affirm the positive symbolism of the seven spirits or seven planets, so too for them Sophia, as the celestial Virgin, possesses only a salvific symbolism; she is never a fallen celestial being, as she is for Valentinian Gnosticism.

For the theosophers, Sophia is experienced as a "tincture," as a spiritual communion. Freher defines "tincture," a technical term that appears throughout theosophic literature, in the following way: "What the Tincture is . . . no tongue can name, or even he that knows it, cannot convey any true notion thereof to an other, but it must be opened by Practice and *Experience*."[14] But if one were to explain the term, it would be by saying that "it is something arising from the Union of Fire and Light"; it is what makes possible the communication between two creatures, for by the tincture "there is represented on one side and perceived on the other, the proper and peculiar Constitution of that Creature, so that without it no Conversation could be between them."

Sophia herself is not a fourth to the Holy Trinity, but rather is the matrix of the divine creative power, and as such is the bride of the Logos, or bridegroom. She, along with the Logos, is intermediary between humanity and God, is the creative power through which all things came to be, and thus is also the spiritual effulgence through whom humanity returns to the paradisal and eternal worlds.[15] Thus, for the theosophers, she is not a mythological being so much as a tincture, an illumination. She illuminates and transmutes man in a mystical marriage that is an inexpressible experience.

For Gichtel in particular, Sophia represented transcendent, immutable unity, and thus

> when Adam broke off from the unity, viz, from the heavenly
> Sophia, and . . . wanted himself to do and create, as his astral
> reason and *ratiocinatio*, understood it, he lost the power of
> the light, and the darkness obtained government of him.
> Which is indeed the origin of sin . . . that we no longer know
> God's light, viz, Sophia.[16]

For the theosophers, Sophia did not fall as in Valentinian Gnosticism— it was man who fell away from Sophia, and to her, to the experience that transcends mere astral reason and offers him direct realization of God's light, man must return in order to be redeemed.

To attain this experience, the theosophers enjoined themselves to complete chastity. This was true of Pordage, certainly, as of the Philadelphians later, it was true of the "woman in the wilderness" and Ephrata communities in Pennsylvania, and it was to some extent even true of Gichtel's "Brethren of the Angelic Life" or "Engelbrüder," who like the Philadelphians regarded men and women more or less equally, and lived in strict, monastic chastity. Among none of the Böhmean theosophers does one find libertinism; all lived exceedingly careful moral lives pledged in troth to the Holy Sophia and the Logos.

To say that there are differences in expression, however, or even in implication, as in the myth of Sophia, is not to say that there are no parallels between the Gnostic views of the cosmos and the theosophic understanding. We have already noted some parallels, including planetary symbolism and Sophia, but have not yet discussed the most important parallels of all. Some modern scholars have defined ancient Gnosticism as characterized above all by the concept of the demiurge, or ignorant creator-god whom man must transcend in order to realize his own true spiritual nature. While there is in theosophy no concept of the demiurge as such—there is in Böhmean cosmology no elaborate mythology of an Ialdaboath, for example—still there is a striking correspondence between the Gnostic demiurge and the theosophers' concept of *spiritus mundi*.

The *spiritus mundi*—or spirit of this world—in theosophy has little mythological significance, but it has eminently practical implications. Probably these implications are most clearly seen in Gichtel's *Theosophia Practica*, where whenever someone Gichtel knows succumbs to a temptation, he or she is said to have fallen prey to the *spiritus mundi*. The demiurge in Gnostic theology is distinguished by its deluded egotism: it is a "jealous God," who wishes to be alone among all Gods. This is essentially the same attitude that the *spiritus mundi* fosters in us; the *spiritus mundi* tries us to see if we will be tempted by this or that. Prayer unites people, but those who fall away into temptation, Gichtel writes, fancy themselves great and fall into disunity: "I want to exalt myself, and to rule over [others] as their head."[17] Thus, such people "now groan under the dreadful burden of the *spiritus mundi*."

Gichtel is here referring to specific people who once were members of his group, but who fell away—due to the same ignorance or egotism that is often attributed to the Gnostic demiurge, but here is called the temptation of the *spiritus mundi*. The spirit of this world draws us toward selfishness, which can take countless forms, but ultimately amounts to self-exaltation in one way or another, and denial of self-transcendence and of higher power or illumination. The spirit of this world tells us that our "astral reason" is sufficient and lures us into complacency, which ultimately means anguish and the absence of spiritual joy and inward peace. All of this reveals a psychological and spiritual understanding in theosophy that, although it closely resembles Gnostic theology in some respects, is peculiarly modern.

Many people cannot resist the testing or temptations offered by the *spiritus mundi*. This testing period Gichtel called the *proba*, and to it he refers on numerous occasions in his letters. In 1710 he wrote a correspondent about his own early years in Amsterdam:

> And when I came to this country, God tried me with many rich women, which temptation by the strength of Jesus, I resisted, whereupon many followers joined me, who indeed were enamored of Jesus, but did not stand in the *proba*, and all except one turned back. [But] here and there good minds heard the voice of the bridegroom and prepared for the marriage.[18]

The *proba* is necessary, according to Gichtel, just as in chivalry the knight is only proven by the testing.

While at first this *proba* might seem rather a simple matter of overcoming temptation, in Gichtel's works it is but one aspect of a complete metaphysics bearing close resemblance to Gnosticism. This metaphysics is a matter, not of fantasizing, but of visionary experience. Gichtel writes:

> It is not a self-imagined thing—What I write is pure experience and intuition; the sufferings [of temptation] are the pangs of labor, at which nature is terrified, and thinks of all kinds of means to protect herself, which gives the *spiritus mundi* opportunities to try us.[19]

If the soul sustains itself against these temptations, it receives a "robe of glory" or a "body of power" from the Virgin that profoundly resonates with ancient Gnostic allegories:

> The Virgin brings the first forming and creating powers as a dowry into the soul, clothes it therewith, and surrounds it with her powers, viz, a body of power, wherein the soul becometh God's servant and priest, and also can step before God and take what it asketh for, as much as it requires for its bodily necessities.[20]

This "clothing" of the soul corresponds well with a similar passage in the "Gospel of Philip":

> The powers do not see those who are clothed in the per-
> fect light, and consequently are not able to detain them. One
> will clothe himself in this light sacramentally in the
> union . . . [T]he woman is united to her husband in the
> bridal chamber. . . . Jesus . . . who was redeemed in return
> redeemed others. . . . It is fitting for each of the disciples to
> enter into his rest.[21]

The parallels here—the opposition of powers to the soul's illumination, the clothing of the soul with light through the power of the Virgin and the inward marriage, the idea that those who are redeemed in return have a responsibility to redeem others—are rather striking.

At heart, testing of soul in wrath is itself not only preparation for death, but the realization of a body of light. Christ adds to our souls his own flesh and blood, "clothing our naked soul, that it can stand in the fire, and this He doeth until the soul can live with our suffering in the fire of God's wrath."[22] The soul must live in the fire of wrath until it becomes like the wrath itself—one with the fire, the soul is purified in this lifetime, and the fire becomes pure light, so it is no longer experienced as fire at all. This process has a parallel in Tibetan Buddhist wrathful deities, upon whom an initiate meditates and which he realizes ultimately as indivisible from the spiritual origin of both good and evil. One who has realized this becomes a "Melchizidekian priest of God," and can take upon himself and burn up in "expiatory sacrifices" the sins of the people[23]

In theosophy as in Gnosticism, then, the empowered soul also has new responsibilities for creation, since it now must truly walk in the path of Christ. But in return, it receives "what it asketh for," which explains perhaps how Gichtel and his brethren survived for many years without any apparent means of support (he was accused by some of being an alchemist or of having secret funds in Germany). The soul is invested with light and filled with joy, but it must in turn bear the burdens of others, and redeem others from the powers of this world. At the same time, its earthly needs will be provided for it, by miracles if necessary.

Thus, theosophers offer a triadic differentiation among religious aspirants that corresponds quite closely to the well-known Gnostic schema of hylic, psychic, and pneumatic man. According to some Gnostic sects, mankind is divided into hylic, or materially fixated people, psychic man (whose primary interest is the human, social world), and pneumatic man, whose aspiration is for a truly spiritual life. Likewise, Gichtel distinguishes between "bestial man," he who "prayeth in the sensual astral man," and the third, who "prayeth in spirit and in truth." This distinction, Gichtel writes, "I have learnt by the illumination of the holy spirit, who opened my understanding and my inward mental eyes."[24] One wonders whether these categories do not truly correspond to archetypal divisions among human beings generally.

Let us turn to summary for a moment. We have seen that even though there are signal differences between ancient Gnosticism (particularly of the Valentinian tradition) and theosophy, these differences amount in the end to differences in means of expression. They are not fundamental. It is true that some of the more scholarly theosophers differentiated their movement from ancient Gnosticism, particularly when accused of being Gnostics reborn. However, they did not reject Gnosticism out of hand, and in some cases affirmed its value. In the meantime, we can see all the major defining characteristics of Gnosticism in theosophy: Sophia, the hebdomad, the symbolism of the bridal chamber and the inward marriage, the demiurge or *spiritus mundi*, the constraints of the "astral" and the necessity of clothing the soul with the robe of glory and perfect light.

So let us conclude with some remarks on the significances of these parallels. We may begin by noting that one need not posit a direct historical connection between theosophy and Gnosticism. Certainly there is no evidence whatever that the central visionary force in theosophy—the spiritual vision, terms, and cosmology of Jacob Böhme—was influenced by Gnosticism. Böhme himself, and all the theosophers who followed after him, insisted that each individual have direct spiritual experience; indeed, in some cases, the visionary experiences came first, and the theosopher then came to Böhme's works as the best explanation for what was happening. Hence, although certain scholarly theosophers were aware of Gnosticism as a historical force in antiquity, none claimed theosophy and Gnosticism to be identical, or even affiliated.

Now, if there was no historical affiliation between theosophy and Gnosticism—other than the fact that both arose in Christianity and are strikingly parallel as modes of visionary spirituality—the parallels between them become all the more significant. For it is one thing to posit some shadowy initiatory continuity through the centuries, as some popular authors might, and quite another to realize that we are dealing here, not with an historical extension of Gnosticism, but with a mode of being—of spiritual seeing—that could reappear in the beginning of the modern era just as it had appeared in the beginning of the Christian era.

If Valentinian Gnosticism, for example, and theosophy were essentially the same mode of visionary Christianity—albeit expressed in slightly different ways, one more mythological, one more psychological—this has ramifications for the study of ancient Gnosticism, and for those who are attracted to Gnosticism in the modern era. Theosophy offers a documented history of practitioners, their problems and triumphs, in ways that such ancient Gnostic collections as the Nag Hammadi Library cannot. As a result, theosophy may well offer insights into aspects of Gnosticism previously obscure.

For the fact is, Gnosticism as a historical movement is truly ancient, and distant from us not only in time, but in ways of thought, while theosophy is peculiarly modern. Closely tied to Greco-Hermetic thought and to mythological ways of experience, Gnosticism is fundamentally foreign to us, and I doubt that it is possible to establish a modern Gnostic tradition, despite recent efforts. However, theosophy arose precisely at the beginning of the modern era, and its insistence on individual experience and its reliance on small groups of like-minded people who are united not by institutional structure or dogma but by their common experiences and practices do seem especially suited to the modern era.

At the same time, there are certainly dangers inherent in such an individualized spiritual practice, and the history of theosophy illustrates this. While none of the major theosophers can be accused of having fallen into libertinism—far from it, in fact—there were certainly libertines such as Abiezer Coppe of the seventeenth century, who like some Gnostic libertines attacked bitterly by Iraneus and Hippolytus, took spiritual freedom to mean license and licentiousness. Nihilism and libertinism appeared in the penumbra of both Gnosticism and theosophy, and one can expect that these are dangers inherent in the visionary movement itself, its shadow, so to say.

But that there exist spiritual deviations or confusions does not invalidate theosophy as a whole, which is remarkably, even strikingly unified and coherent in terminology, cosmology, and visionary experience. Indeed, such deviations or confusions might better be seen as the exceptions that prove the rule—traditional theosophy—is valid. For certainly with its rich history and literature, and many cultures and continents, theosophy presents a visionary path that is extraordinarily unified and yet relies wholly on individual experiential validation. Such a path, whatever its parallels to Gnosticism or Hermeticism, may well speak to us most clearly when it turns us not outward toward dogmatic comparisons but inward toward timeless spiritual experience itself.

CHAPTER NINETEEN

Alchemy and Theosophy

Certainly the place of alchemy in theosophy is difficult to assess. While on the one hand, Böhmean theosophy owes a considerable debt to alchemical terminology that derives from earlier German authors, especially Paracelsus, and to alchemical tradition more generally, on the other hand we find many of the practical theosophers—especially Gichtel—deriding their alchemist contemporaries, not to mention many of the alchemical manuscripts and recipes that came their way. But on the whole, it seems clear that Böhmean theosophers, in particular Gichtel, Pordage, and Kelpius, were deeply learned in alchemy and must be regarded as spiritual alchemists.

But let us begin by defining what we mean. There has developed a controversy, in the last several hundred years especially, over whether alchemy ought to be regarded primarily as a chemical discipline undertaken in a laboratory, or a spiritual discipline, for which the various apparently chemical processes are symbolic. Without wanting to be dismissive, it appears that our theosophers came out on the side of alchemy as primarily a spiritual discipline , but a spiritual discipline that can have definite results in the physical world.

This is most clearly the case with Johann Georg Gichtel, who wrote extensively in his letters about the subject of alchemy. From Gichtel's letters, we certainly see that seventeenth- and eighteenth-century Germany and Holland were hotbeds of alchemical experimentation, that many people were experimenting with recipes that purported to result in transmuting lead or some other metals into gold or into the elixir of life, and that a great deal of money was expended (often quite foolishly) in such efforts. Gichtel himself obviously knew many alchemists, had worked with spiritual alchemy at great length, and made no bones about dissuading people from its pursuit for gain or fame.

Without question, alchemy was rampant during the seventeenth and eighteenth centuries in Europe. Many of the illuminated manuscripts and primary works of alchemy, including numerous unparalleled engravings, date to this time and place, as books such as those of Stanislas Klossowski de Rola amply demonstrate.[1] Courts often had their hired alchemists, and more than one met sudden death when proven a fraud. But not all alchemy can be dismissed as fraud, whatever we might make today of efforts to manufacture gold or an elixir of life. For despite modern denigrations, alchemy inspired not only some remarkable works of art, but a complex philosophy of nature and spiritual discipline as well.

How this is so in theosophy is perhaps best examined in light of Gichtel's extensive letters. In 1703, Gichtel wrote:

> In the year 1666, when I held office at the imperial court at Vienna, a runaway monk of the order of St. Augustine gave the emperor a small grain of tincture, which in dusting the library of his monastery he had found in a chymical book and wrapped up in paper, wherewith in the presence of the emperor two ounces of lead were tinctured and turned into gold.[2]

Gichtel writes matter-of-factly about alchemy here as a reality; he does not doubt that this event happened. But he also writes, in the same letter, that then

> there was scarcely a monastery, courtier, indeed no rich citizen who would not have a share in it and did not give money for the work, which attracted many cheats who obtained money for their "particulars;" then I saw abominable rascality.[3]

Clearly, Gichtel was familiar with much false alchemy, but also with the true.

True alchemy, Gichtel emphasized, was alchemy under the guidance of holy Sophia, alchemy in a religious context. Alchemy separated from that context and become merely a search for gold was perverse and doomed, he wrote. Thus, he wrote in 1702,

> Chymistry enchants minds hungry after gold to such an
> extent that they fancy they are possessed of much knowledge,
> where yet it is hidden in God's wisdom, and none by his own
> authority can open the book of nature. The spirit of Sophia
> must both in chymistry and theology, co-work with our
> understanding, if we are to bring forth anything great.[4]

The true philosopher, he affirms, "must be brought by God out of the
inward ground, viz, out of the heavenly light world of Sophia. . . . [W]e
must be born anew of water and the spirit."[5]

Authentic alchemical mysteries are to be understood only by working
first inwardly, Gichtel continues, and those who work outwardly without
inward purification are grievously deceived: under such circumstances

> Deception is everywhere the end of the art; if it is stupid
> duplicity it deceives itself in opinion and imagination. For it
> runs in a false desire, and seeketh not inwardly in God; but
> outwardly in metals and minerals. . . .
>
> I have often wondered at the doings of such men that
> they love to make experiments before they are annointed by
> God and have received the key to nature, viz, the Holy Spirit,
> which arises from pure unbelief. . . . [N]one will sink down in
> God's will and give Him the honor, wherefore nature is weak
> and cannot show its powers.[6]

Seeking after outward gain through alchemy is a grave error, Gichtel
asserts, and leads into the "wilderness of flesh and the golden calf,"
worst of all when it is self-deception.

Gichtel evidently had a firm understanding of exactly how would-
be alchemists went wrong. He writes:

> I have thrown away more than a hundred such [false]
> processes; if I had them still, I would give them to you for noth-
> ing, warning you at the same time not to spend a penny on
> them, because it is all an imposition—Good N.——has spent
> 60,000 on such work, without finding one certain process.[7]

Gichtel details the exact nature of these processes to a correspondent
in 1697:

> Many a worker in the laboratory obtains a metal which in the
> separation seems rich, and he immediately fancies he has a
> good particular, but when he repeats it, he finds himself
> deceived, and thinks perhaps he has made a mistake in the

process, founding his opinion on his first trial, and seeking
purchasers, that give him money or at least means for experiments, and send the money up the chimney.[8]

Hence, he concludes,

> In this manner *the other noble art* has come to be despised.
> For my precious time is too short to examine and refute the
> processes; it is enough that there is no *solutio corporum nat-*
> *uralis vel vera, sed sophistica*, and only loss of gold.[9]

All these processes were erroneously based in seeking limited "particu-
lars" that can tincture only a few parts of a metal, but the true "particular" "rises out of the universal spring."

Gichtel's understanding of how false alchemy came about was counterbalanced by his grasp of the authentic alchemy that arises out of the
universal spring of divine wisdom. He writes, using Böhmean terminology of course, that

> Even in the philosopher's tincture I find the *turba* [evil wrath-
> fire] and see that the possessors are volatile, and can do little
> good therewith, for the *spiritus mundi* is opposed to them,
> shuts them up in selfhood, and hinders all good; they do not
> know true poverty, and lack the spirit of discretion, and help
> not where they ought to do so, but only where they choose.[10]

Even the adepts are caught in selfishness, and so their alchemical discoveries come in the end to naught. This brings Gichtel to the remarkable assertion:

> Wherefore it is not good to be an adept unless you inwardly
> overcome the turba and bind the devil. Our experience far
> surpasses the philosopher's stone, for one must wrestle and
> strive with gods, and search after spiritual understanding,
> which is God himself in ourselves.[11]

I have read assertions to the effect that Gichtel had been presented with
the philosopher's stone and had refused it on several occasions. While of
course one cannot verify this story, it seems possible, given that here he
affirms directly "our experience far surpasses the philosopher's stone."

In 1703, Gichtel wrote about an acquaintance who sought to sell his
"potable gold" for money, and to argue with Gichtel about it because
Gichtel held that "the gold must radically be opened before it becomes
medicinal, which he wanted to refute." But Gichtel answered him that

the truth would not be elucidated by disputing, because the
work entirely depends upon the radical solution of the gold,
which none, however subtle his understanding, can effect with
spiritus urinae, sal amon., spir. vini, and such like astringent
menstrua, as they call them, and I am more than astonished
that they fancy they can make the aurum potabile and obtain
money for it, since such tincture would amply provide food.

But having noticed that fantasy is always greater and
more daring than truth, I was silent, because I know that at
last the deceit is found out by everyone. Such people know
how to maintain their opinion in so specious a manner, that
they cannot be convinced otherwise than by actual tincturing
before their own eyes, and then being told to their faces that
they are cheats and worthy of the rope.[12]

This is not the voice of a man unsure of himself on questions concerning alchemy.

Gichtel insists time and again that there are authentic adepts, and
that the error of false experimenters consists in trying to live well through
alchemy, in obtaining gold and extending the fleshly life. "These experimenters," he writes, "generally want to obtain a large capital, that they
may rest in the flesh, and be able, as they fancy, to serve God without
crosses, which God hindereth, seeking the good of the soul."[13] These people, as Heinrich Khunrath wrote in his *Amphitheatre*, try to "work without light," whereas Gichtel with all his heart wishes only that he may
have "mercy from God" and understand "the mystery of this our time."[14]

Even great learning is not enough to truly redeem an adept unless he
has the inward light of Sophia. Gichtel writes of one would-be alchemist
who tried to "apprehend from the emblems and hieroglyphics of the
Phoenicians, Egyptians, Brahmins and Greeks, the arcanum of their
worship and theology" but could not, because he "lacks the light of the
astral and metal tincture." "It is very different with me," Gichtel adds,
"because I was cast out of the world before I was married, and besought
God for his Holy Spirit, that he might lead me through the wilderness of
the world, which he mercifully heard, and gave me a trusting, humble,
and tender heart."[15]

From all of this it seems self-evident that Gichtel's theosophy
included an alchemical dimension, and that, precisely because he was
familiar with authentic alchemical transmutations, he was able to discern quacks. Nowhere, however, does he elaborate in a systematic way
just what this authentic spiritual alchemy consisted in; all we get in his

letters are fragmented allusions to this or that controversy or aspect of the alchemical praxis. One can surmise that Gichtel was familiar with laboratory work from his references to working with metals and elements; one can also surmise that his own alchemical practices were primarily inward, and only secondarily natural, because he decried as frauds those who concentrated only on outward alchemical working.

But such conclusions do not exclude the possibility that Gichtel himself practiced outward alchemy, and in fact he was so accused during his lifetime, in more than one instance by Dr. Breckling, who had known Gichtel intimately as a friend, and had then had a terrible falling-out with him. It is true that the Angelic Brethren, Gichtel's group, lived without apparent external support, which caused much speculation. Gichtel's biographer writes: "[None] could understand how it was possible to go on without borrowing or making debts. Breckling himself fell on the rational conclusion that it was impossible to live thus without the philosopher's stone. Therefore he said that Gichtel made gold, that for whole nights he had seen a light on in back-premises, etc."[16]

There are other possible interpretations for the invisible support of Gichtel and his fellow theosophers both male and female, but the most convincing of these in the end is probably the one he himself gave: prayer. It is true that Gichtel was accused of having a hidden fortune in Germany that was sent him in installments, of being a "coiner," of being an alchemist, and much else. But in his own writings he told his correspondents on numerous occasions that his physical sustenance came from God, because he had wholly given up any other means of sustenance than trust in God, who would provide those who asked. These means of keeping body and soul together were not altogether mysterious: wealthy merchants sometimes brought money, others sometimes brought food, and in all those years, Gichtel and his colleagues were always, almost miraculously sometimes, provided for. Prayer during night vigils would also explain the lights shining at night that Breckling mentioned.

Gichtel's works, like Gichtel himself, are assertive, even combative, and do not brook foolishness: they force us to take a stand ourselves. Gichtel was, from all indications, anything but easy to get along with, and quarrelled with almost everyone he knew at one point or another. This irascibility came, in large part, from an intense intellectual discernment, and an absolute refusal to tolerate foolishness or error. These are not qualities that make for easy friendships. But at the same time, Gichtel's forthright assertions about genuine alchemy and its counterfeits force us to admit that if there is a false alchemy, it can only be so by contradistinction to a real alchemy.

That there was an authentic alchemy was apparently also believed by some American theosophers in Pennsylvania from the early eighteenth century onwards. Johann Jacob Zimmermann, who headed the expedition to America of German theosophers until he died and was replaced by Johann Kelpius, was a renowned astrologer, and the community that this group founded in Pennsylvania along the banks of the Wissahickon River was also deeply interested in astrological, alchemical, and Hermetic sciences. This community is reputed to have practiced herbal medicine, thought that the American Indians possessed keys to philosophical wisdom, and above all, held that it was possible through alchemy "to remove all seeds of disease from the human body, thereby renewing youth and lessening the infirmities of age, if not repelling death."[17]

According to Julius Sachse, the Pennsylvania theosophers believed in a spiritual alchemy of the body that could lead to the "indefinite prolongation of human life." Reputedly, all the leaders of the Wissahickon community—including Kelpius, H. Bernard Köster, Justus Falkner, Johann Seelig, and Conrad Matthai—confirmed the possibility of an elixir of life, or in any case of translation into and communication with the afterlife. It is at least possible, given that Kelpius was an astrologer, that some in the Wissahickon community practiced Hermetic studies "only upon nights when the moon and planets were in certain positions," as Sachse claims. Kelpius himself purportedly had a cave that he had made into a hermit's cell, stocked with alchemical books and manuscripts and laboratory equipment.[18]

This preoccupation with alchemy was continued by the second prominent theosophic community in America, that of Ephrata, founded by Conrad Beissel, who came to Pennsylvania in 1720. The Ephrata community, like the earlier Wissahickon group, was a semi-monastic Protestant theosophic order in the wilderness, open to both men and woman. Hermetic science in Ephrata was invigorated by the arrival of Jacob Martin, a "High Philosopher" who arrived about 1762, who was considered an alchemical adept, and who followed Michael Sendivogius (1566–1646). Martin brought with him many alchemical manuscripts and processes.[19]

In fact, Martin built a working alchemical laboratory near Ephrata, and sought the "red tincture," with which Sendivogius had reputedly transmuted lead into 120,000 thalers of gold, and produced the *lapis philosophorum*. No mention of Martin's alchemical work is made in the

Ephrata chronicles themselves, and thus there is apparently little way of determining what the Ephrata community's official position was on physical alchemy along these lines. But one can conjecture that, like Gichtel, the Pennsylvania theosophers were not opposed to physical alchemy, simply recognizing it as subordinate to, indeed wasteful without, the spiritual alchemy under whose aegis physical alchemy could take place.

Perhaps most extraordinary aspect of Pennsylvanian theosophic alchemy may be its historical continuation at least into the late nineteenth and early twentieth centuries. Julius Sachse, in his massive three-volume series on the Pennsylvania theosophers, wrote that the Golden Elixir or elixir of life had indeed been apparently created by the theosophers, and was continued on from generation to generation. Dr. Hugo Hornemann told Sachse that he had been the custodian of the secret since June 1, 1863, his father from 1826 to 1863, Professor Stulig from 1822 to 1826, before this by Michael Richter, and before this by his father, Peter Richter. Sachse himself claimed to have obtained a vial of the elixir in the late nineteenth century.[20]

It is no doubt easy to dismiss such apocryphal tales of alchemy, but the more one examines theosophic works on alchemy during this time, the more one becomes convinced that under consideration is a discipline of transmutation, which does not necessarily involve the prolongation of physical life, but which involves the soul and its translation into the afterlife. Some of the Pennsylvania theosophers seemed convinced that they would not die in an ordinary manner, and were disappointed to learn that in fact they died much like other people do. But this does not alter the fact that many and perhaps all of the theosophers did practice spiritual alchemy, and some physical alchemy as well.

One of the most concise treatises on spiritual alchemy was written by Dr. John Pordage, probably during the 1670s, although not published, in German in a very rare edition, until 1727.[21] However, it no doubt circulated in manuscript form among many theosophic groups, who would copy out by hand and so transmit the most important theosophic works. This treatise explains that the "red tincture," emphasized in so many alchemical treatises as essential for tincturing gold and creating the elixir of life, is the "red tincture of paradise," the "pure sweet blood of Virginal humanity."[22] Pordage in this little work definitely is elaborating a process of spiritual alchemy, a transmutation of the forces in the human soul.

Consequently, Pordage's "Philosophical Treatise on the Real and True Stone of Wisdom" focuses on the planetary forces and their symbolism. He writes about how the forces of Venus (lust) and Mars (anger) must be transmuted into their pure and archetypal forms, how Saturn and Mars signify God's wrath, and how Lucifer's legions are organized in the wrath-fire, how the soul must pass through darkness and corruption in order to be reborn. This rebirth entails a harmony of Saturn, Mercury, Mars, Venus, and Luna; it derives from the soul's purification and tincturing with the "blood of the Virgin," which in turn produces the Pearl of the Virgin, the Pearl of wisdom.

Pordage's treatise exemplifies spiritual alchemy; clearly Pordage is writing about the soul's transmutation and illumination. One could interpret this treatise as providing a spiritual context within which physical alchemy could take place, but there is little in the text to indicate such a possibility, nor was Pordage reputed to have been a practicing physical alchemist. The "red tincture" is clearly conceived in spiritual terms, as is the Pearl of wisdom; this alchemy consists in the purification of the soul and refers to definite stages in that process of purification and illumination. Alchemy was no doubt seen primarily in this way by all the theosophic alchemists.

There are other works that also demonstrate the importance of spiritual alchemy in this theosophic tradition, including one by a member of the Pordage and Leade circle in London, Edmund Brice. Brice's work is called *Centrum Naturæ Concentratum, or the Salt of Nature Regenerated, For the most part improperly called The Philosopher's Stone*, (London: 1696), said on its title page to be a translation of the work of "Alipili," or "Ali Puli" by "a Lover of the Hermetic Science." In his introduction, Brice writes that the purpose of this alchemical book is that "all Men" may "seek and find that inestimable treasure, that deeply lies hidden in themselves, which this small Tract with great clearness demonstrates." *Centrum Naturæ Concentratum* holds that "the Salt of Nature is every where, and in all things to be found ... .. in short, that Animals, Vegetables and Minerals are one and the same in their essence." Thus the author has shown "the Metalline Mine in your own Body," and "how out of it you may prepare Gold, Argent Vive, Copper, Lead, &c.,"[23]

Here again, as in the cases of Gichtel and Pordage, we see that alchemy in the theosophic tradition occupies a kind of middle ground between spiritual and laboratory work. Without question, Brice's treatise insists upon the primacy of spiritual or inner work over laboratory or physical alchemy, but on the other hand, it also implies that spiritual alchemy gives one the essential key with which one can also "prepare

Gold, Argent Vive, Copper, Lead," and so forth. Given the unquestionable influence that Gichtel and the Philadelphian Society circle had upon Kelpius and, to some degree, also upon the Ephrata Cloister, one can certainly postulate that a similar attitude toward alchemy prevailed among the American theosophic circles in the eighteenth century. While Sachse almost certainly was not right in all his details about alchemical work undertaken in Pennsylvania theosophic circles, and whatever one thinks about his claim of actually possessing a tincture handed down from one generation to the next, there is no doubt that alchemy played a role in Pennsylvania theosophic communities right into the nineteenth century, as I have shown in my article "Western Esotericism and the Harmony Society."[24]

Alchemy, in eighteenth-century Pennsylvania, was definitely practiced commonly enough so that an ordinary sojourner might well run across it. For instance, Ezechiel Sangmeister, in his *Leben und Wandel* (Ephrata: 1825), tells the story of how when travelling to visit someone in Oley, Pennsylvania, he became ill, and his acquaintance there, a physician named George de Benneville (1703–1793), cured him with some drops. "This surprised me a bit," wrote Sangmeister, and so he conversed with the doctor for some time. Sangmeister asked whether there was such a thing as a universal gold-tincture, and the doctor "assured me it was something true and real!" In support of this, he showed Sangmeister a glittering gold liquid in a bottle, and "while flowing back and forth it emitted something like shiny sparks." The doctor offered to tutor Sangmeister and to will him the elixir should the doctor die unexpectedly, but Sangmeister, ever suspicious, turned him down and resumed his travels.[25] Clearly, what we now consider alchemy was well within the purview of an eighteenth-century Pennsylvania physician, and was not entirely uncommon in New England.

But there are larger questions to consider as well. Reading Gichtel's letters, the records of American theosophic communities, and the works of Pordage, one is driven in the end to an inevitable decision about alchemy, its nature and authenticity. One is forced to decide whether what Gichtel wrote to his numerous correspondents was true or not. If it was true, then he was in possession of the alchemical secrets, and was able to determine accurately whether this or that would-be alchemist was authentic or not. This is an uncomfortable question for most moderns, schooled from childhood to disbelieve in such things as alchemy, associated for us with medieval, antiquated beliefs. But we in the modern era may have something to learn from theosophic alchemy. Modern physicist Basarab Nicolescu has pointed out at length how the works of Jacob Böhme offer extraordinary insights into a "new Philosophy of Nature," and in fact "bear witness to a possible reënchantment of the world through the encounter between the study of man and the study of the universe."[26] Nicolescu may be right; like O. V. Milosz, he holds that we may now be on the brink of a new, and truly authentic Renaissance, a rediscovery of our place in the world as spiritual beings, a rediscovery of wisdom that once again situates science in its proper place within a spiritual context. Perhaps this is so.

Such a Renaissance probably will not come about without a real understanding that modern science and its preoccupation with only outward things has its origins in the pseudo-alchemy of external experimentation. Modern science has so far consisted in the relentless exclusion of all dimensions other than the quantifiable and merely external—in a way, much the same as false alchemy (the real predecessor to modern chemistry) consisted in outward, experimental searches for wealth, power, and immortality. This the theosophic alchemists, preëminent among which was Gichtel, never tired of deriding. For their theosophic alchemy existed only in a spiritual context; only a pseudo-alchemy looks merely for insights into and power over this world.

A Renaissance might come from the realization that theosophic alchemy offers us as individuals a way of understanding nature—and man as microcosm—in the context of subtle and spiritual significance. Gichtel often reminded his contemporaries who were interested in alchemy that authentic alchemy consists first of all in religious illumination. Without faith in God, without the guidance of Sophia, divine wisdom, without the light of the Holy Spirit, without humility, alchemy is nothing more than a vain science, a seeking for the golden calf and fleshly life, doomed to failure. Theosophic alchemy, on the other hand, according to Böhme, Gichtel, Pordage, or Kelpius, is knowledge of the hidden forces in nature, illuminated by divine wisdom.

If we approach theosophic alchemy in its totality as a spiritual discipline we may find it pregnant with remarkable implications. For precisely *because* theosophic alchemy represents a spiritual discipline may it also represent an alternative to the materialist modern scientistic perspectives whose consequences modern man is now reaping. Ultimately, theosophic alchemy requires us to reconsider our theory of knowledge. Modern science was predicated on the premise of hypothesis, experimental validation, and hypothesis correction: in other words, on experimentation in the outward world. But theosophic alchemy is founded on the premise that outward, experimental knowledge only refers to the physical realm, and that higher knowledge derives from inward observation and from changes in the knower by virtue of knowing. We can know the Pearl of wisdom only by experiencing it, and this experience in turn requires both our previous preparation, and our subsequent change by virtue of having known the Pearl. Modern science is an accumulation of external observations; theosophic science is a transmutation of the knower by what he knows.

Some modern authors, including Philip Sherrard and O. V. Milosz, already look forward to a new Renaissance, and theosophic alchemy might play a pivotal role in such a Renaissance. For in alchemy may be keys both to nature and to human nature, not only on a base level but throughout higher levels as well. It is true that modernity appeared in Europe during the seventeenth and eighteenth centuries—but alongside scientific materialism and atheism was an alternate way of understanding the universe: theosophy. Theosophy does not reject everything except what can be grasped with the hands, but rather understands that knowledge consists in the qualitative relationship between the knower and what is known. This higher knowledge, which has been ignored throughout modernity, may offer even today the keys to the qualitative transformation of the human world. And in any case, we can hardly doubt that enquiry into theosophic alchemy is worth the study; it is a field whose mysteries and richness have too long been overlooked.

CHAPTER TWENTY

Theosophy and Chivalry

It is altogether easy, but wholly false, to regard theosophy as having appeared without antecedents. Jacob Böhme, some modern authors attest, had his first vision, and from this derived the rest of theosophy. Naturally, such a view ignores the debt theosophy owes such diverse sources as alchemy, medieval astrology, and German mysticism including Meister Eckhart and Johannes Tauler, Paracelsus, and Valentin Weigel. As we have seen, inspected closely, theosophy appears more as a summation or culmination of European mysticism from Greco-Roman times onward than as a modern movement *sui generis*. Indeed, as we will shortly see, theosophy stands squarely in the current of major European literature and spirituality: theosophy represents a continuation of the spiritual chivalric tradition.

Antoine Faivre, in his landmark book *Access to Western Esotericism*, discussed at length how eighteenth-century Europe drew extensively on the imagery of the knight and of chivalric traditions, not only in literature but also in the creation of esoteric orders like those of Freemasonry or of the Golden Fleece.[1] One finds chivalric imagery persists, not only in the eighteenth century, but right down to the present day, at first glance strange in an era mostly antagonistic to such things as feudal hierarchies. Undoubtedly chivalric imagery has a deep, one may even say an archetypal resonance in the European imagination. Here, I would like to begin to explore why spiritual chivalry is a major leitmotif in Christian theosophy. But we might begin with a broader context and history.

As Henry Corbin has demonstrated, the Islamic mysticism of Suhrawardi and other Sufi and Ismaili authors has direct antecedents in the Mazdaean "theology of light" that created a spiritual chivalric tradition. Mazdaean and Manichaean traditions both saw mankind as engaged in a cosmic war of the forces of light against the forces of darkness. This spiritual chivalry in Mazdaean, Manichaean, and Islamic traditions bears profound similarities to the spiritual chivalry of Europe. Since the Mazdaean and Manichaean traditions were defeated and eventually lost, they have been denigrated as dualistic, but as theosopher Dionysius Andreas Freher wrote:

> [W]e know very little of Manes and the Manichaeans; all their own writings are lost, except for some short and few fragments, and from them it does not appear they were such fools and monsters as they are still described. I, therefore, for my part will neither excuse nor accuse them.[2]

In fact, I would argue that there are clear parallels between the Gnostic, the Mazdaean, the Manichaean, and the Christian and Islamic spiritual chivalric traditions.

But our scope here is more limited: we will focus on the continuity of spiritual chivalry through Europe from the thirteenth-century to eighteenth-century theosophy. For while it is important to note that there are numerous parallels between Gnostic, Mazdaean, Manichaean, Sufi, and Christian mystical traditions, to do such a comparison justice one would have to devote volumes to it. Here, we will examine how theosophy reflects and in a sense internalizes the Christian chivalric tradition that continued from the middle ages into the modern era, and so may offer a foundation for further comparisons of wider scope.

We may begin by considering the import of St. Bernard of Clairveaux's *De laude Novae Militae* (1136), his treatise in praise of the knights of God. This treatise came during the reign of the Knights Templar, guardians of pilgrims to the Holy Land from Christendom, and was intended to show how knights should not be secular, mercenary creatures, but should undertake all their actions, including warfare, in light of spiritual contemplation. Knights should be engaged in spiritual chivalry, and if they must shed blood, this must happen only for just causes. Knights should be above all spiritual warriors for Christ.

Now we must remember that chivalry has always occupied a peculiar station within Christendom: knights in general, and the Knights Templar in particular, occupied a position midway between the Church and the secular world. There were numerous people in the Christian world who did not want to enter the Church hierarchy proper, but who still wanted to belong to a spiritual order; the Knights Templar, the "Friends of God" of Rulman Merswin, the medieval *fedeli d'amore*, and later the Order of the Rose-Cross, the Order of the Mustard Seed, the Angelic Brethren, and other esoteric groups of the seventeenth and eighteenth centuries fulfilled exactly this function, being esoteric lay spiritual orders.

Thus, St. Bernard's treatise represents a public affirmation of what became in subsequent Christian history a profoundly important aspect of lay spiritual life. These many esoteric, or perhaps mesoteric orders allowed many people to enter into the chivalric life and to conduct themselves along a path that gave events of daily life a profound symbolic import, and that incorporated all aspects of life into this symbolic understanding. Ascetic monastic life had always been seen in terms of the hidden warfare between angels and demons, but through chivalry and the chivalric lay orders, this perspective was applied to the whole of society.

At the beginning of the thirteenth-century, though, when Wolfram von Eschenbach wrote the epic *Parzival*, the story of the holy grail, chivalry was in its flowering as a governing force in Northern European society. Although written in German, Eschenbach's garbled versions of British and French names reveal that the chivalric traditions surrounding the holy grail and the Arthurian legends could be found across Northern Europe. Without doubt, *Parzival* was written as entertainment, and reinforced this general chivalric code for society of that time; it was not primarily an esoteric work.

Yet when we look closely at *Parzival*, we find that it definitely includes esoteric references, a code if you will. This esotericism appears above all in the astrological references in the epic, over which more than one modern commentator has thrown up his hands. To be sure, there are some puzzling astrological allusions in the text, some of which may very well reflect scribal errors. But Eschenbach is emphatic about the most important astrological signs in his epic, and these, which are quite prominent in the work, reveal the same esoteric planetary order and pairings found in numerous later theosophic illustrations and books.

Let us consider exactly what that order is. We begin with the current state of the grail kingdom at the epic's inception. Although we are not told this until later in the work, the hidden grail kingdom is suffering because its king, Anfortas, has suffered a grievous lance wound that will not heal. There are two planets specifically linked to this suffering king: Saturn and the Moon. In chapter nine, for example, the hermit Trevrizent, Parzival's spiritual elder and guide, tells the knight that Anfortas suffers particularly during "the change in the Moon" and when "the planet Saturn [returns] to its mark." These affiliations are repeated numerous times, not only by Trevrizent, but later by the messenger of the grail, Cundrie.

Why are Saturn and the Moon linked to King Anfortas's suffering? Astrologically, this affiliation makes sense for several reasons. Among the traditional seven planets, Saturn is the furthest from Earth, while the Moon is closest, a fact whose significance is symbolically reinforced by Saturn and the Moon representing opposite extremes in associations as well: Saturn, often considered a malign planet, represents limitation or discipline, and also masculine dryness or astringency (and the longest of the planetary cycles, nearly thirty years)—while the Moon, a feminine planet, represents water (and the shortest of the planetary cycles, nearly thirty days).

If Saturn and the Moon represent the greatest planetary extremes, then the next closest pair of extremes are Jupiter and Mercury, who are intermediate between Saturn and the Moon, and Mars and Venus. Like Saturn, Jupiter is male, but is associated with royalty and largesse—in *Parzival*, Jupiter is explicitly affiliated with Feirefiz, Parzival's mottled black and white infidel half-brother whose "god" we are told in the fifteenth chapter, is Jupiter himself. Feirefiz marries Repanse de Schoy, the maiden who carries the grail, and their son is Prester John, a mysterious figure affiliated with the secret knowledge of the Orient. Thus, Feirefiz represents, even in the color of his skin, movement between worlds or realms: infidel and part Moor, he becomes Christian in the Jovial ceremony that nearly concludes the epic, and his son embodies the hidden movement of knowledge between Orient and Occident.

Jupiter is paired with Mercury in this traditional arrangement, Jupiter being male, Mercury hermaphroditic or female. So it is in the Parzival epic as well. For if Feirefiz represents the male Jupiter, and movement between the pagan and Christian worlds, Cundrie la Surziere, the boarish hideous messenger-woman of the grail, represents Mercury. Mercury is hermaphroditic (Hermes being another name for Mercury, the gods' messenger, from which we derive the word "hermetic"). As if to underscore this point, not only is Cundrie not exactly an enticing or angelic feminine figure, not only does she know many languages (Mercury is the planet governing communication and languages), but as if to underscore her ambiguous sexual nature, in chapter ten she is given an equally betusked half-brother, Malcreatiure, who is her male "spitting image," and who is directly associated with the "land of Tribalibot" and the "River Ganges," hence, like Feirefiz, Repanse de Schoy, and Prester John, with Oriental wisdom.

This brings us to the innermost pair of the planetary dyads: Mars and Venus, who represent the chivalric male and female relationship that virtually the whole of the Parzival epic demonstrates in its many knights and ladies. The knight, a Martial figure if ever there was one, is always linked to his lady, who embodies Venus, the female archetype of beauty and love. On numerous occasions in *Parzival*, knights win battles by falling into a state of love-intoxication, perhaps the most striking instance of which is Parzival's intoxication at seeing three drops of blood in the snow, reminding him of his lady Condwiramurs. Naturally, he wins all jousts or challenges in this condition, without being aware he is fighting. Certainly this episode in chapter six reveals how Mars and Venus are ideally united through chivalric combat.

But the triumphant union of Mars and Venus in the Parzival epic comes at the end, when after five years Parzival and Condwiramurs are reunited in the great festival that marks Parzival's taking the place of Anfortas as grail king. It is noteworthy that the epic's final chapter sees the union of Feirefiz and Repanse de Schoy, Parzival and Condwiramurs—and that the previous chapter (fifteen) has Cundrie congratulating Parzival—so that all the planetary associations of the epic come together in harmony finally. Anfortas, representing Saturn and the Moon, Feirefiz as Jupiter, Cundrie and Repanse as Mercury or Hermes, Parzival and Condwiramurs as Mars and Venus, are all conjunct here.

To underscore this planetary harmony, Cundrie announces it in Arabic to Parzival and the other knights and ladies during their festive meeting in the fifteenth chapter. She tells Parzival outright that Saturn (*al-zuhal*), Jupiter (*al-mushtāri*), Mars (*al-hirrīkh*), and the Sun (*ash-shams*) all "point to good fortune" for him. These are all masculine planets, exactly in the esoteric order we have seen exemplified in the epic. For Parzival himself embodies aspects of all these planets, including the Sun, not only because he has an ancestor named "Mazadan,"[!][3] but above all because as new grail king he is the Sun of all the hidden knights and ladies of the grail kingdom.

I have brought Eschenbach's *Parzival* into our discussion because no other medieval work of literature so clearly exemplifies chivalry, especially in relation to the esoteric knowledge of the planets found also in seventeenth- and eighteen-century theosophy. How is it that a medieval chivalric literary work can incorporate the same astrological symbolism as that found six and seven centuries later in Germany, England, and America? It seems unlikely that there was an esoteric order transmitting such knowledge from 1200 A.D. into the beginning of the modern era, although this hypothesis cannot be ruled out. It is much more likely that this planetary order and linking represents an archetypal pattern that recurs from medieval into modern times precisely because it is archetypal.

For the same planetary pattern recurs throughout theosophy. Jacob Böhme, in his book *The Signature of All Things*, tells us that "God must become man, man must become God . . . the earth must become heaven."[4] Subsequently, he explains the process by which this transmutation can take place—and not surprisingly, he offers us exactly the planetary order we have been discussing. "Let the artist well observe this," Böhme writes: "In Saturn he will raise the dead, understand, he will awaken the dead essence which held him captive in his former prison; for he shall turn the earth to heaven."[5] The artist must then pass through Luna, Jupiter, Mercury, Mars, and Venus. Böhme concludes that "This the artist will see, if he be chosen and accounted worthy of God for the work."[6]

We must point out here that Böhme's exposition of the seven planets and their meanings is both more schematic and more complicated than the way this order appears in *Parzival*. This is not surprising, of course, since *Parzival* is a work of literature in which the characters take precedence over the astrological symbolism worked into it, whereas Böhme's work is an Hermetic exposition. Böhme weaves the story of Christ's persecution into the order of the planets, for example, identifying Saturn as the "worldly dominion," the Pharisees as the "spiritual dominion," and Mars as the devil, who all attack Venus (with whom Jupiter and Luna are allied).

With this kind of allegorical planetary order and significance, Böhme reveals stages of individual spiritual practice. Unlike Eschenbach, Böhme tells no story—his work is a combination of spiritual exhortation and exposition. One can better understand Böhme's open discussion of planetary symbolism in relation to spiritual discipline when we consider that in 1200 A.D., European Christianity was relatively unified and offered a traditional structure for daily life not only through the Church and its ritual cycle, but also through chivalry and its traditions. By the time of Böhme, at the beginning of the seventeenth-century, European

Christianity had begun to splinter, and thus the Christian life was much more a matter of individual choice. Chivalry as an outward way of life was gone, and so Böhme offered a reconstituted version of chivalry for the inward, individual life.

Many of Böhme's works are full of complicated terminology drawn from alchemy and other sources, but one work stands out as his clearest and final address to the modern spiritual seeker: the only book Böhme saw to publication during his lifetime, *Christosophia, or The Way to Christ* (1624; present edition established by Gichtel in 1682). This book addresses the soul who seeks the noble Virgin Sophia, or wisdom of God, and early on it refers to

> How the poor soul shall come before God again, and how it is to strive for the noble, knightly crown; what kind of armor it must wear if it would strive against God's wrath, also against the devil, the world and sin, against flesh and blood, against the stars and elements, and against all enemies.[7]

That this is chivalric language could go without saying—but what we must say is that in it we see chivalric language internalized to describe the spiritual struggle of the seeker.

Indeed, Böhme's whole book—a collection of various addresses to the spiritual seeker—represents a transposition of the chivalric relationship between the angelic lady and the knight to the purely individual level. The angelic lady in chivalry may be a Guinevere for King Arthur or a Condwiramurs for Parzival, or a Beatrice for Dante, but in all cases we are looking at literary parallels of the Virgin Sophia, whom Böhme tells us to seek directly. Everything in Böhme's *Christosophia* is designed to reinforce the chivalric struggle against evil and for the angelic Virgin Sophia. No longer is there societal support for the chivalric quest or for jousting and the like—but the same language always referred in part to the inward quest and the inward struggle anyway. Böhme makes this inward component explicit, both for planetary symbolism and for the chivalric relationship to the Holy Sophia.

In medieval chivalric literature, as in the literature of the Provençal troubadours, the knight or poet has a unique relationship with a given lady who is for him the incarnation of Sophia, but for Böhme it is not as much a matter of a particular woman's being metaphysically transparent as it is a matter of the individual soul's passing through the planetary stages, tinctured by the Virgin Sophia herself. As in medieval chivalry, so in Böhme, each individual must experience Sophia for himself. But there is no longer the possibility of confusion between earthly and divine love; everything earthly, in Böhme's view, must become metaphysically transparent, illuminated by its heavenly archetype.

But we should not complicate Böhme's treatise unnecessarily. He stresses that in question is ultimately a simple matter of the soul's turning in humility to God. Böhme writes:

> Dear soul, for this [undertaking] earnestness is required. There must not simply be a repetition of such words. An earnest, resolute will must pursue this or it will not be attained, for if the soul wishes to obtain Christ's conqueror's crown from the noble Virgin Sophia, it must court Her with great love-desire. It must pray for it to Her in Her holiest of Names and must come before Her in highly chaste humility.[8]

Earnest prayer and genuine humility are the essential elements for spiritual transmutation, according to Böhme. A tale such as Eschenbach's *Parzival* exemplifies humility's importance through its characters, but Böhme eschews colorful tales, even colorful alchemical terminology, focusing instead wholly on exactly what is necessary for spiritual practice.

Thus, Böhme's *Christosophia* is in many ways the simplest and most accessible of his works. In it, he advises us to simply sink our souls into the nothingness of God's love, to cease from our selfishness and in true humility to allow God to manifest his will in us. This means that we are to "desire nothing nor [should we] wish to learn anything."[9] We must give up our selfish striving for this or that accomplishment, cease objectifying the divine into something outside ourselves, and simply come to rest in God.

Such advice would appear to be the polar opposite of chivalric questing and its colorful jousts, its heralds and its battles. After all, Böhme's advice requires no outward work or questing at all—rather, it turns us inward and enjoins us to seek for nothing at all. But we should recall that central to the Parzival epic is the hermit Trevrizent, Parzival's spiritual guide, who has relinquished knightly endeavours in favor of the inward life. Without Trevrizent's taking on Parzival's spiritual burden and sins, the rest of the epic and Parzival's becoming grail king probably could not have taken place. The inward life is implicitly pivotal in traditional chivalry, and it is not surprising to find it explicitly central for Böhme's chivalric spirituality.

In a sense, theosophic chivalry is both purer and more open than traditional chivalry. Only a relatively few could be aristocracy or knights in the traditional Christian world. But Böhmean theosophy is open to everyone, and represents the best elements of democracy and hierarchy: its hierarchy is purely mystical, and without any accidents inherent in any institutional framework. No one is born a theosopher knight of the holy Sophia by happenstance—everyone must seek to be worthy of Sophia, must purify their souls and become a knight of Sophia not in name or repute, but in reality.

From all this we can see how theosophic chivalry belongs to the modern era. In modernity, there is no real aristocracy at all, and chivalry must be—as it certainly was for Böhme and the other theosophers—a purely individual matter, a pact or troth between each of us and Sophia, divine wisdom. We can each be knights and ladies who embody the truth precisely to the degree that we make it so in our own lives and in ourselves. Theosophic chivalry is wholly an individual spiritual quest. It is as if in theosophy the essential responsibility of the chivalric life is opened before us in absolute purity, unadorned with literary characters or situations, laid bare as a challenge.

But it is Johann Georg Gichtel, "our champion," the "holy man of God" and "hermit of Amsterdam," who best exemplifies theosophic chivalry. Gichtel often speaks in terms of spiritual warfare and of hand to hand combat with demons or the devil. In December 1699, Gichtel wrote a friend:

> Now how this war is spiritual, you need not be taught. . . .
> [The fire is kindled] which shall be a trial and a temptation,
> but if they remain constant, it shall make them firmer and
> more constant in the love, and bring great joy.[10]

Each aspirant to spiritual knowledge is a knight in combat against the forces of darkness; his jousts are inward and his victories are of the spirit.

But Gichtel also emphasized something that traditional chivalry perhaps did not: the purely inward nature of this combat. The traditional chivalric quest is an outward one, testing oneself against opponents and monsters, against beasts and other knights. Gichtel, however, always points his readers inward, and writes in March 1696 that "since you are inwardly apprehended by God you have the true teacher in yourself, who shall instruct your soulish spirit, and teach you how to pray aright."[11] Further,

> we should require no teacher without us, if we are attended
> by this teacher within us. But since we are not all masters
> in one day, and many trials assail a pilgrim in the wilder-
> ness, our exercised mind can often give useful instruction to
> the unenlightened.[12]

256CONTEXTS

Gichtel does not disparage the need for instruction, nor the importance of living out the chivalric life, but he lays emphasis most of all on the "teacher within us" and on the inward life upon which all outward action must depend. Prayer and wisdom should precede and inspire action.

Gichtel's theosophic chivalry includes the same emphasis upon the angelic or divine feminine that inspired the whole of traditional chivalry, the troubadour poets of Provençal, and Dante. Gichtel and his fellow theosophers speak, in an amplification of the theme we found earlier in Böhme, of "wooing" the Virgin Sophia. In Gichtel's *Theosophia Practica*, in fact, we find elaborately developed allusions to "marrying" Sophia, to the "kisses" of her mouth, and even to a kind of spiritual coitus, if we may so call it. Gichtel writes, for example, in June 1698: "He who is in earnest about the marriage-bed of the Virgin must woo her in right earnest, and testify by deed that he loves her more than his life."[13]

This is chivalric language, to be sure, and there can be no question that Gichtel intends a chaste meaning to his wooing of the Virgin. When Gichtel refers to wooing, or kisses of the Virgin, or the marriage-bed of the Virgin, his terms are always metaphorical; indeed, the Virgin herself is metaphorical for spiritual consciousness, a state of grace. These kinds of references are part of a long tradition in Judeo-Christianity, harking back to the Song of Solomon and ancient Hebrew love poems to divine Wisdom. In Gichtel's theosophic chivalry, as in traditional medieval chivalry, the troth to the divine lady is paramount.

Just as medieval knights are enjoined never to shrink back from their challenges, so Gichtel enjoins us never to shrink back from wooing Sophia "though body and soul languish."[14] We should earnestly seek her in prayer, "praying for a steadfast mind." "For," he continues, "the Virgin desires to have body, soul, and spirit for her own, to nourish and provide for it herself, as a faithful consort for his *other half*."[15] There is indeed a betrothal between the Virgin Sophia and the spirit who longs for her and, Gichtel writes, "our heavenly Virgin is so enamoured of our *limbus* that no man can believe it, but our fickle mind and inconstant will and heart prevent her influence." She is in fact like "our other half," completing us spiritually; she loves us just as we love and long for her.

At the same time, Gichtel warns us that we must keep our spiritual betrothal to the Virgin clandestine. We ought not divulge the secrets of "our chaste virginal bridal bed" but should "keep it [this pearl] secret," for revealing her hidden munificence to the unworthy will both mislead them and endanger us.[16] In question here is an esoteric spiritual discipline manifested in the same metaphoric way found in chivalric literature—but in chivalric literature, one has to search for these hidden meanings and secret truths, whereas in theosophic writing these truths are writ more directly, hence our obligation not to reveal their most hidden realities to the uninitiate. Casting pearls before swine is, after all, of little significance to the swine, who might even get angry that they cannot eat pearls.

There is another implication to Gichtel's admonition for secrecy. Like the knights of the holy grail kingdom in *Parzival*, theosophic knights and ladies travel among other people without revealing who they are. Such a stricture places responsibility for one's enacting of spiritual discipline wholly on oneself; there can be under such an injunction little question of fraudulently assuming the guise of some great spiritual knight or lady, or seeking the approval of others. One's spiritual life is wholly a matter of one's own responsibility, in the theosophic perspective.

Individualized theosophic chivalry seems aptly suited to a modern world that offers no outward support for the chivalric life in the way that the traditional medieval world did with its St. Bernard of Clairveaux, its poets and chivalric storytellers such as Wolfram von Eschenbach. It is a remarkable coincidence that theosophic chivalry—its profound planetary symbolism and its essentially chivalric relationship to the angelic feminine initiatrix Sophia—appeared exactly at the onset of the modern era during the seventeenth and eighteenth centuries. Theosophic chivalry creates an ambience for itself, often a theosophic circle who work with and pray for one another, largely unknown to outward and often hostile society.

Theosophic chivalry, in short, represents a continuation of medieval esoteric knowledge into the modern era in a condensed form. This helps to explain why theosophy is not inherently hostile to Roman Catholicism, even though it is nominally a Protestant movement, and why one of the most remarkable exponents of Böhme and Louis-Claude de Saint-Martin could be Franz von Baader, a Roman Catholic to his death. For while much of Protestantism may have arisen as a protest against Roman Catholic institutionalization, theosophy represents a retrenchment of the German esotericism and mysticism reflected in Catholic medieval authors such as Eschenbach and Eckhart or Tauler—an adaptation of essentially the same principles embodied in Dante's *Divine Comedy* or *Parzival* (especially the divine Sophia or Beatrice) to a more fragmented modern world.

From the circle around Jacob Böhme himself early in the seventeenth-century, through the Angelic Brethren around Gichtel in Amster-

dam, through the circle of Dr. John Pordage and Jane Leade, through the
numerous other lesser-known theosophic groups in Scotland, in Germany and Northern Europe and in Pennsylvania, into the twentieth-century, theosophy has always been somewhat hidden from the surrounding public. Theosophers have not cared about accumulating proselytes
so much as about spiritual realization, and such inner work is better
done in solitude and among others of like mind. In this respect especially, the theosophers seem to have embodied the injunction to the
knights and ladies of the holy grail so many centuries ago: to avoid
revealing to outsiders who they really are. Perhaps they are doing so still.

CHAPTER TWENTY-ONE

Theosophy, Herbal Medicine, Magic, and Astrology

The modern era has consisted in a precipitous discarding, in but a few centuries, of much that is central to the entire human cultural inheritance. Aspects of life that were taken for granted at the time of Shakespeare, around the beginning of the seventeenth-century, were by the twentieth-century largely considered "backward" or "primitive." Among these discarded forms of knowledge are the disparate elements of herbalism, cosmology, medicine, and astrology that came to be known pejoratively as mere "magic" or "occultism." But the fact that these disciplines and ways of understanding—jettisoned by a heady wave of evolutionist, progressivist enthusiasm—are central to theosophy has doubtless contributed to the almost complete neglect theosophic works and authors have languished in to this day. However, in our discussion of theosophy we will not denigrate the "occult" elements of the tradition; we will merely examine them as a natural part of theosophy as a whole.

The precise role that herbal medicine, for example, played in theosophy remains unclear. Apparently Gichtel, the "hermit of Amsterdam," practiced some form of herbal medicine, just as he practiced and was intimately familiar with alchemy both spiritual and practical. He was at least conversant with the healing properties of certain plants, even

259

though he was not a practicing physician. Likewise, Dr. John Pordage—after he was publicly attacked and lost his place as a clergyman in England—made his living as a medical doctor and, in the practice of the day, prescribed certain herbal decoctions or preparations. Johannes Kelpius and the Pennsylvania theosophers also preserved and augmented herbal medicine that they had brought from Germany to the New World, adding to this some American Indian remedies.

Now, this interest in herbal medicine was common in the seventeenth and eighteenth centuries, of course, but for the theosophers, herbalism was not just a matter of convention. Theosophic medicine is based on the "doctrine of signatures," embraced in the writing of the foremost theosopher, Jacob Böhme himself. According to the doctrine of signatures, everything in the natural world bears a planetary or celestial "stamp" or "signature" that governs its properties. In *Signatura Rerum* Böhme writes:

> Every root, as it is in the earth, may be known by the signature for what it is good or profitable, even such a form also has the earth, and it is discerned in the leaves and stalks which planet is lord in the property, much more in the flower; for of what taste the herb or root is, even such an hunger is in it, and such a cure lies therein, for it has such a salt. The physician must know what kind of sickness is risen in the body . . .[1]

Thus, herbal medicine is based in astrological knowledge of "which planet is lord in the property."

But everything in the cosmos can be understood according to the doctrine of signatures, indeed, must be so understood, because medicine in this context is far more than merely fixing what has become broken. In order to practice medicine according to the doctrine of signatures, one must understand not only the planetary signatures of given herbs, but the signatures of given diseases and people as well. One does not, in general, treat a fiery disease with fire; everything is a matter of restoring proper balance or harmony. This balance can include daily habits—such as walking in the sunshine—one's clothing, one's food, one's jewelry, as well as certain herbs. All these things bear astrological signatures that can affect us even to the point of disease, or of healing.

According to traditional astrological medicine, disease represents a planetary imbalance that has gotten out of hand. Thus, the function of traditional medicine is to bring this imbalance back into a general harmony. Such an effort, however, may require an apparently disproportionate or severe remedy that, however extreme it might at first appear, restores an equilibrium to the body. But effects in the body are necessarily more "substantial" than effects in the soul, whose equilibrium and disequilibrium can be more easily affected by precious stones or other outward influences. For illnesses and healing of the body reflect illnesses and healing in the soul.

Hence we can see that theosophic medicine is inextricably linked to astrology, which in turn is a science of the soul and what influences it. The soul, as we will recall, is a "subtle body" made up of a particular astral "constellation" unique to a given individual. Some people are more Solar and Venusian, others Mercurial, others still Saturnine. Understanding these unique combinations, and the kinds of general patterns governing groups of people and even countries or peoples, is essential to understanding human psychology. If modern psychologists seek a field that will yield countless insights into why and how people act as they do, they need seek no further than theosophic astrology.

As we have seen, theosophy is itself in essence a science of the soul's purification and illumination expressed through astrological and alchemical terms. Naturally, this terminology did not have its origin in theosophy, any more than alchemical terms find their origin in theosophy—rather, the theosophers drew upon and condensed into their works astrological and alchemical symbols because these explained what they meant most clearly and succinctly. The fact that they did so also means that theosophy incorporated into itself essential elements of medieval and classical cosmology, while maintaining its primary focus on the spiritual path.

We should note here that theosophy does not reduce planetary symbols—Mars or Venus, for example—to merely psychological meanings, as so much modern psychology tends to do. True, theosophic works such as Thomas Bromley's *The Way to the Sabbath of Rest* or Pordage's *Sophia* refer primarily to the purification and illumination of the psyche, for after all human beings must live and work through the psyche; this is our nature as beings consisting in spirit, soul, and body. But "unconscious" or "subconscious" are pejorative terms foreign to theosophy, which seeks to harmonize and harness all elements in the soul so that it may turn inward and find the peace of the spirit that passes all understanding.

Modern psychology tends to think in terms of "unconscious" or "subconscious," developing theories of "depth psychology" and focusing on dysfunctional or diseased people while regarding a balanced, ordinary psyche as the pinnacle of human possibilities. Theosophy, on the other hand, thinks in much more traditional terms of a hierarchy of being, begining with a balanced, ordinary, fallen human psyche and moving toward its purification, eventually toward its surpassing the human realm and entering the paradisal. It is true that in theosophy entering the paradisal means passing through the wrath-fire, but this has little to do with one's infancy or with childhood trauma, nor with expressing one's anger. One might say that modern psychology aims at bringing a patient up to the point at which the theosophic ascent can begin.

This brings us to an even more fundamental dissonance between modern worldviews and theosophy. Materialism has led most moderns to believe that the cosmos functions by certain purely physical laws, and that events not conforming to these laws must therefore be delusion, illusion, or fraud. But theosophy—which incorporates in a very condensed way so much of antiquity—does not hold to the primacy of merely physical laws; theosophers no doubt acknowledge that certain laws hold for the temporo-spatial world in which we now live, but in the theosophers' experience, it is possible while living in this world to also see and even participate in realms of the soul "above" the space and time that we know. Put another way, a theosopher might say that modern physics examines our temporo-spatial realm and what is below it; theosophy looks at our temporo-spatial world and what is above it.

This theosophic concentration on mapping the realms of the soul, the totality of which they call "eternal nature," necessarily means that theosophers accepts some events that many modern people, schooled in materialism, find not only inexplicable but unacceptable as well. For the theosophic journey entails travelling into visionary realms that are inhabited by beings and landscapes outside our present time and space, who possess subtle bodies of light or of wrath-fire. Theosophers, visionaries who are able to see, touch, smell, and hear these other realms, not surprisingly experience things on this earth that many of the rest of us do not. According to theosophers, hell and paradise are spread out about us now, but we see them not.

As we saw earlier, Dr. John Pordage and his wife and family all experienced some extraordinary events after the "eternal worlds" were opened to them. They were attacked by demons, who surrounded them with sulphurous smells and even imprinted certain images on the walls, ceiling, and windows of the house; but after they passed through this wrath-fire experience, they experienced the paradisal realm, with wonderful scents and odors, surrounded by angels ascending and descending. Opening "eternal nature," entering into theosophic discipline, evidently means that there is then an "opening" into which the realms of the soul can imprint themselves in this world, or at least be glimpsed in and even affect this world.

These kinds of events were by no means limited to Pordage and his family or friends; Gichtel also said that he had wrestled with devils as man to man, and had played all day with angels as with little children, and indeed, much theosophic literature refers to such experiences.[2] Jane Leade, too, gives voice to remarkable experiences she had, some of which broached the apparent barrier we might like to set up between this world and the realms of the soul. The Pennsylvania chronicles, letters, and manuscripts from the eighteenth-century also remind us of such interpenetration of the demonic, angelic, and human realms. The theosophers seem to be telling us that this world is by no means separate from the next or, in theosophic terms, from eternal nature.

According to Thomas Bromley, in his *The Way to the Sabbath of Rest*, those who follow a common spiritual path, and through visionary awakening enter into an angelic community, experience one another's joys and sorrows. This "Union is eminently great," he writes and "There may be some Knowledge of each others Conditions at a Distance, which comes from their being essenced in each others Spirits and Tinctures, which is the Cause of this invisible Sympathy."[3] The tincture is a "spiritual virtue," a penetration of the transcendent into the temporal by which a community of people can participate in one another's spiritual enjoyment. Thus, Bromley writes that the divine tincture can "pierce through all Distance, and reach those that are far absent; because it is not corporeal, nor subject to the Laws of Place or Time."[4]

According to theosophy, paranormal events are simply a stage in the spiritual development whose trajectory Bromley is outlining, and whose nature he is illuminating. Theosophy does not aim at parapsychological experiences including clairvoyance or telepathy; it simply happens, and must be noted as part of one's development. People discover such phenomena by "Experience, who in Absence enjoy such Influences of Spirit and secret Insinuations of spiritual Virtue from one another."[5] These people find that they "cannot but value this spiritual Communion above all Enjoyments in the World; which compared to it, seem but like the basest Metal to the purest Gold." But Bromley—like the spiritual advisors whose writings are collected in the Greek Orthodox *Philokalia*, and like many Buddhist teachers of meditation—advises theosophers not to cling to such experiences; they are merely to be experienced as a natural part of spiritual praxis.[6]

This brings us to a point whose importance cannot be glossed over: the theosophers emphasized that one should not seek unusual, parapsychological phenomena. Bromley warned against such seeking; so too did Jane Leade, herself a prolific visionary; and Gichtel also said that visions and other parapsychological phenomena were notoriously untrustworthy, and could certainly be attributed in some cases not to God but to the devil. Such warnings, from the preëminent authors of the theosophic school, are particularly important because there are numerous instances of parapsychological phenomena among the theosophers. While such events may happen to one travelling the spiritual path, to actively seek them out is to court delusion and even disaster, the theosophers insist.

Be this as it may, however, theosophic writings are replete with incidents inexplicable by modern standards, some of which seem far closer to medieval than to modern times. Like Conrad Beissel after him, Gichtel was more than once accused of being a sort of magician, and in a letter explained the truth as follows:

> Concerning magic, the reason is this: about 1652, my father bought a house near one of the town gates, which had been greatly damaged, together with a beautiful large garden, and had the house rebuilt. After having done so, the report arose that the house was haunted, so that no lock nor bold could hold the spirit, which my late father at first refused to believe, but it was confirmed by an old gardener seventy years of age, who also pointed out a place in the garden where something was said to be buried.
>
> Which induced my father to have three people dig at the place, and they discovered a large chest, but before they could lift it, the watch came by, and as the officer had no instructions, he asked what they did in the garden—upon which the chest vanished. But the astral spirit howled about the house and showed itself, and by its garment people thought it must be a nun, because before the reformation nuns lived in the house. My father having died meanwhile, a magus offered to my mother to call up the spirit, and as he was a papist, he employed many consecrated means, but with all his conjuring he affected nothing.
>
> Which I related in full to N; but I had nothing to do with it; and N. afterwards twisted and perverted it . . .[7]

We may point out two things: first, Gichtel does not doubt the possibility of an astral being or ghost in the house, and second, he had nothing to do with its presence or with the exorcism. As much as anything, the story reflects the kind of world into which our theosophers were born.

But later in his life, Gichtel himself—whose reputation as a spiritual guide had become relatively widespread—was approached on various occasions by people troubled by ghosts. Of one such case, Gichtel's biographer writes as follows:

> Wherefore also, as he had spiritual experience, even people of the Protestant faith came to him, asking his advice. One man ha[d] for ten years after his death followed his wife everywhere, ever asking for her prayers. Everybody whom she questioned said it was the devil, but the woman knew her husband, and could not get rid of the dream, until Gichtel opened to her the ground of her soul, whereupon she attained peace.[8]

Gichtel did not perform an exorcism; he simply "opened to her the ground of her soul, whereupon she attained peace." A ghost, here in Gichtel's view, is a kind of astral parasite, dissolved by spiritual detachment and peace. He demonstrated that spirit is unaffected by the astral realm, and by "penetrating the astral" she was at peace.

But this was simply a passing incident in Gichtel's life; more common was his experience with those who had died and whose posthumous destinies he saw. For example, on January 4, 1703, Gichtel "found the soul of a friend at the gate of paradise, where it was received with great sensible joy." Indeed, with frequency "those members that remained with Gichtel in one mind of Christ and died, sometimes appeared to him from paradise, lovingly embraced and kissed him, that he could hardly bear it in this mortal tabernacle."[9] By contrast, another companion, whom Dr. Raedt purportedly turned to drink, "died at half his proper age, suffering from hellish anguish, and [appeared] to Gichtel after his death, to show him his burning mouth." Only after some time was his soul "humbled, and reliquished the will, and thus it was received into the eternal tabernacles."[10]

In Gichtel's view it is possible, in other words, not only for the soul to pass from wrath-fire into rest, but for someone living to intercede for a lost soul. This in fact Gichtel himself said he did on several occasions, the most notable of which is of course when a friend and benefactor of his had "wooed Sophia" very ardently, and then, disappointed, committed suicide with five self-inflicted wounds. Gichtel at first thought his friend was doomed to hell, but found that, after years of prayer, his benefactor in fact passed into eternal rest through the power of Christ.[11] I mention this episode because, like the other incidents in which Gichtel saw the states of those who had died, Gichtel held that he was able to see into the soul's realm, and was even able to "channel" to the soul Christ's liberating power.

There are numerous other incidents related in Gichtel's letters, each of which forms a variation on this same pattern. One thinks of the time that Friedrich Breckling came to Gichtel distraught over a debt of 1,200 florins he owed, and Gichtel prayed over the matter—until Breckling came to Gichtel along with a wealthy patron who had been seized with faith, and who brought along a present of 1,200 florins. Or of the times that Breckling later—after their falling out—came to Gichtel full of rage, about which Gichtel wrote that he was himself six times seized with this fury:

> I was like a wild beast, the blood in my veins boiled, and if God had not held my tongue, I should for ever have renounced Him. Wherefore I fundamentally understood what are hell and a devil, and a damned soul, and since then the wrath in B. [Breckling] is exhausted, the wrath which he had made his god in him. This is what is called laying down one's life for the brethren. . . . [O]ut of his fire-nature of wrath, a love-fire has come forth.[12]

Gichtel believed he had taken on himself Breckling's wrath and turned it into love, which he "called laying down one's life for the brethren."

What are we to make of stories such as these, taken as a whole? Certainly it would be possible to dismiss them. But in fact they represent a pattern; they fit together integrally within the theosophic cosmology. If a human being does consist in a body, an astral "constellation" or soul, and spirit, and if one whose soul is illuminated by spirit is capable of seeing into the soul's realms—including all its "signatures" by planets—then it follows that souls who share this illumination share spiritual communion in mysterious ways, and might see into and even affect the posthumous destiny of souls, as well as heal the souls of those alive on earth yet.

Given all that we have so far here discussed—herbal medicine and the doctrine of planetary signatures, the nature of the human soul as an astral constellation and posthumous conditions—we can perhaps more easily understand how this cosmology and microcosmology could in turn support folk magical practices both in Germany and in Pennsylvania. In part, of course, magical practices, which include planetary sigils (astrological emblems impressed in particular metals), herbal healing, and the like, were inherited from medieval Europe and continued on as folklore. What we see in the *Three Books of Occult Philosophy* by Cornelius Agrippa is only a codification of beliefs that continued on in Europe—and in Pennsylvania—long after the so-called Age of Reason and the advent of scientific materialism.

But theosophy provides a coherent worldview quite conducive to magical practices as well. Unlike Calvinist Puritanism, for example, Protestant theosophy by no means disavowed its medieval inheritance of sympathetic magic. This is not to say that theosophers entertained witches. But although fear of witchcraft swept the Puritan colonies in eastern North America, the theosophic communities were largely unaffected, chiefly because they had not rejected sympathetic or natural magic but incorporated it into their lives, and perhaps were not as subject to the terror that so many Puritans apparently felt about European folk practices often interpreted as malevolent witchcraft.

Just as many eighteenth-century Pennsylvania Germans incorporated European sympathetic magic into their daily lives, so too, it appears, did the Ephrata community. In the history of Ephrata, even though several times people tried to burn houses down, and even though chimneys were somewhat rickety, there was never any loss by fire in the settlement proper save for two mill fires in September 1747 and September 1784, and these two fires were contained. Given that all the structures in question were made of wood, this is quite a good record.[13]

How was the Ephrata community protected from fire? Perhaps they simply were careful. But from the community's own perspective, they were protected by a kind of ceremonial magic. According to Julian Sachse, the Ephrata buildings were protected in the following manner: a wooden platter was kept on the communion table in the Saal (Assembly room) through certain lunar phases, until the proper day and hour—a Friday during the waning moon, between eleven P.M. and midnight. No iron could be used in the ceremony; ink made from the gall-apples of an oak tree near a graveyard was used, along with a new goose feather for a pen, to draw three circles on opposite sides of the platter. Written in Hebrew were the words *Attah, Gibbohr, Leolam, Adonai,* or in German, "Du bist stark in Ewigkeit Herr," or "The Lord is mighty in all Eternity," along with Christ's last words: *consummatum est.* Inscribed also were the letters AGLA, from the Hebrew, found in much European ceremonial magic.[14]

Four such plates were placed into the four corners of any given building, and no building thus protected ever burnt—but there were other methods of protecting against fire as well. If, for instance, a building were unprotected and caught fire, such a plate could be thrown into the fire in God's name, and the flames would cease. Then too, by reciting the Biblical verse Numbers 11.2, and pouring water into a pan of coals held in the left hand while staring at the fire, some people were held able to control the flames. This technique of sympathetic magic has its analogues and perhaps its origins in European gypsy and Jewish folk practices. Additionally, one might inscribe the Seal of Solomon on a burning building with a piece of charcoal; in fact this was how the burning mills were said to have been saved from obliteration.[15]

We should note that the Pennsylvania German communities also preserved magical verses that, when chanted, were held to be invincible. Interestingly, these magical verses to control fire could be transmitted only on a Friday between eleven P.M. and midnight during a full moon—and only orally to one person of the opposite sex. Such verses were held to be impotent in the hands of pagans or Jews. One such verse reads as follows:

> Feuer, steh still, um Gottes Will:
> Um des Hernn Jesu Christi willen!
> Feuer, steh still, in deiner Gluth,
> Wie Christus der Herr ist gestanden in seinem
>   rosinenn-farbnem Blut!
> Feuer und Gluth, Ich gebeut dir bei Gottes Namen
> Daß du nicht weiter kommst van dannen, Sondern behaltest
>   alle deinen Funken und Flammen.
> (Fire, be still, by God's will:
> As Lord Jesus Christ wills!
> Fire, be still, in your flame,
> As Christ the Lord is in his rose-colored blood!
> Fire and flame, I command thee by God's name
> That you go no further, but cease your sparks and flames.)
> Amen! Amen! Amen![16]

This is definitely a magical command, one that has its analogues in the magic of Greco-Roman antiquity, in Judaism, and in medieval Christianity.[17]

While I have not been able to verify whether this particular spell was indeed in use at Ephrata, the prevalence of *braucherei* or "pow-wow" medicine in Pennsylvania German communities is well-known. Although the particular assertions of Julius Sachse about magic at Ephrata are in some cases not currently verifiable, there is no doubt that Ephrata existed in an eighteenth century society that did accept the possibility of magic, as is corroborated in the whiny "narrative" of Ezechiel Sangmeister, who in his *Leben und Wandel* remarks on numerous occasions that local people often regarded Conrad Beissel as a sorceror or magician, and that he himself thought the same. What is more, Sangmeister complains at one point that virtually anything went at Ephrata, and "such interest in magic and hocus-pocus is common."[18]

One of the most well-known books of Pennsylvania German folk magic is popularly known as *The Long-Lost Friend*, and was published under this title by Johann Georg Hohman in numerous editions in English. However, it is telling that the original German title of this book is in fact *Der lange Verborgene Freund*, which literally means "*The Long Hidden Friend*."[19] The word "hidden" is important because the *Wunderbare Künste* [Wonderful Arts] of the spells in this book date back to such sources as the medieval *Book of Albertus Magnus* and many of them were in common use in Europe and in Pennsylvania before Hohman published them in 1819/1820. It is only that such "arts" were hidden and not discussed publicly to avoid censure—and indeed, Hohman himself met with some criticism from clergy.

Given all that we have already observed about the theosophic worldview, magical practices are quite comprehensible. As we have seen, theosophy regards the entire natural world as a kind of palimpsest upon which is writ the layers of celestial script, the characters that the stars and planets—insignia of the subtle and spiritual realms—represent. The individual human being also embodies such insignia. But above and informing all such phenomena is the spiritual light of divinity. If one can invoke this divine power, then it is possible to accomplish many things, including protecting buildings, ensuring proper rain, avoiding destructive hailstorms, and the like. Petitionary prayer—common to almost all Christians—differs from such magical practices primarily in that the latter entails "markings" such as sigils to concentrate the divine invocation.

In light of the theosophic cosmology and the magical practices it entails, the well-known "superstitions" of the Pennsylvania Dutch and German communities to the present day—including the so-called hex signs on barns to ward off hail or call down rains—become much more understandable as well. These geometrical signs simply represent ways of invoking beneficent divine influences. These influences are generally specific, therefore often planetary, because as we have seen, according to the doctrine of signatures everything in the natural world is governed by such planetary constellations or signatures.

One is not surprised to find, then, among the Pennsylvania Germans, what was called the *wunder-sigel*, or magical amulet. The amulets could protect against evil spirits, could ward off gunshots or stab wounds, and could ensure longevity, riches, and happiness—more or less the way amulets are held to function in Native American, Middle Eastern, Asian, and other cultures around the world. One such amulet was called the *artabel anhängsel*, and consisted in a thin engraved plate of copper, silver, or gold worn around the neck held by a three-strand cord of horse-tail hair cut at midnight, Christmas Eve. Another such charm was called the *Tritheim zettel*, a term perhaps taken from Johann Trithemius (1462–1516), the abbott who schooled Heinrich Cornelius Agrippa (1486–1535), author of *The Three Books of Occult Philosophy* (1533), in "Chymistry, Magick, and Cabalie, and . . . other things."[20]

About the *tritheim zettel* Sachse writes that the "derivation of the characters or their symbolism . . . has not been traced by the writer," but in fact its origin is astrological natural magic like that found in the works of Cornelius Agrippa. Agrippa's *Three Books*—which, like the works of Pico della Mirandola (1463–1494), shows the clear influence of Jewish Kabbalism—includes not only tables of Hebrew characters and their symbolic associations, but numerous tables and astrological sigils associated both with the seven planets and the constellations as well. These sigils are "seals" or "characters" that help invoke the sidereal influences they represent; they represent a magical script that not only reveals to the initiate particular planets or constellations, but also embodies those influences.[21]

With this in mind, we can better understand how Pennsylvania Germans used these sigils: they were impressed upon documents, letters, parts of the body, wherever a particular influence might best be applied. This impress of the *wunder-sigel* onto written works, people, or farm animals, often for healing, was generally accompanied by invocations or prayers that would "seal" the particular influence, channeling divine power in special ways. We must remember that although such practices have been discarded by modern Christianity, they do fit within the cosmology of traditional Christianity so long as the sigil, for instance, is not seen as a power on its own, but as informed by the divine Trinity.

In fact, one could certainly make the argument that this kind of natural magic intensifies direct connections between the natural world, man, the stars and planets, and God that otherwise would be forgotten, as indeed they have been in the modern world. One who impresses a sigil on a document, or on a farm animal, for example, and does so with full consciousness of exactly the forces that the sigil represents, is, like the man or woman who wears a given amulet, renewing the inherent interrelationships between spirit, the soul (or astral realm), and the natural or physical world. Such amulets or sigils, seen in this light, remind us constantly of divine power and how it manifests itself in all the phenomena of this world. Amulets or sigils seen in this light only become questionable when they are viewed as powerful in themselves, and not because they are invested with divine power.

We might point out that here too is a connection between these practices and early Christian Gnosticism. As is well known, some of the Gnostic sects of the first few centuries A.D. were known for creating amulets and inscribed tablets of magical significance. These amulets and tablets, like those of the Pennsylvania Germans, represented an impressing of divine power and sidereal influences into the physical world; they were created in the awareness that everything in the physical world reflects the subtle, planetary or astral realm, in turn a reflection of spiritual archetypes, in turn a manifestation of divine power itself.

So let us recapitulate. It is no accident that theosophy bears so many similarities to medieval cosmology as outlined, for instance, in C. S. Lewis's excellent book *The Discarded Image*. Theosophy is nominally Protestant, of course, but its practitioners are nonsectarian, some, like Franz von Baader, being Roman Catholic, and in reality theosophy is more like a condensation of the unified, hierarchical medieval Christian cosmology as reflected in, say, Dante's *Divine Comedy*, which is marked throughout by astrological symbolism and correspondences. Theosophy incorporates into itself, through the doctrine of signatures, the European Christian inheritance from Greco-Roman antiquity of planetary and elemental symbolism, condensing this body of knowledge into a cohesive and succinct cosmological framework.

For the theosophers, as for people in traditional medieval Christianity, and as for people in Greco-Roman antiquity, the entire cosmos is knit together in a profoundly intricate hierarchy of correspondences and influences. This hierarchy originates, of course, in the unfathomable light of divinity, which all that we here call "magic" invokes and relies upon. Even the parapsychological events that Gichtel's and

Bromley's works, the Ephrata records, and other theosophic sources all report have their origin in God, according to the theosophic under-standing. Miracles, in other words, are not limited to the New Testa-ment and to the past. Theosophers, as we have elsewhere seen, have sought above all to realize in their communities the pure apostolic church, and to truly follow Christ—which means that among them, as among the countless saints of the Roman Catholic and Eastern Ortho-dox churches, miraculous events including telepathy and clairvoyance are possible.

Some in Pennsylvania German communities also held that it is also possible to channel divine energies into the human community through symbols and sigils, insignias that invoke special planetary or angelic power and protection. Such amulets and sigils are simply concrete rep-resentations of how divine power can work in daily life, reminders that, indeed as the Bible says, not a sparrow falls without God's eye upon it. Essentially the same doctrine of signatures that governs herbal medicine governs sigils: the cosmos is organized on certain patterns, and man can enhance or intensify those patterns through sanctified means, through amulets and rituals.

It may help to recall that the "woman in the wilderness" community of Johannes Kelpius and the Ephrata community of Conrad Beissel—and the other Pietist or theosophic communities of the late seventeenth and early eighteenth centuries in Pennsylvania—lived simple lives, much closer to the natural world than most modern people. They farmed, and held services that coincided with the cycles of the moon and with other astrological rhythms—they were, in short, closely attuned to nature's cycles and to the way those patterns reflected the rhythms of the planets and stars. In such a context—a German community truly living in the wilderness—we can see more clearly how this knowledge of nature and of its religious meanings could be reflected in magical practices inherited from Europe.

For in the end, such magical practices or parapsychological events as we have seen among the theosophers—common to German, Dutch, English, and American theosophic communities alike—represent an adaptation of basic theosophic cosmology to particular situations. Gich-tel's visions of peoples' posthumous states, Pordage's herbal medicine and his own visions, Pennsylvania German amulets, all can be under-stood in light of the hierarchical nature of the theosophic cosmos. For plants and metals, like people, reflect astral or subtle principles in man-ifestation. Perhaps those peripheral but sensational aspects of theosophy we have discussed here—the parapsychological dimension—are like the miracles in the New Testament, a test of faith. One can imagine a theosophy without magical elements, as one can imagine a Jesus who was simply a moral man, not God incarnate, but one would be imagining neither theosophy nor Christianity.

PART FIVE

IMPLICATIONS

CHAPTER TWENTY-TWO

Theosophy and Modern Science

It is an interesting coincidence that theosophy in its fully developed, Böhmean form appeared at exactly the beginning of the modern era, just when modern science was appearing. One could imagine few intellectual currents more polarized than modern science, with its rationalist, materialist premises, and theosophy, with all its inheritance from medieval and ancient mysticism, with its openness to and even insistence on the paranormal. The two currents seem utterly in opposition. Yet with all their apparent conflicts, theosophy and modern science not only have common roots in alchemy, they both share experimental approaches to data, and both seek to understand the underlying or hidden laws of existence. Indeed, strange as such an assertion might seem at first, theosophy may offer a means of resanctifying modern science.

But we should begin by considering how modern science and theosophy both derived from alchemy. That both modern science and theosophy were fed by the alchemical current in European tradition cannot be doubted. Theosophic literature, as we have seen, everywhere bears the terms of alchemy from Böhme onwards, and indeed many theosophers were reputed to be themselves accomplished alchemists, including Pordage, Gichtel, and Kelpius. Likewise, many early modern scientists were fascinated by alchemy, with its retorts and tubes, its furnaces and methods of transforming metals or other substances. Alchemy, with its searches for the hidden laws of the cosmos, with its chemical apparati, is today popularly depicted as a foolish precursor to modern chemistry.

In fact, from William Law onward, some have held that modern science itself drew on theosophy for some of its insights. There is, for example, controversy over whether, as Law said, Isaac Newton plowed with Böhme's heifer.[1] And there are certainly philosophical debts owed theosophy, as seen in, for instance, Hegel's considerable and disastrously superficial borrowings from Böhme. But such indebtedness is hard to trace, and not particularly fruitful an avenue of research, for it is far more interesting to trace the common origins of theosophy and modern science, and to see how the two diverged.

If we keep in mind that alchemy flourished during the seventeenth and eighteenth centuries in Europe, that virtually every court was beset by people claiming to have the secret of making gold, we can see how it is that alchemy could give birth to both modern science and to theosophy. For the prevalence of would-be alchemists during this time naturally led to two apparently disparate reactions. On the one hand, those who concentrated on physical, laboratory alchemical work—heating and cystallizing, extracting and boiling substances, often called "puffers," for their bellows used in fanning flames—were the predecessors of modern chemists. But these people had little luck in tincturing gold, and contributed mightily to alchemy's bad reputation. On the other hand, then, appeared "spiritual alchemy," those alchemists who virtually jettisoned laboratory work entirely, insisting instead that alchemy was mainly a science of inward spiritual transmutation.

In antiquity—and for some alchemists to this day—alchemy was considered both a physical and a spiritual science, a transmutation both of the human being as body, soul, and spirit, and of metals or other actual substances. Laboratory work and prayer were complementary. But the modern era—from the seventeenth-century onward—meant that alchemy would itself be transformed into, on the one hand, modern chemistry (which has virtually nothing whatever to do with spirituality), and spiritual alchemy, which often has little to do with laboratories.

Yet whereas spiritual alchemy—alchemy that focuses on transmuting energies in the alchemist himself—definitely retained a profound interest in the laws of the cosmos, and did continue to work with transmuted substances, modern chemistry retained almost no interest whatever in spirituality. Among the well-known English spiritual alchemists, one could certainly name Michael Maier (1568–1622) and Thomas Vaughan (1622–1665) as preëminent—and it is noteworthy that Vaughan was killed in an explosion during the course of chemical experiments.[2] By contrast, one can hardly think of a single major chemist with a comparable interest in spiritual matters.

There are fundamental parallels between the methods of spiritual alchemy and the methods of modern science. Both alchemists and scientists conduct experiments, collect data and, by proceeding along an experimental path, form hypotheses and try to verify them. It is true that alchemy has a religious foundation, and that modern science tends to be areligious or even at times irreligious. But in method, alchemists like scientists tend to keep careful records, to proceed cautiously, and to gain working knowledge through laboratory experimentation that seeks to reveal the underlying or hidden laws of the cosmos.

Despite these fundamental parallels, clearly science and theosophy took radically divergent paths. Modern science moved increasingly—especially during the late nineteenth-century—toward an exclusively rationalist and materialist worldview hostile to religious traditions and to much of the European cultural heritage. Under the spell of social Darwinism, many people began to embrace a worldview based on dogmatic belief in inevitable progress, and therefore rejected our human inheritances of religion, philosophy, art, and literature as belonging to an outmoded past. And in fact, how extraordinary it was and to some degree still is, to look ahead to a human future incomparably more technologically powerful and sophisticated than anything people before have witnessed.

By contrast, theosophy's adherents, while not averse to expanding scientific knowledge in itself, were far more concerned with meaning than with the rationalist, materialist perspectives that most scientists embraced.[3] Theosophy, like modern science, has roots in alchemy—but theosophers sought to preserve the essences of medieval and ancient cosmology and metaphysics that informed alchemy. While modern science turned outward toward a cataloguing of the cosmos, theosophers turned inward toward an experimental verification of what the most seminal religious figures of the past held to be true. Maintaining some aspects of the scientific method—study, documentation, record keeping, experimentation—theosophers sought to map the realms of consciousness and to unveil the inward meaning of all things.

I do not wish to suggest that theosophers stand in opposition to modern science itself, therefore. In fact, one of the greatest theosophers after Böhme, Franz von Baader, in early nineteenth-century Germany, was very much interested in scientific enquiry and was himself responsible for some remarkable inventions, including extremely successful industrial processes. Likewise, as his proposed reading list for would-be theosophers makes clear, Christopher Walton in mid-nineteenth-century London was much interested in at least some aspects of scientific knowledge in his day. There is no inherent bias in theosophy against scientific knowledge or experimentation.

But as the whole of theosophic literature makes abundantly clear, theosophers are utterly uninterested in dogmatic assertions, be they of religious or scientific origin. Obviously, if a scientist were dogmatically to assert that our material world is the only reality and that there is no God, a theosopher who had himself or herself directly experienced that the material world is *not* the only reality and that there *is* God, would be unimpressed. Theosophers are interested in the experiential verification of spiritual truths, and would be quite likely to dismiss the assertions of someone who presumed to deny such experiences out of hand.

Thus, even though modern science and theosophy do have historical roots, and even have some methods in common, there has been almost no dialogue between them. Partly, this is because theosophy remained almost completely hidden during the twentieth century. But additionally, theosophy has had little to say to modern science because, at least during the late nineteenth and twentieth centuries, a materialistic and rationalistic prejudice so prevailed in the scientific world as to exclude religion or mysticism, and to produce what some call "scientism," a dogmatic denial of all but materialist premises.

Yet times have changed. For perhaps the first time in more than a century, some modern scientists appear open to what the European religio-cultural inheritance has to tell us. One finds, with the positing of "morphogenetic fields" and other hypotheses of contemporary physicists, a resurgence of Platonism,[4] and most extraordinary of all, in a book by French physicist Basarab Nicolescu we find a remarkable effort by a scientist to probe into the meaning of Böhmean cosmology. Nicolescu examines the possibility of a "New Renaissance" in the twenty-first-century, a renaissance rooted in the European theosophic inheritance, particularly in the work of Böhme and in the new "Philosophy of Nature" that his understanding can offer.[5]

Nicolescu, himself a distinguished scientist, perhaps thereby has leave to criticize "scientism"—dogmatic materialism—from an explicitly Böhmean perspective. He argues that scientism focuses only on the "wheel of anguish" in Böhmean cosmology, and writes:

> Scientism, with all its philosophical and sociological ramifications, unknowingly repeats the action of Lucifer who, looking behind himself at the magical source of reality, wants to possess it, but is ignorant of the fact that this action means his own ruin.[6]

He adds:

> It is not by chance that this century has seen more and more monstrous wars take place, in this collective madness which represents the process of the mutual destruction of mankind. It is not by chance that we are witnessing more and more indifferently the establishment of violence in our everyday life. . . . Our world is effectively inside the wheel of anguish. . . . But this first triad is not *yet* closed up on itself.[7]

We stand, Nicolescu asserts, on the point of choosing between self-destruction and transcendence, for "we are quite close to the frontier of the magical source of reality."

If modern science has helped lead us to our present situation, with all the danger of destroying humanity and the world that it represents, nonetheless, Nicolescu argues, "modern fundamental science is a part of our culture and can contribute to the re-enchantment of the world."[8] Admittedly, science alone, "cut off from philosophy, can only lead to self-destruction" brought about by ignorance of meaning. At the same time, "philosophy, wisdom, and Tradition" (the sources and guardians of meaning) "as powerless witnesses, await their own withering and their own death."[9] But Nicolescu holds that a new renaissance will bring about a new synthesis of science and philosophy—a science invested with living meaning. Hence, even though science has helped lead to a "new barbarism," it can also in Nicolescu's view, by being combined with theosophic insights, lead to a renewed culture, even a renewed humanity.

Does theosophy hold the keys to a resanctified modern science and a new renaissance? Indisputably, modern science and theosophy have common roots in alchemy, and indeed are strikingly complementary in their experimental approaches to the outward and inward worlds respectively. Additionally, the time may have come when modern science begins to relinquish some of its dogmatic certainties and to investigate meaning. Any investigation of meaning will inevitably lead us inward, and without question the theosophers have a profound understanding of the inward realms and their correspondences to the macrocosm. But whether modern science can be resanctified, whether science can again

be invested with spiritual meaning, whether the world can be reën-
chanted, and modern man can be spiritually reborn—on such questions
as these, anyone who is wise probably will remain silent.

Nevertheless, it is possible to make one observation from a theosophic perspective. Theosophy insists above all on humility, and on the
necessity of direct individual spiritual rebirth. Theosophy is a religious
or spiritual discipline, not a philosophy. Dialogue between science and
theosophy—any recourse to the works of Jacob Böhme or of the other
theosophers we have discussed by modern scientists or theorists—will
ultimately require acknowledgment of theosophy's mysterious religious
nature. Otherwise, theosophy misprized will only feed the destructive
Luciferic cycle that Nicolescu calls the "wheel of anguish." The impasse
of modern science is dogmatic, and theosophy consists in the shattering
or relinquishing of dogma for living spiritual, not merely intellectual or
philosophical truth.

Theosophy is preëminently an individual praxis, an individual
encounter with living meaning. Thus, even though Nicolescu's hopes for
a European cultural renaissance sparked by a Böhmean "philosophy of
nature" represent an interesting possibility, theosophy's real power has
always manifested on a purely individual level, and at times in small
groups or communities composed of, precisely, individuals, each of
whom experiences theosophic revelation directly and in his own way. It
may be that science and spirituality can find points of convergence in
theosophy; it even may be that a "New Renaissance" does await us. But
theosophy is not concerned with mass movements; theosophers insist
only that each of us experience truth for ourselves, and from this alone,
from individual experiences, will future insights come.

CHAPTER TWENTY-THREE

Toward a New Psychology

O riginally, the word *psyche*, taken from a Greek
myth, meant "breath" or "soul." It referred, in
other words, not to the mind conceived as a bundle of
emotions, influences, and tendencies, but to the soul.
Thus, etymologically, psychology is really the science of
the soul. Soul, of course, is intermediate between body—
the physical world—and spirit, the eternal luminous
realm. Alas, this tripartite division of the human being
was largely eliminated in the Roman Catholic and
Protestant worlds, and because much of Western Christian theology came to focus on a simplistic and dualistic
split between only soul and body, the modern versions of
psychology followed this mind-body dualism relatively naturally. Theosophy, therefore, may help us to recover a more complete understanding
of human psychology.

But let us begin by analyzing the soul's nature according to theosophy. Modern Christianity seems to differ little from modern psychology
in envisioning the soul as mind, the amorphous "I-identity" or ego that
controls or inhabits the body. Theosophy, however, offers a different
view. For theosophers, the body is the envelope of the soul; and the soul
itself is really a subtle body, which in turn is the vehicle of spirit, the
luminous eternal archetypal or angelic being at the center of man. Thus,

283

theosophy does not posit a mind-body or a soul-body dichotomy. Rather, theosophers affirm that man is a tripartite being, whose soul is essentially a subtle or astral body intermediate between body and angelic or spiritual being.

This distinction—the intermediate nature of the soul or astral body—is important. According to Böhme, our souls are composite creations, comprised of unique planetary combinations or qualities, complex admixtures of such qualities as possessed by Venus and Mars, Mercury and the Sun, conditioned through zodiacal affiliations. Given our unique natures, we are each called to particular destinies—but are also charged with the common task of purifying ourselves of destructive emotions such as anger, jealousy, and fear. The soul in itself can never be wholly at peace, except inasmuch as it is illuminated by spirit, by its luminous angelic archetype, which in fact *is* peace, joy.

The soul is composed of "animal man" (the bestial, desiring "old man" in us), of emotion, and of rationality. But at the soul's center is spirit, divine illumination. Thus, theosophic discipline consists, as in the Platonic tradition, in the reining in of desire, emotion, and rationality, in curbing all these tendencies and in making sure that none of them get out of hand. For excessive desire, excessive emotion, and excessive rationality all mark demonic or destructive states of mind. The soul can of course discipline itself to some degree, but it will always remain fallen and subject to its bestial inclinations until it is illuminated and transmuted by its spiritual or eternal archetype.

For the soul fell through what Böhme calls "false imagination." In *The Signature of All Things*, Böhme writes:

> The divine light and love were extinguished in Adam because he imagined into the serpent's property, viz. into evil and good, so that the poison of death began effectively to work . . . and the dark impression of the eternal nature's property took possession of him. . . . [H]e was utterly undone, and there was no remedy for him by any creature, neither in heaven, nor in this world; the wrathful death captivated him in soul and body.[1]

Man's Fall came about through imagination—through awakening and manifesting in himself "the dark and poisonful mercurial fire-world." Imagination, here, refers to the soul's contact with the wrathful, dark, confused astral realm. All fallen souls are subject to this realm of fiery wrath and darkness.

How does the soul accomplish its transmutation and illumination? Through prayer and meditation, through the training of the imagination. For if the soul is become fallen through imagination—through its existing in the fallen, wrathful, or demonic world—so too its resurrection is accomplished by means of imagination. Whereas fallen man through false imagination allows himself to be coöpted by the wrathful dark realm, he can also "not speak and incline [his] will into the fire and dark world," but through spiritual discipline of the imagination "God must become man, man must become God."[2]

One must become virginal, pure in heart, must "reverse" the consequences of the Fall of man. Thus, Böhme writes, "whatever will bring forth fruit must enter into its mother from whence it came first to be." This means that the soul must ascend from its fallenness, its degradation, to its primordial and archetypal place and nature. Böhme writes: "The mother of all beings is Sulphur, Mercury is her life, Mars her sense, Venus her love, Jupiter her understanding, Luna her corporeal essence, Saturn her husband."[3] Böhme here is referring to the soul's primordial nature as unfallen planetary qualities, pure Mercury, Mars, Venus, and so forth—made virginal, made the bride of the pure spirit.

The soul must become virginal by being married to its spiritual spouse, through which "the humanity assumed the Deity, and also the Deity the humanity." Essentially, then, theosophic discipline consists in seeing how "God will change the world [cosmos] and transform it again into paradise," in raising earth back up to heaven through love.[4] This is a discipline of the imagination—meaning that the soul is "tinctured" by the powerful spirit of love, permeated and transformed by it. If the false imagination might be conceived as the opening of a channel for the dark and wrathful powers, then authentic imagination consists in an opening for the "harmony of joy and . . . all colors" of the spiritual realm to enter into the soul and eliminate all darkness. Authentic imagination consists in the fallen soul becoming virginal, full of light again—and this experience of light is itself the wedding of soul with spirit.

Authentic imagination leads us, not incidentally, to a fuller understanding of what authentic art consists in from the theosophic perspective. For Böhme, true art does not reflect twisted or fallen man, in all his tortured and wrathful contortions. Rather, says Böhme, just as at the "restitution, where God shall restore that which is hidden, that paradise does again spring forth afresh in the expressed word," so too "the artist does open the same in a part [in degrees] by God's permission."[5] True art, therefore, is at its highest a prefiguration of paradise, and offers us a glimpse into the paradisal realm in all its beauty, joy, and love. This offers us a provocative measure for contemporary literature and the other arts.

We can see, therefore, how the human being is constantly presented with a choice between the two kingdoms: the paradisal and the hellish. This choice or direction of mind is called the *lubet*, which seventeenth-century English theosopher Edward Taylor called a "longing delight." God creates manifestation by means of his *lubet*, or divine will, and man also, as an image of God, has a *lubet*, or will to manifest. But man can manifest through his will either good or evil, either paradise or hellish suffering and wrath. Thus, theosophy is in part a training of the will to manifest paradise, to transform wrath into love.

According to theosophy—as according to Christian mysticism generally—paradise and hell are preëminently mental conditions, qualities that the soul takes on as a result of what it takes a longing delight in. A soul that is wrathful, full of error, and hates God is Satanic; Satan, for the theosophers, is not only a "Creaturely Devil," but a "Spirit of Error," and the "Property of such an Erroneous Spirit."[6] Demons live in the *turba*, or wrath-fire, which is "horrid Tempests or Hellish Blasts," and these "contagions" can afflict a soul, even waste a body. Likewise, a soul that takes delight in the virginal tincture or "Love-fire" of God is restored to a paradisal condition like Adam's before the Fall; it is not subject to the *turba*, but is filled with light and delight.

As we can see, although there is definitely a theosophic psychology, theosophy cannot be reduced to psychology. That is: the *turba* and the virginal tincture are not merely transient psychological states; they are principles in eternal nature, which exists outside of time. Human psychology, therefore, is a profound interplay between eternal principles whose battlefield is the human soul. Theosophic discipline is an inward chivalry, a chivalric battle against the wrath-fire, the vanquishing of darkness by light. The human being, so long as he is alive, can choose between these principles, and the sum of these choices is reflected in one's posthumous state.

Böhme and the theosophers insist, however, on a trinity of principles in the soul that correspond to the divine Trinity. While there are fundamentally two opposed principles—light and dark, love and wrath—this duality is explained in human terms by a ternary of principles, which Taylor defines as follows:

1) The Darkness in us, which longeth after the Light, is the First Principle.

2) The Vertue of the Light, whereby we see Intellectually, is the Second Principle.

3) The longing Power proceeding from the Mind, and that attracteth or impregnateth it self, whence groweth the Material Body, is the Third Principle.[7]

These three principles are really stages in the soul's spiritual realization, which is why Taylor writes that "There is an inclosure, knot, or stop between each Principle." The soul begins in darkness, longing for light; it begins to see the light; its rebirth or impregnating power is its union with spirit.

These three stages are illustrated differently in a table showing the "Seven Spirits of God, or powers of Nature," transcribed by Abraham Van Somerveldt from Böhme himself:

Anger	Hellish	World
1. Astringent, Desire	Hardness, Cold, Covetousness	Cold, Hardness, Bone, Salt
2. Attraction or Compunction of Sense	Compunction, Envy	Poison, Life, Growth, Senses
3. Anguish or Mind	Enmity	Sulphur, Perceivance, Pain
Love	*Heavenly*	*Earthly Kingdom*
4. Fire or Spirit	Pride, Anger, Love-fire	Spirit, Reason, Desire
5. Light or Love desire	Meekness	Venus-Sport, Life, Light
6. Sound or Understanding	Divine Joy	Speaking, Crying, Distinguishing
7. Body or Essence	Heaven	Body, Wood, Stone, Earth, Metal, Herb

From this table, we can see that the fundamental duality between wrath and love, darkness and light, still holds here. Yet this duality can in turn be divided into a ternary, as for example there can be a spirit, its manifestation in love-fire, and its earthly reflection in the soul as reason and desire; the spirit takes on bodily form, or is "impregnated" in matter or the soul.

Theosophy is therefore an ever more complex elaboration of certain fundamental principles; each more elaborate manifestation does not contradict its precedents, but simply traces their ramifications in different realms. Human emotions, in this schema, are manifestations in dif-

ferent circumstances of variations on the essential division between
wrath and love. Covetousness, envy, enmity, anger, pride, are all variations of selfish confused reactions to the outward world; joy and heaven
are non-selfish reactions to unconfused reality. The origins of the former
are wrath; the origins of the latter are love. Demons are of an astringent,
burning, desiring quality; angels are of a luminous, love-filled nature.

This leads us naturally to the questions of how the "seven properties
of nature" correspond to the seven planets, and of how the seven planets
in turn illustrate our spiritual movement from wrath to love. Essentially,
the same symbolism appears both in the seven properties of nature—
which, as C. A. Muses rightly points out, is central to theosophic cosmology and psychology—and in the seven planets. According to Dionysius Andreas Freher, the planets can be ordered as follows in theosophy:

Saturn	Mercury	Mars	Sun	Venus	Jupiter	Moon
(Moon)	(Jupiter)	(Venus)	(Sun)	(Mars)	(Mercury)	(Saturn)[8]

Saturn is traditionally the first in this series because Saturn's astringent,
harsh quality corresponds to the newness of creation, the first manifestation. But central to the whole series is the Sun, which separates the two
ternaries; the Sun represents on the one hand the blasting, wrathful
power (affiliated with Mars), and on the other the illuminating light of
love (affiliated with Venus).

From this series, we can see how each of the planets in the series
can be linked to its complement on the other side of the sun. These
complementary relationships, we will note, link Saturn and the Moon
(the former dry and masculine, the latter moist and feminine); Mercury
and Jupiter (Mercury, the celestial messenger, linked to Christ, Jupiter
linked to God the Father); and Venus and Mars (love and wrath). Moving from the outward complements inward toward the Sun, we can see
how we are really looking at three stages at the center of which is the
Sun; Jupiter and Mercury are intermediate between two male-female
dyads, the "outward" of which is the extreme masculine-feminine pair-
ing of "old Saturn" and the watery Moon, the "inward" of which pair-
ing is Venus and Mars.

We are looking here at a process of psychological transmutation, a
movement inward that does not reject any of the planetary qualities, but
rather incorporates them in a dyadic harmony perhaps most closely akin
to music. The "outermost" and "innermost" planets in this arrangement, Saturn and Mars, are often seen as maleficent, or at the very least

as harsh, but they are paired with their feminine complements, the moon and Venus, who balance them. In fact, the "innermost" of these two planets, Mars and Venus, are by far the most cited planets in theosophic literature, important because they represent the essential regenerated, balanced human psyche.

Let us consider for a moment this dyadic complementarity in more depth. As Marsilio Ficino, the great Renaissance Platonist, pointed out in the fifteenth-century, there are two Venuses: the lower, lustful Venus who is without love, and the celestial, chaste Venus who is love and delight. So too there are two Marses: there is the vengeful, wrathful lower Mars, and the higher, warrior, chivalric Mars. Given the chivalric relationship between the virginal lady and the warrior pledged to her, we can see exactly why Mars and Venus are here archetypally linked in theosophic psychology. We are enjoined to move from the lower archetypes—represented by uncontrolled Mars or wanton Venus—to their higher chivalric, one may say paradisal, forms.

Mars and Venus are identified by Böhme with fire and with light, respectively; they represent the archetypal complementary highest possibilities of human beings. About this Muses writes:

> The joining of fire (Mars) and light (Venus) in the power of the radiant Sol may be said to be the entire summation of the transmutative and transformative process in human nature and capacity, as stated in Boehme's own terminology, and discussed in Freher's *Serial Elucidations*.[9]

Fire without balance is burning fury; light beyond bounds blinds, as does lust. But together, Mars and Venus represent male and female joined in the harmony of marriage in the light of their spiritual sun, Mars representing the warrior's controlled movement and desire, Venus the delights of the earthly paradise, the beautiful archetypal lady.

The total harmony of planets in Freher's tabular representation reveals a spiralling arrangement of the planetary dyads we have discussed around an eye in the center of a triangle. The spiral arrangement produces the form of a heart, whose two sides are composed of the three light planetary dyads on the left (Moon, Jupiter, Venus, linked with their complements) and the three dark planetary dyads on the right (Saturn, Mercury, Mars, within each of which is its complementary planet). Below is the Sun, mediating between the "dark" powers on the right and the "light" planets on the left, part of the continually evolving, or revolving, spiral.

We have here a symbolic diagram meant for spiritual contemplation. It incorporates the symbolism of the eye in the heart, as well as the
symbolism of the Trinity, and of the planets; it demonstrates above all
the complementary and harmonious relationship between different elements of the human soul. Just as in some Asian Tantric illustrations we
see male and female deities in sexual congress, bearing all kinds of symbolic attributes, so too in these European illustrations we see male and
female symbols in dyadic relationships. In all cases the illustrations
reveal archetypal balances, harmonies of the soul and spirit.

We may also note the purity of this symbolism. The planets are
arrayed on either side of the sun, while in the center is the eye within a
triangle. All the energies, in other words, move out of and into the central eye through a heart-shaped spiralling movement. The eye is the
dynamic center of the energies, and each of the planets represents a har-
monic or qualitative change in the spiralling energy of the human soul.
We may note that the energy spiral produces and takes place in the
heart—in the center of the being, at the very center of which is the
observing eye. This is a very simple and profound, indeed a primordial
symbolism, whose significance unfolds as one contemplates it.

Finally, we should point out that the eye—central to countless theosophic illustrations—represents the visionary aspect of theosophy.
"Visionary" here refers not only to the imaginative faculty that sees into
the nonphysical realms, but also to the symbolism of the eye. The eye
represents the observer—meaning that the planetary qualities of the soul
can be observed by the "eye in the soul." This symbolism brings us to
perhaps the most fundamental question of religious philosophy: who we
are. According to theosophy, we are composed of body, soul—with its
dynamic planetary energies—surrounding spirit, the observing eye. We
are the eye with which God sees himself through us.

But according to theosophy, we live in a fallen world, and we are
fallen people. Our energies are often disharmonious; often out of kil-
ter, we become angry, or jealous, lustful, or envious. All these disharmonious emotions represent life lived without love. Hatred, jealousy,
all our destructive emotions mean that during the moments we are
consumed with them, we do not love. When we are filled with love,
conversely, all disharmonious energies are brought into alignment with
one another. We are fallen people—consumed with negative emotions—when we do not love. When we love, we are raised up, resurrected, all our energies tinctured with the red tincture of divine, illuminating love.

Evil derives from lovelessness. All evil arises out of wrath, and wrath entails separation. We cannot hate without having a separate object to hate; we cannot envy without separation from the object we envy; we cannot be filled with rage without being by it separated from everything around us. It is not for nothing we speak of "blind rage." By contrast, love unites. We cannot love without uniting with beings outside ourselves. In the soul, love is the circulating energy spiralling out of the heart's eye-center and back into it again, having passed through and harmonized all the planetary energies. Love is symbolized too in the Sun, who gives freely to all, who bathes all of us in light and warmth, upon whom all nature depends.

Thus, theosophy is a path by which our energies become more and more harmonized, turned from wrath and separation to love and union. It is a gradual transmutation of the entire being, in a real sense a path toward universal love, toward manifesting God on earth, which is after all the essential meaning of following Christ. In all this symbolism theosophy goes well beyond modern psychology, which is, after all, chiefly interested less in fully realizing our human potential than in studying aberrant behavior, less in angels than in demons. If modern psychology seeks to move unbalanced people closer to the balance of ordinary fallen man, theosophic psychology goes well beyond this to focus on how we can not only become balanced, but can love others, and surpass our fallen nature.

Consequently, those who seek a more comprehensive psychological understanding of human beings may well have to take the theosophic view into account. It is all very well to look to chemical imbalances, or to apply lessons taught insects or rats to human beings, or to analyze psychopathology. But eventually we may develop a comprehensive psychology that recognizes man is a spiritual being whose soul is a complex and profound combination of certain energies that need to be harmonized. We need, in short, a psychology that takes into account the human entelechy, and is not merely a means to integrate people into an often inhuman, or only semihuman, civilization. Theosophy may have much to offer us yet.

CHAPTER TWENTY-FOUR

Hierohistory and Metahistory

 Any reader of seventeenth- and eighteenth-century
theosophic texts will be struck by how often spe-
cific dates appear in accounts of theosophic revelations.
Dr. John Pordage's treatise entitled *Sophia* is written in
the form of daily journal entries, and others in his circle
also kept very specific mystical diaries, taking care to
note each day, sometimes the hour when Sophia manifested herself. Probably the most elaborate of these
visionary chronologies is found in the biography and letters of Gichtel contained in *Theosophia Practica*. This
scientific precision in noting the dates of specific revelations reveals a central preoccupation of theosophers
more generally: placing themselves in the context of what I call "hierohistory" and "metahistory."

To understand how this is so, we must begin by examining the theosophic understanding of time, space, and eternity. We have noted elsewhere how theosophy consists in what Thomas Bromley referred to
directly as transcending temporal and spatial restrictions. This transcendence of time and space through visionary states of consciousness, Bromley tells us, in turn allows clairvoyance, telepathy, and a remarkable communion among fellow theosophers, who can share one another's delights
and sorrows even from afar. In essence, according to Bromley and his

293

friend John Pordage, theosophic discipline allows one to enter into eternity, through trance states and visions to enter into realms that exist without the restrictions of time and space to which we are accustomed.

We should point out, further, that there is an hierarchic relationship between these archetypal realms and our present world. When a theosopher enters into the delightful paradisal realm, Pordage tells us, he is seeing a realm not subject to our present temporo-spatial laws; what he sees is not a mere projection of his own fantasies, or an hallucination, but an actual reality more real than this world, more colorful, more beautiful, and above all eternal. This is not to say that the paradisal realm has no space nor time, but rather, that its time and space are much purer and subtler than ours. One could say that there the Biblical affirmation, that a thousand years in the sight of God is but a moment, takes on a renewed meaning. There is in this paradisal realm a "spiritual earth" and there are "spiritual bodies," just as there is an exceeding fine "spiritual matter" in which this realm consists.

Thus, the theosopher is one whose spiritual body is developed and invested with a "robe of light" by Sophia and Christ, who can enter into the paradisal realm itself by transcending his or her earthly body and consciousness. This paradisal realm is the archetype for the present world, which bears the stamp of "eternal nature." But eternal nature includes the fallen, wrathful realm as well, whose influences are felt throughout all nature. This dichotomy between nature red in tooth and claw, and nature as reflection of paradise simply embodies the multiple realms of eternal nature, some of which are fallen, some of which are paradisal. The theosopher is one who is aware of and has passed through all of these, who has become a reïntegrated individual, completed by Sophia, divine wisdom.

With these observations in mind, we can see how theosophy intrinsically focuses on the points at which time and eternity intersect for a particular individual. For even though eternal nature surrounds and informs our world, it is not accessible to us in ordinary states of consciousness. We must individually break through the astral shell with which we surround ourselves, and through prayer and the help of Christ-Sophia, penetrate into eternity. Each of us, according to theosophy, must accomplish this breakthrough for ourselves. Thus theosophers keep track, in accounts such as Pordage's *Sophia* or Gichtel's *Theosophic Practica*, of exactly how and when eternity penetrated time for them.

As a result, theosophic writings often include what I will here call "hierohistory." By this I mean a record of the exact times at which the theosopher, or in some cases a group of theosophers, penetrated into transcendent reality. These times take absolute precedence over the mundane details of daily life. Readers seeking intimate details of how theosophers lived will be disappointed even when reading the private letters of Gichtel, or the diaries of Anne Bathurst, or the treatises of Pordage, or the records of Richard Roach. For these authors are not concerned with recording minutiæ; for them the supremely relevant human history is hieratic history, those times at which the transcendent was revealed.

In the introduction to Gichtel's *Theosophia Practica*, (written in Leyden at Whitsuntide, 1721), we find the following overview of Gichtel's spiritual life with the Angelic Brethren:

> The first divine economy was that of the heavenly father, where the son dwellt in the father, and extendeth from 1664 to 1685, 21 years. The second is that of the son, where the father dwellt in the son, extending from 1685 to 1706, also 21 years.
>
> The third is that of the holy spirit, which proceedeth from the father and the son; which was completed in ten years, extending from 1706 to 1716, during which the holy spirit hath jealously continued the work, both as to the imagination and regeneration.[1]

This "divine economy" or hieratic history bears a striking resembles to that of the medieval Calabrian monk Joachim of Fiore, who proposed a schema of three ages in human history: that of the father, of the son, and of the holy spirit. But the hierohistory of Gichtel and his group is a personal one, consisting in three cycles, the last of which was shortened (and the author cites Matthew 24.22 to exactly that effect).

It is not surprising that the medieval hierohistory of Joachim of Fiore sought to encompass the whole of human history in this threefold schema, whereas the schema affiliated with Gichtel refers only to him and to his circle. The medieval doctrine of three ages reflects the universality of the medieval Christian worldview, whereas the theosophic perspective refers to the actual experiences of its adherents, and focuses therefore on a much more individual trifold series of cycles. Yet both Joachimite doctrines and theosophic doctrines often include prophetic expectations of a coming new era: for Joachimism this was the coming age of the Holy Spirit; for the Philadelphian theosophers, it was the coming *apocatastasis*, or restoration of all things. While certainly divergent, then, theosophy and Joachimism do have much in common.

Now the theosophic hierohistory is essentially a history of "marriages" between the soul and eternity. The word "marriage" here refers to the intersection of time and eternity, those junctures at which the soul is restored its spiritual origin and purpose, its completion much as a man and a woman are made complete by marriage. But this is a marriage of the earthly and the paradisal, not a marriage of man and woman, rather a marriage of the soul and spirit, of the soul and Sophia. Thus

> In each of the divine economies, which are also so many marriages, . . . God hath married our threefold soul into Christ Jesus, hath thoroughly removed and regenerated out of the darkness through the fire into the light, wherein standeth the image and likeness of God and hath clothed and arranged its divine tincture by the baptism of the holy spirit.[2]

The history of these divine marriages is the hierohistory of the soul's regeneration from fire into the light, its return into the "image and likeness of God" through the baptism of the Holy Spirit.

Thus, Gichtel's friend and colleague Johann Ueberfeld wrote the following hierohistory of their marriage feasts:

> The first marriage-feast of the first marriage took place at the end of the year 1673 and at the beginning of the year 1674 (when the divine talent had now gained ten of them). . . . This is the only one of which we have no creaturely knowledge, and which has remained hidden from us in the spirit of God.[3]

The second marriage, "the more glorious," took place in 1683, and lasted until 1685, almost three years. At this "high wedding,"

> in which the heavenly virgin appeared in the *ternarius sanctus*, gloriously transfigured, . . . she married us two brethren in one spirit, and called my brother-husband by name, and went back with us into the year 1668, and informed me that it was that very brother J. G. Gichtel, whose pilgrim spirit she had allowed me to see after the baptism of the holy spirit. What joy this awakened in the spirit to find ourselves in the spirit and nature in God, no tongue can express.[4]

Here, Gichtel and Ueberfeld share in the marriage to Sophia—and even are shown how they were united back in 1668, where their spirits recognized one another.

The successive marriage-feasts are increasingly comprehensive and powerful. In 1690 the second wedding-feast took place, in the midst yet of the ingenerating of the divine love, whereby our dearest savior Jesus Christ clothed himself entirely into our inward and outward form, with all the substance of the creature, thereby indicating that he had now become unto us, what we are.[5]

Another wedding "took place in the years 1705–6, and by God's goodness lasted a year," followed by "the first wedding feast of the third marriage [that] took place at the end of the year 1709 and the beginning of 1710, shortly before the author's departure from this world. . . . On that occasion the virgin appeared in the same form as in 1683, when she made us brethren acquainted with one another, and welcomed us. . . ."[6] The culminating spiritual wedding took place after Gichtel's death in 1716, "which God in his mercy reneweth unto us every year." The spiritual weddings thus were part of a renewable and increasing cycle, in which not only Gichtel, but the other theosophers as well participated.

This hierohistory precedes Gichtel's collected letters in *Theosophia Practica*—but a similar hierohistory follows the letters in the seventh volume of this series as well, so that Gichtel's letters are in effect bracketed in a hierohistorical context. This is not accidental. For just as Gichtel's letters—representing his life in society—are enclosed within a hierohistory, so too the theosophers' lives generally must be understood within the larger context of their hieratic experiences. Eternity embraces and penetrates this temporal life, and for the theosopher this truth takes absolute precedence over any mundane events. The serene correspondence of Louis Claude de Saint-Martin with Baron von Kirchberger about Böhmean theosophy during the outward confusion of the French Revolution exemplifies exactly how inward events are far more important than outward history.

These inward events are not always delightful, however. Gichtel's anonymous biographer notes how, for example, "the first attack of wrath was made on Ueberfeld in the year 1691, about the autumnal equinox, which has always been fatal to the brethren; the wrath devoured his life in one instant."[7] But eventually through the spiritual intervention of prayer, "the love also entered into the wrath and devoured it." Thus, in ten or twelve days Ueberfeld "rose again. Dying in Christ had been great gain for him." Here we see how Ueberfeld, like Gichtel himself, had to struggle with demonic, destructive powers—and that such a struggle they associated particularly with the autumn equinox. Theosophic hierohistory is often directly affiliated with astrological cycles.

The recounting of Gichtel's death at the conclusion of the biography that follows the six volumes of letters perhaps most clearly illustrates how Gichtel's life itself was for the theosophers enclosed within a hiero-history. After mentioning the specific dates of the Virgin Sophia's appearance to Gichtel—1683, 1706, 1709, for example—our author offers the following elaboration:

> [T]he heavenly mother of wisdom revealed herself anew in 1709, December 13, in the same form in the holy ternary; and just forty days before she called home the blessed soldier [Gichtel]. She smiled very brightly upon the yet living theosopher U. [Ueberfeldt], pointing with her finger to the divine light pearl, that in the faithful and deep process in Christ of the true brethren, had become so transparent, and grown to such a degree of strength, that so small a spark had become so great a light, resembling Adam.[8]

Although Gichtel and Ueberfeld were far separated at this time, "at one and the same moment the heavenly virgin appeared also to Gichtel's spirit in the greatest brightness with the divine jewel in the mind."[9]

Now the previous opening of the Virgin and the revelation of the "Virgin's dowry" took place on January 20, 1706, when God "Father and Son embraced himself in the spirits of both, and comprised himself in a mirror of her Divine Wisdom." In the intervening four years, the "light pearl had again to pass through the degrees of the most holy fire out of the holy ternary, and to be polished."[10] Thus, by January, 1710, exactly four years later, "Jesus, the Virgin's son, now for the fifth time brought himself forth a God-man, which is God, praised for ever and ever!" When "God had opened the fifth form of the Virgin's substantiality, the heavenly bride led her bridegroom Gichtel home on the succeeding day, 21 January, 1710."[11]

What are we to make of this exact correspondence of dates? Gichtel died exactly four years and one day after the beginning of the last revelational cycle in his life; and his death was forecast by exactly forty days with another revelation in this larger cycle. Certainly it makes for a remarkable series of coincidences. Perhaps Gichtel's circle made his life conform to this series of revelations posthumously—but such a hypothesis is countered by the voluminous documenting correspondence of Gichtel, Ueberfeld, and the other members of the Angelic Brethren. Ultimately, we are left to concede that Gichtel's life was mysteriously linked with others in his circle, particularly Ueberfeld, and that his spiritual life conformed to definite hieratic patterns.

But we can also draw some other conclusions from these patterns. It is true that Gichtel's circle, by publishing his letters along with this kind of biographical material documenting his hierohistory, produced a hagiography in which he was depicted as a kind of Protestant saint. However, Gichtel's hierohistory implies the possibility that each one of its readers can also experience these kinds of events. In each new case the hieratic events, while conforming to a general pattern of Sophianic revelation, will be unique to a particular individual or group. The documentation of Gichtel's hierohistory is only exemplary, by no means universal.

Here we may make a distinction between millennialism and theosophic hierohistory. Millennialists—including some Philadelphians, and medieval Joachimites as well—mistake individual or even group hierohistory for a universal phenomenon. Millennialists expect an age of the spirit that will encompass everyone on earth; theosophers such as Gichtel, however, chart chiefly individual and group hierohistory. Accordingly, theosophers and small theosophic circles may experience extraordinary spiritual revelations, but these are a result of theosophic discipline and conform to hieratic patterns or cycles. These revelations do not exclude the possibility of a coming universal millennium on earth, but they do not presume or require it.

The concept of hierohistory is most suggestive. Above all, it amplifies and expands our understanding of what history might actually be. Hierohistorians are certainly interested in temporal cycles and dating with great, we may even say scientific, precision. But the hierohistorian also recognizes that the most important events in human life are not merely historical or time-bound in nature. Rather, the most important events are exactly the irruptions of eternity into time, the extraordinary revelations of the spirit to those who are worthy of them. In a mysterious way, the hierophant through theosophy experiences revelations in cyclical archetypal patterns that reflect primordial numbers: three, four, seven, twelve, forty.

There is in such patterns and their significance much that is esoteric in nature. When discussing exactly this question—the remarkable spiritual experiences of Johann Georg Gichtel—with his faithful correspondent Baron von Kirchberger, Louis Claude de Saint-Martin, writing in the late eighteenth-century, wrote "His [Gichtel's] residence at Amsterdam was replete with a crowd of events in the sublime theosophic order, which I had rather tell you by word of mouth than by letter."[12] Saint-Martin did not want to commit himself to paper on the nature of these spiritual events even when writing to his closest confidant on such subjects, chiefly because it is difficult to convey properly their nature through the written word.

Indeed, one can properly speak of an oral tradition in the case of theosophic hierohistory precisely because, even though theosophers developed a special terminology for discussing spiritual transmutation and experience, these terms remained an outward shell, the kernel of which had to be tasted for oneself in order to truly recognize its real nature. This "tasting" was necessarily unique to each individual case, even while conforming to certain general patterns. Thus Saint-Martin, although he did recount the dates of Gichtel's hierohistory just as we have, did not want to comment too much in a letter on the inward meaning of those events even with someone like Kirchberger, much less with someone into whose hands the letter might fall.

Although we will not speculate on the exact nature of these spiritual events—which include the revelation of the Virgin Sophia and the wedding with her—we will make some comments on their significance, beginning by considering their relationship to hieratic time in other traditions. In his remarkable study *Cyclical Time and Ismaili Gnosis*, Henry Corbin considers cyclical time in ancient Mazdaean, Zurvanite, and then more recent Ismaili gnostic traditions. Corbin's observations on the significance of hieratic time in this context are most suggestive. Corbin writes about the ancient Mazdaean religion in Persia, antecedent to Ismaili religion in the same region: "The hieratic nature of time . . . will give it a privileged position for the unveiling of the world of the archetypes."[13]

Such an observation has a special relevance to theosophy. Mazdaism emphasizes liturgical time as the celebration on earth of spiritual events—and thus to celebrate liturgies on particular dates is to unveil the world of spiritual archetypes on earth. This concept, of course, is manifested in all liturgical Christian traditions as well, including the Roman Catholic and Eastern Orthodox. However, it is not found in theosophic Protestantism: in theosophy liturgical time is always internalized or individualized to particular hieratic events, above all because theosophers hold that an outward liturgical calendar can lend itself to "Babel," the outward show of religion without any notion of spiritual or hieratic content. In this sense, theosophy represents a radical reformation, a relentless emphasis upon the paramount importance of actually experiencing the hieratic meaning of the tradition, the "unveiling of the archetypes."

On Christmas Day, 1673, Gichtel experienced the Virgin Sophia, and this in theosophers' eyes made Christmas that year for Gichtel far more than simply an historical remembrance of Christ's birth. Christmas simply as historical remembrance is of little meaning for theosophers; Christmas as an hieratic event in which one is truly reborn in Christ through the Virgin Sophia—here is the true liturgical significance of the date. It is not that theosophy discards the Christian liturgical calendar; theosophy simply emphasizes the hieratic meaning of that calendar, without which meaning it is, after all, little more than a matter of secular history, like dating the fall of Troy. In fact, theosophy represents from its perspective a restitution of Christianity as inward experience and transmutation alone, a restoration of Christianity as hierohistory.

METAHISTORY

But I do not want to overemphasize the individual nature of theosophic hierohistory, for while it is true that theosophy insists upon individual direct confirmation of spiritual realities, those realities have a common delineation in such writings as those of Böhme and Pordage. In fact, some aspects of the more general theosophic hierohistory bear a striking resemblance to certain Persian hierohistories, most notably that of Zurvanism, and particularly in their parallel understanding that our history is "preceded" by a metaphysical history or metahistory. For both Zurvanism and Böhmean theosophy, our current history and world are under the sway of the prince of this world, the *spiritus mundi*, or Satan, in Zurvanism the Angel of Darkness, Ahriman—and this metahistory in turn explains the problem of evil.

Elaborating the Zurvanite myth regarding Ahriman and Ohrmazd will help explain what we mean here. "Zurvan" refers to the Lord of Glory and Light who existed before creation. According to Zurvanite myth, Zurvan made sacrifices and thought to himself that he would create Ohrmazd, the lord of light and creator of this world. But then Zurvan doubted for a moment, and out of this doubt appeared Ahriman, the foul-smelling lord of darkness. Since Zurvan had promised that the first to appear to him would receive the world as his prize, he was obliged to give this honor—prince of this world—to Ahriman. However, Zurvan gave power over creation to Ahriman for only nine thousand years, after which Ohrmazd would be given reign to do what he wished.[14]

The implications of this mythos are especially interesting when we consider them in light of the Gnostic Christian doctrine of the demiurge, on the one hand, and in light of the theosophic doctrines regarding the *spiritus mundi* on the other. For according to the Zurvanite myth, our current world and history are under the sway of Ahriman, the foul-

smelling lord of darkness. Admittedly, Ahriman's reign is limited, but
during his cycle, Ohrmazd, the lord of light, is relegated to a more distant role. This doctrine bears a definite resemblance to the Gnostic
Christian doctrine of the second and third centuries A.D. regarding the
demiurge, the ignorant creator and ruler of this world who, in some
Gnostic cosmogonies, appeared exactly like Ahriman, as the "shadow"
of the true God, arising out of primordial doubt.

Now, I mention these two mythologies, one of which falls under the
aegis of Christianity (albeit deemed heretical), because both relate a primordial fall before the creation of this world—both relate a metahistory
that explains the existence and nature of our present world and time.
Böhmean theosophy offers a metahistory that is strikingly similar to
some aspects of Persian mythology as related by Corbin and Zaehner,
and to some aspects of Gnostic Christianity as well. In all cases, the
mythologies relate what happened "before" time began, explaining how
evil came to be in this present world, and their cosmogonies are strikingly alike, more so than we have space here to elaborate.[15]

But let us turn to Böhme's doctrines on metahistory and the origins
of evil, focusing in particular on his *The Three Principles of the Divine
Essence*. In this book, Böhme elaborates how our present world came
into being, and what preceded it; he explains the nature of Lucifer and
how he came to have power in the present world, as also how that
power is limited. Noting that people wonder how it is man can have
knowledge of what preceded creation, Böhme points out that although
man cannot have "creaturely" knowledge of such things, by looking
within, into his inward visionary glass of divine knowledge, he can
nonetheless see the principles of all things and come to understand the
nature of existence.

According to Böhme, evil does not arise from God directly, and does
not exist in eternal nature in its pre-fallen state. He writes:

> Evil neither is, nor is called God; this is understood in the
> first principle, where it is the earnest fountain of the Wrath-
> fulness, according to which, God calls himself an angry,
> wrathful, zealous God. For the original of Life . . . consists
> in the Wrathfulness.[16]

Life, in other words, derives from the wrathful energy of God; without
it, there could be no creation. Originally, according to Böhme, "Paradise
was in the place of this world," but when Lucifer and nis legions raised
the "Storm" of their rebellion, God created the present world interme-

diate between paradise and hell.[17] Thus creation of this world is instinct with the manifestation of wrathful energies.

Gichtel, as often is the case, helps clarify Böhme's insight here. According to Gichtel, Lucifer is not only the absence of good or divinity, but an embodiment of a principle. Lucifer possesses, as Bernard Gorceix points out in his book on Gichtel, the "creative independence of Satanic power."[18] The dramatic consequences of the devil's fall are writ all about us in the natural world; not acceptable for Gichtel were the sentimental or Romantic views of nature developing during this time in Europe. For Gichtel, Lucifer represented a very real and independent destructive power bent on human damnation, against which we are all bound to struggle, and his wrathful power left its traces in nature herself.

This is an important point. It explains why there is evil and suffering in this world, and it has a corollary—that if there is suffering here below, that suffering has an end. To use Zurvanite terms, the reign of Ahriman is limited, just as to use Christian terms, the reign of Lucifer, prince of this world, has an end. Like Mazdaeism, theosophy teaches an *apocatastasis*, a universal restoration at the end of time. This is not to say, as Leade did, that the demons will be restored to their original place—for some theosophers, including Gichtel, balked at this idea. But it is to say that the end of time means the end of Lucifer's power, the restoration of divine luminosity and the reign of the God of light, just as in Zurvanism, at the end of Ahriman's reign, Ohrmazd has complete power.

For the existence of evil is simply the existence of God's wrath. According to Böhme, it is not so much that God seeks to punish Lucifer for his pride as it is that because of his arrogance Lucifer is unable to participate in God's will to manifest light and joy. Caught up in himself, Lucifer could only participate in the negative, wrathful aspect of divine manifestation. In the entire divine economy of manifestation, therefore, Lucifer and his minions have their place; they are executors of God's wrathful energies in creation. There is in this divine economy, then, an objective, or neutral quality: it is not so much that God singles out sinners and punishes them, as that sinners by sinning forfeit their participation in God's luminous energy and of their own free will choose to participate in the angry, wrathful energies of creation; they homologize their wills with the wrath.

Because this is so, one can accurately say that wrath and, for that matter, evil, preëxist man and nature. The suffering and pain possible in our present world betray the traces of previous catastrophes, of previous strife between good and evil, of the fall of Lucifer and the corruption of

Adam and Eve from their primordial state—all these refer to the existence of previous worlds and cycles before our present time began. As Böhme wrote, "two Kingdoms wrestle in Man," "who is the true keeper of the Tree of Life."[19] Man occupies a central and mediate place in creation, as does nature, midway between the wrathful hellish powers and paradise; man was created in order to remedy the catastrophes whose metahistory is implied in the very existence of evil.

Nature and human nature both bear the marks of what occurred in metahistory, above all the primordial drama of Lucifer, through pride, becoming "loathesomeness" in heaven's sight because he could not put his imagination into God's love and light. For thus heaven spewed him forth. Unable to reünite with God, he "kindled in himself the source or root of the Fire," and sought to possess in himself the "Heart of God," even though he could never accomplish this. He united instead, then, with the "harshness" and "stringency" of the fiery wrath. The consequences of this mythological selfishness are writ everywhere in human history and, for that matter, the natural world. Those who are arrogant and closed to others will themselves suffer—because being arrogant is implicitly to close oneself off from the wellsprings of light and love.

For if human nature and nature bear the marks of Lucifer's fall in the existence of evil and suffering, they also bear within themselves the marks of the kingdom of God, paradise. Paradise is love. Evil is a closing of the self against the other: this is illustrated again and again in the sordid history of crime, illustrated not only in great death camps or gulags, but in brutal daily life in sprawling cities. A demon could not be a demon if it loved; its nature is to delight in suffering and fury. An angel could not be an angel if it did not love; love is its nature, the element in which it basks, and which it radiates. The marvel of human nature is that we can participate in both realms, angelic and demonic: according to theosophy, the choice is freely ours.

Hence, just as Zurvanism—with its doctrine that Ahriman, lord of darkness, has his hand in creation—does not therefore attribute evil to God directly, so too Böhme's theosophy does not "make of God a devil, as some do, who say, God has created the evil," as Böhme himself explicitly said.[20] Rather, the metahistorical mythologies of the reign of Ahriman or of the fall of Lucifer serve to explain exactly the intermediate nature of our present history and world, on which evil has left its marks, and to which it has some access, without making of God a devil.

What is more, these metahistories may serve to explain the meaning of human existence far more adequately than the rather premature modern assumption that history alone can explain existence. For the most powerful implication of theosophic metahistory is precisely this: that metahistory is not finished, not relegated to the past. We human beings participate in metahistory ourselves—these events ante-date our present history, but only by being "above time," hence still ramifying in the present moment. The fall of Lucifer is important to us because it exemplifies a human possibility as well, albeit with less magnitude. We can choose pride and wrath, or humility and love—and metahistory tells us that this choice has ramifications beyond our present lifetime, beyond time, to speak with absolute precision, beyond history.

For according to theosophy, history is enclosed within metahistory, time is enclosed within eternity, and only this gives meaning to our human lives. Böhme writes:

> [A]s we know that all things [in this world] have had a begin-
> ning, so they shall also have an end; for before the time of this
> world there was nothing but the band of eternity, which
> makes itself, and in the band of the spirit, and the spirit in
> God, who is the highest Good, which was always from Eter-
> nity; and never had any Beginning. But this world has had a
> beginning from the eternal band in Time.[21]

The Last Judgment of Christ represents the revelation of our inward natures, be they wicked or good; it is the moment at which time itself comes to an end, and all our acts, once hidden, are revealed. Thus, the Last Judgment is really nothing less than the revelation of how ephemeral time and this world are, and of how they exist within eternity.

If according to theosophic metahistory time and this world bear the signs of Lucifer's fall "before" time began, so too in eternity the Last Judgment exists at the moment "after" which time ends, and all creation is permeated with premonitions of this moment of revelation. Metahis-tory surrounds and permeates us and this world: both the Fall from and the restoration of paradise exist in eternity, hence at this very moment. If the existence of evil is inherent in the wrath of God, hence in creation itself, so too the restoration of paradise is forecast in creation. A Fall in the "past" and a "future" restoration are present realities for us, whose energies we can contact and embody during this lifetime, the fruits of which will manifest when time is no more.

Böhme explains what the end of time really means for us by eluci-dating exactly what happens "after" time:

> [I]n that moment of departing [the Last Judgment] there pass
> away heaven and earth, Sun, Moon, stars, and elements, and
> thenceforth time is no more.
>
> And there then in the Saints, the incorruptible attracts
> the corruptible into itself, and the death and this earthly flesh
> is swallowed up; and we all live in the great and holy element
> of the Body of Jesus Christ . . . this world . . . perishes; and
> we live as children, and eat of the paradisical fruit, for there
> is no terror, fear, nor death any more, for the principle of Hell
> together with the devils (in this last hour) is shut up . . .
>
> And there then this world shall remain standing in a fig-
> ure and shadow in Paradise, but the substance of the wicked
> perishes in that [figure of the world] and remains in the Hell,
> for the works of every one follow after them; and there shall
> be eternal joy over the figures of all things, and over the fair
> fruit of Paradise, which we shall enjoy eternally.[22]

This present world, with all its beauty, is but a shadow of what shall be revealed in paradise, where "there shall be eternal joy over the figures of all things." Here is revealed everything in its perfection, and divine wrath, the lord of shadows and death, Ahriman-Lucifer, shall no longer have dominion; this world will remain as figures or shadows in the light of paradise, in the perfection it had before history began.

It is therefore a mistake to think of Christianity only in historical terms, for according to theosophy, you cannot explain Christianity in terms of history, you can only explain history's existence in terms of metahistory. Commonly, modern Christians see Christianity only in an historical context, as represented in a timeline running from paganism to Christ's birth to the end of time. The wholly secular perspective that holds Christ was simply a wise man, however detested, is only a stone's throw from historicizing Christianity; modern secularism is only a logi-cal extension of historicizing Christianity itself, which to the degree of its historicization is absent a transcendent dimension. Theosophy holds that this view is altogether too limited, and that it utterly ignores the nature of eternity.

For the truth is, what theosophy represents is the exact opposite of "demythologization." Clearly, history itself cannot offer any spiritual resolutions to the dilemmas of our existence. There can be no historical resolution to the problem of evil or suffering. A resolution of the dilem-mas history presents us may indeed only come from metahistory, from the revelation of eternity encompassing us. According to theosophy, only by recognizing how we and our world represent the "field of combat" between hell and paradise, only by recognizing how our "past" and our "future" can be one in eternally existing paradise, does human existence reveal its true dimensions.

HIEROHISTORY AND METAHISTORY: CONCLUSIONS

Hierohistory (the individual record of spiritual revelations) and metahistory (which mythologically explains the spiritual origin and meaning of humanity as a whole) are mutually illuminating and, indeed, inextricably so. For hierohistory is nothing less than the individual experiential confirmation of what is revealed to each of us in our common mythological heritage. This is why we have alluded to Zurvanism—but we could just as well draw on Islamic, Jewish, Hindu, Buddhist, and Taoist metahistories. Not that these are interchangeable—far from it—but they do all suggest that only metahistory (generally expressed in mythology) can redeem us from history. Böhmean theosophy offers us a very clear metahistory; it refuses to let us lapse into a merely historical view.

But this refusal to allow a lapse into mere history derives its power precisely from individual hierohistories. If Böhme had not had visionary experiences, he would not have written *Aurora* or his subsequent books. His writing, like that of all the theosophers, derived directly from his own visions, from seeing into the inward glass of eternity. The voluminous letters of Gichtel in *Theosophia Practica*, the monumental works of Pordage, the visionary treatises of Leade, all, like Böhme's writings, derive not from other authors, but from direct spiritual experience. Indeed, some theosophic works are essentially hierohistories alone, for example, Pordage's *Sophia*.

This is the striking challenge issued by theosophy to a world now grown accustomed to thinking only in historical terms: it tells us on the one hand that there are levels of reality beyond the physical, that there are worlds and beings we cannot see with our eyes nor touch with our hands, that our tiny historical timelines are enclosed within the far greater horizons of metahistory; and on the other hand that we can directly experience the reality of this metahistory and its implications. What is more, theosophy offers these—metahistory and hieratic individual experience—in a precise, documented, one might even say, scientific framework.

For despite its disparagement by dogmatic critics over the centuries, theosophy could be seen as embodying basic scientific principles. Whatever one can say of theosophy, one cannot call it living by belief without experience; its writings are not inherited dogma but, as much as possible, scientific descriptions of the principles informing the cosmos. Each of the theosophers, like a scientist, undertakes to validate or corroborate those descriptions on his own. Böhme so delights authors such as Pordage or Louis Claude de Saint-Martin because what Böhme describes both corresponds to and explains their own experiences and knowledge, independently developed. Independent corroboration of a general model for understanding—is this not after all a definition of modern scientific methodology?

Theosophy, therefore, may offer an opportunity for the conjunction of science and religion, so often today seen as bitter opponents. For theosophy offers a profound religious cosmology—a metahistory—based in and requiring individual confirmation. To those unattracted by a demythologized Christianity, theosophy offers a remarkable alternative; to scientists for whom objective observation and development of a schematic understanding is important, theosophy offers exactly that. In a very real sense, theosophy might be termed religious science.

But we must not forget that theosophy is religious. Although there can be no doubt that theosophy offers cosmological insights, those insights cannot be divorced from their religious context without distortion. Böhme, Gichtel, Pordage, Leade, Kelpius, were deeply religious people, and all their writing flows from their religious understanding. With this proviso in mind, however, theosophic metahistory and hierohistory unquestionably have much to teach us. In a skeptical, often irreligious and shallow era, theosophy may open to us altogether unexpected religious heights and depths that we have hardly begun to sound.

CHAPTER TWENTY-FIVE

Revelation, Authority,
and the Apostolic Tradition

When one scans the whole of Christianity's history, one cannot help but be struck by the incongruity of Christ's striking radicalism and the dogmatic formulations and institutionalism that developed centuries later. How does one reconcile the Inquisition with the words and life of Christ himself? This is not an idle question, for it places in the foreground a fundamental problem in the entire history of Christianity, a problem of our own day as much as any other. But if we consider this question historically, and then turn to Böhmean theosophy, we will find that our theosophers offer a direct and vital answer to it.

Essentially, we are considering the relationship of tradition and revelation here, and the tension between these two is at the heart of Judeo-Christianity. In the twentieth-century, many writers felt this tension in an acute way, visible in such works as T. S. Eliot's "Tradition and the Individual Talent," or Gershom Scholem's "Revelation and Tradition as Religious Categories in Judaism." Whereas revelation begins or informs a given religious tradition, as the tradition is transmitted from generation to generation, it has a tendency to become sclerotic or ossified, hardened and brittle. This hardening means that eventually those who themselves manifest the revelation are seen by the tradition as radical and dangerous.

This tension is archetypal in Judeo-Christianity, as we can see from the life of Christ himself. It seems impossible to deny that Christ's life as reflected in the Gospels reveals a definite conflict with ecclesiastical authorities. Christ said that he came not to overthrow but to fulfill the law, yet he was seen by the scribal authorities not as an embodiment of revelation, only as a threat. His replies to doctrinal challenges were difficult to refute, and we can see how the traditional religious authorities soon sought for a way to eliminate him. Yet paradoxically, we must remember, he embodied the revelation at the center of the very tradition that opposed him; in the life of Christ we see tradition seeking to eliminate the exemplar of the revelation that ought to crown or inspire it.

When we look at the development of the medieval Roman Catholic Inquisition, therefore, even though this use of torture and murder to enforce doctrinal assent is completely in opposition to the words of Christ himself as recorded in the Gospels, it makes sense if we consider that the archetypal drama represented by the rationalist scribal theologians and Christ is to be repeated throughout Christian history in various guises. It appears, in other words, that Christianity itself is doomed to repeat in various forms the fundamental conflict between those who represent the dangerous power of revelation, like Christ, and those who for rational, dogmatic reasons, oppose them.

We do not have room here to address such topics as Gnosticism generally, and the range of spiritual perspectives it represented during the early years of Christianity. But we can point out that the Gnostic texts we possess certainly indicate the Gnostics believed revelation was absolutely not fixed and incarnate only in the life of an historical Christ. Rather, the Gnostics held that, to be authentic, revelation must be a continuing process in which we too can participate. Scripture is not fixed; indeed, to truly participate in the Christian Gnostic tradition, one must receive revelation oneself. This is why there are numerous Gnostic writings, some collected in the *Nag Hammadi Library*, that amount to new spiritual revelations—records of visionary encounters with Christ, with the living spiritual powers of the tradition.

But Gnosticism was suppressed and eventually eliminated by what came to be known as orthodox Christianity, meaning historicist Christianity, and indeed, the history of Christianity includes many subsequent examples of the same phenomenon. One thinks of John Scotus Erigena during the ninth-century, of Johannes Eckhart during the thirteenth-century, both officially condemned and eventually more or less exonerated, of Quirinus Kuhlmann, burned in Moscow in the seventeenth-century, of the conflict in Eastern Orthodoxy between the hesychast mystic Gregory Palamas and Barlaam the Calabrian—these are exemplary of the conflict inherent in Christianity between representatives of doctrinal orthodoxy, and those who come too close to the dangerous radicalism of Christ himself.

This question does not confront Christianity alone. Islam does offer examples of spiritual men and women who were murdered or exiled by a hostile, ostensibly orthodox mob. And at the center of Judaism's history, too, is a conflict between the orthodox and the mystics. Gershom Scholem writes: "As long as there is a living relationship between religious consciousness and revelation there is no danger to the tradition from within. But when this relationship dies, tradition ceases to be a living force."[1] Only the Kabbalists in Judaism, Scholem continues, have fully confronted this question of the tension between revelation and tradition, for the Kabbalists "were in no sense of the word heretics. Rather, they strove to penetrate, more deeply than their predecessors, into the meaning of Jewish concepts." They took the step from Talmudic tradition to mystical, lived experience.[2]

It is no coincidence that we consider Kabbalism here. For the Christian theosophy of Jacob Böhme has long been regarded as bearing a close affinity with Kabbalism, and indeed having been influenced by it. Some recent authors even have argued that Böhme represents an excellent introduction to some concepts of Lurianic Kabbalism.[3] But regardless of whether this is true or not, it is certainly true that Gnosticism, Kabbalism, and Böhmean theosophy have one fundamental commonality: all of them insist that the individual must directly experience and in this way extend the essential revelation of the tradition. For all three, tradition exists as a context within which spiritual revelation can be continued and amplified.

This emphasis upon revelation—of direct experiential contact with the heart of the spiritual tradition—naturally leaves some room for innovation or, to put it another way, amplifying different aspects of the central revelation. Gnosticism, Kabbalism, and Böhmean theosophy each allow, indeed, almost mandate doctrinal expansion or refocusing on the basis of direct spiritual experience. Thus the Kabbalist Isaac Luria can develop his extraordinary doctrines; thus Jane Leade and some of her Philadelphian theosophers could develop their doctrine of universal restoration; thus Böhmean theosophy in general could develop its emphasis on the Virgin Sophia.

This is not to say that there is no conservative tendency in Gnosticism, Kabbalism, or Böhmean theosophy. Some Böhmean theosophers,

Johann Gichtel in particular, came to oppose Leade's doctrinal innovation of universal restoration. There are both conservative and innovative
wings in theosophy. But we must emphasize that none of our theosophers regarded themselves as heretical in the sense this word is used by,
say, the Inquisitional arbiters of orthodoxy. In other words, all our
theosophers were motivated by a sincere desire to embody and to carry
on the apostolic Christian tradition in its purest form. Their doctrinal
innovations, amplifications, and corrections come directly out of this
sincere desire, indeed, paradoxically, out of their conservative devotion
to the primordial apostolic revelation.

This brings us to a critical point: the question of authority. What is the
origin of authority in Christianity? There are essentially two sources, one
external or institutional, consisting in dogmatic formulation requiring
assent, and the other inward and inspirational. Naturally these are not
utterly opposed to one another, for doctrinal formulation provides a necessary context within which inward experiential confirmation takes place.
Everyone participating in the Christian tradition must combine these two;
there is simply a spectrum of combinations, from the absolute Inquisitional
requirements for dogmatic affirmation of rigid orthodoxy to the almost
total affirmation of inspiration in prophetic illuminist Protestantism.

Yet it is a mistake to characterize Böhmean theosophy as belonging
wholly to the latter, for spiritual authority among the theosophers comes
from a unique combination of doctrinal formulation and spiritual discipline—drawing on the German medieval mysticism of Tauler and the
Friends of God, on St. Dionysius the Areopagite, Eastern Orthodoxy
and the Desert Fathers, as well as on the devotional and doctrinal traditions embodied in Böhme's works—while simultaneously insisting upon
inward, individual confirmation of these doctrines. Böhmean theosophy
embodies a paradoxical combination of elaborate theocosmology and
insistence on personal realization; the theosopher's authority derives
from a mastery of both, but requires individual revelation above all.

From this emphasis upon individual revelation—on direct individual experience of spiritual reality—derived Böhme's denunciation of
"Babel," meaning the outward forms of institutionalism and dogmatic
assent without inward spiritual realization. Babel, for Böhme and subsequent theosophers, is a broad term whose amplitude includes all those
Christians who attend church, or even are representatives of Christianity, but who have not inwardly begun to truly follow Christ. Dogmatic
assent, for Böhme, does not make one Christian; only actually realizing
in oneself spiritual truth and striving to transmute wrath into love makes

one Christian. Christianity means the soul's transmutation, nothing less; what remains otherwise is only Babel, empty words or worse.

Böhme therefore strongly condemns those who are members of the "stone church," Christians in name only, who self-righteously attack others as "heretics" but themselves have no love. Indeed, so far are such would-be Christians from authentic Christianity, they "persecute, curse, and damn" "with words other people who are not of their name and opinion."[4] This is a situation of which Böhme had firsthand knowledge, having endured public vilification by Pastor Richter and others ever since his visionary revelations became more widely known. It is not that Böhme attacks such people in kind; it is only that he recognizes their real nature in his writing, so as to point his reader toward direct spiritual realization.

Direct spiritual realization is the source of Böhme's own authority in writing, and it is the true source of the apostolic Christian tradition as he sees it. In Böhme's perspective, the apostolic Christian tradition is not a matter of temporal succession through the historical transmission of the Roman Catholic or other churches; for him, being a Christian in the apostolic tradition means participating in the essential Christian revelation itself, not only following, but indeed *living* Christ. This perspective was later elaborated by theosophers such as Gottfried Arnold, who in his history of Christian doctrine and heresy was willing to admit some "heretics" as members of the apostolic tradition. In this tradition, outwardly expressing orthodoxy is not so important as inwardly experiencing the divine through what we may call *orthosophy*.

According to Böhme, the devil offers us a hypocritical coat that, when we put it on, gives the illusion of godliness, but beneath it lies cloaked pride, envy, and anger. These pernicious properties turn a human being into a beast, even though he has human form and the outward appearance of godliness. Such a one may very well espouse "orthodoxy," but these are mere words. He who is sincere must "here be at war against himself, if he wishes to become a heavenly citizen."[5] His fighting is not of the tongue or sword, but of mind and spirit, and following this inward battle against selfishness, pride, and wrath is itself orthosophy, wise self-governing.

The theosophers, therefore, affirm that the only true apostolic tradition is that which is engaged in the inward battle against pride, envy, and wrath. Only from this comes true authority, and only this marks those who are truly Christian, not just in name but in reality. One must remain steadfast in this battle even if the whole world appears to be against one, never giving ground, for spiritual hierarchy has nothing to do with worldly or institutional positions. Like the desert fathers and mystics of all generations, including St. Dionysius the Areopagite, Böhme affirms a hierarchy of those who have achieved inward victories against selfishness and anger.

From a theosophic perspective, those who embody the true apostolic Christian tradition may no doubt, like Christ himself, be treated badly by the world, but their spiritual purification or transparency will bear fruit in the next life. Böhme was not quite as millennialist as the English Philadelphians later in the seventeenth-century, but he did affirm that there would come an "age of the spirit" with considerable affinity to Joachim of Fiore's schema. Whenever time ends, then is an "age of the spirit" that Böhme, like countless Gnostics and Kabbalists, identified with the Biblical Enoch, who was transported into heaven. Of Enoch, Böhme writes in *Mysterium Magnum*, "His ecstasy was not death and not a laying aside of nature and creature; rather, he entered the *mysterium* between the spiritual and external world, as into Paradise."[6]

This Enochian "age of the spirit" refers primarily to a transcendence of time and space through visionary ecstasy, a trance journey. Such trance journeys are exemplified throughout the subsequent history of theosophy; Johann Gichtel, John Pordage, Jane Leade, and countless other lesser known theosophers—some of whom kept meticulous mystical diaries—all saw "eternal nature" and paradise with their inward eyes. We tend to think of the phrase "end of time" as referring to a historical end to linear time, but Böhme and the other theosophers are referring primarily to an "age of the spirit" that is an entry into timelessness, precisely an "end to time" by realizing a timeless state of the spirit, what Jane Leade called "Enochian Walks with God."

One can readily see that an Enochian journey of the spirit is a radically different origin for spiritual authority than is ordinarily accepted within Christianity. Over two millennia, Christianity in its various wings has developed a remarkable body of doctrinal interpretation and institutional structure; but at the same time, it has developed a certain resistance to the prophetic dimension of the tradition. Certainly we can think of no major theologian in the past several centuries, Berdyaeu excepted, who affirms even indirectly the prophetic or Enochian origin for Christian spiritual authority that is essential within Böhmean theosophy.

Yet the argument that our theosophers (including Gichtel, Pordage, Leade, Kelpius, and Beissel) put forward in different ways is difficult to refute: if miracles and prophetic revelation are possible in Biblical times, why is this impossible today? Logic alone tells us that the prophets and those to whom revelation came in antiquity were human too, separated from us only by time and distance. And what is time and distance to eternity? The Ephrata chronicles tell us that the revelations of the spirit among our European and Pennsylvanian theosophers rivalled those of Biblical times. If Pentecost is possible among the apostles, is it not also possible in a circle of theosophers in the wilderness?

But this brings us to the most important point of all. For if we follow the implications of this argument to its necessary conclusion, we must admit, with the Gnostics and Kabbalists, that since revelation did not cease in antiquity, it is therefore possible to find new scriptures revealed today. Generally associated with Protestantism is a belief in the Bible as literally true, and fixed forever. But our theosopher Protestants offer a Kabbalistic interpretation of scripture, as witness Böhme's enormous and elaborate exegeses of Genesis in his *Mysterium Magnum*. What is more, like the Gnostic Christians of antiquity, our theosophers openly assert the possibility of new revelations with scriptural authority.

This is an assertion of great import. It is true, of course, that other world religious traditions leave room for continuous revelations suited to particular eras—indeed, the history of Buddhism shows continuous development or amplification, as witness the *bodhisattva* doctrine, for example, implicit in early Buddhism, only made explicit later. Tibetan Buddhism has a history of "hidden scriptures," or *terma*, that are revealed at special moments when they are needed most. Even Judaism and Islam—like Christianity, religions of the word and the book—have traditions of continuous revelation, chiefly in the mysticism of Kabbalism and Sufism or Ismailism. But nonetheless, it surprises us to find a similar view of revelation espoused by, for example, Jane Leade of late-seventeenth-century London.

Leade, after all, felt compelled to offer the doctrine of universal redemption even against her own inclinations; and her writings include quotations from Christ given her in vision that embrace this doctrine, which has a long history in Christianity stretching from Origen among the church fathers to John Scotus Erigena in the ninth-century. She was told in vision that the time had come for this doctrine to become known, perhaps because of the time's religious decadence and as an affirmation that God's mercy is inexhaustible. Certainly not dogmatic, Leade nonetheless was convinced of the authenticity of her revelations, even though some fellow theosophers had doubts.

My point here is not to elaborate this controversy within theosophy, but to examine its implications, not to judge Leade in particular, but to consider the principle of prophetic revelation she represents. Are we to believe that visionary revelation is confined only to great antiquity? Logically, this seems unlikely. But if revelation is not confined to the past, how do we judge the authenticity of a given modern revelation? This is a critical question, and one that is partly answered by a contemporary accusation against William Law that he considered the works of Böhme and Pordage as virtually scripture.

If like Law we recognize the Böhmean theosophic discipline we have been discussing here as a continuous, single apostolic tradition directly descended from the original Christian revelation, then we are still setting boundaries upon the nature of revelation. It is true that the breadth of accepted revelation in theosophy is much greater than that in historicist Christianity, but ultimately, for the theosophers there is only one way to determine the authenticity of a given revelation: through prayer and one's own inward revelation. In theosophy, only what Catholic mystic Augustine Baker called the "inward teacher" can finally distinguish authentic from inauthentic. Thus, when Johann Gichtel heard of Jane Leade's revelations, and her embrace of universal redemption, he at first withheld judgment, until after much prayer and some study of Böhme he concluded that she was wrong on this point. Likewise, in his letters to Baron von Kirchberger, French theosopher Louis-Claude de Saint-Martin at first was undecided about Leade, and after much reflection agreed in general with Gichtel. Both Gichtel and Saint-Martin were willing in principle to accept new visionary revelations, but those revelations had to be confirmed by their own inward teachers.

Here is the fundamental premise of theosophy: that being Christian means not only rational doctrinal assessment or historicist knowledge, but actual spiritual realization of one's own, through which alone one can truly distinguish authentic revelation. For, the theosophers say, if we have not ourselves experientially realized what it means to live in Christ, all our distinctions and judgments are based in comparison and ratiocination rather than direct knowledge. While rational comparison has its place, needless to say, our theosophers would affirm nonetheless that even more important is grounding in direct metaphysical understanding.

Theosophy, then, differs from theology because it encompasses an entire spiritual discipline and requires the transmutation of a whole being. From this derives its revelations and its cosmology, as reflected in the works of Böhme, Pordage, Leade, and our other visionary theosophers. Theosophy does not exclude the possibility of new revelations to us; indeed, one mark of authentic spiritual realization is precisely such visionary revelations. Thus, although theosophy may be in conflict with what is often regarded as orthodox Christianity (the kind of orthodoxy that created the Inquisition), theosophy is not heretical but, like Christian Cabala and Gnosticism, represents a profound movement to experientially realize the apostolic heart of the Christian tradition.

This is why theosophers often appended to manuscripts circulating privately, quotations from Eastern Orthodox and Roman Catholic mysticism alike, as indeed sometimes from Gnostics and church fathers, particularly St. Clement of Alexandria, and Origen. Theosophers see themselves as embodying through their spiritual practice the apostolic Christian tradition itself, exemplified by all those who penetrate the merely astral shell, who reject the blandishments of the *spiritus mundi*, and who truly realize in themselves the marriage of Sophia and Christ, bride and bridegroom, in the ultimate triumph of love over wrath. For only here, theosophy tells us, is there possible an apostolic union of the Christian traditions.

Conclusion

Certainly theosophy has not received much scholarly attention to date, nor has its influence been fully charted. That this is the first specific work in English devoted to the subject in depth—following on the heels of my own *Theosophia: Hidden Dimensions of Christianity*—tells us a great deal about the movement's obscurity. But the theosophers themselves would not, I think, be too concerned about this neglect, nor about whether they had influenced the course of modern science or society in general. It is interesting to consider how much figures such as John Milton, Isaac Newton, Friedrich Hegel, or William Blake were influenced by Jacob Böhme and the other theosophers. But from a theosophic perspective, inspiring scientists, philosophers, or artists is not where the importance of theosophy lies. Theosophers focused wholly on direct spiritual experience, and the only influence they desired was to point people toward such experience.

There is, of course, some evidence to suggest that theosophy inspired the poetic visions of Milton and Blake, as Désirée Hirst detailed in her study *Hidden Riches*. Whether, as Law held, Newton was inspired by Böhme is somewhat more controversial, but it is indisputable that Hegel derived his philosophy by diluting Böhme's extraordinarily rich and complex visionary theosophy and converting it into a rationalist framework. As we have seen, it is not surprising that theosophy could influence fields as disparate as poetry and art, philosophy, and science. In fact, one cannot but suspect that not only has theosophy been more inspirational in these fields than has previously been acknowledged, but what is more, theosophy still has the potential to inspire modern artists, philosophers, and scientists.

Of course, one must keep in mind while considering matters of philosophical, literary, and scientific influence that theosophy is part of an esoteric current in Western thought that includes Hermeticism and Neoplatonism, alchemy and Rosicrucianism, all of which are linked together.[1] Theosophy itself—although it is definitely a single discipline, a coherent tradition stretching across several continents and centuries— is in its derivations syncretic, and in turn feeds into a host of later esoteric streams. Consequently, attempts to single out specific influences theosophy might have had, always must be hedged with the cautionary awareness that such influences are part of larger, often hidden currents in European and American history.

For example, one can find countless Rosicrucian illustrations—German, Dutch, French, and English—dating to the late-seventeenth and eighteenth centuries, almost all of which derive from, or were at least strongly influenced by, theosophic sources. These Rosicrucian illustrations tend to be much more complex and diagrammatic than their more strictly theosophic counterparts or sources. In many cases, the Rosicrucian illustrations, being much more catalogical than theosophic illustrations, are clearly intended to include every fundamental aspect of the created cosmos, to incorporate the whole of Jewish, Christian, and Hermetic knowledge into single works. Partaking of Kabbalistic, Hermetic, alchemical, and theosophic sources, such works can arguably be classed numerous ways, and certainly reveal the syncretic and yet unified nature of this tradition.

Here, I have concentrated almost exclusively on Böhmean theosophy alone, even though I have made numerous references to other forms of Western esotericism. But we should also recall that the Hermetic practitioner or Christian Kabbalist, whether alone or in a small group, works within a perspective very much akin to Böhmean theosophy, one that overlaps it on many points. Indeed, there is some reason to suspect that despite apparent differences, Christian Kabbalists and alchemists have much more in common with one another than with, say, dogmatic Christianity of any sort. Thus it is not always easy to distinguish between these different forms of Western esotericism, and in fact theosophy might best be considered in the context of Hermetic and Kabbalist esoteric traditions.

In other words, although there are many disputes or differences among theosophers themselves, not to mention differences between alchemists, theosophers, and Rosicrucians, when we step back and consider all these traditions together, they do appear like a palimpsest, all part of essentially the same manuscript but forming layer upon layer, or aspect upon aspect of it. Hermeticists, alchemists, and theosophers all work within a common esoteric tradition that has not at all been adequately examined, and although it would require a work at once encyclopaedic and insightful, much of the groundwork for such a broad study has already been laid.

Obviously, close study of given esoteric groups will reveal their diversity. As Frances Yates and Christopher McIntosh have pointed out, it is extremely difficult to tell exactly what "Rosicrucianism," for example, really was. Especially during the eighteenth-century in northern Europe, there was a bewildering variety of esoteric groups or "orders," many and perhaps all of which were influenced by the theosophers. There are countless disputes among esoterists within any given larger grouping—often a matter of more insightful authors such as Saint-Martin separating themselves from somewhat baser groups interested in "psychic manifestations."

But stepping back from all the theosophers and theosophic communities we have examined in this book, we can see how they, taken together, form a real unity. Separated in time and even by continents, working often without knowledge of one another, our theosophers' works reveal a striking coherence. Their journals reveal similar experiences; their books reveal each to be working alone within a larger context that joins them all. Theosophy—stretching from Böhme through Pordage, Gichtel, Kelpius, and Beissel on into the nineteenth and twentieth centuries—is without question continuous, an experimental discipline within which, if certain conditions are created, certain spiritual results seem to follow, each time suited to those who participate.

Yet we can say more. For as we have seen, theosophy bears some striking resemblances to ancient Gnosticism. It is, of course, unclear exactly how much theosophers such as Gichtel or Pordage knew about second- or third-century Valentinian Gnosticism, for example—but on the other hand, we need not posit direct knowledge of ancient Gnosticism by theosophers in order to recognize that there are real parallels between the two traditions. Indeed, the publication of the Nag Hammadi library—and the forthcoming publication of many theosophic texts, which today are more inaccessible than the ancient Gnostic works—allows illuminating, previously impossible comparisons between these two movements, extensive comparisons beyond the scope of this work.

We can, in fact, consider theosophy as a modern manifestation—a particularly coherent discipline—of Western esotericism more generally, which includes a whole range of related perspectives or traditions. Among these are Hermeticism, alchemy, Kabbalism, Christian Kabbalism, and Rosicrucianism, as well as Neoplatonism, (manifesting especially in the ninth-century mysticism of John Scotus Erigena and in the medieval German mysticism of Johannes Tauler and the Friends of God, as well as the minnesinger and troubadour tradition whose highest representative was Dante). Situating theosophy historically in this context would require an encyclopaedic study again far beyond our present scope—but here, in our conclusion, we can at least point out the range of possible future enquiries.

Naturally, though, if we consider theosophy along with all these other historically disparate figures and movements, we would have to propose a theory of what I have come to call "ahistorical continuity." By this I refer to exactly the kind of parallels between ancient Gnosticism and modern theosophy that we have considered earlier in this book. How are we to explain such parallels in the absence of convincing proof that all theosophers read, or even had access to information about, ancient Gnostic sects? A theory of ahistorical continuity would suggest—along essentially Platonic lines—that theosophers pursued a spiritual discipline producing knowledge or results fundamentally akin to the perspective of Tauler, or Erigena, or, for that matter, some sects of ancient Gnosticism, particularly Valentinian.

In other words, ahistorical continuity is not "perennialism." "Perennialism" or "the perennial philosophy" holds that all religious traditions have at their center common or perennial insights. Ahistorical continuity refers only to a single religious tradition, however broadly conceived, and means that within this context there are always inherent certain spiritual possibilities. In the case of Judeo-Christianity, we can see that although there are numerous forms of esotericism—as diverse as Kabbalism, Hermeticism, Gnosticism, mysticism, and theosophy—later authors or spiritual figures do tend to recapitulate perspectives quite similar to their predecessors'. This theory says nothing about parallels between such extraordinarily diverse cultures as Chinese Taoist and Native American—it holds only that within a given tradition there exist spiritual possibilities that are periodically rediscovered or realized, regardless of whether the sucessor is aware of his predecessors or not.

Hence we have the concept of universal restoration or redemption voiced by Origen early in the Christian era, by John Scotus Erigena in the ninth-century, and by Jane Leade in the eighteenth-century. This concept—a spiritual possibility within the Christian tradition—is rediscovered in an ahistorical continuity. To say this is to cast no judgment on the concept—it is only to point out that evidently Christianity contains within itself the possibility of such a perspective, and this possibility is occasionally actualized by various Christians. It is true that such a perspective may well be condemned by other Christians as heresy, but from an observer's viewpoint Christianity might be seen as a constellation of different perspectives, all of which may be actualized at one or another time, and thus "heresy" implies a divergence from a monolithic dogmatic unity that historically does not exist.

The tradition as a whole, in other words, is multifaceted, but recapitulates in different forms what are essentially the same perspectives. And we may go further than this. For the ahistorical continuity of a doctrine such as universal redemption derives from the periodic re-realization, by subsequent people, of certain spiritual experiences validating the doctrine. We cannot tell the motivations or experiences of Origen or John Scotus Erigena, for example, but Jane Leade tells us that she only came forward with this doctrine after being told in visionary experiences that it was her mission to do so. Certainly Erigena and Origen, too, most likely embraced the doctrine only after being convinced through some kind of inward validation. The experiential confirmation precedes the public affirmation of the doctrine—and might best be seen as contacting an understanding beyond time or space, and latent in Christianity.

In fact, Jane Leade wrote of exactly this in her book *A Fountain of Gardens* (1700), where she discussed the "college of the magi," or the "theosophic college." The *Fountain of Gardens* consists in a spiritual diary that records events in Mrs. Leade's life during the late 1670s. On December 15, 1678, she records a particular insight into the uniting of the "*Contrarieties* in Nature," only after which " Opening and Spiritual Parly" was she "cast as into a *Trance*, and had all [her] outward Senses drowned, and was brought by the Spirit into such a place, that was as the Scene of another World."[2] This place was the "Magia-School," or "the school of the magi," or the "theosophic college," which exists in a realm "clear as crystal," inhabited by angelic beings with "clarified Bodies."

This realm of the "theosophic college" is above time and space as we currently conceive of them. It is entered by going into the "Watch-Tower of the silent Mind." It is like a "*Holy Island*" beyond the "Coast" of this world, upon which coast "thou art not to stay." Entering it is "a restoring to the Cœlestiality of that Kingdom, to which ye have been Alienates."[3] Consequently, "all of Mortal Language was to be excluded. For all was understood by the operation of the Magia: here was no Speech, but all Power acted."[4] In fact, as a "young Novice" in this school, Leade was "suddenly . . . bound" and then as suddenly freed, demonstrating to her the power and "Soveraignty" of the celestial inhabitants. They are not bound by laws of time and space, but work through the power of magia-thoughts.

Here, in this college of the magi, is taught the "new Science" of the "Angelical Philosophy." Here we are called to "be Couragious to draw off from the Shoar of all mortal Things." Thus, the first rule is to "*unlearn* and *unknow* all, which the wise rational Spirit hath in its refined Morality disciplin'd and exercised our Senses in."[5] We are called to "fly above" the elemental regions of the "Sun, Moon, and Stars" and learn "Heavenly Philosophy." No one here can waver between two worlds; one must live either below, in the "leaden" realm of the senses, or rise up to the "Wisdom-School," "New-born in this High & Cœlestial University."[6]

I am not suggesting that the ahistorical continuity of the Christian mystical tradition derives from a series of experiences precisely like those of Leade. But this concept of a supra-temporal, "Angelical" or "Cœlestial University" does describe well how authors or spiritually inclined people in strikingly different times, even on different continents, can all participate in parallel spiritual experiences. There does appear to be a kind of "college of the magi," a "place" beyond the shores of temporality in which our authors do learn. Entering this "place," the theosophers assert, requires leaving behind our pride in our own rationality, and ascending beyond the realm of the senses.

While there are certainly numerous distinctions to be made among the various forms of Christian mysticism, theosophers do share these fundamental requirements for the spiritual path. Theosophy consists in a mapping out of spiritual experiences through diaries and books; more than many mystics, theosophers offer us cosmological and psychological maps of the terrain that they have covered. This terrain, if we are to accept them at their word, is supraphysical and supratemporal, and thus even if we do not accept the concept of a more or less literal "theosophic college" of angelical philosophy, we still can accept that when these maps are taken together and collated, they do reflect a common reality.

For there is, after all, a kind of camaraderie of the spirit. It is no coincidence that the German and English theosophers identified themselves with Johannes Tauler, for example, or that Christopher Walton in the mid-nineteenth century is fascinated with Dionysius Andreas Freher of the early eighteenth-century, or that many of the theosophers identified themselves with Eastern Orthodox authors. It is possible, as Petrarch once said, to regard an author long dead as more of a friend than someone next door. I have written this work in order to introduce just such readers to this neglected school whose faculty span the centuries, and whose significance is yet to be fully assessed.

Notes

INTRODUCTION

1. There are a number of books in English that do offer very helpful information on theosophy: See Arthur Versluis, *Theosophia: Hidden Dimensions of Christianity* (Hudson: Lindisfarne, 1994), and Antoine Faivre, *Access to Western Esotericism* (Albany: SUNY Press, 1994). See also Pierre Deghaye, "Jacob Böhme and His Followers," in *Modern Esoteric Spirituality*, A. Faivre and J. Needleman, eds. (New York: Crossroad, 1992); Nils Thune, *The Behmenists and the Philadelphians: A Contribution to the Study of English Mysticism in the Seventeenth and Eighteenth Centuries* (Uppsala: Almqvist, 1948), and Désirée Hirst, *Hidden Riches: Traditional Symbolism From the Renaissance to Blake* (London: Eyre and Spottiswood, 1963); for an interesting view of Böhme and science, see Basarab Nicolescu, *Science, Meaning, and Evolution, the Cosmology of Jacob Böhme* (New York: Parabola, 1992).

2. Antoine Faivre, "Le courant théosophique (fin xvi–xx siècles): essai de périodisation," *Politica Hermetica* (Paris: L'Age de'Homme)7 (1993): pp. 6–41, also in Faivre, *Accès de L'Ésotérisme Occidental II* (Paris: Gallimard, 1996), pp. 45–163; see also Antoine Faivre, *Philosophie de la Nature: Physique sacrée et theosophie* (Paris: Albin Michel, 1996); Antoine Faivre and Rolf Zimmerman, eds., *Epochen de Naturmystik* (Berlin: Erich Schmidt, 1979); Jean-Paul Corsetti, *Histoire de l'ésotérisme et des sciences occultes* (Paris: Larousse, 1992); Serge Hutin, *Les Disciples Anglais de Jacob Böhme* (Paris: Denoel, 1960); Alexandre Koyré, *Mystiques, spirituels, alchimistes du xvi siècle allemand* (Paris: Gallimard, 1971); Peter Koslowski, *Die Prüfungen der Neuzeit: Über Postmodernität, Philosophie der Geschichte, Metaphysik, Gnosis* (Wien: Passagen, 1989); specifically on Böhme see Pierre Deghaye, *La Naissance de Dieu ou La doctrine de Jacob Boehme* (Paris: Albin Michel, 1985) and Alexandre Koyré, *La Philosophie de Jacob Boehme* (Paris: Vrin, 1929); for a more general context, see Karl Frick, *Licht und Finsternis*, 2 vols (Graz: Akademisches, 1975) and Will-Erich Peuckert, *Pansophie*, 2nd ed. (Berlin: 1956), as well as the definitive survey of New Age writings and their origins in Western esotericism by Wouter Hanegraaff entitled *New Age Religion and Western Culture: Esotericism in the Mirror of Secular Thought* (Leiden: Brill, 1996).

3. On methodology, see Antoine Faivre, "Questions of Terminology Proper to The Study of Esoteric Currents" and Wouter Hanegraaff. "On The Construction of 'Esoteric Traditions,'" in *Western Esotericism and The Science of Religion* (Leuven: Peeters, 1998), pp. 1–10 and 11–62. See also Wouter Hanegraaff's excellent article, "Some Remarks on The Study of Western Esotericism," in *Esoterica: The Journal of Esoteric Studies* I (1999), i: 3–19 [http://www.esoteric.msu.edu/].

4. Arthur Versluis, ed., *Wisdom's Book: The Sophia Anthology* (St. Paul: Paragon House, 2000).

CHAPTER 1. BÖHME

1. See Andrew Weeks, *Boehme: An Intellectual Biography of the Seventeenth-Century Philosopher and Mystic* (Albany: SUNY Press, 1991), pp. 9, 40–43.

2. This is particularly well documented in the case of Zen Buddhism—one might even go so far as to suggest that Böhme's spiritual illumination parallels the pattern of *satori*, or awakening.

3. See Weeks, op. cit., p. 39.

4. See Augustine Baker, O.S.B., *Sancta Sophia, or Holy Wisdom* (London: Burns Oates, 1905); original publication *Sancta Sophia, or Directions for the Prayer of Contemplation* (Doway: Patte and Fievet, 1652). Baker writes of the "secret paths of divine love," and observes that "it is said of Perfect Soules, that they may judge of these matters by their owne supernatural Light"(I.iii), noting that "lay-persons may be spirituall Guides to Religious, yea, woemen" (I.75–77). But necessary above all is "a Divine Internal Teacher, for the "Interiour Illumination and Inspiration of Gods Holy Spirit . . . is to be acknowledged the only supreme Master" (I.101, 93–94). One has to wonder exactly how far Baker is from Protestant mysticism in his affirmations, or how much one can distinguish between Protestant and Catholic mysticism, so close, indeed intertwined are they.

5. See Weeks, op. cit., p. 94.

6. Böhme, *The Aurora*, III.42. Throughout my citations of Böhme's works, I use the translated English titles of his writings, which are available in numerous editions both in German and in English translation. In all editions, there are chapter and paragraph numbers, to which all citations here refer. Hence *Aurora* III.42 should be read as *Aurora,* Chapter III, § 42.

7. Ibid., III.45,47.

8. Ibid., III.56.

9. Ibid., *Contents*, §19.

10. Ibid., §27.

11. Ibid., §28.

12. Ibid., XX.50–51.

13. Ibid., XX.87.

14. Ibid., XXVI.142.

15. See Böhme, *The Three Principles of the Divine Essence, Preface*, §2.

16. Ibid., §21. Pennsylvanian theosophy at Ephrata was to make these lines almost literal: Beissel's monastic theosophers both male and female met for services every midnight.

17. Ibid., I.10.

18. Ibid., II.1.

19. Ibid., XI.30.

20. Ibid.

21. "Of the Threefold Life in Man," §23.

22. In French on Böhme, see Alexandre Koyré, *La Philosophie de Jacob Böhme* (Paris: Urin, 1929), and Pierre Deghaye, *La Naissance de Dieu, ou La doctrine de Jacob Boehme* (Paris: Albin Michel, 1985).

23. Böhme, *The Signature of All Things*, I.1.

24. Ibid., I.6.

25. Ibid., I.15.

26. Ibid., IX.1.

27. Ibid., IX.35.

28. Ibid., XII.19.

29. Ibid., XII.20.

30. Ibid., XII.30.

31. Ibid., XV.20.

32. Ibid., XII.37.

33. See Böhme, *Christosophia* §16, 17.

34. Ibid., §26.

35. Ibid., §32.

36. Ibid., V.vi.4.

37. Ibid., V.viii.1.

38. Ibid., VI.2, "Treatise on the Supersensual Life."

39. Ibid., VI.9.

40. See esp. VI.38.

41. Ibid., IX.103.

42. Ibid., VI.8.

CHAPTER 2. JOHANN GEORG GICHTEL AND HIS CIRCLE

1. See, on Gichtel's early years, Bernard Gorceix, *Johann Georg Gichtel, Theosophe d'Amsterdam* (Delphica: L'Age d'Homme, 1975), pp. 17–18. I have drawn on Gorceix's account, an important twentieth-century book on Gichtel, but have relied primarily on original source material.

2. See Gichtel, *Theosophia Practica* (Leyden: 1722), VII.34–35, hereafter "Gichtel." See the ms. translation by C. W. Heckethorne (1868–1869) in Dr. Williams's Library, London. Pagination refers to the 1722 edition.

3. Ibid.

4. Gichtel, II.742–744.

5. Gichtel, VII.63–67.

6. Gichtel, VII.72–74.

7. Gichtel, VII.185.

8. Gichtel, VII.188–189.

9. Gorceix, op. cit., p. 31.

10. Ibid.

11. Gichtel, VII.212–213.

12. Gichtel, VII.340–341.

13. See, for more on Gichtel's monumental project, Gorceix, pp. 33–34.

14. Gichtel, III.2091–2092.

15. Ibid., III.2117.

16. Ibid.

CHAPTER 3. THE LUCID VISIONARY SCIENCE
OF DR. JOHN PORDAGE

1. Baxter, *Reliquiae Baxterianae*, p. 77, quoted in Thune, pp. 14–15.

2. See Serge Hutin, *Les disciples anglais de Jacob Böhme* (Paris: Didier, 1960), p. 82.

3. See Rawlinson Ms. 833, Folio 63.

4. Ibid.

5. Pordage, *Innocencie Appearing Through the Dark Mists of Pretended Guilt* (Cornhill: Blunden, 1654), pp. 72–73.

6. See Gichtel II.742, where he relates his 1664 illumination in prison.

7. Pordage, p. 73.

8. Ibid., p. 74.

9. Ibid., p. 75.

10. Ibid.

11. Ms. Rawl. D 833, p. 130; see Thune, p. 51.

12. See *A Most Faithful relation of two wonderful passages which happened very lately* . . . *in the parish of Bradfield* (London: James Cottrell, 1650).

13. *Innocencie Appearing*, op. cit., pp. 14–15.

14. Ibid., p. 17.

15. *Innocencie Appearing*, p. 2.

16. Ibid., p. 79.

17. This story is recounted in *A Fountain of Gardens*, I.17 ff.

18. We are sorely lacking a complete edition of Pordage's works at this time.

19. Pordage, *A Treatise of Eternal Nature* (London: 1681), preface.

20. Ibid., pp. 105, 107.

21. *Theologia Mystica* (London: 1683), p. 2.

22. Ibid., p. 7.

23. Ibid., p. 16.

24. Ibid., p. 31.

25. Ibid., p. 34.

26. Ibid., pp. 37–38.

27. Ibid., pp. 68–69.

28. Ibid., pp. 87, 92.

29. Pordage, *Göttliche und Wahre Metaphysica* (Frankfurt/Leipzig: 1715/1746) II.ii.26.

30. Ibid., II.iv.12, p. 222.

31. Ibid., p. 260. The German reads: "Von den Englischen Leibern aber können wir nicht sagen daß sie nach Gottes Bilde gemacht sind: weil Gott keinen organischen oder weckzeuglichen Leib hat wie die Engel: sondern die h. Dreiheit offenbahret sich als ein ewiges Auge das in dem flammenden herzen der ewigen Liebe seinen beständigen Sitz hat welche . . . in dem Tempel-Leib des h. Geistes wohnen, ohne alle Gestalt . . ."

32. Pordage, *Ein gründlich Philosophisch Sendschreiben von rechten und wahren Steine der Weissheit, aus dem Englischen übersetzt* (Frankfurt: 1727), p. 4.

33. Ibid., p. 7.

34. Ibid., pp. 11–16.

35. *Mundorum Explicatio* (London: 1661), preface, n.p.

36. Ibid., p. 40.

CHAPTER 4. JANE LEADE, THE PHILADELPHEANS, AND THE DOCTRINE OF UNIVERSAL RESTORATION

1. See Thune, pp. 68–69; see also *The Wars of David*: The Preface of the Publisher; see also Leade, *Sechs unschätzbare durch göttliche Offenbarung und Befel ans Licht gebrachte mystische Tratätlein* (Amsterdam: 1696), pp. 413–415.

2. Pordage, *Theologia Mystica*, op. cit., "To the reader," p. 2.

3. For speculation on which Knyphausen is in question here, see Thune, p. 86. Dodo von Knyphausen may have been Mrs. Leade's supporter, or it may have been Georg Guillaume Knyphausen, who wrote *Entretiens solitaires d'une âme dévote avec son Dieu* (Amsterdam: 1697).

4. Walton, *Notes and Materials*, p. 508.

5. Ibid.

6. Ibid., p. 509.

7. Ibid.

8. Ms. Rawlinson, D 833 p. 169; see Thune, p. 88.

9. Ibid.

10. Ibid., p. 134; Thune, p. 90.

11. *The Declaration of the Philadelphian Society of England*, p. 5.

12. Ibid., pp. 6–7.

13. See Thune, p. 115.

14. On the bizarre confusion that produced the accusation Mrs. Leade had an illegitimate child, see Thune, p. 128. The journal *Theosophical Transactions* carried a report that a holy child had been born in Beyreuth, Germany, an announcement that—given the belief among some that Mrs. Leade was the woman mentioned in the apocalyptic book of Revelation—was interpreted in Germany to mean that Mrs. Leade had had an illegitimate child in Beyreuth. Thune rightly terms this accusation "absurd." On Eva von Buttlar, see Arthur Versluis, *The Mysteries of Love* (St. Paul: Grail, 1996), pp. 123 ff.

15. See Thune, p. 123.

16. *The State of the Philadelphian Society*, op. cit., p. 7; Thune, p. 131.

17. See Leade, *The Wars of David and the Peacable Reign of Solomon* (London: 1700), p. 1.

18. Roach, Ms. Rawl. D 833, p. 172; Thune, p. 136.

19. Ibid., Ms. Rawl. p. 66; Thune, p. 136.

20. John Scotus Erigena, J. O'Meara, trs., *Periphyseon* (Dumbarton Oaks: 1987), V.918B, C, pp. 591–592.

21. Gichtel, op. cit., I.325.

22. Ibid., III.2444.

23. Ibid., V.3130.

24. See Gichtel, op. cit., VII.328.

25. Ibid., VII.329.

26. Leade, "A Revelation of the Everlasting Gospel-Message," p. 1.

27. Ibid., p. 25.

28. Leade, "The Enochian Walks with God," p. 58.

29. Ibid., p. 60.

30. Cp. Rev. 20: 10, 14, 15. These verses do refer to the beast and the false prophet being thrown into the fire and being tormented "for ever and ever." This is the "second death." What is meant by this, however, is a matter for deep study, and certainly subject to interpretation.

31. Leade, "Enochian Walks," p. 61.

32. Leade, "Everlasting Gospel," pp. 25–26.

33. Roach, *The Imperial Standard of Messiah Triumphant; coming now in the Power and Kingdom of his Father, to Reign with his saints on Earth* (London: 1727), pp. 189–204.

CHAPTER 5. DIONYSIUS ANDREAS FREHER, ALLEN LIPPINGTON, AND WILLIAM LAW

1. Adam McLean may publish the collected works of Freher in the next several years, in concert with the Bibliotheca Philosophica Hermetica of Amsterdam.

2. C. A. Muses, *Illumination on Jacob Böhme: The Work Of Dionysius Andreas Freher* (New York: King's Crown, 1951), p. 3.

3. See Donovan Dawe, *Skilbecks: Drysalters, 1650–1950* (London: Skilbeck Brothers, 1950), p. 3.

4. Dawe, op. cit., p. 46.

5. See Muses, op. cit., p. 25, and Dawe, op. cit., p. 49.

6. Law, "The Spirit of Love," in *William Law: A Serious Call to a Devout and Holy Life and The Spirit of Love* (New York: Paulist Press, 1978), p. 375.

7. Muses, op. cit., pp. 23–24.

8. Law, op. cit., p. 392.

9. Ibid., p. 429; italics added.

10. Ibid., p. 482.

11. Ibid., p. 483.

12. Ibid.

13. See Charles Williams, *The Descent of the Dove* (New York: Meridian, 1956), p. 196; Rufus Jones, *The Luminous Trail* (New York: Macmillan, 1947), pp. 124–125; see also E. P. Rudolph, *William Law* (Boston: Twayne, 1980), p. 118.

CHAPTER 6. JOHANNES KELPIUS AND PENNSYLVANIA THEOSOPHY

1. See Julius Sachse, *The Pietists of Provincial Pennsylvania* (Philadelphia: Sachse, 1895), I.150. See also Oswald Seidensticker, *Der Deutsche Pionier* (Cincinnati: 1870), pp. 67–75; as also K. Klein, "Magister Johannes Kelpius," in *Festschrift Seiner Hochwürden D. Dr. F. Teutsch* (Hermannstadt: 1931), pp. 57–77. As Peter Erb remarks in his *Johann Conrad Beissel and the Ephrata Community* (Lewiston: Mellon, 1985), p. 40 the best general source for this field remains Sachse. There are problems with Sachse's work, chiefly in that some documents from which he drew cannot currently be located; but compared to the problems with other sources for the Kelpius and Ephrata histories, like the confabulated "diary" of Ezechiel Sangmeister entitled *Leben und Wandel*, Sachse remains very useful. Jeffrey Bach's *Voices of the Turtledoves*, Ph.D. Diss., Duke University (1997) is an excellent contemporary resource, but does not deal with Kelpius.

2. See Seidensticker, op. cit., and Klein, op. cit.; see also Sachse, I.222.

3. Peter Miller, cited in Sachse, I.249

4. See Johannes Kelpius, *The Diarium of Magister Johannes Kelpius*, J. Sachse, trs. (Lancaster: 1917), in *The Pennsylvania-German Society, Proceedings and Addresses*, Vol. XXV, p. 9, hereafter cited as *Diarium*.

5. See Ernst Benz, *Die Protestantische Thebais* (Mainz: 1963), pp. 95–96. Benz's work is marred by some surprising errors, including his resurrection of James [sic] Pordage, who actually died in 1681, to greet along with John [sic] Bromley and Jane Leade the pilgrims from Germany in 1693.

6. See Revelation XII, 1–6, especially "And there appeared a great wonder in heaven, a woman clothed with the sun, and the moon under her feet, and upon her head a crown of twelve stars. . . . And the woman fled into the wilderness, where she hath a place prepared of God, that they should find her there a thousand two hundred and threescore days."

7. Kelpius, *Diarium*, pp. 13–14

8. *Diarium*, p. 21.

9. Sachse, op. cit., I.79.

10. See, for its brief discussion of Kelpius in relation to Ephrata, *Chronicon Ephratense* (Ephrata: 1786), Kap. XXXIII. There is an English translation under the same title (Lancaster: Zahm, 1889).

11. This story is related by Sachse, I.153. Kelpius's life and work still await a full scholarly examination.

12. This kind of story is not uncommon in the theosophic tradition; similar examples are to be found in Gichtel's *Theosophia Practica*.

13. Kelpius's letters quoted can be found in Sachse, I.129 ff.

14. Ibid., p. 130.

15. Ibid.

16. Ibid., p. 133.

17. Ibid., p. 163.

18. Kelpius, *Diarium*, pp. 80 ff.

19. Ibid., pp. 86 ff.

20. Ibid., p. 100.

21. Sachse, I.219.

22. Johannes Kelpius, *A Short, Easy, and Comprehensive Method of Prayer*. Christopher Witt, trs. (Philadelphia: 1761), p. 1, available in the *Esoterica* archives at http://www.esoteric.msu.edu/.

23. Ibid., pp. 34–35.

24. This version of Kelpius's death is told by Sachse, I.244–246.

25. Ibid., I.247.

26. The most comprehensive historical overview of Ephrata's history is Julius Sachse, *The German Sectarians of Pennsylvania*, 2 vols. (Philadelphia: 1899–1900), although Sachse does have a tendency to romanticise and embellish. A good corrective is the recent Ph.D. dissertation of Jeffrey Bach, already cited. See Sachse, I.39; on Haller, see *Chronicon Ephratense*, Kap. I. According to the *Chronicon*, Haller's circle did hold meetings in the forest; it is unlikely they were Rosicrucian, however.

27. See Jeffrey Bach, *Voices of the Turtledoves: The Mystical Language of the Ephrata Cloister*, Ph.D. Diss., Duke University (1997), pp. 433–453 on the problematic nature of Rosicrucianism in Ephrata studies.

28. Beissel, quoted in Sachse, *Sectarians*, I.53.

29. *Chronicon Ephratense*, op. cit., Kap. IV, pp. 21, 25.

30. On the Conestoga community, see *Chronicon Ephratense*, Kap. V and VI; see, on the sect called the "Newborns," George Michael Weiss, *Der in der Amerikanischen Wildnuß* . . . (Philadelphia: Bradford, 1729); see also Sachse, *Sectarians*, I.430.

31. See *Chronicon Ephratense*, Kap. XVI, pp. 97–98.

32. Ibid. See also the precise dating of the ecstatic visions of Catharine Hummer in Kap. XXXIII. See also on this Sachse, I.273, 275.

33. On Beisselian dietary restrictions, see the *Chronicon Ephratense*, Kap. XIV; see also the unpublished Beissel ms. *Diœtetetica Sacra: die Zucht des Leibes, Zur Heiligung der Seelen beförderlich Aus richtigen Natur Gründen* (Pennsylvama Historical and Museum Commission, Ephrata Cloister, Ephrata, Pennsylvania).

34. See Sachse, *Sectarians*, II.152.

35. Arnold is discussed as a direct influence on Ephrata, as is Gichtel, in *Chronicon Ephratense*, Kap. XXXIII.

36. In the final chapter of *Chronicon*, Beissel is said to have made peace before he died with everyone with whom he had quarrelled.

37. On the quarrels with the Eckerlings, see *Chronicon*, XXVII and XXVIII. See also Peter Erb, *Johann Conrad Beissel and the Ephrata Community* (Lewiston: Mellon, 1985), pp. 26–27, and Sachse, II. 172–173.

38. Erb., p. 24.

39. There are a number of alchemical and astrological manuscripts of Jacob Martin in the Pennypacker Collection of the Pennsylvania Historical and Museum Collection, belonging to his Ephrata period. See Bach, op. cit., pp. 422 ff.

40. On Hummer's initial seven days and nights in trance, and her visions of heaven, see Chronicon, Kap. XXXII. See also Erb, op. cit., p. 355. It is interesting that Hummer's experiences correspond strikingly with those of John Pordage, who was said by Jane Leade to have spent up to two weeks at a time in trance.

41. Erb, p. 358.

42. Ibid., p. 365.

43. See Erb, op. cit., passim.

44. Readers are advised to examine Thomas Mann, *Doctor Faustus*, Ch. VIII, and its interesting description of Ephrata music.

45. Erb, p. 186.

46. Ibid., p. 190.

47. Sachse, II.176 ff., 238 ff.

48. See Erb, op. cit., translated from *Deliciae Ephratenses, Pars. I, oder des ehrwürdigen Vatters Friedsam Gottrecht, . . . Geistliche Reden . . .* (Ephrata: Typis Societatis, 1773). What Erb labelled "First Sermon" is actually Beissel's *Dissertation on Man's Fall*, as pointed out by Jeffrey Bach in *Voices of the Turtledoves*, Ph.D. Diss. (1997).

49. Erb, p. 113.

50. Ibid., 113–114.

51. Ibid., p. 114.

52. Ibid.

53. Ibid., pp. 118–119.

54. Ibid., p. 121.

55. Ibid., p. 122.

56. Ibid.

57. Ibid., p. 131.

CHAPTER 7. CHRISTOPHER WALTON
AND HIS THEOSOPHIC COLLEGE

1. Christopher Walton, *An Introduction to Theosophy, or the Science of the Mystery of Christ*(London: Kendrick, 1854), p. xviii.

2. See, for a very extensive discussion of religious pluralism in Europe and America, Versluis, *American Transcendentalism and Asian Religions* (Oxford: Oxford University Press, 1993), passim.

3. Ibid., p. vii.

4. Ibid.

5. Walton, pp. vii–viii.

6. Ibid., p. xiii.

7. Ibid., pp. 491–499.

8. Ibid., pp. xviii–xix.

9. Ibid., p. 505.

10. Ibid., p. 506.

11. Ibid., p. 507.

12. Ibid., pp. 507–508.

13. Ibid., p. 509.

14. Ibid., p. xv.

15. Ibid., p. ix.

16. See "Theosophy and Modern Science" in this volume.

17. See Louis Claude de Saint-Martin, *Theosophic Correspondence 1792–1797*, E. B. Penny, trans. (Exeter: Roberts, 1863; Theosophical University Press, 1982), appendix.

18. *The Letters of A. Bronson Alcott*, R. Herrnstadt, ed. (Ames: Iowa State University Press, 1969), pp. 417, 67–26.

19. Ibid., p. 469, 69–20.

20. Ibid., p. 470.

21. Ibid.

22. See Charles William Heckethorn, *The Secret Societies of All Ages and Countries* (London: 1875; New York: University Books, 1965), 2 vols., I.205.

23. See Christopher Walton, *Memorial of Law: Notes and Materials For an Adequate Biography of the celebrated Divine and Philosopher William Law, Comprising an* Elucidation *of the Scope and* Contents *of the* Writings of *Jacob Böhme, and of his great Commentator, Dionysius Andreas Freher* (London: Walton, 1854).

24. The copies of Walton's works I have drawn on can be found at the University of Richmond Library, Richmond, Virginia, and at the Bibliotheca Philosophica Hermetica, Amsterdam.

25. Walton, illustration, ibid.

26. Walton, ibid.

27. Walton, *Notes and Materials*, epigraph.

28. Walton, p. 143.

29. Ibid., p. vi.

30. Ibid., p. 252.

31. Ibid., p. 252.

32. Ibid., pp. 252–257.

33. Ibid., p. 237.

34. Ibid., p. 240.

35. Ibid., pp. 497–505.

36. Ibid., p. 589.

37. Ibid., p. 591.

PART TWO. INTRODUCTION

1. Böhme, *Christosophia*, VI.37–38.

CHAPTER 8. THE DIVINE NATURE

1. Böhme, *Aurora*, XIII.86.

2. Ibid., XIII.98–99.

3. Böhme, *Theoscopia*, §14.

4. Ibid., §44.

CHAPTER 9. THE DIVINE EMANATION OF WORLDS

1. See Leo Schaya, *The Universal Meaning of the Kabbala* (Baltimore: Penguin, 1973), p. 108.

2. *Christosophia*, V.i.19.

3. Ibid., V.ii.6.

CHAPTER 10. THE FALL OF LUCIFER, HUMANITY, AND NATURE

1. Böhme, *Six Theosophic Points*, I.64.

2. Ibid., II.4.

3. Ibid., II.1.

4. See *Christosophia*, VIII.21–23.

5. Ibid., VIII.80.

CHAPTER 11. SPIRITUAL REGENERATION

1. Böhme, *Six Theosophic Points*, V.33.

2. Ibid., V.44.

3. Ibid., IV.16.

4. Gichtel, I.30.

5. Ibid.

CHAPTER 12. ANGELOLOGY AND PARADISE

1. Böhme, *Aurora*, XII.1.

2. Ibid., XII.15–18.

3. Ibid., XII.111.

4. Ibid., XII.116; see Matthew 21.30.

5. Edward Hooker, *The Triple Crown of Glory* (London: 1697); Walton ms. I.1.12, preface, p. 21.

6. Gichtel, II.1253.

7. Böhme, *Christosophia*, VI.28–29.

8. Samuel Pordage (attrib.), *Mundorum Explicatio or, The Explanation of an Hieroglyphical Figure* . . . (London: Lodowick Lloyd, 1661), p. 40, notes likely those of John Pordage.

9. I will explore the topic of Kabbalah and Christian Theosophy in a forthcoming article. On this subject, see W. A. Schultze, "Jakob Böhme und die Kabbala," *Zeitschrift für Philosophische Forschung* 9 (1955): 447–460.

CHAPTER 13. THE SCIENCE OF IMAGINATION

1. Böhme, *The Three Principles of the Divine Essence*, XVI.50.

2. Ibid., XVI.34.

3. Ibid.

4. Ibid., XVI.43.

5. Ibid., XVI.37.

6. Ibid., IV.66.

7. Gichtel, II.1011.

8. Ibid., II.1016.

9. Ibid., II.873.

10. Gichtel, II.873–874.

11. See W. B. Yeats, intro., Patanjali, *Aphorisms of Yoga* (London: Faber, 1938), I.41, p. 42

12. Gichtel, II.660.

13. Gichtel, I.317–318.

14. Böhme, *Theoscopia*, §8.

15. Edward Taylor, *Theosophick Philosophy Unfolded* (London: 1691), "Some Words Explained".

16. Pordage, *Theologia Mystica* (London: 1683), p. 69.

17. Ibid., pp. 51–52.

18. Böhme, "Of the Supersensual Life," in *The Signature of All Things*, p. 270.

19. Ibid.

20. Böhme, "Discourse between two Souls," in *The Signature of All Things*, pp. 286–288.

21. Ibid., p. 295.

CHAPTER 14. THE EYE IN THE HEART

1. Dante's Beatrice, whose name means thrice beatific, is essentially an incarnation of Sophia, the Virgin of Holy Wisdom who plays such an important role in Böhmean mysticism on one hand, and Eastern Orthodoxy on the other. Sophianic mysticism is found throughout the Christian tradition, and is not the invention of Jacob Böhme by any means.

2. While *Herzens-spiegel* is undoubtedly not by Tauler, perhaps we can spare the anonymous author the indignity of being called "Pseudo-Tauler."

3. See *The Rosicrucian Emblems of Daniel Cramer*, Adam McLean, ed. (Grand Rapids: Phanes Press, 1991).

4. The full title of van Haeften's work is *Schola Cordis sive aversi a Deo cordis ad cundem reductio et instructio*; the full title of Pona's work is *Cardiomorphoseos sive ex corde desumpta Emblemata sacra*. See, for a full discussion of such works, Mario Praz, *Studies in Seventeenth-century Imagery* (Rome: Edizione de Storia, 1975), pp. 151–156.

5. As to the connections between Tauler's mysticism and that of the Böhmenist school: one finds references to Tauler in the scholarly works of the theosophers, including Gottfried Arnold, as well as in unpublished manuscripts of the time attributed to Tauler and circulated widely in theosophic circles.

6. See Christopher Geismar, *Bilder zu Jakob Böhme*, Dissertation, Hamburg, 1990, 2 vols., I.39.

7. Joel 2.12, 13: "Therefore also now, saith the Lord, turn ye even to me with all your heart, and with fasting, and with weeping, and with mourning. And rend your heart, and not your garments, and turn unto the Lord your God, for he is gracious and merciful, slow to anger, and of great kindness, and repenteth him of the evil."

8. Adam McLean has worked on an edition of Leade's collected works for the Bibliotheca Philosophica Hermetica in Amsterdam; when it will appear is unknown.

9. See Thomas Bromley, *The Way to the Sabbath of Rest, or the Soul's Progress in the Work of the New-Birth* (London/Germantown, Pa.: C. Sower [Sauer], 1759), pp. 30–31.

10. Ibid., p. 32.

11. Ibid., p. 36.

12. Ibid., p. 44.

13. Ibid., p. 52.

14. Ibid., p. 56.

15. Pordage, *Theologia Mystica* (London: 1683), p. 16.

16. Ibid., p. 32.

17. Ibid., p. 34.

18. As to lost manuscripts: to this day, we must read Pordage's main works in German, for the original English manuscripts have disappeared, and only the translations into German remain, placing us in the strange position of having to translate back into English works originally written in that language.

CHAPTER 15. THE PHYSIOLOGY OF THE SOUL

1. *The Philokalia*, G. Palmer, P. Sherrard, K. Ware, trans. (London: Faber, 1981), II.106.

2. Ibid., II.110.

3. Ibid., II.108.

4. *Meister Eckhart, Sermons and Treatises*, M. O'C. Walshe, trans. (Longmead: Element, 1987), I.177.

5. *Johannes Tauler, Sermons*, M. Schrady, trans. (New York: Paulist, 1985), p. 37.

6. Dr. Williams's Library, Ms. I.1.37.

7. Ibid., unpaginated; author's copy.

8. Gichtel, *Theosophia Practica: Eine kurze Eröffnung und Anweisung der dreyen Principien und Welten im Menschen* (Berlin/Leipzig: 1696, 1779), p. 16.

9. Gichtel, op. cit., I.25.

10. Ibid., I.40.

11. Gichtel, op. cit., I.25.

12. *Philokalia*, op. cit., I.26–27. St. Isaiah the Solitary lived during the end of the fourth-century A.D., and his advice here is characteristic of his entire tradition.

13. Philokalia, III.268 ff.; III.336, 337.

14. Gichtel, op. cit., V.3857 ff.

15. See Ernst Benz, *Die Protestantische Thebais, Zur Nachwirkung Makarios de Ägypters im Protestantismus des 17 und 18 Jahrhunderts in Europa und America* (Mainz: Akademie der Wissenschaften, 1963), p. 10; Arnold's edition of Makarios was entitled, in full, *Denckmal des Alten Christenthums, Bestehend*

in des Heil. Macarii Und Anderer Hochleuchteter Männer aus der Alten Kirche (Leipzig: 1716).

16. See Böhme, De Electione Gratiae, i.5,6.

17. Gichtel, op. cit., V.3130.

18. *Pseudo-Dionysius: The Complete Works*, C. Luibheid, trans. (New York: Paulist Press, 1987), p. 149.

19. Gichtel, III.2040.

20. Gichtel, V.3659.

21. Gichtel, III.1905–1906.

22. Ibid.

23. Ibid.

24. Gichtel, III.1908.

25. Henry Corbin, *Spiritual Body and Celestial Earth: From Mazdean Iran to Shi'ite Iran*, N Pearson, trans. (Princeton: Bollingen, 1977).

26. Ibid., pp. 158–159.

27. Gershom Scholem, *On the Kabbalah and Its Symbolism* (New York: Schocken, 1969), p. 122.

CHAPTER 16. TURNING WRATH INTO LOVE

1. Bromley, op. cit., p. 50.

2. Ibid., p. 36.

3. See Pordage, *Göttliche und Wahre Metaphysica*, III.10; this passage appears in Thune, p. 59.

4. See *Apparatus ad historiam ecclesiasticam novam*, Coburg, Germany, I.13, and Thune, p. 55.

5. Gichtel, III.2091–2092.

6. Gichtel, II.1095.

7. Gichtel, VII.185.

8. Gichtel, VII.188.

9. Gichtel, VII.195.

10. VII.197.

11. VII.268.

CHAPTER 17. PENETRATION OF THE MERELY ASTRAL

1. See Ioan P. Culianu, *Magic and Eros in the Renaissance* (Chicago: University of Chicago Press, 1987).

2. See my discussion of this community in chapter 4. See also Julius Sachse, op. cit.

3. See Thune, pp. 131–132.

4. Gichtel, *Theosophia Practica*, I.70.

5. Ibid., I.320.

6. Ibid., I.334.

7. Ibid., II.643–644.

8. Ibid., II.980.

9. II.1016.

10. II.1011.

11. II.900.

12. VII.216.

13. See Thune, pp. 146–147.

14. The existence of an essentially Gnostic worldview that reappears in Manichaeism, in Ismaili gnosis in Islam, and in Böhmean theosophy is suggested numerous times in the many works of Henry Corbin.

CHAPTER 18. THEOSOPHY AND GNOSTICISM

1. Dionysius Andreas Freher, "The Substance of a Conversation betwixt a German Theosophist and an English Divine, Mr. W. and Mr. J.," n.d., ms. copy, Dr. Williams's Library, p. 18.

2. Ibid.

3. Ibid., p. 20.

4. Ibid.

5. Ibid., p. 21.

6. Ibid., p. 23.

7. Kurt Rudolph, *Gnosis* (San Francisco: Harper, 1983), p. 179.

8. Ibid., pp. 67–68.

9. Freher, op. cit., p. 55.

10. Quoted in Christopher Walton, *Law's Memorial*, p. 207.

11. Ibid.

12. Ibid., pp. 207–208.

13. *The Nag Hammadi Library* (San Francisco: Harper, 1977), pp. 98 ff.

14. Freher, "Conversation," p. 47.

15. See, for an extended discussion of Sophia in Christianity generally and in theosophy particularly, Versluis, *Theosophia*, op. cit.

16. Gichtel, III.2117.

17. Gichtel, I.339.

18. Gichtel, I.592.

19. Gichtel III.2040.

20. Ibid.

21. *Nag Hammadi Library*, pp. 142–143.

22. Gichtel, II.1095.

23. Ibid.

24. Gichtel, II.732.

CHAPTER 19. ALCHEMY AND THEOSOPHY

1. See Klossowski de Rola, *The Golden Game: Alchemical Engravings of the Seventeenth-Century* (New York: Braziller, 1990).

2. Gichtel, op. cit., V.3333. See Bernard Gorceix, *Johann Georg Gichtel, Théosophe D'Amsterdam* (Delphica: 1975), p. 22.

3. Ibid.

4. Ibid., V.3329.

5. Ibid., V.3322.

6. Ibid., V.3329–3330.

7. Ibid., V.3211.

8. Ibid., V.3210–3211.

9. Ibid., V.3211.

10. Ibid., V.3188.

11. Ibid.

12. Ibid., V.3343.

13. Ibid., V.3336.

14. V.3343.

15. Ibid., V.3337.

16. Gichtel, VII.264.

17. See J. Sachse, *The German Pietists of Pennsylvania* (Philadelphia: Stockhausen, 1895), I.111 ff.

18. See Sachse, I.73, 212 ff., 112.

19. See Jacob Martin, *Philosophische Schriftstellen and Processe, auf daß Jahr 1762 and Hernach*, unpublished ms., Pennypacker Collection, Pennsylvania Historical and Museum Commission, Ephrata Cloister no. 52, ms. 46. See Bach, *Voices of the Turtledoves*, Ph.D. Diss. (1997), pp. 425–426.

20. See Sachse, I.112, 207.

21. The title in German is *Ein gründlich Philosophisch Send-schreiben vom rechten und wahren Steine der Weissheit*. There is a copy in the British Library; another copy I consulted is in the private Bibliotheca Philosophica Hermetica, Amsterdam.

22. Ibid., p. 4.

23. Edmund Brice, *Centrum Naturæ Concentratum, or the Salt of Nature Regenerated*, for the most part improperly called *The Philosopher's Stone* (London: 1696), pp. 66, 84–85

24. See Arthur Versluis, "Western Esotericism and the Harmony Society," *Esoterica: The Journal of Esoteric Studies*, I (1999) i: 20–47, [http.//www.esoteric.msu.edu/].

25. See Ezechiel Sangmeister, *Leben und Wandel* (Ephrata: Bauman, 1825), volume II. See the translation by B. Schindler entitled *Life and Conduct* (Ephrata: Historical Society, 1986), VII.60. As Felix Reichmann demonstrated in the *Pennsylvania Magazine of History and Biography* 68 (1944): 292–313, Sangmeister's book was most probably largely written by Joseph Bauman, his publisher, drawing on the *Chronicon* and Sangmeister's letters. See on this point, Erb, *Johann Conrad Beissel*, op. cit., p. 40. However, this does not eliminate the significance of the Sangmeister story, which does in this one instance, at least, reflect some facts. Alchemy was practiced by some in eighteenth-century Pennsylvania. On the prevalence of alchemy in colonial America, see Arthur Versluis, *The Esoteric Origins of the American Renaissance*, forthcoming. There was in Oley, Pennsylvania, a sect called "Die Neugeborene," or "The Newborns," on which see Georg Michael Weiss, *Der in der Amerikanischen Wildnuß* . . . (Philadelphia: Bradford, 1729).

26. Basarab Nicolescu, *Science, Meaning, and Evolution: The Cosmology of Jacob Boehme* (New York: Parabola, 1991), p. 109.

CHAPTER 20. THEOSOPHY AND CHIVALRY

1. See Antoine Faivre, *Access to Western Esotericism* (SUNY: 1994), pp. 177 ff. on aspects of the chivalric imagination in the eighteenth century.

2. Freher, *Five Conferences* . . . , British Library 5785, f. 241. C. A. Muses pointed to the parallels between the ancient Babylonian and other so-called dualistic traditions of antiquity, and the Böhmean understanding of evil, its origin and meaning. See Muses, *Illumination on Jacob Boehme*, op. cit., p. 75.

3. From Ahura-Mazda, the Persian word for the spiritual Sun of the cosmos.

4. Böhme, *The Signature of All Things*, X.50 ff.

5. Ibid.

6. Ibid.

7. See Böhme, *Christosophia*, I.26.

8. Ibid.

9. Ibid., IV.33.

10. Gichtel, 2511.

11. Gichtel, II.1253.

12. Gichtel, II.1263.

13. Gichtel, II.916.

14. Gichtel, I.957–958.

15. Ibid., Italics added by this author.

16. Ibid.

CHAPTER 21. THEOSOPHY, HERBAL MEDICINE, MAGIC, AND ASTROLOGY

1. . Böhme, *The Signature of All Things*, VIII.37.

2. Gichtel, III.1908.

3. Bromley, *The Way to the Sabbath of Rest* (London; Germantown P A.: C.Sower, 1759), p. 36.

4. Ibid.

5. Ibid.

6. Ibid., pp. 37 ff.

7. Gichtel, op. cit., V.3785–3787.

8. Ibid., VII.215–216.

9. Ibid.

10. Ibid.

11. Ibid., I.335.

12. Gichtel, VI.1847.

13. See J. Sachse, *German Pietists in Pennsylvania*, op. cit., III.372.

14. Ibid., III.373.

15. Ibid., III.376.

16. Ibid., III.377.

17. See, for example, *Magika Hiera: Ancient Greek Magic and Religion*, C. Faraone and D. Obbink, eds. (New York: Oxford University Press, 1991). The theosopher's fire-chant is a binding spell, of which there are examples in countless traditional cultures around the world.

18. Ezechiel Sangmeister, *Leben und Wandel* (Ephrata: Bauman, 1825). II.127. If it is true that Sachse cannot always be trusted, this is even more true of sources like Sangmeister, who exemplifies the term "chip on his shoulder." Even the *Chronicon Ephratense* cannot be completely relied upon, in that it represents hagiography full of allusions and vague phrasing. At the same time, given the well-known prevalence of magic in Pennsylvania German communities, the presence of such practices at Ephrata is almost certain. See, for an accessible overview of materials, *Pennsylvania Dutch Folk Spirituality*, Richard Wentz, ed. (New York: Paulist Press, 1993), esp. pp. 147 ff. See also my earlier remarks on "Sangmeister."

19. See Johann Georg Hohman, *Der lange Verborgene Freund, oder: Getreuer und Christlicher Unterricht für Jedermann, Enthaltend: Wunderbare und probmäßige Mittel und Künste* (Reading: 1819). See also Edwin Fogel, *Beliefs and Superstitions of the Pennsylvania Germans* (Philadelphia: American Germanica Press, 1915); see also Alice Rix, "The Reading Witch Doctor's Sway Over the Trusting and the Ignorant," *North American* 208 (May 22, 1900): 16 pp., and the work of Ann Hark, *Hex Marks the Spot* (Philadelphia: Lippincott, 1938), which does suggest the prevalence of "pow-wow" into the twentieth century at least.

20. See Agrippa, *The Three Books of Occult Philosophy* (London: Chthonios Books, 1987 ed.), p. iv.

21. See Agrippa, op. cit., pp. 68, 244–252, 317–323, 438–446 for various signs and sigils.

CHAPTER 22. THEOSOPHY AND MODERN SCIENCE

1. See Stephen Hobhouse, *Selected Mystical Writings of William Law, Edited with Note and Twenty-four Studies in the Mystical Theology of William Law and Jacob Boehme and an Inquiry into the Influence of Jacob Boehme on Isaac Newton*, 2nd ed. (New York: Harper, 1948).

2. See Arthur Edward Waite, *The Works of Thomas Vaughan* (New York: University, 1968), pp. vii ff.

3. Not all scientists of the nineteenth-century were rationalist, materialist Aristotelians: Louis Aggasiz, the renowned scientist at Harvard, argued for a Platonic approach to human and natural history that directly confronted Darwinian evolutionism. Aggasiz's arguments on this subject bear rereading today,

for it may well be that we have reached a time when such views can again be considered and may bear fruit.

4. I am referring here to the work of Rupert Sheldrake.

5. See Basarab Nicolescu, *Science, Meaning, and Evolution: The Cosmology of Jacob Boehme* (New York: Parabola, 1991).

6. Ibid., p. 77.

7. Ibid., p. 86.

8. Ibid., p. 104.

9. Ibid., p. 111.

CHAPTER 23. TOWARD A NEW PSYCHOLOGY

1. Böhme, *The Signature of All Things*, VI.x.2.

2. Ibid., VI.x.43, 53.

3. Ibid., VI.x.56.

4. Ibid., VI.x.67.

5. Ibid.

6. See Edward Taylor, *Jacob Behmen's Theosophick Philosophy Unfolded* (London: 1691) glossary.

7. Ibid.

8. See Dionysius Andreas Freher, *Paradoxa Emblemata*, figure 100, Dr. Williams's Library, Ms. I.1.76.

9. C. A. Musés, *Illuminations on Jacob Boehme: The Work of Dionysius Andreas Freher* (New York: King's Crown, 1951), p. 150.

CHAPTER 24. HIEROHISTORY AND METAHISTORY

1. Gichtel, I.[§50].

2. Ibid., I.[§52].

3. Gichtel, I.[§64].

4. Gichtel, I.[§65].

5. Ibid., I.[§68].

6. Gichtel, I.[§77].

7. Gichtel, VII.268.

8. Ibid., VII.339–342.

9. Ibid.

10. Gichtel, VII.341.

11. Ibid.

12. Louis Claude de Saint-Martin, *Theosophic Correspondence 1792–1797*, E. B. Penny, trans. (Exeter: Roberts, 1863; Theosophical University Press, 1982), p. 140.

13. Henry Corbin, *Cyclical Time and Ismaili Gnosis* (London: Kegan Paul, 1983), p. 10.

14. Ibid., pp. 15–17.

15. The terrain of comparative religion surveyed by Corbin needs much more examination and elucidation; the parallels between Persian, Sufi, and Gnostic and other Christian theosophic texts will no doubt prove to be mutually illuminating.

16. Böhme, *The Three Principles of the Divine Essence*, I.2.

17. Ibid., V.27.

18. See Bernard Gorceix, *Johann Georg Gichtel: Théosophe d'Amsterdam* (Paris: L'Age d'Homme, 1975), p. 89.

19. Böhme, *Three Principles*, XX.

20. Böhme, *The Aurora*, XIII.64.

21. Böhme, *Three Principles*, XXVII.4.

22. Ibid., XXVII.19, 20.

CHAPTER 25. REVELATION, AUTHORITY AND THE APOSTOLIC TRADITION

1. See Gershom Scholem, *The Messianic Idea in Judaism*, "Revelation and Tradition as Religious Categories in Judaism," p. 292.

2. Ibid.

3. See, for example, Weeks, op. cit., pp. 204–205 on the Kabbala and Böhme generally; see more specifically Wolfgang Huber, "Die Kabbala als Quelle zur Anthropologie Jakob Böhmes," *Kairos* 13 (1971): 131–150.

4. Böhme, *Mysterium Magnum*, VII, p. 664.

5. Böhme, *Six Theosophic Points*, VI.x.6 ff.

6. Böhme, *Mysterium Magnum*, VII.274, quoted in Weeks, p. 200.

CONCLUSION

1. See, on questions of Western esotericism and definitions thereof, the works of Antoine Faivre, for example, the indispensable *Access to Western Eso-*

tericism (SUNY Press, 1994), *Accès de L'Ésotérisme Occidental II* (Paris: Galli-mard, 1996), and *L'ésotérisme* (Paris: Presses Universitaires, 1992) as well as, for a different overview, Jean-Paul Corsetti, *Histoire de l'ésotérisme et des sci-ences occultes* (Paris: Larousse, 1992).

2. Jane Leade, *A Fountain of Gardens: or, A Spiritual Diary of the Won-derful Experiences of a Christian Soul, under the Conduct of the Heavenly Wis-dom; Continued for the Year MDCLXXVIII* (London: 1700), III.324.

3. Ibid., III.327.

4. Ibid., III.325.

5. Ibid., III.329–330.

6. Ibid., III.335.

Selected Bibliography

Acta Philadelphica or Monthly Memoirs of the Philadelphian Society. London: 1697.

Alcott, Bronson. *Concord Days.* Boston: Roberts, 1872.

———. *The Letters of Bronson Alcott.* R. Herrnstadt, ed. Ames: Iowa State University Press, 1969.

———. *Tablets.* Boston: Roberts, 1868.

———. *Table-talk.* Boston: Roberts, 1877.

Alleman, George M. *A Critique of Some Philosophical Aspects of the Mysticism of Jacob Boehme.* Philadelphia: University of Pennsylvania Press, 1932.

Andersson, Bo. *Du solst wissen es ist aus keinem Stein gesogen: Studien zu Jakob Böhme's Aurora, oder, Morgenröte im Auffgang.* Stockholm: Almqvist, 1986.

Anonymous, *A Reall and unfeigned testimonie concerning Jacob Beme of Old Seidenburg, in Upper Lausatia, or, The letters of two learned Germans, both acquaintances and lovers of this author, called Teutonicus: the first is an epistle of H. D. V., T. to H. P. V., H., dated the 3 of Octob. stilo novo, anno 1641, the second is an epistle of A. V., F. to D. O. B. J. O. S. the 21 of Octob. anno. 1641 / translated out of High Dutch, for benefit and information to those that read his writing.* London: 1649.

Ante-Nicene Fathers, 10 vols. Edinburgh: T.T. Clark; Grand Rapids: Eerdman's, 1990.

Arnold, Gottfried. *Das Geheimnis der Göttlichen Sophia.* Leipzig: 1700; Stuttgart, Frommann, 1963.

———. *Historie und Beschreibung der Mystischen Theologie.* Stuttgart: Frommann, 1969 (facs. 1703 ed.).

———. *Sämmtliche geistliche Lieder.* C. Ehmann, ed. 1856.

———. *Unpartheiische Kirchen-und-Ketzer-Historien.* Frankfurt: 1699–1700: 2nd ed., revised and expanded, Schafhausen: 1740–1742.

Atala, Karin. *A Study of the Nature of Reality and Language in J.Bohme's "Aurora" and G. W. F. Hegel's "Vorlesungen über die Philosophie der Religion."* Catholic University of America: Ph.D. Diss., 1988.

Aubrey, Bryan. *Influence of Jacob Boehme on the Work of William Blake.* Durham: Ph.D. Diss., 1982.

———. *Watchmen of Eternity: Blake's Debt to Jacob Boehme.* Lanham, Md.: University Press of America, 1986.

Ayshford, Robert. *Aurora Sapientia, that is to saie, The Daiebreak of Wisdome Of the three Principles and beginning of all in the mysterie of wisdome in which the ground and key of all wisdome is laid open, directing to the true understanding of God, of Man, and of the whole world, in a new and true triune wisdome Physisophie, Theologie, and Theosophie. tending to the Honour of God, Revelation of the true wisdome and to the service of the Sixt Church att Philadelphia* By Her Minister called by the Grace of God to beare witness of God and of Jesus Christ. 1629.

Baader, Franz von. *Erötische philosophie.* Frankfurt: Insel, 1991.

———. *Sämmtliche Werke.* Leipzig: Scientia, 1963 (Reproduction of the Franz Hoffman edition, Leipzig, 1851–1860).

Bach, Jeffrey. *Voices of The Turtledoves: The Mystical Language of the Ephrata Cloister,* Ph.D. Diss., Duke University, 1997.

Bachchan, Harbans R. *W. B. Yeats and Occultism; A Study of his Works in Relation to Indian Lore, the Cabbala, Swedenborg, Boehme, and Theosophy.* Delhi: Motilal Banarsidass, 1965.

Baden, Hans Jürgen. *Das religiöse Problem der Gegenwart bei JakobBöhme.* Leipzig: J. C. Heinrich, 1939.

Bailey, Margaret L. *Milton and Jakob Boehme.* New York: Haskell, 1964.

Barker, C. J. *Prerequisites for the Study of J. Boehme.* London: Watkins, 1920.

Bastian, Albert. *Der Gottesbegriff bei Jakob Böhme.* Kiel: Ph.D.Diss., 1904.

Benz, Ernst. *Der vollkomene Mensch nach Jacob Böhme.* Stuttgart:Kohlhammer, 1937.

———. *Adam. Der Mythus vom Urmenschen.* München:Otto-Wilhelm-Barth, 1955.

———. *Der Prophet Jakob Boehme: Eine Studie über den Typusnachreformatorischen Prophetentums.* Wiesbaden: Steiner, 1959; Mainz: Verlag der Akademie der Wissenschaften, 1959.

———. *The Mystical Sources of German Romantic Philosophy.* Allison Park, Pennsylvania: Pickwick, 1983.

Berdyaev, Nicolas. *The Beginning and the End.* R. M.French, trans. New York:

Harper, 1952 (Original: Opyt Eschatologuicheskoy Metaphiziki [Tvorchestvo i Objektivizacia]).

———. *The Meaning of the Creative Act.* Donald Lowrie, trans. London: Gollancz, 1955 (Original: Smysl tvorchestva [The Meaning of Creativity]. Moscow: G. A. Lemana and S. I. Sakharov, 1915).

———. *The Destiny of Man.* Natalie Duddington, trans. New York: Harper, 1960.

Bethea, Dean Wentworth. *Visionary Warfare: Blake, Hamann, and Boehme against Ideology.* University of Tennessee: Ph. D. Diss., 1989.

Betti, Mario. *The Sophia Mystery in Our Time.* London: Temple Lodge, 1994.

Beyreuther, Erich. *Geschichte des Pietismus.* Stuttgart: Steinkopf, 1978.

Bieker, J. *Das Menschenbild Jakob Böhmes.* Münster: Ph.D. Diss., 1945.

Blau, Joseph. *The Christian Interpretation of the Cabala in the Renaissance.* New York: Columbia University Press, 1944.

Böhme, Jakob. *Aurora.* London: 1910.

———. *Dialogues on the Supersensual Life.* New York: Ungar, 1957.

———. *Sämtliche Schriften*, 11 vols. Will-Erich Peuckert, August Faust, eds. Stuttgart: Frommann, 1955–1961. [Facsimile of the 1730 Gichtel edition]

———. *Six Theosophic Points.* Ann Arbor: Univ. of Mich. Press, 1958.

———. *The Way to Christ.* P. Erb, trans. New York: Paulist Press, 1978.

———. *Theosophische Beschreibung der Tinktur der Weisen und der Curaller Krankheiten, aus des Gottseligen Jacob Boehme's Schriften herausgezogen von einem Liebhaber göttlicher Weisheit.* Leipzig und Berlin: Christian Ulrich Ringmacher,1780.

Bornkamm, Heinrich. *Luther und Böhme.* Bonn: Marcus und Weber,1925.

Breckling, Friedrich. Landesbibliotek Gotha, Handschrifte, A310, no. 15, 69 pp., "Briefe von und an Breckling."

Brice, Edmund, "trans." Ali Puli. *Centrum Naturae Concentratum.* London: 1696.

Brinton, Howard. *The Mystic Will.* New York: Macmillan, 1930.

British Museum. *Jacob Boehme: An Extract from the Catalogue of Printed Books of the British Museum.* London: Clowes, 1922.

Bromley, Thomas. *The Way to the Sabbath of Rest, or the Soul's Progress in the Work of the New Birth.* London: 1655 (Reprinted 1692, 1710).

Brown, Robert. *The Later Philosophy of Schelling: the Influence of Boehme on the Works of 1809–1815.* Cranbury, N.J.: Associated University Presses,

1977.

Buber, Martin, *Zur Geschichte Des Individuationsproblem Nicolaus von Cues und Jakob Böhme*. University of Vienna: Ph.D. Diss., 1904.

Buddecke, Werner. *Verzeichnis von Jakob-Böhme-Handschriften*. Göttingen: Häntzschel, 1934.

——. *Die Jakob Böhme-Ausgaben*. Göttingen: Hantzschel. 1 Teil, 1937; 2 Teil, 1957.

——. *Die Urschriften I*. Stuttgart: Fromann, 1963.

——. *Die Urschriften II*. Stuttgart: Fromann, 1966.

Bulgakov, Sergei. *A Bulgakov Anthology*. J. Pain, N. Zernov, eds. Philadelphia: Westminster Press, 1976.

——. *Sophia: The Wisdom of God*. Hudson: Lindisfarne, 1993.

Certeau, Michel de. *The Mystic Fable*. Chicago: University of Chicago Press, 1992.

Cheney, Sheldon. *Men Who Have Walked With God*. New York: Knopf, 1945.

Cioran, Samuel. *Vladimir Solov'ev and the Knighthood of the Divine Sophia*. Waterloo, Canada: Wilfred Laurier University Press, 1977.

Corbin, Henry. *Avicenna and the Visionary Recital*. Princeton: Princeton University Press.

——. ed., *Le Combat Pour l'Ame du Monde*. Paris: Berg, 1980.

——. *Creative Imagination in the Sûfism of Ibn 'Arabî*. Princeton: Princeton University Press, 1969.

——. *Spiritual Body and Celestial Earth, From Mazdaean Iran to Shi'ite Islam*. Princeton University Press, 1977.

Coulianu, Ioan P. *The Tree of Gnosis: Gnostic Mythology from Early Christianity to Modern Nihilism* San Francisco: Harper, 1992 (originally *Les Gnoses dualistes d'Occident*. Paris: Plon, 1990.

Dawe, Donovan. *Skilbecks: Drysalters, 1650–1950*. London: 1950.

Deghaye, Pierre. *La Doctrin ésotérique de Zinzendorf*. Paris: Klincksieck, 1970.

——. *La Naissance De Dieu*. Paris: Albin Michel, 1985.

Deussen, Paul. *Jakob Böhme: Über sein Leben und seine Philosophie*. Leipzig: F. A. Brockhaus, 1922.

Dionysius. *The Complete Works*. Colm Lubhéid, trans. Mahwah: Paulist Press, 1987.

Dornseiff, Franz. *Das Alphabet in Mystik und Magie*. Leipzig und Berlin: Teubner, 1922.

Dowson, M. E. *The Confessions of Jacob Boehme*. London: 1920.

Drott, Heinrich Arnim. *J. Böhme und J. G. Hamann. Eine vergleichende Untersuchung*. Freiburg: Ph.D. Diss., 1956.

Eckartshausen, Karl von. *Magic: The Principles of Higher Knowledge*. G. Hanswille and D. Brumlich, trans. Scarborough, Can.: Merkur, 1989.

Ebertin, Elsbeth. *Der erleuchtete Gottmensch und Christusverehrer J. Böhme*. Görlitz, 1924.

Ederheimer, Edgar. *Jakob Böhme und die Romantiker*. Heidelberg: Winter, 1904.

Elert, Werner. *Die voluntarische Mystik Jakob Böhmes*. Berlin:Trowitzsch, 1913.

———. *Jakob Böhmes deutsches Christentum*. Berlin: Runge,1914.

Ensign, Chauncey David. *Radical German Pietism (c. 1675–1760)*. Boston Univ.: Ph.D. Diss., 1955.

Erb, Peter. *Johann Conrad Beissel and the Ephrata Community: Mystical and Historical Texts*. Lewiston: Edwin Mellen, 1985.

———. *Pietists, Protestants, and Mysticism: The Use of Late Medieval Spiritual Texts in the Work of Gottfried Arnold*. Metuchen, Scarecrow Press, 1989.

———. *The Pietists*. New York: Paulist Press, 1983.

Evans, E. Lewis. *Boehme's Contribution to the English Speaking World*. Kiel: Ph.D. Diss., 1956.

Faas, Robert. *The Divine Couple: Writings on the Christian Mysteries of Eros*. St. Paul: Grail, 2000.

Faivre, Antoine. *Access to Western Esotericism*. Albany: SUNY Press, 1994.

———. "Le courant théosophique (fin XV–XX siécle): Essai de périodisation." *Politica Hermetica* 7(1993): 6–41.

———. *Eckhartshausen et la théosophie chrétienne*. Paris: Klincksieck, 1969.

———. "Eglise intérieure et Jérusalem céleste." In *Cahiers de l'Université St. Jean de Jérusalem*. Paris: Berg, 1976.

———. ed. *Epochen der Naturmystik, Hermetische Tradition im wissenschaftlichen Fortshritt*. Berlin: Erich Schmidt Verlag, 1979.

———. *L'ésotérisme: que sais-je?* Paris: Presses Universitaires, 1992.

———. *L'ésoterisme au XVIIIème siècle en France et en Allemagne*. Paris: Seghers, 1973.

———. ed. (with J. Needleman). *Modern Esoteric Spirituality*. New York: Crossroad, 1992.

————. *Mystiques, Théosophes et Illumines Au Siècle des Lumières.* Olms Verlag, Hildesheim, 1976.

————. *Philosophie de la Nature: Physique sacrée et théosophie XVIII–XIX siècle.* Paris: Albin Michel, 1996.

————, and Wouter Hanegraaff, eds. *Western Esotericism and The Science of Religion.* Leuven: Peeters, 1998.

Faust, August. *Die Handschrift Jakob Böhmes: Ein Hinweis.* Breslau: Historische Kommission für Schlesien, 1940.

Feilchenfeld, Walter. *Der Einfluss Jacob Böhmes auf Novalis.* Berlin: Ebering, 1922.

Florensky, Pavel. *The Pillar and Foundation of Truth.* Princeton: Princeton University Press, 1997.

Franklin, N. V. P. *"His Most Hideous Pilgrimage": The Presence of Jacob Boehme's Christian Theosophy in William Blake's "The Four Zoas."* Swansea, Wales: M.A. Thesis, 1979.

Frensch, Michael. *Michael-Sophia in Nomine Christi.* Great Barrington: Golden Stone, 1990.

Frick, Karl. *Die Erleuchteten.* Graz: Akademisches, 1973.

————. *Licht und Finsternis,* 2 vols. Graz: Akademisches, 1978.

Gabel, Sister Generose. *James Joyce, Jacob Boehme and the Mystic Way.* University of Wisconsin-Madison: Ph.D. Diss., 1977.

Gem, S. H.. *The Mysticism of William Law.* London: 1914.

Gerhardt, Ferdinand August. *Untersuchung über das Wesen des mystischen Grunderlebnisses. Ein Beitrag zur Mystik Meister Eckharts, Luthers und Böhmes.* Greifswald: Ph.D. Diss., 1923.

Gibbons, B.T. *Gender in Mystical and Occult Thought: Behmenism and Its Development in England.* Cambridge: Cambridge University Press, 1996.

Gichtel, Johann Georg. *Eine kurze Eröffnung und Anwesung der drei Prinzipien und Welten im Menschen.* Leipzig: 1696; newly edited version by Agnes Klein: Schwarzenburg: Ansata, 1979.

————. *Theosophia Practica,* 7 vols. Leyden: 1722.

Giese, Fritz. *Die Entwicklung des Androgynenproblems in der Frühromantik.* Langensalza: 1919.

Godwin, Joscelyn. *The Theosophical Enlightenment.* Albany: SUNY Press, 1994.

Gorceix, Bernard. *Flambée et agonie. Mystiques du XVIIe siécle allemand.* Paris: Editions Prèsence, 1977.

————. *Johann Georg Gichtel: Théosophe d'Amsterdam.* Paris: L'Age D'Homme, 1975.

Greaves, James Pierrepont, and Christopher Walton. *Behmen, Law, and Other Mystics on the past, present and future, with regard to Creation, Written from a Knowledge of the Philosophy of Jacob Behmen.* London: 1847–1848.

————. *Letters and Extracts,* 2 vols. London: Chapman, 1845.

————. *The New Nature in the Soul.* London: Chapman, 1847.

————. *Triune Life: Divine and Human.* Francis Barham, ed. London: 1880.

Grunsky, Hans. *Jacob Boehme als Schöpfer einer germanischenPhilosophie des Willens.* Hamburg: Hanseatesche, 1940.

————. *Jacob Boehme.* Stuttgart: Fromann, 1956.

Günther, Graf zu Solms-Rödelheim. *Die Grundvorstellung Jacob Böhme's und Ihre Terminologie.* München: Inaugural Diss., 1960.

Hanegraaff, Wouter. *New Age Religion and Western Culture: Esotericism in the Mirror of Secular Thought.* Albany: SUNY Press, 1998.

Hankamer, Paul. *Jakob Böhme: Gestalt und Gestaltung.* Hildesheim: Olms, 1960.

Hartley, Thomas. *Paradise Restored. . . . A Short Defence of the Mystical Writers.* London: 1764.

Hartmann, Franz. *Lichtstrahlen vom Orient.* Leipzig: n.d..

————. *Personal Christianity, a Science: The Doctrines of Jacob Boehme, the God-Taught Philosopher.* New York, 1919; reissued New York: Ungar, 1957.

Heinze, Reiner. *Das Verhaltnis von Mystik und Spekulation bei Jakob Böhme.* University of Münster: Ph.D. Diss., 1972.

Heller, Arno. *Die Sprachwelt in Jakob Böhmes Morgenröte.* University of Innsbruck: Ph.D. Diss., 1965.

Hirst, Désirée. *Hidden Riches: Traditional Symbolism from the Renaissance to Blake.* London: Eyre, 1964.

Hobhouse, Stephen. *Selected Mystical Writings of William Law, Edited with Notes and Twenty-four Studies in the Mystical Theology of William Law and Jacob Boehme and an Inquiry into the Influence of Jacob Boehme on Isaac Newton.* New York: Harper, 1948.

Hoffmeister, Joachim. *Der Ketzerische Schuster; Leben und Denkendes Görlitzer Meisters Jakob Böhme.* Berlin: Evangelische, 1975.

Hooker, Edward. *The Triple Crown of Glory.* London: 1697.

360   SELECTED BIBLIOGRAPHY

Hughes, E. M. *The Theology of William Law and the Influence of Boehme*. London: Ph.D. Diss., 1952.

Hutin, Serge. *Les Disciples anglais de Jacob Boehme aux XVIIe et XVIIIe siécles*. Paris: Editions Denoël, 1960.

Hvolbek, Russell H. *Seventeenth-Century Dialogues: Jacob Boehme and the New Sciences*. University of Chicago: Ph.D. Diss., 1984.

Irmler, R. *Revolution des Herzens: Jakob Böhme, heute*. Lorch: Weber, 1974.

Janz, Bruce. *Jacob Boehme's Theory of Knowledge in Mysterium Magnum*. University of Waterloo: Ph.D. Diss., 1991.

Jecht, Richard. *Jakob Böhme und Görlitz. Ein Bildwerk*. Görlitz,1924.

Jones, Rufus M. *Studies in Mystical Religion*. London: Macmillan,1909.

———. *Spiritual Reformers in the Sixteenth and Seventeenth Centuries*. London: Macmillan, 1914.

Jungheinrich, Hans-George. *Das Seinsproblem bei Jakob Böhme*. Hamburg: Hansischer, 1940.

Kämmerer, Ernst. *Das Leib-Seele-Geist Problem bei Paracelsus undeinigen Autoren des 17. Jahrhunderts*. Wiesbaden: Steiner, 1971.

Kelpius, Johannes. *A Short, Easy, and Comprehensive Method of Prayer*. Christopher Witt, trans. Philadelphia, 1761.

Kim, Sunoon. *The Formative Factors in Jacob Boehme's Understanding of God*. Temple University: Ph.D Diss., 1971.

Kocher, Kurt E. *Jakob Böhme: sein Werk und seine Aussage*. Dannstadt-Schauerheim: Heko, 1975.

Konapacki, Steven. *Frustration and Promise: Jacob Boehme's Language Theories in the Aurora oder Morgenröte im Aufgang*. Ann Arbor: University Microfilms, 1977.

———. *The Descent Into Words: Jakob Boehme's Transcendental Linguistics*. Ann Arbor: Karoma, 1979.

Korycinski, K. *Anxiety and Creative Mysticism in the Works of Boehme*. Dundee: M.A. Thesis, 1982.

Koslowski, Peter. *Die Prüfungen der Neuzeit: Über Postmodernität, Philosophie der Geschichte, Metaphysik, Gnosis*. Wien: Passagen, 1989.

———. ed. *Die Philosophie, Theologie und Gnosis Franz von Baaders: Spekulatives Denken zwischen Aufklärung, Restauration und Romantik*. Wien: Passagen, 1993.

Koyré, Alexandre. *La Philosophie de Jacob Boehme*. Paris: J. Vrin,1929.

———. *Mystiques, spirituels, alchimistes du xvi siècle allemand*. Paris: Gallimard, 1971.

Krüger, Gustav. *Die Rosenkreuzer.* Berlin: 1932.

Lamech and Agrippa. *Chronicon Ephratense.* Ephrata: 1786; translation, Lancaster: 1889.

Law, William.. *The Way to Divine Knowledge: being several dialogues . . . preparatory to a new edition of the works of J. Böhme, and the right use of them.* London: 1752.

——. *The Spirit of Love. Being an Appendix to the Spirit of Prayer.* London: W. Innys, and J. Richardson, in Pater-Noster Row, 1752.

Leade, Jane. *Enochian Walks with God.* London: Edwards, 1694.

——. *A Fountain of Gardens: or, A Spiritual Diary of the Wonderful Experiences of a Christian Soul, under the Conduct of the Heavenly Wisdom; Continued for the Year MDCLXXVIII.* London: 1700.

——. *The Heavenly Cloud Now Breaking.* London: 1681.

——. *The Revelation of Revelations.* London: 1683.

Leese, Kurt. *Von Jakob Böhme zu Schelling: Eine Untersuchung zur Metaphysik des Gottesproblems.* Erfurt: Kurt Stenger, 1927.

Lemper, Ernst-Heinz. *Jakob Böhme: Leben und Werk.* Berlin: Union, 1976.

Liem, Ann. *Jacob Boehme: Insights into the Challenge of Evil.* Pendle Hill , 1977.

Ludovica, E. (pseudonym: Else Ludwig). *Jakob Boehme, der Görlitzer Mystiker.* Bad Schmiedeberg: Lothar Baumann, 1909.

Massingham, H. J. *The Tree of Life.* London: Chapman, 1943.

Maxse, R. *The Reception of Jacob Boehme in England in the 17th and 18th centuries.* Oxford (Brasenose College): B. Litt. Thesis, 1934.

McIntosh, Christopher. *The Rose Cross and the Age of Reason.* Leiden: Brill, 1992.

Merkur, Dan. *Gnosis: An Esoteric Tradition of Mystical Visions and Unions.* Albany: SUNY Press, 1993.

Mikeleitis, Edith. *Das Ewige Bildnis.* Berlin: Georg Westermann,1942.

Miller (Guinsberg), Arlene. *Jacob Boehme: From Orthodoxy to Enlightenment.* Stanford University: Ph.D. Diss., 1971.

Molitor, Franz Josef. *Philosophie der Geschichte, oder Über die Tradition.* Münster, Thessing'schen, 1827, 1834, 1839, 1853.

Möseneder, Karl. *Philipp Otto Runge und Jakob Böhme.* Marburg: J.G. Herder-Institut, 1981.

Muses, Charles. *Dionysius Andreas Freher: An Inquiry into the Work of a Fundamental Contributor to the Philosophic Tradition of Jacob Boehme.* Columbia University: Ph.D. Diss., 1951.

———. *Illumination on Jakob Boehme: The Work of Dionysus Andreas Freher.* New York: King's Crown, 1951.

Nicolescu, Basarab. *Science, Meaning, and Evolution: The Cosmology of Jacob Boehme.* Rob Baker, trans. New York: Parabola, 1991. Translated from *La Science, Le Sens, Et l'Evolution.* Paris: Editions du Felin, 1988.

Nigg, Walter. "Heimliche Weisheit." *Mystisches Leben in der evangelischen Christenheit.* Zurich, 1959, 146–173.

Nobile, E. *I limiti del misticismo di J. Boehme.* Naples: 1936.

Oetinger, Friedrich Christoph. *Die Lehrtafel der Prinzessin Antonia.* Berlin: de Gruyter ed., 1977.

———. *Sämmtliche theosophische Schriften.* Stuttgart: 1858.

Pältz, Eberhard. *Jacob Böhmes Hermeneutik. Geschichtsverständnes und Sozialethik.* University of Jena: Habilitationschrift, 1961.

Paschek, Carl. *Der Einfluss Jacob Böhmes auf das Werk Friedrich von Hardenbergs Novalis.* University of Bonn: Ph.D. Diss., 1967.

Penny, A. J. *An Introduction to the Study of Jacob Boehme's Writings.* New York: 1901.

———. *Studies in Jacob Böhme.* London: Watkins,1912.

Peuckert, Will-Erich. *Das Leben Jacob Böhmes.* Jena: Eugen Diederichs, 1924.

———. *Die Rosenkreutzer. Zur Geschichte einer Reformation.* Jena: 1928.

———. *Pansophie.* Berlin: Erich Schmidt,1956.

———. *Gabalia: Ein Versuch zur Geschichte der magia naturalis im 16. bis 18. Jahrhundert.* Berlin: Erich Schmidt, 1967.

Pietsch, Roland. *Die Dialektik von Gut und Böse in der Morgenröthe Böhmes.* University of Innsbruck: Ph.D. Diss., 1975.

Poiret, P. *Bibliotheca Mysticorum selecta.* Amsterdam: 1708.

———. *Theologiae Christianae juxta principia Jacobi Boehmii,teutonici, Idea Brevis et Methodica.* Amsterdam: 1687.

Popp, Karl Robert. *Jakob Böhme und Isaac Newton.* Leipzig: S.Hirzel, 1935.

Popper, H. *Jacob Böhme: Doctrine of a Natural Language.* Bristol University: Ph.D. Diss., 1958.

Pordage, John. *Göttliche und Wahre Metaphysica.* Frankfurt/Leipzig: 1715/1746.

———. *Sophia: The Graceful Eternal Virgin of Holy Wisdom, or Wonderful Spiritual Discoveries and Revelations That the Precious Wisdom Has Given to a Holy Soul.* London: ca. 1675.

———. *Theologia Mystica, or the Mystic Divinitie of the Aeternal Invisibles, viz. the Archetypous Globe.* London: 1683.

———. *A Treatise of Eternal Nature with Her Seven Eternal Forms.* London: 1681.

Pordage, Samuel. *Mundorum Explicatio.* London: 1661.

Powell, Robert. *The Most Holy Trinosophia.* Great Barrington: Golden Stone Press, 1990.

Rainy, C. A. *Selections from Boehme.* London: 1908.

Reguara, I. *Objetos de Melancolia (Jacob Boehme).* Madrid: Ediciones Libertarias, 1984.

Renz, Joan. *Yeats and the Germans: A Dramatic Kinship Once Removed.* University of Conneticut: Ph.D. Diss., 1979.

Ricards, Philip Chayton. *Visionary Mysticism: A Study of Visionary Mystical Experience as it informs the works of Jacob Boehme and William Blake and its Importance for the Philosophy of Religion.* Claremont Graduate School: Ph.D. Diss., 1987.

Richter, Liselotte. *Jakob Böhme. Mystische Schau.* Hamburg: Hoffman and Campe, 1943.

Roach, Richard. *The Imperial Standard.* London: 1727.

Roos, Jacques. *Les Aspects littéraires du mysticisme philosophique et l'influence de Boehme et de Swedenborg au début du romantisme: William Blake, Novalis, Balanche.* Strasbourg: Heitz, 1953.

Sachse, Julius. *The German Pietists of Provincial Pennsylvania.* Philadelphia: Sachse, 1895.

———. *The German Sectarians of Pennsylvania*, 2 vols. Philadelphia: Sachse, 1899–1900.

———. trans. *The Diarium of Magister Johannes Kelpius* (Lancaster, Pa., 1917). *The Pennsylvania-German Society, Proceedings and Addresses* XXV. Lancaster, Pa., 1917.

Saint-Martin, Louis Claude de. *Des Erreurs et de la Verité.* Edinburgh: 1775.

———. *Les Ministère de l'Homme Esprit.* Paris: 1802.

———. *Œuvres Majeures.* R. Amadou, ed. Hildesheim: Olms, 1973 et seq..

———. *Tableau Naturel.* Edinburgh: 1782.

———. *Theosophic Correspondence.* E. B. Penny, trans. Exeter: Roberts, 1863;

Theosophical Publ. House rpt..

Santucci, James. "On Theosophia and Related Terms." *Theosophical History* II.3(1987): 107–110.

——. "Theosophy and the Theosophical Society." London: Theosophical History Center, 1985.

Schäublin, Peter. *Zur Sprache Jacob Boehmes.* Winterthur: Keller, 1963.

Schmitz, Heinz, Deghaye, P., Vieillard-Baron, J-L., et al., eds., *Jacob Boehme ou l'obscure lumière de la connaissance mystique.* Paris: J. Vrin, 1979.

Schneider, Robert. *Schelling und Hegels schwäbische Geistesahnen.*Würzburg-Aumühle: 1938.

Scholem, Gershom. *Kabbalah.* Jerusalem: Keter, 1974.

——. *Origins of the Kabbalah.* Princeton: Princeton University Press, 1987.

Schrade, H. *Abraham von Franckenberg.* Heidelberg: Ph.D. Diss., 1923.

Schrey, Rudolph (Schreyer, Lothar). *Die Lehre des Jacob Böhme.* Hamburg: Hanseatische, 1924.

Schuchard, Marsha Keith. *Freemasonry, Secret Societies, and the Continuity of the Occult Traditions in English Literature.* University of Texas at Austin: Ph.D. Diss., 1975.

Schuhmacher, Käthe. *Die Signaturenlehre bei Paracelsus.* Köln: Ph.D. Diss., 1953.

Schulitz, John-Robert. *Einheit in Differenz: Die kabbalistische Metamorphose bei Jakob Bohme.* University of Michigan: Ph.D. Diss., 1991.

Schwarz, Hermann. *Der Gottesgedanke in der Geschichte der Philosophie.* Heidelberg: 1913.

Secret, Françoise. *Les Cabalistes chrétiens de la renaissance.* Paris: Dunod, 1964.

Sheldon, James Gail. *The Orientation of Nicolas Berdyaev: His Relation to Jacob Boehme, Fyodor Dostoyevsky, Friedrich Nietzsche, and Henrik Ibsen.* Indiana Univ.: Ph.D. Diss. 1954.

Silberer, Herbert. *Probleme der Mystik und ihrer Symbolik.* Wien:1914.

Soloviev, Vladimir. *The Meaning of Love.* London: 1945.

South, Mary Anne. *A Suggestive Inquiry into the Hermetic Mystery.* London: 1850; New York: Julian, 1960.

Spunda, Franz. *Das mystische Leben Jakob Böhmes.* Freiburg: Bauer, 1961.

Steiger, Isabel de. *Memorabilia.* London: Rider, n.d..

Steiner, Rudolf. *Mystics of the Renaissance: Jacob Boehme, Meister Eckhart, Paracelsus, Giordano Bruno, Tauler.* London: 1911; Gordon, 1991.

————. *Theosophy.* New York: Rand, 1910; Leipzig: Altmann, 1908.

Stewig, Christiana. *Böhmes Lehre vom innern Wort in ihrer Beziehung zu Frankenbergs Anschauung vom Wort.* München: Ph.D. Diss., 1953.

Stockum, Th. C. van. *Zwischen Jacob Böhme und Johann Scheffler.*Amsterdam: Noord-Hollandsche Uitgevers, 1967.

Stoeber, Michael. *Evil and the Mystic's God: Towards a Mystical Theodicy.* University of Toronto: Ph.D. Diss., 1990.

Stoudt, John. *Sunrise to Eternity.* Philadelphia: University of Pennsylvania Press, 1957.

Struck, Wilhelm. *Der Einfluss Jakob Böehmes auf die evangelische Literatur des 17. Jahrhunderts.* Berlin: Junker and Dünnhaupt, 1936.

Susini, Eugène. *La Philosophie de Franz von Baader.* Paris: Vrin, 1942.

Swainson, William. *Jacob Boehme, the God-taught Philosopher.* London: 1905.

————. *Jacob Boehme: The Teutonic Philosopher.* London: Rider, 1921.

Taylor, Edward. *Jacob Behmen's Theosophick Philosophy UNFOLDED; IN DIVERS Considerations and Demonstrations, SHEWING The Verity and Utility of the several Doctrines or Propositions contained in the Writings of that Divinely Instructed AUTHOR. ALSO, the principal treatises of the said author abridged. And answers given to the remainder of the 177 theosophic questions, Propounded by the said JACOB BEHMEN, which were left unanswered by him at his death.* London: Tho. Salisbury, Inner-Temple Gate in Fleetstreet. 1691.

Thune, Nils. *The Behmenists and the Philadelphians: A Contribution to the Study of English Mysticism in the 17th and 18th Centuries.* Uppsala: Almquist and Wiksells, 1948.

Trinick, John, *The Fire-Tried Stone (Signum Atque Signatum): An Enquiry into the Development of a Symbol.* London: Watkins, 1967.

van den Broek, R., and W. Hanegraaff, eds. *Gnosis and Hermeticism.* Albany: SUNY Press, 1997.

Versluis, Arthur. *American Transcendentalism and Asian Religions.* New York: Oxford University Press, 1993.

————. "Bronson Alcott and Jacob Böhme." *Studies in the American Renaissance* 16 (1993), 153–159.

————. *Gnosis and Literature.* St. Paul: Grail, 1996.

————. *The Hermetic Book of Nature.* St. Paul: Grail, 1997.

————. *The Mysteries of Love: Eros and Spirituality.* St. Paul: Grail, 1996.

————. *Theosophia: Hidden Dimensions of Christianity.* Hudson: Lindisfarne,

1994.

———. *Wisdom's Book: The Sophia Anthology.* St. Paul: Paragon House, 2000.

———. *Wisdom's Children: A Christian Esoteric Tradition.* Albany: SUNY Press, 1999.

Vetterling, Herman. *The Illuminate of Görlitz or Jakob Böhme's Life and Philosophy.* Leipzig: Markert and Petters, 1923.

Waldemar, Charles. *Jakob Böhme der schlesische Mystiker.* München:Goldmann, 1959.

Walker, A. Keith. *William Law: His Life and Thought.* London: S.P.C.K., 1973.

Walsh, David. *The Mysticism of Innerworldly Fulfillment.* Gainesville: University Presses of Florida, 1983.

———. *After Ideology.* San Francisco: Harper, 1990.

Waterfield, Robin. *Jacob Boehme: Essential Readings.* Wellingborough: Aquarian, 1989.

Weeks, Andrew. *Boehme: An Intellectual Biography of the Seventeenth-Century Philosopher and Mystic.* Albany: SUNY Press, 1991.

Wehr, Gerhard. *Jakob Böhme in Selbstzeugnissen und Bilddokumenten.* Hamburg: Rowohlt, 1975.

———. *Die Deutsche Mystik.* Bern: Otto Wilhelm Barth Verlag, 1988.

———. *Esoterisches Christentum.* Stuttgart: Klett, 1975.

———. *Jakob Böhme: Der Geisteslehrer und Seelenführer(Fermenta Cognitionis 4).* Freiburg: Aurum, 1979.

Weigel, Valentin. *Sämtliche Schriften.* Will-Erich Peuckert, Winfried Zeller, eds. Stuttgart: Frommann Verlag, 1964.

Weinfurter, Karel. *Man's Highest Purpose: The Lost Word Regained.* London: Rider, n.d.

Weiss, George Michael. *Der in der Amerikanischen Wildnuß Unter Menschen von verschiedenen Nationen. . . .* Philadelphia: Bradford, 1729.

Weiss, Victor. *Die Gnosis Jakob Böhmes.* Zürich: Origo, 1955.

Wentzlaff-Eggebert, Friedrich Wilhelm. *Deutsche Mystik zwischenMittelalter und Neuzeit.* Berlin: Walter de Gruyter, 1944.

Zalitis, Emma D. *Stock, Bud, and Flowers: A Comparative Study of Mysticism in Böhme, Blake, and Coleridge.* Purdue University: Ph.D. Diss., 1981.

Ziegler, Leopold. *Menschwerdung,* 2 vols. Summa Verlag, 1948

———. *Überlieferung.* München: Hegner, 1949.

Index